The
Florida Boom
of the **1920s**
and How It
Brought on the
Great Depression

BUBBLE IN
THE SUN

———✦❖✦———

CHRISTOPHER
KNOWLTON

Simon & Schuster
New York London Toronto Sydney New Delhi

Simon & Schuster
1230 Avenue of the Americas
New York, NY 10020

First Simon & Schuster hardcover edition January 2020

SIMON & SCHUSTER and colophon are registered
trademarks of Simon & Schuster, Inc.

For information about special discounts for bulk purchases,
please contact Simon & Schuster Special Sales at 1-866-506-1949
or business@simonandschuster.com.

The Simon & Schuster Speakers Bureau can bring authors to
your live event. For more information or to book an event, contact
the Simon & Schuster Speakers Bureau at 1-866-248-3049
or visit our website at www.simonspeakers.com.

Interior design by Lewelin Polanco

Manufactured in the United States of America

1   3   5   7   9   10   8   6   4   2

Library of Congress Cataloging-in-Publication Data
Names: Knowlton, Christopher, author.
Title: Bubble in the sun : the Florida boom of the 1920s and how it brought on the Great
Depression / Christopher Knowlton.
Description: First Simon & Schuster hardcover edition. | New York :
Simon & Schuster, 2020. | Includes bibliographical references and index. |
Summary: "Christopher Knowlton, author of Cattle Kingdom and former Fortune writer,
takes an in-depth look at the spectacular Florida land boom of the 1920s and shows how it led
directly to the Great Depression"— Provided by publisher.
Identifiers: LCCN 2019034981 (print) | LCCN 2019034982 (ebook) |
ISBN 9781982128371 (hardcover) | ISBN 9781982128388 (paperback) |
ISBN 9781982128395 (ebook)
Subjects: LCSH: Real estate development—Florida—History—20th century. |
Real estate investment—Florida—History—20th century. | Land speculation—
Florida—History—20th century. | Financial crises—Florida—History—20th century. |
Depressions—1929. | Florida—Economic conditions—20th century.
Classification: LCC HD266.F6 K67 2020 (print) | LCC HD266.F6 (ebook) |
DDC 333.3309759/09042—dc23
LC record available at https://lccn.loc.gov/2019034981
LC ebook record available at https://lccn.loc.gov/2019034982

ISBN 978-1-9821-2837-1
ISBN 978-1-9821-2839-5 (ebook)

To Pippa and to the memory of my grandmother
Ruth Bull Rathbone, who gave me Florida.

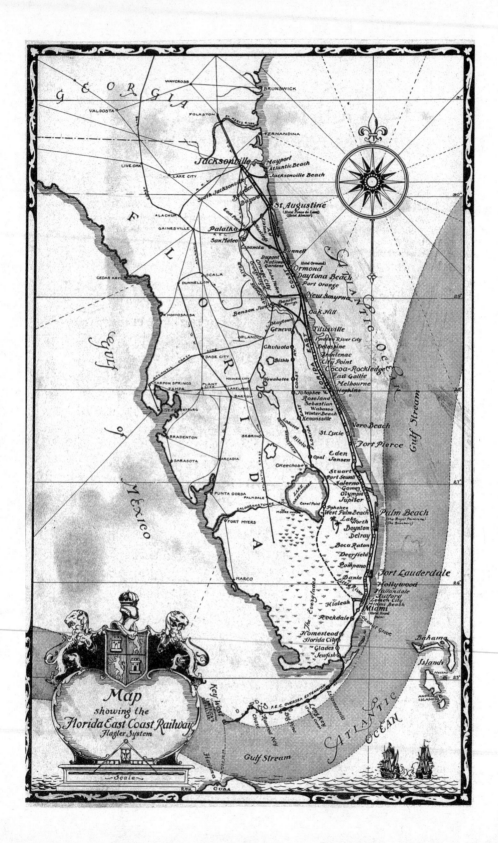

Map
showing the
Florida East Coast Railway
Flagler System

Did *any* of these people know what they were doing—could *any* of them see even an inch beyond their own affairs, or realize what hopelessly inconspicuous, enormously unimportant atoms they were in that great surging sea that was modern America?

—T. H. WEIGALL, *Boom in Paradise*

CONTENTS

INTRODUCTION

At high tide on the clear morning of January 10, 1926, to the squalling of circling gulls, the *Prinz Valdemar*, a five-masted steel-hulled barkentine, weighed anchor. With the help of two tugboats, she prepared to navigate the narrow channel known as Government Cut that led into the turning basin of Miami Harbor. Her captain and crew of eighty were understandably impatient: they had waited ten days for their turn to be towed into the crowded harbor. Many of the crew stood at ease at her deck railings and watched the tugs at work. As they knew well, the *Prinz Valdemar* was a dinosaur of the great age of sailing ships and, at 241 feet long, likely the largest vessel ever to enter the harbor. Built in Denmark in 1891, she had weathered many transatlantic crossings and countless storms at sea until the outbreak of World War I, when the German navy deployed her as a blockade runner. In a later incarnation, she had hauled sacks of coconuts up from Nicaragua. The plan now was to convert her into a floating hundred-room hotel to help meet the acute housing shortage in Miami, which, like the rest of Florida, was in the midst of an epic building boom.

Thirty-six other ships, mostly steamships and schooners, already jammed the inner harbor, vying for berths and wharf space to unload their cargos of building supplies. The steamers were tied up three deep at the city piers. An additional thirty-one ships lay at anchor outside the harbor, awaiting their turn to enter, loaded with enormous amounts of lumber— millions of feet, by one estimate—to say nothing of the wallboard, plumbing fixtures, and roofing materials destined for various construction projects up and down the coast.

Precluded from entering the port, passenger ships arriving from Havana, New York, and as far away as San Francisco had resorted to anchoring off the coast and ferrying their passengers ashore on launches and tenders. At night, with their rigging lit, the forest of masts and rows of bright portholes suggested an ethereal, glittering city bobbing on the horizon.

But nothing seemed more fantastical than what was actually happening onshore. From the deck of the *Valdemar*, the crew could see the skeletons of a dozen new steel and concrete skyscrapers sheathed in scaffolding and jutting into the sky, creating a new urban skyline where only one multistory structure had existed just eighteen months before. Three tall hotels along the bay-front area of downtown Miami—the Columbus, the Watson, and the Everglades—were framed in steel girders but remained unfinished. Behind them rose the Meyer-Kiser Bank Building on Flagler Street, also still under construction, and the three-towered McAllister Hotel. Tallest of them all was the recently completed Miami Daily News Building a few blocks north. The year before, the newspaper had set a world record when it published a 504-page edition in twenty sections, loaded with real estate ads and weighing 7.5 pounds—requiring fifty railcars full of newsprint to produce. To celebrate its unprecedented success, the paper had built this twenty-six-story skyscraper and crowned it with an elaborate tiered bell tower modeled on the Giralda tower that sits atop Seville Cathedral in southern Spain.

Pandemonium raged on Miami's city streets—and on the streets of all the new cities and towns that had sprung up along both coasts of Florida during that decade. "My first impression, as I wandered out into the blazing sunlight of that bedlam that was Miami, was of utter confusion," remembered Theyre Hamilton Weigall, a twenty-four-year-old Australian-born, London-based journalist who arrived in Florida by train at the peak of the boom and stood stunned among the screeching motor horns and the deafening cacophony of rivet guns, drills, and hammers. "Hatless, coat-less men rushed about the blazing streets, their arms full of papers, perspiration pouring from their foreheads," he recalled. "Every shop seemed to be combined with a real estate office; at every doorway, crowds of young men were shouting and speech-making, thrusting forward papers and proclaiming to heaven the unsurpassed chances they were offering to make a fortune. . . . Everybody in Miami was real estate mad."

Building projects in the Greater Miami region totaled $103 million in 1925 ($1.5 billion in today's money), a huge figure for the day. But an embargo imposed by the Florida railroads in September 1925 had compounded the chaos and overcrowding in the harbor and on the city's streets. Lacking the requisite warehousing, logistics, and labor, the railroads had been overwhelmed by the avalanche of building materials pouring into the state. Until order could be restored, the tracks repaired, and new warehouses built, all cargo into Florida was now banned, except fuel and perishables. A milk bottle shortage emerged; ice had to be rationed; local cows, deprived of feed, began to starve. By year-end 1925, thousands of railroad cars were backed up in Jacksonville and other gateways to the state.

One enterprising businessman tried to smuggle in a railcar full of building bricks under a layer of ice, in the guise of a shipment of lettuce. Others tried to move their supplies in by steamship and schooner, and when that didn't work, by truck, clogging the highways in and out of the state—highways still rough and already jammed with automobiles, all bound for the new promised land of Florida, dubbed the last American frontier. Adding to the chaos at the piers and railroad stations were the endless stacks of crates, the beginnings of what would be a record citrus crop bound for northern markets—but at the moment, going nowhere. The Miami dockworkers seized on the demand for their services to strike for better wages—60 cents per hour, up from 45 cents. Soon thereafter 1,800 telegraphers went on strike, too, hampering communications.

Nowhere was the speculation as feverish as it was along the waterfront of Dade County, where prices for bare plots of land were doubling and tripling, seemingly overnight, including those that had yet to be dredged from the bays. As property values exploded, the speculation extended to the selling and reselling, numerous times in a day, of paper options on these parcels. Land sales caused small riots where crowds literally threw checks at the developers—in such numbers that they had to be collected in barrels.

Seminole Beach was bought for $3 million one day, then sold three days later for $7.6 million. One Miami real estate office sold $34 million worth of real estate in a single morning.

But the construction boom in Florida was by no means limited to the coasts. Countless inland communities were under development as well. In addition to the celebrated subdivisions of Miami Beach, Coral Gables, Boca Raton, and Davis Islands were literally hundreds of others—by one estimate, 970—of varying sizes around the state with names that evoked garden-like settings or tropical Spanish paradises, such as Jungle Terrace, Altos del Mar, Opa-Locka, and Rio Vista Isles.

Many of these developments were being built around golf courses that were a major selling point in every resort's lavish brochure. In fact, the state was on its way to boasting the world's largest concentration of golf courses, a distinction it holds to this day. In all likelihood, some twenty million lots were for sale across Florida. As Willard A. Barrett, a writer for the financial publication *Barron's*, noted, to occupy them all would require a Florida population of sixty million—or roughly half the existing population of the United States at that time. Problematically, Florida, by the late 1920s, had only one and a half million residents, although that was up 50 percent from the start of the decade. Nevertheless, that didn't discourage outsiders from spending more than $1 million per day to buy up Florida property in 1925. By then, the Florida land boom had evolved into a historic investment frenzy. Barron G. Collier, who had purchased more than a million acres in southwestern Florida—a parcel larger than the state of Rhode Island—very likely became the nation's first billionaire, at least on paper, when the value of his Florida holdings spiked during this period. "Something is taking place in Florida to which the history of developments, booms, inrushes, speculation, and investment yields no parallel," reported the *New York Times* in March 1925.

As the *Prinz Valdemar* entered Government Cut, the Clyde Line ship *George Washington*, loaded with one hundred impatient passengers bound for New York, began to sound its ship's whistle, announcing its intention to depart the harbor the moment the *Prinz Valdemar* had cleared the channel. At that moment, an accident occurred that seemed foreordained. Someone ignored a command, or missed a signal, or a gust of wind blew in from offshore, or the tide shifted—no one could be entirely sure which of these factors was most responsible for the mishap that followed.

The huge gray-hulled sailing ship bumped up against a sandbar, swung sideways, and wedged itself across the mouth of the eighteen-foot-deep channel. As the tide began to recede, the weight of the outgoing seawater swung the giant keel out from under the vessel so that her cargo of supplies shifted. The old ship, her iron sides grinding, groaning, and creaking, capsized in a slow-motion pantomime that took an agonizing four minutes to play out, allowing her crew ample time to leap overboard into the lukewarm, blue-green waters of Biscayne Bay. As her five masts gradually genuflected, water rushed over her gunwales until she came to rest on her side, half submerged, so that she stoppered the channel like a cork in a bottle, preventing all but the smallest boats from passing in and out of the harbor.

Frantic efforts were made to right the great ship. Thick ropes called hawsers were cleated to her decks and hauled by the tugboats to try to pull her upright. When these efforts failed, a pair of dredging vessels were assigned to carve out an eighty-foot-wide temporary channel that could bypass around her. Both dredgers struck coral and broke down. A second vessel, the steamer *Lakevort*, tried to squeeze past the wreck only to run aground herself, further complicating the salvage operation.

Meanwhile, on board the *George Washington*, now trapped in the harbor, hysteria mounted. The governor's office in Tallahassee was flooded with telephone calls and telegraphs demanding that Governor John Martin fire the harbormaster. Overnight all the frantic building construction up and down the East Coast was forced into a near-complete standstill. By now, the state's entire transportation system—its rails, its roads, and its seaports; the infrastructure that built and sustained the great boom—was either clogged, stalled, or broken.

This forced recess gave developers a chance to review their projects. One by one, in offices across the state, they pulled out their drawings and their blueprints, their contracts and their budgets, and spread them out on their drafting tables to reconsider every nuance of their ambitious plans. A few of them, after doing so, decided that the prudent course of action was to pull back a little. In Wall Street parlance, they opted to take some of the risk off the table; but they would be the exceptions.

The 1920s are best remembered as the era of the flapper, jazz, the automobile, radio, Prohibition, and rum-running. But in isolation, perhaps nothing reflects better the spirit of this rollicking decade than the remarkable sequence of events that transpired in Florida. Impressive skyscrapers had been built before, and a few suburbs had been drawn up in places such as Shaker Heights, Ohio, but not on the colossal scale of what occurred in Florida during the twenties. Up and down both coasts, entire cities were mapped out, or platted, from scratch, with much of the land somehow dredged up out of swampland or sand, and sold, seemingly overnight, to the property-famished public.

The great Florida land boom would prompt the country's greatest migration of people, dwarfing every previous westward exodus, as laid-off factory workers, failing farmers, disaffected office clerks—anyone unemployed or seeking a better quality of life—boarded southbound trains or climbed into their Tin Lizzies and made their way to this emerging land of opportunity, touted as a tropical paradise. Six million people flowed into the state in three years. In 1925 alone, an estimated two and a half million people arrived looking for jobs and careers, and, for a time, found them in the building trades. As one observer wrote: "All of America's gold rushes, all her oil booms, and all her free-land stampedes dwindled by comparison with the torrent of migration pouring into Florida."

Florida, which began the decade as America's last frontier, would end the decade as the country's most celebrated playground—and its favorite retirement destination. Furthermore, it quickly became the bellwether for every important social and economic development of the period, and has remained a bellwether ever since.

And yet historians and economists have largely overlooked the boom's larger significance, specifically its direct impact on the severity and duration of the Great Depression that followed. Most cite the stock market crash of 1929 as the event that heralded the Depression. In fact, the bursting of the great Florida land bubble was the more pivotal event—the one that truly, if tragically, triggered the nationwide economic and social trauma that followed, and the one that helps explain why it lasted so long and was so devastating. The land boom, not the stock market, was the true catalyst for the disasters that befell the nation as overvalued housing and property prices everywhere began to collapse in the wake of the Florida debacle. The eroding economic fundamentals and collapsing consumer confidence finally reached Wall Street and pulled down the stock market, bringing an end to the frantic nationwide party so aptly named the Roaring Twenties.

In short, the great Florida land boom was one of the most consequential financial manias in US history, and yet to this day, it has never received the attention it deserves. One reason for this has been the paucity of economic data to fully explain the event—in particular, limited government statistics from the era relating to home prices, household wealth, and foreclosures. Another reason is that the significance of the boom has not been understood in a broad enough historical and business context. One goal of this book is to remedy those omissions and oversights. Another goal is to tell the story through the experiences of the characters who led the boom and were most responsible for its magnitude and repercussions.

The stars of the story are the handful of daring men who, eager for fame and wealth, took enormous risks to open up Florida for real estate development and then chased the boom to its ruinous conclusion. (Other than one rich widow on each coast, Florida's developers at the time were all men.) Chief among these are "the uncrowned kings" of real estate: Carl Fisher in Miami Beach, Addison Mizner in Palm Beach and Boca Raton, George Merrick in Coral Gables, and David Paul "D.P." Davis in Tampa and St. Augustine.

Fisher, a former bicycle racer still addicted to speed and excitement, chain-smoked cigars, often chewing off their butts and swallowing them. Sloppy, crude, and profane, he was also terrifically clever, with a genius for promotional gimmicks and publicity stunts. Mizner, the son of a diplomat, had previously prospected for Klondike gold in the Yukon and fought as a heavyweight boxer in Australia. An affable and eccentric bon vivant and raconteur, he collected Spanish religious relics and surrounded himself with a coterie of friends and animals—including a pair of Chows and a monkey that he carried around on his shoulder named Johnnie Brown. Merrick, by contrast, was an idealistic, ruggedly handsome part-time poet and churchgoing workaholic. For years, he had planned how to convert his father's grapefruit orchards into an ideal city. And finally, the dapper, pencil-thin Davis was a former newsboy and shoe salesman. He had worked on the Panama Canal and operated a lucrative ferry concession in Jacksonville before becoming a real estate broker. Blindly driven, arrogant, and wildly overconfident, he appeared to possess the Midas touch.

All four of these men were daring gamblers, bold promoters, and consummate showmen. Each had grown exceptionally rich during the decade, accruing fortunes of between $50 million to $100 million, equivalent to $690 million to $1.38 billion in today's dollars. But before long, each would find himself physically taxed and morally challenged. By the decade's end, they would write the script for how flamboyant and hyperbolic real estate developers and promoters should, or could, behave.

One earlier player's importance is such that he cannot be omitted from this narrative: the Gilded Age oil tycoon Henry Flagler. By creating the state's first empire of railroads and resort hotels, he built the infrastructure backbone and provided the template for all of the madcap development that followed. Our story will begin with him, in St. Augustine, a few decades before the boom.

Nor is the historical record complete without mentioning the men and women who stood up for the preservation of Florida's environment, which found itself under siege by dredgers, road builders, and property developers. Among these, none is more important than the author Marjory Stoneman Douglas, daughter of the editor in chief of the *Miami Herald*, who, during the twenties, came of age, built her house, and found her cause. She spent much of her long career doing everything in her power to protect Florida's one-of-a-kind ecosystem and, in particular, its Everglades. The evolving understanding of the ecology of tropical wetlands during this period—of just how much environmental change these mangrove swamps, salt marshes, and wet grasslands could endure—is an integral aspect of Florida's land boom, relevant today in light of the threats presented by global warming and rising sea levels that have put so much of the state's wetlands, wildlife, and valuable real estate in peril.

The epic Florida land boom and its collapse—replete with its greed, excess, corruption, and comeuppance—also provides useful lessons for us today. In particular, it throws light on the threats posed by rampant speculation and overleveraging. But the boom's underlying causes also merit study. Contributing mightily to the calamity at the end of the twenties were the loose lending standards across the country. Such lending was used in conjunction with two relatively new and suddenly popular financial instruments: home mortgages, which more than tripled in volume during the decade, and installment credit loans for the purchase of cars and home appliances, which more than doubled. They fueled the boom and pushed personal indebtedness to unsustainable levels. Corruption and fraud, too, would play their parts, especially in Florida, which quickly became the epicenter of the era's property speculation, attracting gangsters, crooks, and double-dealing bankers. Finally, the story has import because the Great Depression was the most traumatic social and economic calamity in the nation's history. Its staggering dimensions and devastating worldwide impact make it all the more vital that we understand its origins, if we are to avoid repeating our mistakes.

Back in Miami Harbor, it would take twenty-five days to dredge and dynamite a new channel and a full forty-two days to remove the *Prinz Valdemar*'s masts, pump out her hold, extract her $200,000 worth of ruined and water-soaked cargo, and then right her and refloat her. But when the ship was finally towed ashore and the channel cleared, the character of the boom had changed. Unbeknownst to the millions of Americans participating in the frenzy, the entire teetering, speculative housing house of cards in Florida and across the nation as a whole—much like the capsizing *Prinz Valdemar*—had begun to topple.

1

THE LAST FRONTIER

1

THE PHARAOH OF FLORIDA

One afternoon in early January 1878, a well-dressed middle-aged man with a walrus mustache and a handsome square head of graying hair stepped off the train in St. Augustine, Florida. His seven-year-old son, his twenty-two-year-old daughter, her husband, and his sickly wife stepped down after him. The family had made their ninety-hour journey from New York to Florida on doctor's orders, looking for sunshine, warmth, and clean air to help the wife recuperate from tuberculosis. They had stopped for one night en route in Savannah, Georgia, to break up the long trip.

It was couple's first holiday in many years, and the farthest they had ever been from Cleveland, where they had spent most of their married life, or from New York City, to which they had recently moved. They were Henry Morrison Flagler and Mary Harkness Flagler, and, thanks to Mary's incurable illness, they lived a socially monastic existence: they rarely went out and never entertained. In the prior seventeen years, they had spent only two nights apart. Most nights, the Flaglers would sit at home, and he would read to her; or if she slept, he would sit up late, reading in a chair positioned just outside her bedroom so that he could hear her if she called out to him.

St. Augustine, the oldest city in the country, was reputed to boast Old World Spanish charm, which it did, but the best hotel there—really, the only adequate hotel—was noisy and ramshackle. Worse, it was filled with coughing consumptives, many of them confined to wicker wheelchairs. The couple found the accommodations disappointing and depressing. The establishment's food, which consisted of canned meats and canned vegetables accompanied by an assortment of tarts and meringues, was virtually inedible. The young people in the party found nothing to do. The Flagler family stayed for only one night.

Apart from the northernmost counties that bordered Georgia and the nearly adjacent northern towns of Jacksonville and St. Augustine, Florida in the 1870s remained a largely unsettled and undeveloped wilderness of dense pinewoods, impassable palmetto jungle, and tangled mangrove swamps. Scraggly beards of gray Spanish moss hung from huge cypress trees and live oaks along the riverbanks. The farther south you went, the swampier the state became. A few tiny fishing villages had sprung up along the sandy coasts, but the vast interior was largely unexplored—a land of watery saw grass and shallow lakes and jungle hammocks where the bay laurel and myrtle competed with the oaks and the palmettos, and where bromeliads, or air plants, sprouted from the tree branches. The state could accurately be described at the time as America's last frontier. Roads were virtually nonexistent. Stern-wheelers lazily plied the inland waterway between St. Augustine and Jupiter. The largest town was Key West, with its population of ten thousand, situated at the far end of a string of coral reef islands off the southern tip of the peninsula. Local industry consisted of a few lumber mills in the north, some early phosphate mines, and a smattering of citrus groves. A pair of failed coconut plantations had left a line of nonnative coconut palms swaying over the beaches along a stretch of the central coast.

Four years would pass before Henry Flagler returned to St. Augustine. When he did, it would be his turn to be ill and in need of recuperation. Fifty-two years old and widowed, he was recovering from a liver ailment that had hospitalized him in New York City the month before. During the intervening years, a number of changes had occurred in his life. Mary had died of her tuberculosis in May 1881. His son, Harry, eleven, was now being raised by an aunt back in New York. Flagler himself was semiretired from running the world's largest and most profitable business enterprise, the monopoly known throughout the world as the Standard Oil Trust. Thanks to his founding stake in the business, Flagler had become stupendously wealthy.

Freed from caring for an invalid wife, freed from the obligations of parenthood, and freed from the burdens of running a vast and vilified enterprise, he was looking for something new to do with his free time and his giant fortune. He was about to find what he was looking for in St. Augustine—a new occupation and career—and it would lead to one of the most extraordinary second acts in American business history.

Henry Flagler was born in upstate New York in 1830, the son of a rural Presbyterian minister of German Palatine stock. At fourteen, he left home to join his older half brother, who was working at a general store run by a maternal uncle in Republic, Ohio. Quiet, shrewd, dutiful, and keenly attentive to detail, Henry showed a natural aptitude for business. By age thirty-one, married with one daughter, he had made the substantial sum of $50,000 ($1.1 million in today's dollars) trading grain and selling alcohol. Impatient to make more, he rolled his entire stake into a salt manufacturing business in Saginaw, Michigan, hoping to take advantage of the Civil War boom in salt as a food preservative. Unfortunately, he and his partner entered the business too late and ran into ferocious competition in an industry that had overexpanded. When demand for salt evaporated at the end of the war, their company collapsed. Flagler lost his entire $50,000 and another $50,000 that he had borrowed from his in-laws, the Harkness family. He was forced to return to trading grain.

Two years later, his debts paid off, he entered the kerosene refining business, teaming up with an equally meticulous and ambitious young neighbor, eight years his junior, whom he knew from his early grain trading days. His new colleague's name was John D. Rockefeller. Together with a third partner, an Englishman named Samuel Andrews, who was an expert in kerosene refining, the three formed the partnership of Rockefeller, Andrews, and Flagler. Once again, the Harkness family staked their son-in-law in the business, doubling their initial investment to $100,000. This time he did not disappoint them. He and his partners quickly consolidated the nascent Ohio kerosene and oil refining business, with a view to better controlling both price and supply. For the next fifteen years, Flagler and

Rockefeller, who soon lived a few doors down from each other on fashionable Euclid Avenue in Cleveland, walked to and from work together, side by side, dressed in their silk top hats, long coats, and gloves, two well-heeled Victorian gentlemen intently discussing their shared enterprise. Theirs would remain, Flagler acknowledged, "a friendship founded on business rather than a business founded on friendship." When the company relocated to New York City, Rockefeller and Flagler continued to live around the corner from each other on East Fifty-Fourth Street in Manhattan.

Today the business is understood to have been Rockefeller's creation, and Flagler's formative contribution has been largely forgotten. But it was Henry's idea to consolidate the industry by buying up all of their small competitors, thus avoiding the fate that befell his salt venture. It was also his idea to secretly demand price concessions from the railroads (10 percent to 15 percent rebates in the early years, more in later years), in return for guaranteed shipments. These concessions allowed the partners to undercut their competition on price, forcing most out of business or into merger agreements with the fast-growing firm. And finally, it was his idea to create the secret trust structure that would allow the company to expand across state borders and combine with other large corporations. It was this last decision, implemented by the firm's clever attorney, Samuel C. T. Dodd, that gave birth to the Standard Oil Trust, the greatest wealth creator the world had seen since the best days of the Dutch East India Company and the British East India Company in the seventeenth and eighteenth centuries.

Flagler's innovations were easily the most significant contributions to the organization's historic success—and Rockefeller knew it. When asked during testimony before Congress if it was his idea to form the oil trust, Rockefeller replied, "No, sir, I wish I'd had the brains to think of it. It was Henry M. Flagler." As he admitted freely to others over the years, "The key to our success was Henry Flagler."

By the time Flagler stepped back from the business in his early fifties to pursue other ventures—ones where he could have complete control— the Standard Oil Trust had a market capitalization of $154 million, or $4.1 billion in today's money, and reigned as the world's largest industrial enterprise. But its exponential growth had only just begun. When John D. Rockefeller, who stayed on in the business, finally retired from the company in 1918, the Standard Oil companies had paid him hundreds of millions in dividends and distributions. His stock holdings in the company made him the world's richest man.

But even as early as the 1880s, controversy engulfed Standard Oil. The public judged it to be a tyrannical monopoly, ruthless and destructive; its management team, greedy and predatory. The muckraking reporter Ida M. Tarbell, whose father's refinery had been steamrolled by the company, wrote a long and scathing exposé for *McClure's* magazine, later published as a book in 1904 called *The History of the Standard Oil Company* that prompted several investigations, which in turn led Congress to pass the Sherman Antitrust Act of 1890.

The question that nagged at the government and the general public was a simple one: How corrupt were the Standard Oil founders? When examined under oath, they chose a campaign of silence and obfuscation, which only exacerbated their public relations problem. In one exchange in 1882, when advised by an investigating committee's attorney that there was a rising tide of sentiment against the company, Flagler lost his composure:

"It suits me to go elsewhere for advice, particularly as I am not paying you for it!"

The government's attorney was ready with a riposte.

"I am not paying you to rob the community, I am trying to expose your robbery."

Robbery might have been an exaggeration, but collusion, skullduggery, and kickbacks were not. A few years later, documents revealed that in order to keep politicians in line and supportive of their enterprise, Standard Oil lent them money and made other "investments" in their careers. Let's call these what they were: bribes. Such behavior was not unusual at this time, when everyday business practices, particularly those west of the more refined cities of New York, Philadelphia, and Boston, resembled a bareknuckle brawl. Businessmen did what they felt was necessary to survive. Meanwhile, politicians were famously receptive to the largesse that came their way.

It is unlikely that Flagler felt any remorse for the actions he had taken at Standard Oil. Yet it must have been a relief for him to escape the press scrutiny and the controversy that enveloped the oil company. He clearly wanted to have more fun, too. A new woman in his life would make that possible. Her name was Ida Alice Shourds. She was pretty and blue eyed and possessed a profusion of red hair as well as a notoriously hot temper. A failed stage actress, she previously had been one of the caregivers for Flagler's wife. Alice was also eighteen years his junior, socially ambitious, and not averse to spending his money.

For the first time in his adult life, Flagler went out to restaurants and to the theater. He rode horseback on his thirty-acre estate in Mamaroneck, New York, and raced trotters against his Standard Oil friends and colleagues. He even joined the Larchmont and New York Yacht Clubs and bought his first yacht, a fifty-foot sloop. As he told a companion in 1886, "For about fourteen or fifteen years, I have devoted my time exclusively to business, and now I am pleasing myself."

St. Augustine in 1882 during Flagler's second visit was no longer a town filled with consumptives. In fact, it had begun to attract society types, the class of men, remarked Flagler, "one might encounter in the great watering places of Europe." However, there was still very little to do. Flagler found himself taking daily walks down narrow St. George Street, where the old colonial buildings on both sides featured crooked second-story balconies. He would continue around the Plaza de la Constitucion, and perhaps over to Castillo de San Marcos, the old Spanish fort on the waterfront, and then back to the hotel, passing along the route other gentlemen who were staying at his hotel, equally at a loss as to what to do with themselves.

Flagler would return to St. Augustine the following December, this time on his honeymoon, newly married to Alice. And he returned again the year after that. "I liked the place and the climate, and it occurred to me very strongly that someone with sufficient means ought to provide accommodations for that class of people who are not sick, who come to enjoy the climate, have plenty of money, but could find no satisfactory way of spending it."

As it happened, he was just such a person. In the prior years, Flagler had discovered how much he enjoyed developing real estate. He had overseen the construction of Standard Oil's first office tower in New York City: a handsome ten-story, eighty-six-foot-wide structure at 26 Broadway in Lower Manhattan (once the home address of Alexander Hamilton). He had also rebuilt his Mamaroneck estate on Long Island Sound in 1882, adding extensions and redecorating the forty-room frame house with, among other fixtures, massive brass and crystal chandeliers of his own design that weighed nearly one thousand pounds. He went so far as to construct a two-hundred-foot breakwater, importing sand to convert the rocky shoreline into his own private beach.

Now he had the architectural drawings for a massive world-class hotel that would offer state-of-the-art amenities. In keeping with the Spanish influence still evident in St. Augustine, the structure would be mostly Moorish in design. If all went well, Flagler would build the grandest resort hotel in the country, surpassing even Potter Palmer's 1875 Palmer House Hotel in Chicago. His larger goal, he told a friend, was to turn St. Augustine into the Newport, Rhode Island, of the South.

He hired two young architects for the project: Thomas S. Hastings (the son of a close friend) and Hastings's partner, Brazilian-born John Merven Carrère, both of whom had studied at the École des Beaux Arts in Paris and worked for the esteemed firm of McKim, Mead & White in New York. It was to be Carrère and Hastings's first major commission. Later in life, Carrère recounted the young partners' jubilation when Hastings returned from a meeting with the news that they had been awarded the plum assignment. Hastings burst into the office and began throwing things at Carrère: " 'We are going to Florida! We've got a million-dollar hotel to build there!' Then we simply proceeded to smash everything we could lay our hands on, our office boy ably assisting us. Of course, we didn't know anything about hotels." Thanks to the start that Flagler gave them, the young firm would go on to become one of the most celebrated architectural practices of the day, renowned for works in the Beaux Arts style and for such iconic commissions as the New York Public Library, the Frick Collection's building on Manhattan's Upper East Side, and the Russell Senate Office Building in Washington, DC.

Excavation began on December 1, 1885. It would take two years and $2.5 million to construct the hotel on a site that had once been a mosquito-infested swamp. Lumber was cut in the Palatka region of Florida and shipped to the site by barge and rail. The carved and dressed oak that would adorn the interior was made in New York and shipped down by coastal schooners. Coquina gravel was sourced from the neighboring island of Anastasia, mixed with concrete, and then poured to create walls four feet thick.

Rising four stories high, topped by a pair of medieval turrets that jutted even higher, the Hotel Ponce de León towered over the Spanish colonial town of St. Augustine. Flagler, who oversaw every element of the design, surrounded the structure, which sprawled over five acres, with a tropical palm garden and a fragrant orange grove. The building was built to last. It still stands today as the imposing main campus building of Flagler College.

Dolphin fountains flowed at the east and west entrances. Over the main entryway, carved mermaids supported a shield bearing the hotel's name. Vine-covered verandahs and loggias lined with spiraling terra-cotta columns opened into a dome-covered rotunda, its floor laid with brightly colored Moroccan mosaics. Carved figurines and naval ornaments recalled the era of the sixteenth-century Spanish discoverer Ponce de León. The dining room seated seven hundred and featured soaring stained-glass windows designed by Louis Comfort Tiffany. Flagler furnished the 450 rooms and suites of varying sizes with Flemish carpets, silk draperies, and furniture made of rosewood, walnut, and mahogany. Steam heat and electric lights, both considered novelties at the time, became important new amenities. Initially, the bathrooms were not en suite, but as tastes changed, Flagler added them.

When the furniture arrived by steamship in late 1887, the tycoon himself was down at the pier to meet the shipment. Removing his topcoat, he helped the workers transport the new furnishings to the hotel. The grand opening of the Ponce de León was on January 10, 1888. It garnered immediate acclaim despite its high prices: $35 per night ($899 in today's dollars) for a suite and full board. Despite the cost, wealthy visitors from the North would soon fill the hotel to capacity, and it quickly earned a sterling reputation for its food and service—and for its clientele. Charles A. Dana, the editor of the *New York Sun*, an art connoisseur, and one of a long list of prominent figures who arrived for a stay, told the *Florida Times-Union*, "The Ponce de León had more pretty girls in it than any hotel I ever saw in my life." Florida's reputation as a premier resort destination was born.

The resort hotel was largely a nineteenth-century innovation, one whose rapid adoption around the world would be spurred by the arrival of the railroad. Luxury urban hotels, per se, were not new; they had evolved from the coaching inns of medieval Europe. One of the earliest in Europe was London's Mivart's Hotel, which opened in 1812 and today is known as Claridge's. The early railway hotels, such as the Victoria and the Adelaide at London's Euston Station, followed soon after in 1839, the product of growing urban populations and industrialization. At first, these were little more than glorified dormitories. The Swiss would put their stamp on this new class of accommodation for the wealthy by offering exceptional service at hotels like the Schweizerhof (1845) on the Lake of Lucerne and the two hotels in Zurich built by Johannes Baur : the Baur en Ville (1836) and the Baur au Lac (1844). It wasn't long before neglected palaces—and in some cases monasteries—in German spa towns, along the French Riviera, and in the Italian Lake District were being retrofitted into palatial hotels.

In the United States, the Tremont House in Boston, completed in 1829, was the first to offer indoor plumbing and running water and what was to become the design standard: rows of private rooms with locking doors arrayed along long interior corridors. Each room sported a jug of water, a bowl, and a bar of soap. It wasn't until Ellsworth Statler built the Hotel Statler in Buffalo in 1907 that a bathroom with a shower or a tub became a standard feature in every room. Still, the Tremont kicked off a competition among US cities and hoteliers to build the largest, swankest,

most comfortable hostelry available, fronted by the most elaborately ornamented facade the developer could afford.

By the 1880s, large resort hotels along the railroads were being built as
vacation destinations for those who could afford them, but especially for
America's burgeoning class of well-to-do entrepreneurs, bankers, and in-
dustrialists, few of whom yet owned second homes. And for the country's
Gilded Age titans, these grand resort hotels—ostentatious, luxurious, and
potentially highly profitable—quickly became trophy assets that offered
a way to diversify one's wealth away from the source of one's fortune and
into more financially stable real estate. They also added to one's social status and prestige. The practice continues to this day, with many billionaires
owning highly visible resort properties as integral parts of their investment
portfolios, and for their own amusement.

However, no one had ever assembled a collection of resort hotels on
the colossal scale that Flagler would do in the last years of the nineteenth
century.

2

A RAILROAD GOES TO SEA

Even before the Ponce de León was finished in 1888, Flagler began work on a second ambitious hotel directly across the street. The giant Alcazar was intended for a slightly less affluent clientele. A square-shaped hotel built around a central courtyard, it would boast a bathing casino, which is to say a swimming pavilion replete with steam baths (single bath: $1.50), massage rooms (massage at bath: $1; outside: $2), and gym equipment. The 120-foot indoor pool was fed by an artesian well (exercise and plunge: 50 cents). Other facilities included a 15,000-square-foot dance floor lit with five hundred incandescent lights, ship shuffleboard, and tenpin and candlepin bowling, while a colonnade at the front of the building housed an array of luxury boutiques. The hotel's facade paid homage to the *Alcázar* palace in Seville, Spain. The Hotel Alcazar initially slept 250; 40 more rooms were added later when a fourth floor was built. The hotel cost Flagler $1 million to build, equivalent to $26.6 million in current dollars. Today it houses municipal offices, shops that cater to tourists, and the Lightner Museum, which is devoted primarily to Gilded Age antiquities. A cafe occupies the sloping floor of the empty indoor swimming pool.

Railroads would necessarily play a starring role in Flagler's growing empire. Fortunately, he already possessed a solid understanding of this business. The financing and building of the railroads had been the great business story of his youth, impossible to ignore. And for years, he had negotiated freight rates with the midwestern railroads on behalf of Standard

Oil. Starting in late 1885, he began to buy up and combine the small East Coast railroads in the north of Florida.

Flagler soon acquired the Jacksonville, St. Augustine, and Halifax River Railroad, followed by the St. Augustine and Palatka Railroad, and finally the St. John's Railroad. Collectively, these became known as the Florida East Coast Railway, or the FEC, on being chartered in 1895. To make the distinct pieces work together, he removed all the narrow-gauge tracks that had been built using light rails and replaced them with the more standard sixty-pound rails and 4-foot-8.5-inch gauge tracks (gauge denotes the distance between the two rails). He replaced the steam locomotives with five new McQueen engines that had a top speed of sixty miles an hour. He also constructed his first bridge, over the St. Johns River.

The railroads gave Flagler enormous power and leverage within the state, as each company was an unregulated monopoly. They also came with a bonus: he could avail himself of massive land grants available only to the railroads. In 1899, for example, the Florida legislature would set aside ten million acres of land to be awarded to anyone willing to build new railroads that enhanced the state's nascent infrastructure. Flagler took full advantage. Claiming eight thousand acres for every mile of track that he laid, he temporarily seized control of two million acres of land at no additional cost. When the federal government contested this deal, Flagler took actual possession of far less, but a still-substantial 210,000 acres. He then added vastly to this acreage through deals with other Florida companies and outright purchases of land.

To cultivate, develop, or simply sell off all the land that he now owned, he founded the Model Land Company and its various subsidiaries. He would use the land company to promote agricultural projects of various kinds—orange and pineapple groves being chief among them—draining and then selling land to farmers and plantation operators at prices that initially ranged from $1.50 to $5.00 an acre, payable in three or four yearly installments at 8 percent interest. In other cases, he went into the construction business, erecting single-family homes, which sold for $1,500 each. The company even planned and promoted colonies along the east coast of the state designed specifically for Swedish, Norwegian, Danish, and

Japanese immigrants to the United States. By now, Flagler had morphed from a hotelier into a full-fledged real estate developer.

To run his railroad efficiently, he needed passengers and freight to run in both directions, in and out of the state. Building supplies were streaming nicely southward, but he needed cargoes of vegetables and fruit to return northward as well. As the system matured, contentious arguments would arise over the rates his railroad charged and the preferences he gave to certain shippers—Cuban purveyors of pineapples, for instance. Eventually public opposition would grow in reaction to the inordinate power the various Flagler enterprises wielded within the state, but, by then, they were virtually unstoppable, as was Flagler.

As the organization grew in size and complexity, Flagler gathered around him a team of exceptionally able men to run his various enterprises. For chief engineer, he recruited a man named Joseph C. Meredith, who had overseen the construction of a giant pier in Tampico, Mexico. Meredith, who loved a challenge, was something of an authority on the uses of reinforced (with iron rods) concrete, the newest building material. He in turn recruited workers from as far north as New York City, with offers to pay their $12 rail fare down to Florida and daily wages of $1.25, which was 25 cents above the norm of the time.

White laborers—a mix of Greeks, Italians, and Germans—moved the earth to build the dikes and the roadbeds. Much of the work would be undertaken in grueling, hot, sunbaked conditions. Mosquitos, poisonous brown recluse and black widow spiders, ten-foot-long American alligators, and a variety of venomous snakes were ever-present dangers. Smudge pots were used to keep the bugs at bay. The clearing and soil moving was done by hand, using machetes and wheelbarrows.

Most foremen believed that black workers were better suited to hot conditions, so more African American men were hired during the sweltering summer months. It was also thought that black laborers excelled at cutting and clearing operations but not at any of the skilled jobs such as carpentry. A rare exception was Dana A. Dorsey, a black carpenter with only a fourth-grade education. The son of former Georgia slaves, Dorsey would go on to build rental housing for black workers in Miami and eventually became one of Florida's first black millionaires. Needless to say, there was not a single black foreman. The railroad wasn't above hiring convicts, either, at a cost of $2.50 per month, even though the convict leasing system was well known for its brutality toward its workers.

By 1888, Flagler owned a section of track that reached as far south as Daytona, about a third of the way down the east coast of Florida. At Ormond, just north of Daytona, he bought a small hotel, renovated it, expanded it, and renamed it the Ormond Beach Hotel. He soon added an eighteen-hole golf course, which was still a novelty in the United States at the time. Then in 1892 he extended the railroad even farther south. By November, it had reached New Smyrna. Hugging the coast, it arrived at Cocoa later that year. It reached Rockledge in February 1893, and Fort Pierce in January 1894. By this time, eager to build another resort hotel, Flagler had a specific destination in mind: a site sixty-eight miles farther south.

Sailing his yacht along the coast the year before, he had stumbled on a slender, sandy barrier island about two-thirds of the way down the Florida coast. He secretly explored the island by mule cart and on foot. Only three-quarters of a mile wide, it was situated between a freshwater ocean inlet called Lake Worth Lagoon and a section of ocean where the Gulf Stream happened to swing close to shore, creating surprisingly balmy temperatures. The deserted, palm-lined beaches were beautiful; the sand bountiful and soft to the touch. He wrote to a friend, "I have found a veritable paradise." Flagler would name the island's tiny village Palm Beach. On a site overlooking Lake Worth Lagoon, he began to build the Royal Poinciana Hotel.

This hotel would be his most ambitious structure yet. In fact, it would be the largest wood hotel in the world and possibly the world's largest wooden structure. Initially able to accommodate 800 guests, the Royal Poinciana eventually boasted 1,081 hotel rooms. At its peak, the resort would employ a staff of 1,400: a waiter for every four diners, a chambermaid for every three rooms, and a bellboy in every hallway. The announcement of the hotel's construction, and the news of the sheer scale of it, sparked one of the earliest Florida property booms. Prices for lots of raw land in the vicinity of the hotel jumped from $150 to $1,500 an acre.

In the spring of 1893, with construction well under way, Flagler decided to move his predominantly black work crews out of the nearby impromptu shantytown known as the Styx. He relocated them to a new two-hundred-acre settlement he'd created on the opposite shore of Lake Worth, a grid of streets soon to be renamed West Palm Beach. From then on, the workers would row across Lake Worth in the morning to their jobs on the construction site and then row home in the evening. By this deliberate act, Flagler accentuated the divide between the workers on one side of his tracks and the future well-to-do patrons of his resort hotels on the other. He had, in effect, created the two worlds of the haves and the have-nots, and set a negative precedent for later developers. The socioeconomic divide between these two groups would grow more pronounced during the 1920s.

Flagler discouraged the use of horses and automobiles on Palm Beach Island. Wicker wheelchairs, also known as pedicycles, or, later, by the more derogatory term "afromobiles," became ubiquitous at his hotels. Two hundred black chairmen were employed for $5 a day to pedal hotel guests around his hotel properties, to local attractions, or to the beach.

When the Royal Poinciana, charging $100 a night, proved to be another instant success, Flagler mirrored his St. Augustine strategy and added a second giant and opulent resort hotel, this one on the ocean side of Palm Beach Island. He would name it the Palm Beach Inn, and only later changed it to the Breakers. Today the Breakers, which has burned down twice, is a Florida landmark and the only one of the properties Henry Flagler built that survives as a resort hotel.

In the winter of 1894–95, Florida suffered a series of horrific freezes. Citrus crops, vegetables, and even coconut palms wilted and died across the northern two-thirds of the state. The economic impact was immediate: the year before, Florida groves produced 5.6 million boxes of oranges; the year following the freeze, that number was down to 150,000 boxes. The fruit-bearing trees lost 90 percent of their fruit-bearing branches. Flagler was determined to protect his various investments, chief among them his railroad, which now depended heavily on local agriculture. He doled out money to the farmers; he gave away seeds, packing materials, and other essentials to help them keep their businesses afloat. And he did much more, lending his credit to stabilize local banks. In short, Flagler kept the crisis from spiraling out of control, which could have cost him ten years of effort and expense.

According to local legend, a backwoods widow named Julia Tuttle actively lobbied him at this time to extend his railroad down to her coastal village, once the site of a Seminole Indian trading post. She was willing to gift him one hundred acres of her land—she owned a 640-acre homestead along the Miami River at Key Biscayne—and one of her neighbors would match that amount, knowing full well that their remaining property would soar in value. When the Key Biscayne area of Florida escaped the harsh winter freezes, she seized upon this fact and sent Flagler sprays of citrus branches in full bloom to prove the point, which may have helped to sway him. Flagler made the journey down to visit her, selected a new hotel site, and struck a deal with Tuttle. Before long, he had yet another hotel under construction: the Royal Palm, with its mansard roof, its signature "Flagler yellow" exterior, and its green trim. Here, too, black workers were relegated to the outskirts of town, in an area then known as Colored Town (later renamed Overtown), which soon became an overcrowded slum. He also built a railroad station, the first city streets, some modestly priced housing, and various waterworks, although they didn't extend to Colored Town. As was so often the case, the railroad's arrival had the desired effect of literally putting the town—Miami, as it was soon named—on the map.

Julia Tuttle did not waste her opportunity, either. She immediately built a large hotel of her own, the Miami Hotel, completed in 1896. Sadly, she did not live long enough to witness the full effects of the Florida boom or to see Miami transform from a small town to a metropolis. She died of meningitis two years later at age forty-nine. Her wooden hotel caught fire a year after that and burned to the ground.

Meanwhile, Flagler's succession of projects—hotels built in concert with the extension of the railroad—was proving to be extraordinarily costly. He would complain to an interviewer in 1909, "If it wasn't for Florida, I'd be quite a rich man today." He was exaggerating his penury. When he began his construction spree, Flagler's net worth ranged between $10 million and $20 million, but that fortune had soared. By 1900, his thirty-thousand-share equity stake in the Standard Oil Trust was throwing off $1.2 million a year in dividends. He borrowed against that money and occasionally sold shares back to the company when cash grew tight. Flagler was able to spend $45 million on the railroad, another $12 on the hotels, and $1 million on steamships. Millions more were spent on charitable activities that included the building of local churches, which helped to soften his image with the locals. The hotels, despite being seasonal in nature, eventually proved profitable. The railroad, however, never broke even during his lifetime.

By 1904, Flagler had nearly completed his resort hotel empire. He would call it the Florida East Coast Hotel Company. He also owned two electric and water utility companies and four land companies. To these he would add a steamship service to Cuba and the Bahamas (where he bought yet another hotel, the Colonial). He remained actively in charge of the so-called Flagler System until 1909, at which point he delegated day-to-day control of the enterprise to a president, James R. Parrott, a graduate of Yale University and Yale Law School, who had served as his chief legal advisor for decades.

Despite the giant scale of this empire, Flagler remained largely unknown to the general public. This was by choice. He would grant only three major interviews during these later years, and even in these, he revealed little of himself or his motivations for building his empire.

There may well have been a reason why Flagler presented such an implacable facade to the public, his image notably at odds with those of the showmen developers who came after him. For one thing, he had a great deal of sorrow and unhappiness to hide. He had lost a child of only three years in age early in his first marriage. Then, of course, he had lost his beloved first wife, Mary, to tuberculosis. In 1889 he lost his only other daughter, Jennie Louise, who died after a troubled pregnancy; the newborn child herself lived only a few hours. In addition, Flagler had grown estranged from his only son, Harry, who moved to Florida after graduating from Columbia University but spent only two years working for his father before retreating to Manhattan. There he spent the rest of his life immersed in the world of classical music, eventually founding a symphony orchestra that would merge with another to form the New York Philharmonic. In his will, Flagler left his son only a small portion of his fortune, some 5,000 shares of Standard Oil stock, complaining that "my son has not shown for me the filial regard that would make me inclined to do more for him," and stipulating that Harry be disinherited if he attempted to contest the will.

Worse yet, Flagler's second marriage, to Ida Alice Shourds, had proven disastrous. She squandered his money on clothes, yachts, and lavish entertaining, throwing a succession of charity balls in St. Augustine at which she wore increasingly risqué clothing. Always irascible and erratic in her behavior, she grew noticeably more so. Unable to bear children, she became inordinately interested in other people's newborns and compiled a large scrapbook of their photographs that she obsessed over. Soon she became delusional, announcing that she was engaged to marry the czar of Russia and whispering to household staff that she planned to murder her husband. Alice began to carry on discussions with imaginary people and absent relatives and to throw violent tantrums. In 1895 she was finally committed into the House of Dr. Choate Sanitarium in Pleasantville, New York; eight months later, she was briefly released, but the delusions soon returned. She locked herself in her bedroom with a Ouija board, which she consulted for hours at a time, and, at one point, she attacked a visiting doctor with a pair of scissors, badly lacerating his face and hands.

Alice was institutionalized for a second and final time in March 1897. At this point, she seems to have descended into a constant state of paranoia and outright insanity, talking to imaginary people, filling notebooks with incoherent scribbling, rouging her cheeks with the dye from her yarn, blackening her eyebrows with burnt cork, and rubbing the cream served with her coffee into her hair as a tonic. As one account put it, "she lost her reason." In June 1899 she was declared mentally incompetent. Flagler would send her flowers twice a week for the rest of his life, but after her second incarceration, he never saw her again. She lived on for another thirty years, far outliving him and dying of a stroke in 1930.

At the time of Alice's second incarceration, in 1897, Flagler, now sixty-six, began an affair with a North Carolina belle named Mary Lily

Kenan, who was thirty-seven years younger than he. When her parents objected to the relationship, he gave her a thousand shares of Standard Oil stock, then trading for around $600 a share, and bought her jewelry valued at more than $1 million. He was determined to marry her and resolved to find a way to do so.

Flagler began by moving his legal residency to Florida. There he lobbied the legislature to draft and pass a new law that allowed for divorce on grounds of insanity—up until then, adultery was the only legal cause for divorce. The legislation easily passed both the Florida House of Representatives and the Senate and was signed into law by the governor in April 1901. Two months later, Flagler was able to divorce Alice. It was subsequently revealed that he had lavished gifts on Florida legislators, following the familiar Standard Oil playbook.

He finally married Mary Lily in August 1901. As a wedding present, he built for her, on the edge of Lake Worth in Palm Beach, one of the Gilded Age's most splendid private homes: Whitehall. Designed by Carrère and Hastings in their favored Beaux Arts style, this marble masterpiece was dubbed "the Taj Mahal of North America" by the *New York Herald*. It combined Greek and Roman architecture with French and Italian Renaissance motifs, and endures today as the Flagler Museum. The 4,400-square-foot front hall, known as Grand Hall, featured seven different types of marble and was the largest room in any of the great Gilded Age mansions: 110 feet wide by 40 feet deep. The dining room seated fifty. Upstairs were sixteen guest suites, each with a different design, evoking a famous epoch in world history.

Flagler personally oversaw every detail of Whitehall's construction and decorating. Perhaps because Mary Lily left such matters to him, his third marriage appeared to be a happy one, at least initially. She was quickly welcomed into the social set in Palm Beach, where she was admired for her grace and charm, and especially for her generosity: she liked to give out silver trinkets and snuffboxes as gifts. The third Mrs. Flagler enjoyed dancing, playing the piano, and singing, and took an active interest in local cultural events. She began to entertain grandly. Eventually, however, rumors would emerge that Mary Lily drank too much and, more ominously, that she was addicted to the opiate laudanum. The couple drifted apart in the ensuing years, estranged by his age and growing frailty; Flagler soon began abstaining from attending his wife's social events. He was elderly now and had begun to lose his eyesight; then he began to go deaf as well.

In response to his growing infirmities, he retreated deeper into his work. At one point, in the summer of 1907, a newspaper reported that the seventy-seven-year-old entrepreneur had suffered a nervous breakdown. As Flagler told the journalist Edwin Lefèvre in 1909, "I don't know of anyone who has been successful, but that he has been compelled to pay some price for success. Some get it at the loss of their health, others forego the pleasures of home and spend their years in the forest or mines; some acquire success at the loss of their character, and so it goes. Many prices are paid."

As he entered the final decade of his life, Flagler grew preoccupied with fulfilling one last grand ambition, and it may well have been his goal from the beginning: to extend the railroad to the remote island town of Key West. He seems to have understood early on that the eventual opening of the Panama Canal could mean enormous business opportunities for the deep port on the island, but only if it could be linked by rail to the mainland. Coal, for example, could be delivered there to the US Navy, now patrolling the Caribbean. Trade with Cuba presented yet another opportunity, especially after the island fell under American purview following the Spanish-American War of 1898. Cuba, a rich source of sugar, tobacco, pineapples, bananas, and coffee, was just a short ninety-mile steamship ride from Key West. Conceivably, Pullman cars full of tourists could be carried by steamship to the island and back. Flagler is said to have gathered his engineers at the terminus of the railroad south of Miami in early 1904 and announced, "Gentlemen, the railroad will go to sea." He had saved this, his riskiest project, for last—a $15 million engineering marvel that would be disparaged by the press as "Flagler's Folly." The Key West Extension seemed as improbable and preposterous a project as would the building of a new Egyptian pyramid.

The 155 miles of track from Miami to Key West would take eight years to complete, between 1904 and 1912, at a cost of $35 million. It would stand as a dazzling feat of engineering on a par with the building of the Hoover Dam. The once-skeptical press would describe it as "the Eighth Wonder of the World." To carve through the Everglades south of Homestead, Flagler's men used a pair of floating dredges that worked side by side. They dug up the mud and the sedimentary rock known as marl and dumped it between them to construct a causeway and railroad bed, creating their own parallel channels as they chewed their way through the great swamp toward Key Largo.

When the railroad finally reached the ocean, the project grew infinitely more complex. Meredith and his men would need a fleet of ships to proceed. Flagler bought, leased, or had built an armada that included some nine paddle-wheel steamers, sixty-three gasoline-powered launches, five tugboats, forty-six barges or lighters that varied in length from 20 feet to 157 feet (to be used for driving pilings, mixing cement, or ferrying cargo), thirteen floating dredges, and a dozen quarter boats, or houseboats, to be used as dormitories.

Linking up the Florida Keys required thirteen separate stretches of track, varying in length from .02 miles to 28.4 miles over water that ranged in depth from 10 to 30 feet. Each was a distinct project with its own obstacles. Waterproof cofferdams were constructed so that the concrete could be poured to make the piers and viaducts that would carry the railroad bed over the water. The Long Key Viaduct, one of the first great engineering problems, required 186 separate eighty-foot reinforced concrete arches in order to span 2.15 miles of open water. It would take 286,000 barrels of concrete to build a structure that resembled a Roman aqueduct. The Seven-Mile Bridge from Knight's Key to Little Duck Key, the longest of the open-water expanses, took four years to build and included a swiveling drawbridge over the deepest stretch of water.

The Panama Canal was the only project on the continent at the time to compete in scale with the Key West Extension. With 102 steam shovels deployed for more than a decade, the canal project dwarfed Flagler's railroad to the sea, but in technical terms was less of an engineering feat. There was another important difference: Flagler's extension was entirely privately funded.

Heat, humidity, and bugs made for the most arduous working conditions yet. Fresh water was so scarce on the Keys that tanker cars were used to ship in supplies of it, or the water was pumped out of the Everglades into large holding tanks. During the day, most of the men wore improvised screened hats made from cheesecloth and wire. Long-sleeved shirts and gloves helped to protect against the cacti, mosquitoes, spiders, and fire ants. The mosquitos rose in black swarms after five o'clock in the afternoon, discouraging anyone from venturing outdoors. The workers slept in bunkhouses with as many as sixty-four men to a dorm. Many slept on bunk beds in the hold of a quarter boat.

It was a six-day workweek for the 2,500 workers. Sundays were spent writing letters to loved ones at home or exploring Miami or the Keys. Paid monthly in gold coin, many of the workers promptly drank or gambled away their earnings. According to one newspaper account, "the very great majority will wend their way to a groggery and there remain until the cop scoops them in or their money is gone." Whiskey, at $5 a quart, could easily consume a large portion of a paycheck.

All went relatively smoothly until the night of October 17, 1906, when an unexpected hurricane blew onto the Keys. The railroad crews, using unreliable homemade barometers, were caught by surprise. Quarter boat no. 4, carrying on board 145 sleeping men and tethered to the pilings at Long Key Viaduct, was torn from its mooring. The gigantic surf of the storm smashed the vessel to pieces against the new concrete piers before sweeping the debris out to sea. Only forty-nine survivors were rescued over the following days, most found clinging to wreckage and floating in the Gulf Stream, one of them blinded by the salt water and sun. Another twenty men drowned when the steamship *St. Lucie* sank in the pitch dark later that same night.

How did Flagler respond to this sudden loss of life? Perhaps it is no coincidence that the hurricane occurred in late 1906, and Flagler suffered his nervous breakdown in 1907.

Eleven more men would die when the tugboat *Sybil* sank in another hurricane in 1909. Dynamite, which was used daily, killed an additional twenty-one men in accidents of various kinds, and maimed another dozen. One worker, drunk and asleep on the tracks, was run over by a train. In total, the project claimed 158 lives and injured another 81.

At the end, it was a race against time—the time left in Flagler's life. In the final year of the project, with the frail tycoon weakening, they pushed on even harder, ramping up the number of men and adding shifts to get the work done. They chose his eighty-second birthday as a deadline for completion and missed the date by less than a month. When the railroad was finished on January 21, 1912, Flagler, deaf and nearly completely blind, was in failing health, but he could still walk with the aid of a cane. He rode down to Key West in his private railcar to the celebratory ribbon cutting, accompanied by his wife, the Florida governor, and a handful of state dignitaries. They arrived to find a crowd of some five thousand, who cheered the old man and waved flags. He disembarked gingerly to blaring boat horns and drumrolls of the Cuban National Band.

A podium had been set up at the railroad station. In his remarks, Flagler spoke of all the changes that he had witnessed in Florida over the prior decades: When he broke ground on the Ponce de León in December 1885, there were only 1,500 to 2,000 people living in St. Augustine. There was not a single house between the city and East Palatka. Ormond had only 150 inhabitants; Daytona, about the same. Everything south of Daytona was virtual wilderness, including the sixty miles between Palm Beach and Miami. "I traveled over it riding behind a mule and a cart. . . . Palm Beach had three houses, two families living in two of them and an old bachelor in the third house. Coconut Grove perhaps had three or four houses—nothing south of that. Today there is a very large population, and that whole country is filled with an industrious and prosperous people, and thousands of comfortable homes exist where desolation existed only twenty-five years ago."

At one point in the celebration, a chorus of schoolchildren serenaded Flager. As he listened, he turned to an official and remarked, "I can hear the children singing, but I cannot see them."

If Flagler had not inherited his father's reticence, as he claimed, or perhaps if he had granted more interviews and minded less seeing his name in print, the story of what he accomplished in Florida would be better known today. His railroad-to-sea project remained overshadowed by the construction of the Panama Canal, which was completed two years later, in 1914—much as Flagler's earlier career had been eclipsed by the career of his partner, John D. Rockefeller. There was also the fact that his railroad never earned back the enormous investment required to build it.

Back in Palm Beach, Flagler lived on for another fifteen months. In May 1913 the old tycoon fell on the marble stairs in Whitehall and broke his hip. He complained to the minister of the nearby Royal Poinciana Chapel, "I was old and blind and deaf; was it fair to make me lame?" He never recovered. He died on May 20, at age eighty-three.

Thanks to his taciturn public persona, Henry Flagler's obituaries were understandably somewhat broad-brush, extolling him for converting the Florida peninsula from wilderness into one long luxury resort, and for being perhaps the greatest construction genius America had yet produced. The fact that one of the nation's richest men had become the nineteenth century's greatest entrepreneur and that he had accomplished so much in the second act of his life seemed all the more remarkable to the press of the day.

All that was true, but the encomiums overlooked the larger story of what Flagler had accomplished. By virtually inventing the resort towns of Ormond, Palm Beach, Delray, Deerfield, Fort Lauderdale, Homestead, and Miami, and by building the Florida East Coast Railway the length of Florida to service them, well before there were decent roads, Flagler had laid down the main infrastructure artery—the freight lifeline—for the next great boom in the state's astonishing development. Thanks to these improvements, and Flagler's early investments in land, agriculture, banking, and utilities, Florida would grow from being arguably the poorest state in the union to having the country's third largest population and fourth largest economy today. "Indeed, no individual has had a greater or more lasting impact on a state than Henry Flagler has had in Florida," a recent biographer has written.

Flagler had created a blueprint for how resort development could be accomplished and demonstrated the soaring heights a developer could reach if he or she had the funds and the willingness to dream big enough. His imitators stood in the wings, with plans of their own, eager to build on what he had begun or to put their own marks on the unique terrain of the state. Fittingly, most of them would arrive in Florida on the very railroad that Flagler had built—at such a great cost in wealth and human lives.

3

✦◆❏◆✿◆❏◆✦

NEW ARRIVALS

By the time of his death, Henry Flagler had created in Florida what the author Henry James, after a visit, described as "a hotel civilization." If you had the money to afford Flagler's expensive resorts, you were granted access to this new community, whether you were a member of the old guard or one of the nouveau riche. This was especially true in Palm Beach, the toniest of the developments, where "nothing counts but lucre," according to the editor of the New York scandal sheet *Town Topics: The Journal of Society*. In Palm Beach, the only important social distinction that mattered (and still matters today) was the one between the ordinary wealthy and the extremely rich. Fittingly, at the very top of the social heap were those who arrived in Florida by private yacht or, better yet, in their own private railcar. During this period, which fell at the end of the Gilded Age, "The nearest thing to a real aristocracy in America was the private-car peerage," according to the *New Yorker* writer Alva Johnston, "and Palm Beach had the world's most snobbish rail road yard—a Newport-on-wheels, an exalted trailer camp for the gold-encrusted Pullmans of the New World nobility."

Flagler had created a winter playground for the wealthy, but it was active for only six to eight weeks each winter and was largely boarded up in the summer months. The resort towns would remain no more than winter retreats until better and more numerous roads could be built, freeing potential year-round residents from their dependency on the railroad.

Meanwhile, popular pastimes at the Royal Poinciana and the Breakers consisted of bicycling, which was a hugely popular hobby at the turn of the century, and also golf, swimming, croquet, and shooting. You could take aim at exotic plumed shorebirds, such as egrets and herons, from the decks of boats, or you could stand on the sand and take potshots at pelicans and seagulls. In Miami, the lifestyle was similar, revolving around Flagler's Royal Palm Hotel, where the yellow and green clapboard structure catered to a similarly upmarket clientele, offering tea dances and soirees on a daily basis, as well as lawn tennis and swimming lessons.

Part of the fun and lure of the grand hotels, which socially reigned supreme from 1830 to 1930, was that they offered guests who were not of royal lineage all the luxury and grandeur once available only to the Old World's royal families. Housed in highly theatrical neoclassical structures, these hotels could provide great comfort and obsequious levels of customer service, always a winning combination. In this pampered environment, "The customer is always right," the great hotelier Cesar Ritz was the first to proclaim.

As everyone was on holiday, there was the unspoken understanding that the usual social constraints could be relaxed somewhat, which meant, of course, more drinking, gambling, and other forms of carousing. In fact, the grand hotels helped to break the social taboos that once forbade women from dining alone or smoking cigarettes in public. They even encouraged ever-deeper décolletages. Paradoxically, the very success of these grand hotels set in motion the cultural changes and trends toward informality that would cause them to fall out of favor.

The economic devastation in Europe caused by World War I hurt their prospects as well. On the Continent, the leading grand hotels fell into disrepair in the years following the war. In the United States, many grand hotels, such as the Royal Palm in Miami, were built in great haste and were lightly constructed out of timber. Gas lighting, big kitchens, and shoddy electrical wiring created serious fire hazards. Many would burn to the ground.

The bulk of the so-called New World nobility who frequented these grand resort hotels possessed fortunes that were the direct outcome of the country's rapid industrialization, most of them derived from investments in oil, coal, steel, sugar, real estate, mining, finance, and automobiles. As these fortunes grew, a younger generation of wealthy visitors arrived in Florida: the sons and daughters of the founders of these great enterprises. For them, the hotels were less of a novelty and more of a relic of the bygone belle époque. It wasn't long before the members of this younger generation tired of the formal hotel suites and began to play with the idea of building their own private homes for use during extended winter stays. These were the first stirrings of the land boom that would mark the 1920s. Whitehall had offered a superb example of what was possible, and so did a splendid new estate under construction; it was called Vizcaya.

If Flagler's Whitehall was Palm Beach's first great stately home, Villa Vizcaya would be Miami's. Named in honor of the Spanish explorer Sebastián Vizcaíno, who discovered Biscayne Bay, the estate was built on the waterfront in 1914, two miles south of the city. Whereas the funds to build Whitehall came from a great fortune made in oil, the money behind Vizcaya derived from the mechanization of agriculture; more specifically, from the sale of grain harvesters. The house was the winter home of James Deering, son of the founder of the Deering Harvester Company, which had merged with the McCormick Harvesting Machine Company in 1902 to form International Harvester. The company soon made the Deering family one of the wealthiest in the country. James, who was the vice president of the merged company, was an elegant lifelong bachelor who liked to be shaved each morning by his personal valet in front of a large gilt mirror. He spoke three foreign languages fluently, wore a pince-nez, and walked with a Malacca walking cane—a popular accessory of aristocratic gentlemen of the late nineteenth century. He favored pearl-gray bespoke suits and owned six hundred neckties. He already owned a house on Lake Shore Drive in Chicago, an apartment in Manhattan, and leased a house on Rue Spontini in Paris during the summer months.

Initially, Deering had envisioned building a Spanish villa, but the design quickly morphed into a predominantly Venetian-style structure with Palladian elements spread across its three-story facade. Even before the impressive structure was completed, Deering had amassed a warehouse full of artwork and statuary on trips to Europe with his architect, F. Burrall Hoffman Jr., and his designer, Paul Chalfin, who had once worked for the famed interior decorator Elsie de Wolfe. Both men were united in their determination that the estate be a work of art. "Must we be so grand?" Deering is said to have moaned as Chalfin rummaged through crumbling French and Italian villas and palaces, buying up entire rooms, medieval altars—even a fireplace from a chateau that once belonged to Catherine de' Medici, a powerful queen of France in the mid-1500s. One schooner brought in 110 tons of marble and 779 crates of household effects that had taken eleven days to load in the Port of New York.

Villa Vizcaya endures today as a museum of European decorative arts. Most of the elaborate formal gardens, however, are gone, with the exception of those immediately adjacent to the house. Originally, they stretched over 180 landscaped acres that included a walled garden, a fountain garden, a maze garden, a tropical garden, and a theater garden. A giant baroque stone barge in the shape of a galleon was erected in the water off the front of the house in part to serve as a breakwater. It was ornamented with statues of nude sea-girls carved by Stirling Calder, father of the sculptor Alexander Calder. Although somewhat dilapidated, the barge remains standing today. As the sea level has risen—more than a foot since its construction one hundred years ago—the barge appears to be sinking into the bay. It is worth noting that before the 1920s, and before the proliferation of the automobile and the internal combustion engine, sea level rise was limited to one foot per one thousand years. From 1930 onward, the rate would increase to one foot per one hundred years, a rate that today is accelerating once again.

The house itself, built around an open courtyard, is a clever synthesis of Renaissance, baroque, rococo, and neoclassical architectural styles. It was largely completed in two years, although Colombian landscape architect Diego Suarez, who deserves credit for the stone barge idea and design, did not complete the gardens until 1923.

For a time, at least 10 percent of the population of Miami was involved in the construction and maintenance of this extraordinary estate. Once the villa was up and running, it required a full-time staff of thirty that included a superintendent, a chief engineer, a boat captain, a boat engineer, a garage supervisor, a chauffeur to drive the Rolls-Royce, a poultry man, and a fishing guide, not to mention the cooks and the housemaids. The gardens and extended property employed another eighty or so. Fond of yachting and deep-sea fishing, Deering kept his eighty-foot cruiser *Nepenthe* and his forty-five-foot fishing launch *Psyche* moored in the waters off the front of the villa. Although Miami had been "dry" since 1913, Deering shipped in $27,000 worth of wine to fill his wine cellar.

According to one story, possibly false, Deering threw a stag dinner party for friends at Vizcaya that featured a performance by the entire chorus line of the Ziegfeld Follies, two of whom stayed on to marry Miami men. Another story, this one verified, is that William Randolph Hearst first met the Hollywood actress and former Ziegfeld girl Marion Davies, with whom he had a thirty-year extramarital affair, at a pool party at Vizcaya in 1918. Another source of salacious gossip was the secret passageway that linked Deering's suite to the suite immediately next to his—an egress clearly designed for late-night assignations. The suite itself featured a seventeenth-century bed believed to have once belonged to Lady Hamilton, wife of the British ambassador to Naples, Italy, and mistress of Lord Nelson.

When in residence, Deering could be found seated in a white wicker chaise longue in the open courtyard, clad in a white linen suit and wearing his pince-nez as he read the daily newspapers. Some of celebrated society artist John Singer Sargent's finest watercolors were painted of the loggia and terraces at Vizcaya—as well as a handful of more personal nudes of the Vizcaya workmen. A longtime sufferer of pernicious anemia, Deering had the use of the house for only nine winters. Accompanied by a nurse, his private physician, his personal secretary, and his valet, he would die at age sixty-five in 1925 on the French luxury liner SS *Paris* on a return trip from Paris.

Construction projects such as Vizcaya began to draw both the professional and working classes to Florida in significant numbers. For the first time, opportunities existed for employment beyond menial jobs in agriculture or on the staff of the Flagler hotels. Bankers, lawyers, architects, artisans, contractors, interior decorators, real estate agents, and journalists arrived on the coattails of the wintering rich, recognizing that the tropical frontier was now fertile ground for business.

Chief among these new prospectors was the handful of figures that would end up playing starring roles in the great land boom of the 1920s.

The first to appear was a handsome, square-faced twenty-five-year-old New York law student named George Edgar Merrick. In the fall of 1911, he sat staring out a Pullman car window at the blur of passing loblolly pines as his train rumbled through the forests of Georgia and crossed the border into Florida. His life and his future career had just been upended by an alarming piece of news: a few days earlier, word had reached him by telegraph that his father, who was suffering from heart disease, had taken a turn for the worse and lay bedridden and desperately ill. The family needed George to come home to take over managing its extensive grapefruit planation. Any plans he might have had to pursue a career of his own were put on hold. On the train that day, Merrick struggled to contain his bitterness. He was returning, as he wrote in an autobiographical short story, "like the beaten prodigal son" to assume the role of hired hand to his sick, irascible father.

The Reverend Solomon Merrick, a Congregationalist minister with a degree from Yale Divinity School, had moved his family to the area south of Miami from Duxbury, Massachusetts, in 1899, when George, the oldest of six children, was twelve years old. The Merricks were looking for warmer, healthier climes after having lost a four-year-old daughter to diphtheria. With little idea of the challenges awaiting them, Solomon and his wife, Althea, had bought a 160-acre homestead, sight unseen, with their life savings of $1,100. Their accommodations consisted of a two-room shack, two small cabins, and a barn built out of barrel staves. They scratched out a living growing vegetables and grapefruit on what turned out to be a poor parcel of land. As a young boy, George delivered their homegrown produce to Flagler's newly built Royal Palm Hotel on a homemade mule cart, bouncing along the area's sandy, rutted roads. At the docks in Miami Harbor, he helped load the family's cabbages, peppers, eggplant, and potatoes onto Flagler steamships bound for Nassau and Cuba.

Even as a boy, George Merrick aspired to more than farming and selling produce. Highly idealistic and blessed with a modicum of literary talent, he wrote lyric poetry and earnest short stories. One of his stories, called "The Sponger's Delilah," won a literary contest in 1910 and was published in the *New York Evening Telegram*. When he floated the idea to his parents that he might want to pursue a literary career instead of the law, his father met the suggestion with derision. Now the point was moot: neither career was open to him. George was returning to Florida with his "silly, futile, empty, hopeless dreams" reduced to, as he wrote, "pithy, wilted stalks."

And yet, secretly, he had not given up all hope of doing something creative and innovative. Merrick had been inspired by a visit to Frederick Law Olmsted Jr.'s Forest Hills Gardens in Queens, New York. The son of the famous landscape architect of Central Park, the junior Olmsted was, like his father, a chief proponent of the City Beautiful Movement that had caught the imaginations of many urban planners on both sides of the Atlantic at the turn of the century. Forest Hills Gardens, still under construction, was a well-publicized American realization of these novel ideas: a mixture of green spaces, tree-lined boulevards, and Arts and Crafts–style Tudor housing in a tranquil, parklike setting where residents could live harmoniously with nature.

The visit to Forest Hills Gardens gave George an idea for how to transform his family's grapefruit plantation into a more profitable enterprise. Assuming he could make or raise enough money, he envisioned converting the property into a humane small city, an Olmsted-like planned community where every municipal requirement, every architectural feature, and every landscape detail could be worked out in advance to ensure its overall beauty, function, and harmony. He imagined seven grand entrances, winding streets and waterways, elegant plazas, neoclassical fountains, and harmonious tree-lined subdivisions.

Unlike his literary aspirations, which would never be fully realized, George Merrick's dream of building an ideal community in Florida would come to stunning fruition over the ensuing years, thanks in large part to his impressive work ethic. His father would die of congestive heart failure within a year of George's return to Miami, but, by then, George was staying up late at night to sketch out the details of his project. Coral Gables would emerge as one of the largest and most ambitious planned communities in the country, and it would set the standard for countless other developments, sparking imitators up and down the Florida coast throughout the 1920s. For a period of time, George Merrick would be the most famous land developer in the country.

The next significant figure to appear on the scene was a young woman named Marjory Stoneman Douglas. She, too, was twenty-five years old when she arrived by train in Miami in September 1915. Like Merrick, she had shown a precocious talent for writing, and also like Merrick, her home life had been challenging. Her parents separated when she was six, and she grew up an only child in her maternal grandparents' house in Taunton, Massachusetts, in the custody of her mother and her aunt Fanny. Her mother, to whom she was close, was high-strung, childlike, and so mentally unstable as to require repeated stays in a sanitarium. In order to pay for Douglas to attend Wellesley College, the family rented out a room in their house, and her aunt dipped into her savings. At Wellesley, Douglas excelled at her studies, especially at elocution—from the outset, she was a fearless public speaker. In 1912, her senior year, she was editor in chief of her Wellesley senior yearbook. That same year, her mother died of breast cancer.

The dislocations and troubles of her childhood made Marjory, as she would say later in life, "a skeptic and a dissenter." She also considered herself something of an ugly duckling, and the facts bear this out. As she wrote in her memoirs, "During my entire four years at college, no man took me to a dance, or even to lunch." Not surprisingly, she married one of the first men ever to notice her or pay her much attention: Kenneth Douglas, an older, courtly fellow she met in a library in Newark, New Jersey. He was the church and social service editor of the *Newark Evening News* newspaper but would prove to be a singularly poor choice for a husband. Thirty years her senior, he was an unrepentant con artist who specialized in forging checks. Her uncle described him as "a threshold case"—in other words, an alcoholic. Within a year of their marriage, Kenneth was serving six months in prison for passing bad checks. When he attempted to repeat the offense shortly after his release, she resolved to leave him.

By moving down to Florida, she hoped to restart her adult life. That would entail getting a divorce, although securing one would require two years of residency in the state. Her father, Frank B. Stoneman, living in Miami, had offered to take her in and sent her money for the train fare to Florida. She had not seen him since she was six years old.

As luck would have it, her father was the founder and editor in chief of the *Miami Herald*, one of two newspapers serving the small but growing population of Miami, which now numbered some five thousand residents. His success as a newspaperman was hard won. He had failed at a variety of business ventures, including opening the first grocery store in Billings, Montana, and later selling lubricating oil to factories in Providence, Rhode Island. Frank had moved to Orlando, Florida, in the late 1890s to open a law practice, but after a few years of struggling there as an attorney, he accepted an old flatbed press in return for the forgiveness of a debt. In 1903 he moved the printing press down to Miami to start the first evening paper, assisted by two partners and his girlfriend and eventual second wife, Lilla Shine, who was a great-great-granddaughter of Thomas Jefferson.

They named the paper the *Miami Evening Record*. Four years later, they made an acquisition that caused the business to stumble financially. The paper was reorganized as the *Miami Herald* with Henry Flagler's secretive financial backing and Flagler's former railroad lawyer, Frank Shutts, serving as its new publisher. By then, Shutts was the most successful attorney in Miami. Shortly after Flagler's death, Shutts would quietly purchase the paper from the tycoon's estate; he would make a substantial fortune from the investment as the circulation soared. Frank Stoneman would continue to serve as the editor in chief of the *Herald* until his death in 1941.

The train ride down from New York City took two days. On the morning she arrived in Miami, directionless, her marriage a shambles, Douglas's main worry was what her father and her new stepmother would think of her—and of the awful mess that she had made of her young life. She stepped down from her Pullman car into the morning heat and humidity. With time to kill before her father was scheduled to meet her, Marjory decided to explore the town. She walked the grid of Miami streets with its dingy collection of boardinghouses and its nondescript wood-frame commercial buildings. The largest structure by far was Flagler's yellow and white Royal Palm Hotel.

In a few minutes, she reached the waterfront and stood there staring out at Biscayne Bay. A light breeze was blowing, and the slanting sun imparted glints of gold to the blue-green waters. "It was magnificent," she recalled years later. "There were schools of mullet jumping in the sunlight, and flocks of birds turning and wheeling so their white wings would catch that light." The humid air was dense with tropical promise and laden with citrus smells and faint jungle odors. The smells and the brilliant sunshine—"this wonderful white tropic light," as she called it—stirred an early childhood memory of her father lifting her up to pluck an orange from a blossoming tree in the gardens of the Tampa Bay Hotel while on a family holiday; now once again she could smell that tree's aroma: pungent, liquory, and sweet. With that memory came a sudden affinity for this strange new place: "I recognized it as something I had loved and missed and longed for all my life."

Her rapport with Florida would only grow in intensity as she found her mission in life and her voice as a writer. Douglas's chief cause would become the preservation of the nearby Everglades, the vast tropical wetlands that originally encompassed four thousand square miles in the southern half of the state. The Everglades were already the site of rancorous battles over land use, and those battles would become an ongoing postscript to the Flagler era. For her conservation work, Douglas would be awarded the Presidential Medal of Freedom in 1993—when she was 103 years old and still a formidable advocate for the environment.

Returning to the train, Douglas reboarded the Pullman and sat waiting, full of apprehension, her suitcase by her side. Eventually she heard a man approaching and someone shouting to him a greeting: "Morning, Judge!" Frank Stoneman swung himself aboard the train at the far end of her railcar. Unbeknownst to Douglas, her father had won an election for circuit court judge, although Governor Napoleon Broward had denied him the job and refused to ratify his election after the newspaperman wrote a series of editorials critical of Broward's rash and scientifically ill-informed plan to drain the Everglades. The incident nevertheless had earned Stoneman the nickname "Judge."

He strode down the aisle of the Pullman with his Panama hat in one hand, a tall, imposing figure with a handsome head of graying hair, a prominent Roman nose, and intelligent and kind hazel eyes. He seemed at ease and quietly confident. As Marjory rose to greet him, he took a slight step backward in surprise—and she instantly guessed why. She was just five foot two and had none of her mother's beauty, nor did she have any of the charming curly hair that she had possessed as a child, the last time her father had seen her. In fact, she was a rather plain-looking young woman. "My face was always a bit crooked, and if anything, it had become crookeder," she wrote in a 1987 autobiography, *Voice of the River.* Her stringy, mousy hair fell limply at either side of her face. "He expected a pretty girl, but now I wasn't." As she watched, he regained his composure with an effort. "Hello, sweetheart," he said softly. "Hello, Father," she answered. Then he leaned forward and kissed her on the cheek, and they were reunited, as she later described it, "with no fuss and feathers."

When the position of society editor for the *Miami Herald* opened up unexpectedly a few weeks later, he offered his daughter the job, making her the newspaper's first female reporter.

On January 5, 1918, a little more than two years after Marjory Douglas's arrival, the next prominent player in Florida's improbable chain of events hobbled down off Flagler's train. His name was Addison Cairns Mizner. At forty-five, he was a large, burly man weighing more than 250 pounds. With a crutch tucked under each arm and one leg in a cast, he needed to be helped off the train at the West Palm Beach station. Accompanying him, each extending a hand, were his two traveling companions: an attractive young nurse named Joan Bates and a tall, strikingly good-looking man named Paris Singer, who sported a salt-and-pepper goatee.

Mizner had recently reinjured an old ankle injury from childhood. The incident happened after he offered three hitchhiking teenagers on

Long Island a car ride, only to have them attack and mug him. In the fight that ensued, and before the ruffians made off with his wallet, one of them kicked Mizner hard in his bad ankle. The new break had required surgery and left Mizner bedridden for months. It was while recuperating in a Manhattan apartment set up for him by the celebrated British hostess Lady Alexandra Colebrooke that he met her friend Paris Singer, an heir to the Singer Sewing Machine Company fortune. The two men began chatting. They had much in common. Both enjoyed mingling in high society, and they shared a love of European architecture, painting, and antiques. They quickly became fast friends.

Their original plan had been to make a trip to Guatemala to look at Spanish colonial architecture and perhaps to collect some colonial-era artifacts and antiques. Singer had gone so far as to book tickets on the United Fruit Company boat to Puerto Barrios on the Gulf of Honduras and train tickets for the journey on to Guatemala City. But just a week before their departure, an earthquake leveled much of Guatemala City and neighboring Antigua. The two friends elected to head to Palm Beach instead for rest and relaxation.

Both had a good reason for wanting to escape New York during that biting cold winter of 1918: Mizner, because his architectural practice on Long Island had dried up with the onset of World War I, leaving him unemployed and virtually broke; and Singer, because he had recently ended a tempestuous and exhausting affair with the renowned modern dancer Isadora Duncan.

Both men had eclectic backgrounds. Addison Mizner, the son of a US diplomat, had spent a few years in his early teens in Guatemala, where his father served as the minister plenipotentiary (roughly equivalent to US ambassador) to several Central American countries. Addison's higher education, after he was denied admission to the University of California, consisted of attending the University of Salamanca in Spain for a year. There he discovered his love of all things Spanish. Although he remained spottily educated and a poor speller, Mizner could draw well and was also an accomplished watercolorist. Perhaps more surprisingly, he could embroider beautifully.

A few years later, around 1892 or 1893, his family persuaded him to accompany his brother William, who had been hired as a ship's doctor, on a trip to China. The hope was that the journey would discourage Addison from becoming an artist—or, worse, an architect, an occupation that his father considered to be "the lowest form of long-haired, flowing-cravat ass extant." When Mizner returned to San Francisco, unreformed and unrepentant, he apprenticed himself as a drafter to Willis Polk, a celebrated West Coast architect. He worked with Polk from 1894 to 1896, eventually being promoted to a partner in the practice. Both men contributed to the *Lark*, a local avant-garde literary magazine.

In November 1897 Addison joined his brothers William and Wilson on an expedition to the Klondike in Alaska to search for gold, hiking over the steep Chilkoot Pass and then rafting down the Yukon River to Dawson to join the first group of gold seekers. Addison, with his architectural background, was assigned to help lay out the new boomtown, which soon swelled its population to over ten thousand. He later worked a claim, amassed a respectable "purse," and then lost most of it to the Canadian tax authorities. Mizner later tried to launch a career as an architect in Honolulu but ended up sketching for tourists, painting miniature ivories, and helping to restore family portraits for the Hawaiian royal family. During these years, he traveled to Samoa, the Philippines, Siam, and India. In Australia, he boxed under the nickname "Whirlwind Watson from Frisco."

Addison's good friend, the mystery writer Arthur Somers Roche, objected to the description of Mizner during his early years in Florida as a fat man: "He is merely large, of brain and heart as well of body, and every ounce of him is concocted of roguery and gayety and mischief and laughter. It needs a great frame to contain tremendous mirth." Witty and a fine raconteur, Addison had achieved some early literary notoriety for having coauthored (with the novelist and playwright Ethel Watts Mumford) *The Cynic's Calendar of Revised Wisdom* an annual list of cleverly altered proverbs, such as: "Where there's a will, there's a lawsuit," "Many are called but few get up," or "A word to the wise is resented."

When Mizner moved to New York to resume his architectural career, two childhood friends, Theresa (Tessie) Fair, and her sister, Virginia, known as Birdie, had provided him with excellent entrees into the city's high society. The sisters were heirs to a fortune from the Comstock

Lode—their father, James Graham Fair, was one of the four silver kings of Virginia City, Nevada, and San Francisco, who shared in the spoils of the so-called Big Bonanza, the country's richest silver deposit. Both daughters had married wealthy, prominent New Yorkers.

The sisters introduced Mizner to their generation of friends in New York and Newport, a number of whom later became important clients for him in Palm Beach. Tessie also introduced Mizner to the architect of Rose-cliff, her mansion in Newport. He was the celebrated Stanford White of McKim, Mead & White. Until White was murdered in cold blood a year later while watching a performance at Madison Square Garden's rooftop theater, Mizner was loosely associated with White's firm, often doing brownstone renovations and smaller work that White outsourced to him. As Mizner remarked years later, "I worshipped him, for he was my God." Until the Great War broke out, and business dried up fourteen years later, Mizner operated a successful, if small, architectural practice in New York City and on Long Island, mostly designing country houses for New Yorkers.

In his spare time, he had begun to buy up ancient relics from the financially imperiled Catholic dioceses of Guatemala—furniture, vestments, and crucifixes—to sell to the public, to decorate the homes of his architectural clients, and for his own collection. He described himself as "the greatest Cathedral looter in the world." A lover of animals, he also bred Chows on Long Island. Flamboyant and bohemian, Mizner was known to shop on the streets of Manhattan clad in Chinese garb, such as a silk dressing gown and pajamas.

The Paris-born Paris Singer, meanwhile, was one of twenty-four children that his father, Isaac Singer, had sired with an assortment of wives and mistresses. The elder Singer bequeathed to his son a large fortune that included, among other grand residential properties, the massive 115-room Oldway Mansion near Torquay in the southwest of England. Singer promptly rebuilt the mansion in the style of the Palace of Versailles. A reckless spender, he allegedly garaged fourteen cars at the estate and kept his yacht, *Nille*, moored off the coast. At the outbreak of World War I, he lent the entire property to the American Women's War Relief Fund for the rehabilitation of servicemen wounded in the war. By that time, Singer was estranged from his wife and living in the United States. He also happened to own a four-bedroom cottage on the beach in Palm Beach, which he had bought the year before while vacationing there with Isadora Duncan.

Singer's tempestuous affair with Duncan had lasted ten years. A celebrated beauty and the progenitor of modern dance, Duncan was politically outspoken, mercurial, unfaithful, and overly fond of alcohol—so much so that Addison Mizner once dubbed her "Is-a-bore-when-drunken." In 1910 Singer and Duncan had a son together, the second of the two children that she bore out of wedlock with her lovers. In April 1913 both children, Deirdre, six, and Patrick, two, died in a tragic accident on the outskirts of Paris. They were seated with their nanny in a chauffeur-driven car that drove off a bridge into the River Seine. The chauffeur escaped, but the children and their nanny drowned, throwing the lovers' relationship into a downward spiral.

The couple's final rupture occurred following one of Duncan's performances at the New York Metropolitan Opera—at a dinner dance that Singer had hosted in her honor at Sherry's Hotel. During the meal, he presented her with a diamond necklace, fastening it around her neck as guests applauded. Later in the evening, after a few too many glasses of champagne, she made the mistake of teaching a handsome young man the Apache tango in front of the assembled crowd. Apparently, she danced too intimately for Singer's taste, because he grew agitated and then enraged. Finally, he stormed over and flung the pair apart. According to Duncan, he then shoved her so hard that she struck a wall and fell to the floor, bruised. "I was so indignant at the injustice of his action that I rose and, tearing the diamond necklace from my throat, flung it in his face." The diamonds scattered across the ballroom. Speechless with rage, Singer marched out, leaving the rest of the guests to collect the diamonds off the floor. Back at their hotel, the couple fought again, at which point Singer departed for good, abandoning Duncan with no money to pay their hotel bill. She would be forced to pawn her new broken necklace.

Idling outside the train station on that warm January day in 1918 when Paris Singer, Addison Mizner, and the nurse Joan Bates arrived in Palm

Beach was a gleaming new Buick touring car that Singer had purchased in advance by telegraph. Singer climbed behind the wheel and drove his guests across a rattling wood bridge and into Palm Beach. Singer's cook and her husband, who was Singer's butler-valet, followed behind in a taxi with the luggage.

Over the next few years, Mizner and Singer together would popularize an important new architectural aesthetic that was to alter the Florida development landscape. Socially and culturally ambitious, they were also destined to shake up the staid and money-oriented Palm Beach society. To a large extent, they would mold the town in their own images and anoint themselves gatekeepers of the smart set. Then Mizner would go one step further: he would concoct a scheme to build from scratch a new, even grander and more exclusive Palm Beach where he could reside as the king of the haut monde and the occupant of its most impressive waterfront castle.

In the fifteen years following Henry Flagler's death, his FEC Railway had opened the peninsula to significant new development, causing the populations of the towns up and down the east coast to expand exponentially. Furthermore, his railroad had brought to Florida a new generation of wealthy young people, as well as the cast of characters who would shape the great land boom to come.

But the rails were only one piece of the infrastructure puzzle needed to set the frenzy of Florida's land boom in full swing. Good roads would be an essential requirement as well. And the man who did more than anyone else to bring better roads to Florida was a former bicycle racer and race-car driver from Indiana named Carl Graham Fisher, who had arrived in Miami in 1910 already remarkably successful and in possession of a large fortune. Although Fisher could not have been more different temperamentally from Flagler, he, too, was blessed with drive and resourcefulness and would conjure up his own remarkable second act in Florida.

4

BALLYHOO

Carl Fisher loved to go fast. In today's parlance, Fisher was an adrena-
line junkie—in love with speed and determined to get where he was
going ahead of everyone else. As Fisher put it himself, "I just like to see
the dirt fly."

Carl Fisher was born into a middle-class family in Greensburg, Indiana, in 1874. His father, a small-town lawyer, became a bad alcoholic,
which caused his parents to separate when he was young. The oldest of
three boys, Carl was born with astigmatism so severe that he was barely
able to read the blackboard at school. He dropped out at age twelve. Despite his impaired eyesight, he was an avid reader, a gifted athlete, and a
gleeful show-off. The best ice-skater in Indianapolis, he could also walk
on stilts that stood a full story high, stand on his head, tightrope walk, and
outrun most of his classmates running backward. In fact, one of his two
wives would recall that he was nearly as nimble with his feet as with his
hands. When he finally bought his first pair of glasses, at age thirty-one,
they were a pair of round horn-rimmed spectacles. These, along with the
floppy hats he wore to hide a bald head, gave him the distinctive rumpled
appearance for which he became nationally known.

Squat and slope shouldered, Fisher would grow into a dimple-grinning
boozer, an avid poker player, and an unrepentant womanizer who peppered his talk with profanity. He chewed tobacco—sometimes smoking a
cigar at the same time after biting off and swallowing the cigar's tip. When
he married his first wife, Jane, in late 1909, she was twenty-four, and he

was thirty-five, but she was smitten: "He was all speed. . . . I found him so dazzling I could hardly look at him."

Fisher, nicknamed Skipper, was addicted to speed from a very early age. When the safety bicycle, the prototype for the modern bicycle, began to replace the high wheelers—also known as ordinaries or penny-farthings— he and his brothers learned to fix their flat tires and opened a bicycle repair shop, which soon evolved into a dealership. Fisher spent most of his time away from the shop racing bikes rather than repairing them. One of the men he raced against, Barney Oldfield, would become a lifelong friend and a celebrated race-car driver.

With the advent of the automobile, Fisher was the first person in Indianapolis to own one: a three-wheeled French-made De Dion–Bouton that featured an early internal combustion engine. Before long, he was racing Winton motorcars at fairgrounds and racetracks across the Midwest, often against his pal Barney Oldfield. In 1904, on the Harlem Race Track outside Chicago, Fisher set the world speed record over two miles of dirt track, driving a Premier Comet at 60.6 miles per hour. A car dealership soon followed: Carl Fisher Automobiles, which sported a lavish showroom and dozens of makes and models of both passenger cars and motor trucks. It may have been the first auto dealership in the country.

Fisher was a born salesman. His first real job had been as a news butcher (newsboy) on the railroad. He boosted his sales of chocolate, fruit, and newspapers by pinning the picture of a naked woman under his apron and flashing it at the male passengers, a tactic that usually induced a laugh and helped him get their attention. During this period, Fisher won a national contest for selling the most copies of Robert Ingersoll books. Known as the Great Agnostic, Ingersoll was the Dale Carnegie of the day, espousing a life of self-empowerment, "free of envy, hostility, and frustration." Fisher embraced Ingersoll's theories and his self-help philosophy—so much so that after he made his great fortune, the multimillionaire had a complete twelve-volume set of Ingersoll's books bound in Moroccan leather for his library.

Fisher had a special talent for showmanship, or ballyhoo, the popular term of the day for outlandish promotional stunts, pranks, or gimmicks

used to win over customers. For example, to help sell a particularly dura-
ble model of safety bicycle, Fisher announced to the press his plan to toss
one off Indianapolis's tallest building, offering a brand-new one for free
to whoever retrieved and returned the damaged vehicle to his shop. The
police were called to the scene, but he managed to elude them just long
enough to heave the contraption off the roof. Soon afterward, Fisher built
the world's largest penny-farthing, twenty feet tall, and rode it conspicuously through the streets of the city. In another celebrated stunt, he rode
a bicycle over a tightrope strung between two twelve-story buildings—
although he took the precaution to affix safety guide wires to the handle-
bars. On another occasion, he released a thousand balloons over the city,
one hundred of them tagged with lucky numbers, guaranteeing a free Pope
bicycle to anyone who managed to recover and redeem one of the tagged
balloons. The event created a local sensation.

When Fisher began to sell automobiles, he dreamed up more stunts. In
the most famous of these, he removed the engine from a Stoddard-Dayton
and hung the now-much-lighter automobile from a hot air balloon in place
of the basket. Then he flew the balloon over Indianapolis. "The novel
spectacle was one never before seen in any part of the world," reported the
Indianapolis News, "and the people forgot their business affairs and worries
while they stood gaping in open-eyed astonishment as the giant balloon
and its unusual load drifted lazily across the city." Fisher stood at the steering wheel, waving to the crowd below while his friend, the famous balloon-
ist George Bumbaugh, walked round in the back of the car "as though he
were on a curbstone waiting for a streetcar." A few hours later, Fisher drove
the car back into town with the balloon folded up in the trunk of the car.
Unbeknownst to the public, it was actually a duplicate vehicle, its engine
still intact, which a friend had surreptitiously driven to the landing site.
Photos of the stunt garnered his auto dealership nationwide publicity.

It was on this occasion that his wife-to-be, Jane Watts, first laid eyes on
Fisher: as he floated leisurely overhead in his hot air balloon, waving down
at her. They soon met, and a year later he married her, without much ceremony, advising her only a few days before the ceremony that if she wanted
a priest to administer the vows, then she would need to find one because

he didn't know any. (Fisher was promptly sued for breach of promise by another girlfriend, a suit that he settled out of court.) He proceeded to be just as casual about his vows after he and Jane were married. On their honeymoon trip, the couple cruised down the Mississippi River to New Orleans in his new custom-built motor yacht. When they reached the fabled city, he left her alone in the boat overnight while he caroused in the brothels with two of his male friends. It wasn't long before he was conducting an affair with his secretary. When Jane complained, he somehow managed to reassure her: "Why, you little wench, I love you. I wouldn't trade you for two skunks." Living with Fisher, she realized, "was like living at a circus."

And yet, many of his accomplishments were more than publicity stunts. Fisher was a bona fide entrepreneur. Recognizing that automobiles needed better headlights for driving after dark, he bought a third interest in a novel automobile headlight system that had been rejected by all the major auto companies. Instead of kerosene, it used compressed acetylene in its gas lamps. He renamed the company Prest-O-Lite, expanded it, and found a way to distribute replacement canisters overnight. Despite the volatile nature of the gas and a series of factory explosions, the product was a commercial hit. He and his partners sold the business to the industrial chemicals manufacturer Union Carbide Company in 1913, and Fisher personally pocketed $5.6 million in Union Carbide stock—the equivalent of $144 million in today's dollars. If Fisher had left this money in Union Carbide stock, it would have appreciated twentyfold over the ensuing years. But he had other plans for his winnings.

One such plan was the Indianapolis Motor Speedway, a crushed-stone track for auto races that he and three partners, all close friends, built for $75,000 some five miles west of the city. The four men incorporated their new company with $250,000 of capital; Fisher took on the role of president.

The very first race, a three-day, three-hundred-mile speed and endurance event, got off to a rocky start, literally, as the track disintegrated into ruts and potholes. On the first day, a race car flipped over, killing both its driver and the riding mechanic. The following day, a car hit a pothole, catapulted one hundred feet off the road, and killed a second riding mechanic and two spectators. By the third day, the track had deteriorated to the point where Fisher was forced to end the race at the 235-mile mark.

Despite the setback, Fisher was undaunted. He was well acquainted with the dangers of racing, including the risk of fatalities. In Zanesville, Ohio, in 1903, he'd been at the wheel of a custom-built Mohawk racer when it blew a tire and went careening off the track. According to the *Zanesville Times Recorder*, "John Goodwin, known all over the city, who was acting as special policeman at the fair, was directly in front of the machine and was struck fairly by it, and was thrown under it. Hamilton Shutts of Roseville, an old soldier, aged about sixty-one years, was severely crushed by being caught between the machine and the wire fence." Shutts died at the scene.

Fisher and his partners rebuilt the track's surface, this time using 3.2 million glazed and vitrified bricks hand laid on their sides over two inches of level sand. They also banked the turns and added higher concrete retaining walls. The project was completed in two months in the fall of 1909, and Fisher was ready to try again. Eighty thousand spectators turned out to watch the track's first five-hundred-mile race. There would be one fatality from a flat tire at the halfway mark and a separate but nonlethal pileup that took out four cars, leaving one upside down and smoking. The crowd loved it. Over the next sixteen years, Fisher would promote the Indianapolis 500 into the largest single-day sporting event in the country, drawing more than 150,000 spectators annually to what came to be known as the Brickyard.

Not all of Fisher's ideas had a profit motive. In October 1912, at a meeting of leading auto men at Das Deutsche Haus, a cultural center in Indianapolis, he proposed that the industry build a coast-to-coast highway stretching from Manhattan's Times Square to San Francisco's Lincoln Park. "A road across the United States!" he exclaimed from the podium. "Let's build it before we're too old to enjoy it."

Fisher even devised a scheme to fund the project: he persuaded the industry's carmakers, dealers, suppliers, and jobbers to each contribute a small percentage of their annual sales to a construction fund that would not be touched until $10 million had been raised. This was at a time

when twenty-eight of the forty-eight states spent a total of only $11 mil-
lion annually on their roads; the rest spent nothing. Most of the nation's
roads were dirt and rutted and often muddy or otherwise impassible for
horse-drawn carts, let alone for automobiles. Originally conceived of as
the Coast-to-Coast Rock Highway, the road would become better known
as the Lincoln Highway. Fisher was credited with raising the money that
made the venture possible, and he did so by making the case that the highway would be a boon to auto sales. Notably, Henry Ford, who believed that
the government should build the roads, refused to contribute. The Lincoln Highway, dedicated in 1913 and largely completed two years later,
ran parallel to what is today Interstate 80. Riding the road in a military
convoy in 1919 would give then Lieutenant Colonel Dwight Eisenhower
the idea for the national highway system, which became a reality with the
passage of the National Interstate and Defense Highways Act of 1956.

The great business boom of the 1920s would be driven largely by auto
sales and the industries surrounding the automobile: steel, petroleum, machine tools, auto parts, paint, glass, and highway building—industries that
midwestern men such as Fisher, Ford, and Flagler, from Indiana, Michigan,
and Ohio, respectively, had built from scratch. Needless to say, the importance of the automobile's rise, and the arrival of the so-called Automobile
Age, would have enormous significance in the larger American narrative.
Perhaps no other advancement has so altered the way Americans work and
play. As sociologist William F. Ogburn argued as far back as 1938: "the
invention of the automobile has had more influence on society than the
combined exploits of Napoleon, Genghis Kahn, and Julius Caesar."

The auto industry would be instrumental in creating the consumer-
goods-oriented society that we inhabit today. It would contribute to the
emergence of the vast expanse of American suburbs, where it soon changed
the architecture of the American home by adding carports and then ga-
rages to bungalows and single-family residences. Equally important, it
brought an end to rural isolation and largely freed the homemaker from
the house. The automobile gave its owner the flexibility to work, shop, and
play wherever he or she desired. A car allowed for distant vacations and
access to better medical care; it even added a kind of insurance policy that

permitted one to escape to a new location if circumstances required it—a factor that would contribute heavily to the great migration to Florida that was to follow shortly.

Not all the changes brought by the automobile were positive ones. Derivative vehicles, such as the tractor, soon put out of business the uncompetitive small farmer with his mule. Traffic congestion was another negative. We think of traffic as being a recent problem, but it snarled and clogged New York City streets twice a day, at rush hour, as early as the 1910s. Meanwhile, the automobile's contribution to global warming would not be fully understood for another sixty years.

Fisher followed up his Lincoln Highway idea with the plan for a similar north-south route that would link Chicago and Upper Michigan with Miami. The Dixie Highway route was actually a pair of roads—an east route and a west route—converging in Florida and linked along the way by connecting roads like the rungs on a ladder. Because of the parallel routes, the highway would encompass some 5,786 miles, far exceeding the length of the Lincoln Highway, and it would take more than a decade to complete. In 1915 a caravan of fifteen cars calling themselves the Dixie Highway Pathfinders' Tour made the journey from Indianapolis to Miami to publicize the project, arriving in October with Carl Fisher in the lead vehicle.

It was no accident that the highway ended in Miami. Fisher knew by now what he was going to do for his next act. Like Flagler, he had chosen to become a real estate developer. The parcel that he had settled on developing, originally named Alton Beach, would become much better known as Miami Beach.

Fisher and his wife, Jane, had discovered Miami for the first time in 1910, the year before he sold the Prest-O-Lite Company. John Levi, the skipper of Fisher's forty-five-foot motor yacht, was cruising the boat up the coast of Florida when he discovered the village on Biscayne Bay. He wired Fisher that the town was worth a visit. The Fishers traveled down by train and liked Miami immediately. They already owned a second Indiana home on

Lake Michigan, but Miami had more to offer. Both the weather and the fishing were better, and the couple could boat all year round. Plus Fisher saw development opportunities everywhere he looked. They bought their first Miami house from a brochure, sight unseen. Fisher proceeded to make his first small investment in a bay-front subdivision called Point View, where one of the earliest Miami developers, Locke T. Highleyman, was using dredgers to convert a mangrove swamp into a tidy shoreline and an exclusive residential neighborhood.

According to local lore, the moment that kick-started Fisher's second career came when he offered financial aid to a failed coconut farmer named John Collins. The seventy-two-year-old Collins owned a long strip of oceanfront land on a barrier island across Biscayne Bay. Collins and his son-in-law, Thomas Pancoast, had attempted to build a two-and-a-half-mile wooden bridge across the bay to improve the efficiency and enhance the value of his latest farming venture: the first avocado plantation in the United States. With the bridge still a half mile from the far shore, Collins had run out of money. The bridge to nowhere sat unfinished for a year or so while Collins shopped around for the funds to complete it.

In her biography of her ex-husband, Jane describes their first encounter with Collins on a clearing on the island: "He was a very short man. He had a white beard—it was a white goatee—and the whitest shirt and the bluest suit that I had ever seen. He wore a bow tie, a polka-dot blue-and-white tie. It impressed me to see a man so immaculately dressed standing amidst all this wild territory." The local lawyer Frank Shutts, originally from Indianapolis, who had worked for Henry Flagler's railroad before opening a Miami legal practice, brokered the deal.

In return for the $50,000 loan that Collins needed to complete the bridge, Fisher received 200 acres of prime land on the south-central portion of the island. This consisted of a mile of property that stretched between the ocean and the bay. Two months later, he bought an additional 150 acres from a pair of prominent locals, brothers J. E. and J. N. Lummus. The three parties would each play an important role in the ensuing development of the island, although it was Fisher who brought most of the money and inspiration to the project. His parcels, flanked by the others', would one day become the prime commercial real estate section of Miami Beach. The shrewd lawyer Shutts, who was also the publisher of the *Miami Herald*, eventually bought 47 acres situated between the parcels owned by Fisher and the Lummuses.

Jane believed the project would be an expensive mistake. When Fisher took her to inspect the property by boat, they entered from the bay side, rowing up a channel lined with dense mangroves. "Mosquitos blackened our clothing," she wrote. "Jungle flies, as large as horse flies, waited for our blood. . . . Other creatures that made me shudder were lying in wait in the slimy paths or on the branches of overhanging trees. The jungle itself was as hot and steamy as a conservatory. . . . What on earth could Carl possibly see in such a place?"

But Fisher insisted that he knew what he was doing. Standing with her on the soft sand on the ocean side of the long neck, the surf breaking toward them in slow, white rollers, he sketched out his vision for the area. It would be half beach resort and half playground. "In that moment, Carl's imagination saw Miami Beach in its entirety, blazing like a jewel with hibiscus, oleander, poinsettia, bougainvillea, and orchids, feathered with palms and lifting proud white towers against the sky," Jane recalled. "But I looked at that rooted and evil-smelling morass and had nothing to say. There was nothing a devoted wife *could* say."

Fisher was correct about one thing: the sand. Light gray-brown in color, the crystal-quartz sand had a fine grain somewhere between sugar and powder. It was soft underfoot, easy to brush off, and lovely to look at. And it stretched down the wide, pristine beach for uninterrupted miles.

Before he could proceed with his plans, Fisher would need to remove the rattlesnakes. His neighbor J. N. Lummus, who would be the first to put Miami Beach lots on sale, had eradicated seventeen from his development: "When you kill one," he advised, "tie it to a stake, and another one will be coiled there the next morning." Next, Fisher needed to do away with the alligators, the numerous raccoons, and the thousands of rats—in the latter case the introduction of cats would help. Finally, he needed to clear the mangrove trees. When laborers, hacking laboriously at the dense growth in a process called "swamp chopping," failed to do the job, Fisher retrofitted some Indiana farm equipment into a machete plow to cut the plants off at knee level. The plow was so large and so heavy when assembled that the Collins Bridge, which opened in 1913, could not support it. It had to be moved onto the island by barge, along with a big tractor to pull it. But the system worked. Fisher left the roots of the mangroves in place, with plans to bury them under sand. Next, he drove rows of pilings into the mud and began to build retaining walls to hold back the water along the shore of the bay. To these he affixed bulkheads made of timber, fastening them to the pilings with steel cables.

His great insight was to recognize the value that the latest type of dredges—suction dredges—could bring to his project. They sucked up from the bay floor a stinky soup of sand, mud, and marl, some three million cubic feet of it, and deposited it on top of the mangrove stumps, raising the level of the land some five feet and creating a tidy shoreline where docks could be built and boats moored. This new coastline would be expensive, costing him $10 per foot, but Fisher realized that he and J. N. Lummus, working in partnership, could create land where none had existed before.

This was grueling toil for the workers involved. The mosquitoes and sandflies were so bad that the men tucked newspapers into their socks to protect their ankles from being bitten. Dredges broke down; pipes ruptured or clogged with weeds and then had to be repaired by divers. But the dredges, operated by 150 men from the James Clark Company, of Baltimore, using a pair of digging boats, two anchor boats, two oil tugs, fifteen barges, and a handful of supply boats, gradually turned sand bars such as Belle Isle into actual islands, and pulled other new islands out of the bay. As his friend the humorist and actor Will Rogers quipped, "Carl discovered that sand could hold up a Real Estate sign." Fisher understood that these new islands needed to be protected from storms, but otherwise there seemed little limit to what could be accomplished inside Biscayne Bay.

These tactics—excavating mangrove swamps or other types of swamps and saltwater marshes; building new barrier islands; erecting bulkheads and seawalls; and dredging in ways that removed natural breakwaters or barriers to storms and altered shorelines or changed current flows—were the beginnings of a new pattern of coastline development in the country. This pattern would one day lead to disasters such as the flooding of New Orleans during Hurricane Katrina in 2005, and other disasters in Florida whose effects were compounded by the removal of the mangroves and the misconceived networks of canals, dikes, and levees built by the US Army Corps of Engineers.

The dredge churns, once pumped into place, created new land that needed to dry—or, more accurately, to cure. The resulting landfill was bright white and concrete hard. Topsoil could then be spread on top, followed by the planting of palms, flowering shrubs, or ornamental flowers.

Before too long, Fisher had created a brand-new, if somewhat artificial, tropical paradise suitable for a subdivision. Roadbeds could be made from crushed limestone that he barged in from the mainland. To create the front lawns, each individual sprig of grass was planted by hand by dozens of black workers—mostly women and children—crawling on their hands and knees and pushing baskets of Bermuda grass in front of them, a laborious process known as sprigging. In December 1913 Fisher opened the Alton Beach Realty Company. He sold lots on the waterfront for $1,875, and for as little as $500 if they were a few blocks inland.

All of Fisher's developments, as well as virtually all of the others on the island, would be racially restricted in the decades to come, as was the prevailing custom in most upscale resort areas. The so-called Caucasian clause in the deeds prohibited anyone but a white person from buying a parcel of land. The contractual language typically read: "Said property shall not be sold, leased, or rented in any form or manner, by any title, either legal or equitable, to any person or persons other than of the Caucasian Race, or to any firm or corporations of which any persons other than of the Caucasian Race shall be a part or stockholder."

The day-to-day racial prohibitions and restrictions actually went much further. For example, blacks were forbidden to drive an automobile in Miami Beach. This law was eventually rescinded in 1918, but only because white tourists arriving with black chauffeurs for the winter season complained vociferously when they weren't allowed to use them. Owners of large houses could keep black servants in their servants' quarters, but otherwise blacks were permitted on the island only during daylight hours to work in service or as gardeners.

The restrictions against buying property or frequenting the hotels often applied to Jews as well as blacks. Anti-Semitism had been on the rise since the arrival in the United States of large numbers of Jewish immigrants from Eastern Europe starting in the 1880s. Exceptions to the restrictions were often made for wealthy or prominent "assimilated" Jews who ran investment banks or successful corporations. Fisher's correspondence in later years is full of letters of exception he wrote for friends such as yeast company president Julius Fleischmann, taxicab magnate John Hertz, and department store mogul Bernard Gimbel, granting them access to his hotels or privileges at his clubs. Fisher liked to think of himself as a fair person, staunchly unbiased, but for business purposes, he was quite willing to share in the prevailing bigotry of the day. It wasn't until 1948 that the US Supreme Court eventually ruled such race covenants unenforceable. The Fair Housing Act of 1968 would ban the practice altogether.

Fisher spent $65,000 to build his own house, a three-story Italian Renaissance–style waterfront mansion he called the Shadows. Over the next two years, he expanded his Alton Beach development, adding a golf course, tennis courts, and a tennis clubhouse. He organized an annual regatta on the bay that included speedboat races, in which he took part. In fact, Fisher won an early race skippering one of his own cruisers. Next, he added his first small hotel, the Lincoln, with only thirty-six rooms. In his hotels, as in his own homes, he would insist on big, comfortable furniture: "No sissy furniture a man won't sit on," were his instructions to Jane, who oversaw the decorating. Two eight-story office buildings followed, as well as the thoroughfare that came to be called Lincoln Road. By 1915, there were seventy-seven blocks, twelve miles of road, two more small hotels, and a large grandstand overlooking the bay for watching the motorboat races. This was also the year Miami Beach opened its first nightclub, Olin Finney's Casino.

Fisher threw money at every element of his project, intoxicated now with a Flagler-like dream of an empire. It was no longer just his wife who worried about the extravagance of his plans. "Many of his friends thought he was troubled with what the French call May flies in the dome," recalled the journalist and author Kenneth Roberts. When Fisher decided to build a major resort hotel on the island, the $2 million Flamingo Hotel, in partnership with Jim Allison, his former Prest-O-Lite partner, he was so short of cash that he needed to borrow the money to cover his half of the cost. By now, he had bet his entire fortune, aside from his share of the Indianapolis Speedway and his vacation homes, on the Alton Beach development.

Although Fisher feigned boundless optimism, he was, in fact, worried. The pace of lot sales was slow to take off. He concluded that it was not enough to sell the empty lots; he would need to build "spec" houses on them, at $4,000 apiece. But even that failed to kindle the boom. The warm climate alone was not enough of an inducement to bring people as far down the coast as Miami. And the truth was that his barrier island was simply too far from the mainland. It took potential home owners too long to cross the Collins Bridge to do their grocery shopping or for their kids to attend school. A faster access route to the island was needed. Fisher and the other developers on the Beach began to lobby for a new causeway. At last, with financial help from the city, construction began on the two-lane County Causeway across the bay. Delayed by the outset of the First World War, it would not be finished until 1920.

Desperate by now, Fisher and the other developers along the beach, including the Lummus and the Collins-Pancoast families, tried a number of tactics to boost their land sales. They gave away lots in return for strict promises that the buyers would build homes of a certain size. They hired a well-known auctioneer named Edward E. "Doc" Dammers from Delray Beach to organize a three-day auction. Dammers, a former eyeglass salesman who would play a central role in neighboring Coral Gables in the years to come, interspersed the auctioning of empty lots with drawings for free sets of china, cut glass, oriental rugs, and gold watches. All of this helped, but it still wasn't enough.

Determined to try something new, in 1917 Fisher opened a fishing club called the Cocolobo Cay Club with two junior partners. Together they bought a pair of small islands in the Florida Keys, an hour south of Miami by speedboat. The idea was to use the lure of memberships in the fishing club to help Fisher sell high-end Miami Beach real estate. But the club, accessible only by boat, soon became much more than that. Many of Miami's movers and shakers signed up for membership and would join him there for cocktails and fishing—men such as the banker Ed Romfh, who later became Miami's mayor, and Miami's top lawyer, Frank Shutts, who was also the powerful publisher of the *Miami Herald*. Members could radio ahead the size of their party and request that elaborate seafood lunches be prepared in advance or reserve one of the cottages or guest rooms for a stay on the beach. Three local fishing guides were available to take members to the best locations in the surrounding waters to catch the still-prevalent sailfish, marlin, king mackerel, grouper, snappers, and porgies, or, closer to shore, bonefish, ladyfish, and tarpon.

Next, Fisher bought a large swimming pool complex from the Collins-Pancoast family. He added a Dutch-style windmill to circulate the pool water and expanded the beach casino into an elaborate complex that he eventually named the Roman Pools. He even began work on a polo field and imported the ponies and the players to play on it. Intrigued by the sport, he learned how to play.

Despite all these efforts, despite over $2 million spent on masterminding the dredging, the waterside grandstands, the golf course, the Roman Pools, the spec houses, the fishing club, four small hotels, and the big one still under construction (the Flamingo), Fisher could not get the land sales moving. They had grown only modestly, from $40,000 in 1916 to $52,000 in 1917. Although houses had begun to speckle the island, there were not enough of them to achieve the kind of success that he and his neighbors envisioned.

When the United States entered the First World War in April 1917, Fisher and the other early developers expected to see their plans put on hold. To their surprise, the war brought new tourists and new sales prospects to Miami, many of them the kind of people who might otherwise have traveled to the French Riviera for their vacations. At last, sales began to improve.

When the Great War ended in November 1918, the foundation for a classic real estate boom was finally in place. By then, the basic infrastructure was built—railroads, roads, causeways, and bridges—in large part thanks to Flagler and Fisher, in addition to many other smaller players up and down both coasts and across the country. The nation, having fought and won a traumatic war, was eager to have some fun, and an exotic new American Riviera beckoned.

As 1919 unfolded, Carl Fisher made two final and critical changes to his business strategy. The first was to switch his target audience, which had always been the elderly and the retired rich, most of whom still favored Palm Beach over Miami, and always would. As he told *Business* magazine a few years later, "I was on the wrong track. I had been trying to reach the dead ones. I had been going after the old folks. I saw that what I needed to do was go after the live wires. And the live wires don't want to rest." He would concede the superrich and the old money to Palm Beach. Instead, Miami Beach would be for the nouveau riche; for men like Fisher himself, especially those from the industrial Midwest; men who were younger, still making their fortunes, and looking for fun ways to spend their new wealth. He would appeal to them with the sort of activities that appealed to him: contests, races, and other events that featured sports celebrities. Henceforth, Miami Beach would become "a youthful city of indeterminate social standing," in the words of social historian Charlotte Curtis.

Fisher's second change in tactics was equally radical: he raised his land prices by 10 percent, in part to give the appearance that his lots were appreciating rapidly in value. And to further promote that perception, he offered a return guarantee of 6 percent "to any customer in Miami or elsewhere who purchased lots from us and are not well pleased with their investment." He assured his buyers that, from then on, he would be raising prices by 10 percent every year. Ten percent was an exceptionally attractive rate of return; 10 percent that seemed virtually guaranteed was even more attractive. Fisher, in trying to stoke a small fire, was about to fuel a conflagration.

Behind the scenes, other factors had contributed to the marked improvement in sales. Chief among these was the wide proliferation of the automobile. The machines that Fisher had raced, sold, and promoted back in Indiana had evolved into bona fide consumer products, viable and cost-effective substitutes for the horse and buggy. The automobile, more than the railroad, the streetcar, or any other factor, turned the American landscape from raw land into real estate. It did so by making the land accessible and thus developable: its value could be easily established, enhanced, and commodified. Land then became a far more salable product, one that benefited landlords, lenders, contractors, and real estate agents, to say nothing of the purchasers and renters of that property. Nowhere was this truer than in Florida. And nowhere in Florida was it truer than in Miami Beach, where the road built over the Collins Bridge and the new County Causeway (renamed MacArthur Causeway in 1942) at last made the resort developments there commercially viable—by making them accessible to cars. Miami Beach was on its way to becoming the most widely publicized and most famous resort destination in the country.

Fisher was now forty-three years old but still full of vitality. "This is only the beginning," he announced presciently in an ad that appeared in the *Miami Metropolis* newspaper late in 1919, adding that he planned to further enhance Alton Beach the following year with "a polo club house, a church, theater, schoolhouse, six store buildings, and ten Italian villas ranging from $10,000 to $35,000 each."

The Roaring Twenties would play to all of Fisher's formidable strengths as an entrepreneur and promoter, as well as to his every weakness. He would respond to the boom with his inimitable creativity and flair and his unrivaled talent for ballyhoo. Henry Flagler, in a conversation shortly before he died in 1913, remarked to a friend, "Those men and women there [in Miami] are like boys and girls. They have never been hurt, and they know no fear." The old tycoon understood that there is always a price to be paid for excessive risk taking and for financial naiveté. Even if Fisher had been aware of Flagler's admonition, he was unlikely to have heeded it. Blinded by his excitement as badly as by his astigmatism, he would fail to see the frothy boom for what it was: a bubble in the sun.

2

GRAND PLANS

5

⊷•⊱◦✥◦⊰•⊶

A SPANISH DREAMSCAPE

Almost immediately after his arrival by train in Palm Beach with Paris Singer in 1918, Addison Mizner fell ill, first with an apparent heart attack and then with a bout of pneumonia. Joan Bates, who eventually became Singer's second wife, managed to nurse the architect back to health, although he would never regain his robust boxer's constitution.

Soon after his recovery in early April, the two friends made a day trip down to Miami to visit Vizcaya, the fabulous James Deering estate overlooking Biscayne Bay. The trip gave Addison inspiration for the type and scale of construction that could be accomplished in Florida if one had clients of sufficient means. Fortunately, in his friend Singer, he had found one. Of course, to have a successful career as an architect, he would need many more.

He knew by now what type of an architect he hoped to become: a society architect, much like Stanford White, whom Mizner had befriended and idolized in his early years in New York. White, who earned his fame with his classical rendition of the Washington Square Arch constructed at the foot of Manhattan's Fifth Avenue, also designed the second Madison Square Garden building, at the corner of Twenty-Sixth Street and Madison Avenue, working in an Italian and Moorish architectural idiom. The central tower of that structure featured the first of many American renditions of the much-admired Giralda tower in Seville. White and his celebrated partners in the firm of McKim, Mead & White were the rare architects whose reputations were such that they weren't beholden to the kind of financial pressures from contractors and lenders that necessarily compromised aesthetics in the interests of cost or efficiency. The legacy of the great firm is a portfolio of the country's finest neoclassical public buildings, social clubs, and libraries, and two dozen of its grandest private homes. McKim, Mead & White would also get credit for the lovely, stately interiors of the White House, which the writer Henry James would describe admiringly as "excellent extensions and embellishments," thanks to a renovation project completed during Theodore Roosevelt's presidency.

Much as White had done, Mizner wanted to design and build grand houses from scratch for the wealthy, not the bungalows, warehouses, and brownstone renovations that he had accepted out of desperation when he began work as an architect in New York fourteen years earlier. As it turned out, he would find himself in the right place at a most fortuitous time because the hotel culture of Palm Beach was rapidly evolving into a "cottage" culture of grandiose homes, following in the tradition of haunts such as Newport, Rhode Island; Lenox, Massachusetts; and South Hampton, Long Island, where the wealthy ostentatiously displayed their riches and competed to outdo one another with their outsized mansions.

The arrival of the rich, in large numbers, implied a maturation of the economy and suggested that a solid foundation had been laid for a healthy economy based on real estate, and perhaps even a boom. Popular resorts, it was commonly thought, had an almost Darwinian evolution: first, they were discovered by writers, artists, and academics; following them came the "nice" millionaires, who didn't flaunt their wealth and valued their privacy; these were then followed by the "naughty" millionaires, who did flaunt their wealth by building extravagant houses, opening social clubs, throwing grand balls, and, in general, consuming conspicuously. The latter was the moment when an architect on the scene could succeed beyond his wildest imaginings—and Florida was rapidly approaching that stage. In the social historian Cleveland Amory's view, there was one final step in this evolution, which he simply, and aptly, described as "trouble."

To succeed as a society architect, one needed to satisfy the aspirations and ambitions of an especially demanding clientele. The greatest challenge was figuring out how to please these clients without necessarily pandering to their whims, which were likely to result in homes that were an aesthetic mess from an architectural perspective. It also helped if you could manage to enjoy your clients' company and hold your own conversationally. Mizner could do both.

In the first volume of his memoirs, Mizner describes meeting the formidable Mrs. Stuyvesant Fish at a dinner party in New York. An eccentric society doyenne, Marion Graves Anthon Fish was famous for her wit and for throwing outlandish parties, including birthday parties in honor of her favorite pets. She immediately endeavored to put Mizner in his place: "I have been listening to your chatter and am disappointed. Harry [Lehr] said you were amusing. I spent a part of the afternoon looking over your *Cynic's Calendar*. It's not bad, but there are a few that aren't very original. The one about Folly, for instance. Racine said that when he said . . ." She proceeded to quote a half page of the French dramatist's writing to Mizner, who didn't speak the language.

The architect listened attentively and gave her "my most innocent blue eyes" as he prepared his reply. When she finished, he answered: "You know, Racine wasn't exactly original, either, for Confucius said five hundred and fifty years BC . . ." Mizner proceeded to count to one hundred rapidly in Chinese. "Of course, he was a little more flowery, but he had such a beautiful way of putting things."

Mrs. Fish gave him a stern glance before she looked away.

"I had crossed swords with the greatest wit in society and gotten away with it," he recalled. Perhaps so, but he hadn't entirely fooled her. Several months later, she remarked, "You are the only person I know who's not afraid of me and dares to be impudent."

The first commission Paris Singer offered Addison Mizner was modest. He wanted him to redesign the beachfront bungalow where the two friends were living. Mizner proposed that the structure be converted into a Chinese villa featuring brightly colored walls, a pagoda roof, and elaborate ornamental fish carvings along the eves. It would be surrounded with a bamboo fence and a *paifang*, or Chinese welcome gate. Singer was delighted with the concept, and in a matter of months, the renovation was complete. The man of luxury added the final touch himself: a five-foot-long stuffed alligator that he mounted on the roof.

Then one day, while walking at the southern end of the Palm Beach island and discussing architecture, the two men came across a particularly attractive parcel of bare land. Singer asked Mizner what sort of building he envisioned being built there. Mizner, no fool, didn't hesitate: "A Moorish tower, like on the south coast of Spain, with an open loggia at one side facing the sea, and on this side a cool court with a dripping fountain in the shade of these beautiful palms." A few days later, standing on the edge of Lake Worth, Singer challenged him again to visualize a fitting structure. Mizner responded: "It is so beautiful that it ought to be something religious—a nunnery, with a chapel built into the lake, with a great cool cloisters and a court of oranges; a landing stage, where the stern old abbess could barter with boatmen bringing over their fruit and vegetables for sale; a great gate over there on the road, where the faithful could leave their offerings and receive largesse."

Singer proceeded to buy the property, which was the former site of a tourist attraction called Joe's Florida Alligator Farm. A jungle trail through the property would be widened and renamed Worth Avenue. Here Singer announced plans to build a convalescent hospital and social club for shell-shocked veterans of World War I. He directed Mizner to draw up a set of plans, offering him a salary if he would stay on in Florida through the spring and summer and oversee the project as the de facto general contractor. The actual builder would be a former carpenter named Cooper C. Lightbown, who was to collaborate with Mizner on many later commissions and one day become mayor of Palm Beach. Mizner accepted Singer's offer without hesitation. In the ensuing months, he closed his dormant New York architectural office on Park Avenue, sold his Long Island home, and settled permanently in Florida with his two Chows. "I was in love with Palm Beach," he would write in his memoirs, "and Mr. Singer had fired me with a dream."

Addison Mizner deserved the most credit for popularizing a particular architectural aesthetic known as the Spanish Colonial Revival style, which would soon become one of Florida's most distinctive visual traits. He was among the first to take the previously unadorned adobe and hacienda architecture of early California settlements and missions and add to it the baroque features found on the churches, cathedrals, and castles of Spain and Central America, including the florid plaster detailing on their facades that were full of elaborate displays of pinnacles, shields, and neoclassical columns. The broader style of Mediterranean Revival went further and combined Spanish, Italian, Mediterranean, and Moorish architecture—although the Spanish influence predominated.

Before Mizner's arrival in Florida, most of the smaller houses being built in Palm Beach were American Craftsman, or so-called Arts and Crafts. Such houses, featuring low-pitched gabled roofs, spacious front porches, and tapered columns, had begun to populate middle-class suburbs around the country. The grander Palm Beach houses had followed Flagler's Whitehall in the Beaux Arts style, among them the white Theodore Frelinghuysen house designed by Hoppin & Koen on Barton Avenue. A few had veered off into the formal Greek Revival style, such as Frederick Guest's mansion, Villa Artemis, designed by F. Burrall Hoffman Jr.

Mizner paired the tropical setting with the architectural style aesthetically best suited to it. As he explained years later, "Northern architecture didn't register. I couldn't get away from the fact. There was one New England colonial house that was placed in the midst of coconut trees, and it was an abortion. The house wasn't bad—it had good simplicity—but in Florida it was out of the picture." The Spanish mode, by contrast, harmonized with the environment perfectly.

This style came to be championed by architects on both coasts of the United States because it resulted in open-air buildings well suited to the near-tropical climate and terrain of California and Florida, both of which had obvious historical Spanish antecedents. These buildings were not only attractive but also functional in these warmer climes: they were built with thick insulating walls made of cool adobe covered in stucco, and they featured porches, open loggias, or arcades, and large, often sunken, terraces. Invariably, the roofs were of red barrel mission tile.

Mizner had first encountered Spanish architecture in Guatemala as a boy and while studying in Salamanca, Spain, a few years later. He already possessed a deep appreciation for everything Spanish or Spanish influenced, especially Andalusian architecture with its Moorish influence, enclosed patios, and orange tree courts. Before his arrival in Florida, Mizner's portfolio already included two buildings in the Spanish vernacular on Long Island.

The construction work on his first Florida building would not be as easy to execute as Mizner had hoped. Few of the workers he hired had any significant construction experience, let alone the ability to read a blueprint. The requisite building materials were scarce. The right kind of clay, for instance, had to be imported from Georgia. He decided to start from scratch by opening a veritable trade school where his workers could learn to lay bricks and apply stucco. He bought a local blacksmith shop and converted it into an ironmonger. He built kilns and a sawmill.

These initiatives would become the basis of the Mizner Industries, a collection of factories and workshops that produced the roof and floor tiles, the heavy oak furniture, and the iron grillwork and sconces for most of the Spanish colonial homes built in the surrounding area throughout the twenties. In charge of the landscaping as well as the construction of the club, Mizner also built greenhouses to grow ornamental plants. He would devote almost as much care and attention to the outdoor spaces as to a building's rooms.

Despite his girth and his limp, Mizner threw himself into the project, chain-smoking cigarettes while he cajoled and charmed his workers. At one point, he helped to talk the carpenters' union out of striking, in part by threatening to move the project to California. Unusual for an architect of his day, Mizner actually knew how things were made and the best techniques for making them. He was an inveterate do-it-yourselfer. Recalled Singer, "When he could find no one to carry out his orders, he set to with his own hands and made the thing he wanted. He could do this for he is, like the architects of the Middle Ages, a master of all the crafts that serve his profession. He paints, carves wood, and works in metals, knows all about the making of glazed pottery, and his wrought iron is second to none in Old Spain."

The war ended just as the building approached completion. Acknowledging that there was no longer a need for a convalescent hospital, Singer and Mizner quickly repurposed and reconfigured the structure as a private social club for Palm Beach residents and their guests. The name was changed from the Touchstone Convalescents' Club to the Everglades Club, and a Palm Beach institution was born.

The Everglades was not the first club in Palm Beach. The Sailfish Club, a fishing club, and the Palm Beach Country Club both preceded it by a couple of years. Of even more prominence was Colonel Bradley's Casino (later Bradley's Beach Club), which had opened in 1898, a high-stakes gambling venue for nonresidents. The Everglades Club, however, was on a different scale altogether. The resulting edifice, one of the handsomest Mizner would ever design, set a new standard for Florida.

The Mediterranean palace was an instant hit with members and tourists alike. It was lovely, inside and out, from its filigreed grillwork and massive, elaborately paneled wood doors, to the painted timber and beamed ceilings; from the Moroccan-style cloister archways and arcades, to the marble patio, red-tiled floors, and sunken orange court. Mizner furnished it lovingly with heavy dark-wood Spanish antiques, and couches and chairs upholstered in velvet damasks. At night, all of it was bathed in the soft yellow light from the iron sconces and the enormous, dangling, double-tiered chandeliers.

A short golf course, measuring 2,830 yards, followed soon afterward, along with three tennis courts. The tennis pro was hired away from the Piping Rock Club on Long Island. Ten rental villas known as maisonettes arose in varying pastel colors on an adjoining property. Eighteen new Buick automobiles, parked in a garage across the street from the club, were bought solely for the use of the members occupying the club's various apartments.

As the president and owner, Paris Singer was in total control of the club from the outset, and he made sure that the membership understood that. Only 350 men were invited to join the first year—and only for a single year. He reserved the right to select the group all over again the following year, blackballing whomever he chose. He upped the number to 500 for the second year. Dues were $275 annually for couples; $175.50 for single men. Guest lists for large parties at the club required his preapproval.

Ladies' use of the premises was limited to the first floor. He then went one step further, establishing a new, more informal resort apparel based on what was commonly worn on the French Riviera: Singer's favored attire of "striped shirts, colorful sweaters, baggy pants, and espadrilles." Evening attire remained strictly formal. As he confided to Mizner before the launch, "If we start things off right, the club will make Palm Beach the winter capital of the world. There is no place in Europe to compare with the climate; all that is needed is to make it gay and attractive. It's up to you and me."

They succeeded. The club was an instant success. Mizner recalled hiding behind some palms to eavesdrop on the guests, hoping to overhear some unbiased criticism of the new building. "Craig Biddle and Birdie Vanderbilt were three feet from me. They couldn't have been more complimentary," he recalled. "In fact, there were very few knockers, and I sneaked up to my rooms with a trance of pleasure."

Within weeks of the club's opening on February 4, 1919, Mizner landed commissions to build four private homes. The first of these was from Eva Cromwell Stotesbury, soon to become the grand dame of Palm Beach, earning the sobriquet Queen Eva. As the pampered second wife of a senior J. P. Morgan partner who had recently announced that he'd achieved a net worth of $100 million, she could spend whatever she wanted on anything she wanted. And what she wanted was a very grand house on the ocean in Palm Beach to be called El Mirasol (the Sunflower). The estate would eventually include a thirty-seven-room mansion, a twenty-car garage, a private zoo, a movie theater, and an oceanfront Moorish tearoom. A few days after the Everglades Club opened, Mizner noticed her pacing out and measuring the terraces of the new club. Spotting an opportunity, he asked if he could assist her in any way. "Oh, Mr. Mizner," she replied, "you have made me so discontented with the plans I have had done for 'El Mirasol'; I don't think I will ever be content with them after seeing this." A few weeks later, she fired her architect and hired Addison Mizner.

The Mizner Mediterranean Revival style was on its way to becoming the dominant architectural template of Florida, as well as emblematic of the boom and all of its attendant romance and glamour. Mizner himself was well on his way to becoming the era's foremost society architect and one of the preeminent architects of his generation.

Ultimately, Mizner's professional success as an architect would fail to satisfy him. He thirsted for something more, if only to escape the uncertainty of what had always been a peripatetic life. "My ups and downs had been like riding a see-saw," he noted in his memoirs. Still, he would insist in his later years that he had never wanted to be one of "the vulgar rich." At the same time, Mizner admitted to having something of a Santa Claus complex: "I like nice things and comforts and always wanted to make presents." So while he might not have aspired to be one of the vulgar rich, he had no objection to one day being every bit as wealthy—and socially prominent—as they were. That would become his next goal, and his ultimate undoing.

6

MERRICK'S IDEAL CITY

After the armistice brought an end to the Great War in November 1918, anyone contemplating real estate development in Florida and serious about how their buildings should look felt obliged to see firsthand Addison Mizner's work in Palm Beach. One such aspirant was George Merrick, who drove up from Miami in 1919 to tour the Everglades Club and inspect a few of the new Mizner residences with his uncle, the illustrator Denman Fink.

The two men resolved during their Palm Beach visit that the Coral Gables project, now taking final shape, would need to be in the Mediterranean Revival architectural idiom. Their approach, however, would differ from Mizner's because they would not be building grandiose clubhouses or homes for the ultrawealthy who favored Palm Beach, nor for the nouveaux riche now drawn to Carl Fisher's Miami Beach. They planned to target a wider potential market: the middle class, who couldn't afford grand waterfront properties but wanted something nicer and more permanent than the rudimentary facilities of a tent camp or an auto park. By now, Merrick and Fink were working on blueprints for a project on a scale grander than anything Mizner or Fisher had yet envisaged.

In the prior five years, Merrick's project, Coral Gables, had taken shape as a small city with a surrounding suburb—"a balanced city," as he described it. His father had dreamed once that the Merrick homestead would one day encompass a retirement village for clergymen and college professors as well as for families of modest means, and this notion had influenced

George's thinking. It helped that his property and his lots were well inland and would be much more affordable to the general public.

All of Merrick's advance planning and design ensured that the development would boast a distinctive and harmonious look. Unlike the haphazard and unplanned growth of most suburbs and cities of the day, the conception of Coral Gables had been worked out well in advance—every aspect, right down to the uniform design of the lampposts and the location of the sewers, drains, and telephone poles. All the Spanish street names were taken from Washington Irving's two books *Tales of the Alhambra* and *A History of the Life and Voyages of Columbus*. Merrick believed this planning would help to inspire his buyers' confidence that they were making sound investments in a carefully managed and well-run community.

It was not the first such planned community in Florida. Credit for that would go to Bostonian entrepreneur Harry Seymour Kelsey, who sold his Waldorf restaurant chain to purchase a hundred thousand acres in Palm Beach County and founded Kelsey City in 1919 with plans drawn up by the Olmsted Brothers.

By now, Merrick had acquired the experience and know-how to proceed with the launch. He had worked for a variety of local real estate companies as a broker and then as an investor, selling entire blocks of land and then later selling the smaller lots that made up those blocks. He had been elected secretary of the Dixie Highway Council, which was locally promoting the new road. Merrick had even served one term as a Dade County commissioner, where he learned the nuances of urban planning. Along the way, he managed to build up a nest egg of some $500,000. As he commented to a newspaper reporter a few years later: "I worked night and day to build up a nucleus for the Coral Gables, which consistently grew in my dreams. I never told anyone my plans, but as my profits in real estate grew, I bought adjoining land. The hundred sixty acres the family originally owned increased to three hundred acres, then to five hundred, a thousand, and finally to sixteen hundred." By 1927, the suburb had grown to three thousand acres, with space to accommodate fifty thousand homes.

When he eventually possessed enough land and capital to begin construction work in 1919, Merrick launched his first small project under his own banner, George E. Merrick Company. He had partners to help him fund and sell each deal. The ten-acre Fernway Park sold well enough to allow him to quickly move on to three other small subdivisions, which he platted in quick succession: South Bay Estates, North Miami Estates, and Twelfth Street Manors. When these sold out, he was ready to go it alone on his giant Coral Gables project. The dress rehearsals were over.

Despite a near monomaniacal focus on his vision for Coral Gables, Merrick found time to socialize. In 1913 he met the woman he would marry, Eunice Isabella Peacock, a recent graduate of the Trenton Model Finishing School for Girls. A very attractive young woman from one of the founding families of neighboring Coconut Grove, she had numerous admirers and wasn't above playing them off against one another. Merrick joined her list of suitors. It did not hurt his chances that, by 1914, he boasted a net worth of more than $300,000 ($7.6 million in today's money), his family owned a very sizable citrus plantation, and he drove a fancy Hudson Model 6-40 open touring car with a convertible top.

The couple married in 1916 at her parents' home and then spent ten days honeymooning in central Florida, which they toured by car. They would have no children. Strains emerged early in the marriage, particularly over Eunice's desire to escape Florida in the sweltering summer months. She made an annual pilgrimage to see relatives in the North every year, leaving a plaintive Merrick behind to write letters expressing how desperately he missed her:

"I feel like boarding [the] train straight to you . . . miss you every minute. . . . Bushels of love, George."

"Hello, Sweetheart. Hope arrived safely. Am terribly lonesome already. Love, George."

A recurring theme in his letters to her was her failure to reply: "I have driven three mail clerks crazy inquiring for a letter from you. Fourth one threatens to shoot me if I ask again. . . . Write immediately if only to save my life!" In one letter that he wrote to his wife on bank stationery, he joked that she had "an overdraft on matter of letters . . . [that] will not be tolerated by Bank of George E. Merrick, lover and sole proprietor of Eunice I. Peacock Merrick Love Account. Deficiency must be taken care of in 5 days or proper proceedings will be initiated. . . . I send you my deep all love of my heart, and I am missing you lots and lots all ready. Good night my dear, dear wifie girl. Your old Iggie."

At one point in 1917, to further research his Coral Gables project and see what Florida's other early developers were up to, Merrick traveled the state with a small group of friends on a sixteen-day auto party. As the "gear-jammer," he did all the driving—all 1,100 miles of it—averaging twenty miles per hour in his brand-new White Motor Company seven-passenger touring car. Among those accompanying him was Eunice; his mother, Althea; his best friend, a lawyer named Clifton Benson; and Benson's wife. "Left hotel early. Some trouble with gas again. Breakfast at Kissimmee—Crane's restaurant—poor place. Fine brick road all the way to Kissimmee but bad beyond Osceola County, beyond Polk County line. Fine asphalt road to Haines City. Ice cream there.... Fine lake region near Winter Haven. Freight train stropped by mules on track. Road poor at Winter Haven then poor all the way to Lakeland. . . . Fruit for lunch. Uninteresting country from Lakeland to Tampa." They had three flat tires on route. Then, in 1920, he and Eunice made a holiday trip to Cuba to see the original Spanish colonial architecture in its native setting. They wandered the streets taking note of the barrel-tiled roofs, the courtyards that featured tiled fountains, the pale-colored stucco-walled buildings, and the churches with bell towers.

He found time that same year to publish a book of poetry titled *Songs of the Wind on a Southern Shore and Other Poems of Florida*, illustrated by his uncle Denman Fink. His publishing house, the Four Seas Company, also published early works by William Carlos Williams, Gertrude Stein, William Faulkner, and Conrad Aiken. Like its other authors, he had to subsidize the cost of publication. The poems celebrated Florida's natural beauty and Merrick's possibly unrequited love for his wife. The first couplet of the Walt Whitman–esque title poem reads: "I ripple the fronds of the cocoanut palms, / As I join with the voice of the sea / The somnolent swell of the mystical psalms / That I breathe from the quivering tree."

The book was featured in the windows of a few Miami stores and received polite reviews. Merrick sent inscribed copies to his friends. He took special care to send a copy to a local writer whose work he had recently come to admire: Marjory Stoneman Douglas. Her column in the *Miami*

Herald often began with a poem of her own. He inscribed a copy of the volume to her, noting how he was working "very modestly in the same field." He assured her that "none of your good ones will get by this *one* reader without being fully appreciated, I am, Yours respectfully, Geo. E. Merrick." It seems likely that the two met on this basis. They would remain lifelong acquaintances if not close friends. Some years later, Merrick hired Douglas at $100 a week to write ads and publicity to promote Coral Gables.

As he readied for the launch, Merrick hired an experienced team of men to work for him. Foremost among these was his uncle Denman Fink, the celebrated illustrator whose work appeared in publications such as *Scribner's Monthly* and the *Saturday Evening Post*. Fink's job as artistic advisor was to ensure that the winding streets, the boulevards, the entryways, the plazas, the promenades, and the public parks were of a uniform design and aesthetically pleasing, replete with the look of antiquity.

Merrick also hired a handful of architects, led by Phineas Paist, a Philadelphian who had worked on Villa Vizcaya. Paist would design the public buildings, oversee the overall color scheme, and ensure compliance to strict building codes. His initial title was "supervisor of color." Next in prominence on the team was a celebrated landscape architect named Frank M. Button, who had designed Chicago's Lincoln Park. His job was to create the parks, the canals, and the streetscapes, using a variety of tropical trees and blooming shrubs but leaving examples of the original orange and grapefruit trees where possible. Button laid out a plan for the first 1,200 acres, charging Merrick a dollar an acre for his services. By late 1924, Button's 130 landscaper workers had planted fifty thousand tropical trees, shrubs, and flowering plants—mostly palms, jacaranda, African tulip, wild fig, tree ferns, and bougainvillea.

Together Paist, Button, and Denman Fink would design the iconic multistory Douglas Entrance (La Puerta del Sol) out of coquina stone, a sedimentary rock composed of shell fragments, at a cost of $1 million. It was widely imitated at other developments around the state. With office buildings attached, it was the grandest of the four entrances to the development that were actually built. A total of eight had been planned.

Finally, to design individual spec homes, Merrick hired his cousin H. George Fink, Denman's nephew and a local architect who had spent six years designing buildings for Carl Fisher on Miami Beach. Two thousand homes would be built in the development between 1921 and 1927, luring buyers from twenty-nine states. Every aspect of each house—the style of the roof, the design of the window casements, the color of the stucco or the awnings—had to be reviewed, "passed up by architect and artist so that there may be no clash against the general scheme of things." After the first few years, the adherence to the Mediterranean Revival style began to loosen, and, to add some variety, seven villages were designed, each with a distinctive motif such as Chinese, French Norman, and Cape Dutch.

In a decision every bit as crucial as hiring the architects, Merrick managed to persuade Edward "Doc" Dammers to head up sales and serve as his "real estate counsel." Dammers had already made a name for himself as a superb salesman and auctioneer, hawking real estate at Delray Beach and Miami Beach. He was a familiar sight to the community, pigeon-toed in his white spats and saddle shoes, his beribboned straw boater tipped jauntily to the side as he waved a rolled-up brochure in one hand in a slightly threatening manner or gesticulated wildly, always exhorting his audience to buy before it was too late or launching into one of his signature lyrical tirades.

"What is it, I ask you, that makes our citizens different?" he would begin. "Women more beautiful, men more dashing, enterprise more daring, while the song of the bird, the color of the flower, the smile of little children are all aglow and have to them a charm, a divine thrill unmatched the world around." Who could resist such appeals? In the case of one auctioneer, Charlie Powell in St. Petersburg, Doc's pitch was so compelling that he once found himself bidding on the lots that he himself was selling—to the point where his purchases quickly exceeded his commission.

The popular Doc Dammers would eventually be elected the first mayor of Coral Gables after the city was incorporated. To head up his sales force, Dammers in turn hired George Cummings, in the words of one competitor, "as brilliant a sale manager as ever hazed millions out of a group of prima donnas." Together Dammers and Cummings would assemble a large sales force for Merrick, most of them clad in the white plus-four golf knickers, which became the signature attire of the Florida real estate broker.

As the launch date approached, it became clear that the scale of what Merrick envisioned vastly exceeded his $500,000 initial investment. He was forced to scramble to find a bank to help fund the operation, at first without success. Then he ran into an old college friend named C. F. Baldwin, who ran an insurance company in Miami, and Merrick persuaded him to finance the construction of the first one hundred homes.

In one of their first advertisements, the sales team touted the fact that popular investment expert Roger Babson, whom they described as "the foremost economist of the country," was recommending that everybody buy suburban real estate now. Their pitch concluded by asking, "With lower costs of plots and building, with every convenience at your command— why should anyone not prefer an ideal home at Coral Gables?" Merrick and his team had successfully taken Mizner's Mediterranean style and incorporated it into a beautiful planned community that had everything a contemporary buyer could possibly ask for. In a literal sense, the stage was set for the boom that followed. Flagler's hotel civilization would soon be transformed into a subdivision civilization.

In November 1921 the first lots and homes went on sale.

Few people who knew Merrick would be surprised at the scale of the success he was about to achieve. As the Florida journalist Charles E. Harner noted, the man exuded success: "Standing six feet tall, blond and with the handshake of a blacksmith, he was confidence personified." It would not be long before both the local and the national press would be describing George Merrick as "a truly great man," "one of the most remarkable men in America," and, of course, "a genius." As his partner Denman Fink observed later, "There was a man I would have gone through hell and high-water for." Doc Dammers echoed the sentiment, describing Merrick as "one of the finest men who ever drew the breath of life."

At Coral Gables, Merrick had taken much of the uncertainty out of the development process even before he broke ground. The question was no longer would he be successful—that was a given. The more pertinent question was how he would handle his immense success when it arrived.

7

GREAT MIGRATIONS

George Merrick's new city, Addison Mizner's new club, and Carl Fisher's Miami Beach were perfectly timed to meet the onslaught of a sudden new migration. And in sheer numbers, the flow of people to Florida in the mid-1920s would exceed any of the great land rushes of the past: the 300,000 or so to California from 1848 to 1852, for instance, or the 50,000 to Oklahoma in 1889. By 1925, it would be conservatively estimated that 4,000 people were entering Florida daily by car, an additional 3,000 by train, and hundreds more by ship. In total, some 2.5 million entered the state that year alone. According to one participant, it was "like the possessive pilgrimage of army ants or the seasonal flight of myriad of blackbirds." Although the resident population reached 1.5 million by the end of the decade, this figure overlooks the enormous number of vacationers and seasonal or part-time residents—"snowbirds," second-home home owners, or retirees—who came and went regularly, to say nothing of the vast tide of people who would arrive strictly to invest in the land boom.

The boom did not quite begin at the start of the decade. The US economy stalled from January 1920 to July 1921 as industrial production levels, which had ramped up in wartime, ran into the realities of lower postwar demand. This sharp eighteen-month postwar recession was exacerbated when the nation's central bank, the Federal Reserve, founded in late 1913, raised its key interest rate, the discount rate, to stem losses in the value of gold, to which the US currency was pegged. Companies were forced to lay off workers and shutter factories.

Fortunately, this postwar recession was relatively short-lived. The two key drivers of the economy at the time, housing and automobiles, rebounded quickly. From then on, housing starts would grow at a rate of 883,000 per year until 1929—more than twice the rate of any comparable period—as suburbs began to spring up around the country's major metropolitan areas, offering single-family homes as an alternative to cramped urban living. Auto sales, which had dipped for a year or so, showed an even more dramatic recovery. In 1919 there were eight million cars on the road; by 1930, that number had jumped to twenty-six million, at which point, 87 percent of US households owned a registered vehicle—a figure ominously near the market's saturation point and hinting at a serious potential problem for the nation's largest industry should anything go wrong with the US economy, which, of course, it did. The ongoing electrification of the country also contributed to the rapid economic recovery. And thanks largely to electrification, productivity would surge during the decade, as shops, factories, and streetcars found ways to exploit uses for the new power. Output per man hours jumped 72 percent nationwide between 1919 and 1929.

However, the prospects for the American farmer were not nearly so rosy. When Europe's grain farmers returned to work and brought their crops back onto the global market following the war, commodity prices began to fall. Automation brought on by tractors, combines, threshers, and bailers would keep the downward pressure on crop prices for years to come. Throughout an otherwise prosperous decade, small farmers and sharecroppers would struggle to make a living, especially those growing grain. Dairy farmers and fruit growers, including those in Florida, fared much better. In all, some four million farmers would be forced to sell up and move on in search of other lines of work, continuing the exodus from farm country to urban areas around the United States. These enduring problems would snowball and contribute to the national tragedy of the Dust Bowl once the Depression began.

With hindsight, it would become clear that the underlying health of the national economy during the twenties was more fragile than it seemed at the time. Most of the income gains during the decade would go to the wealthy, adding to the already considerable income disparities and social inequality and weakening the underpinnings of a society that still lacked a social safety net. Such problems are uncomfortably familiar to those who lived through the financial crash of 2008–09 and its aftermath, particularly in the American heartland, where profound economic anxiety produced anger at the urban elites, resentment of immigrants, and ominous stirrings of economic nationalism.

When the recession ended in 1921, even the nation's roads were finally ready for the boom—and would do their part to contribute to it. A vascular infrastructure of highways had begun to emerge, spreading from city to city, from city to town, from east to west, and, finally and most importantly, from north to south, allowing the population to move about by car. Many of the county roads, including in Florida, remained primitive in spots, narrow paths made of sand-clay mixtures, or even pine straw laid down a foot thick over dirt tracks. Such straw roads had the virtue of being cheap to build: $40 per mile versus $1,000 per mile for sand-clay surfaces. Fisher's Dixie Highway, by contrast, was a generous eighteen feet wide, with much of it paved. It gathered various feeder roads into two broad arteries that ran from the northern midwestern states all the way down to Florida, and then down opposite coasts of the Florida peninsula. The plan was for the two roads to convene at a southern hub, Miami, although for that to happen, a road through the Everglades, known as the Tamiami Trail, still needed to be constructed at considerable effort and expense. Work on the trail had begun in 1916 but stalled for lack of funds.

Kenneth L. Roberts, a reporter for the *Saturday Evening Post* and later known for popular historical novels such as *Northwest Passage,* accepted a commission from the Tampa developer D. P. Davis to write a book extolling the virtues of Florida. In it, Roberts described witnessing firsthand the Florida migration on the Dixie Highway at its peak in 1925:

> *Hour after hour, day after day, week after week, month after month . . . an articulated serpent 1,500 miles in length—an endless serpent whose joints, composed entirely of automobiles, slipped easily over the ground in some spots and labored more violently in others, but on the whole managed to wriggle forward at a rate of*

about thirty miles an hour. In this ever-flowing stream one could
find every known brand of automobile and every imaginable
human combination. Trucks and limousines and coupes and little
tin cars purred and wheezed and roared and clanked and boomed
along the road, democratically and tenaciously clinging to their
places in the 1,500-mile procession.

The trip down to Florida from the North required patience. In 1920 the best a driver could hope to accomplish was 170 miles per day along the Dixie Highway. Five years later, 200 miles per day was doable; by 1931, 300 miles. But the distance was at least manageable in a few days' time; by contrast, a similar auto migration to California for those seeking a new and better life there easily took ten days. The two states would compete for settlers and tourists throughout the decade, using advertising campaigns that touted their ideal weather and their Riviera-like lifestyle at the ocean's edge.

California, less of a new frontier at this point in history, had its own particular allure during the decade. It offered high-paying jobs in a burgeoning oil industry, in a nascent aviation industry, in agriculture, in shipping, in construction, and in a rapidly expanding motion picture industry based in the new township of Hollywood. In fact, the state's population would grow at a rate comparable with Florida's during the decade (some 50 percent off a much larger base). It would have its own celebrated land developers such as the newspaper magnate Harry Chandler, although few of them captured the imagination of the press in the way that Florida's developers did. And Chandler's development of land around Los Angeles was less explicitly about making fast money and flipping real estate. Much of California's population growth during the decade stemmed from the declining fortunes of farmworkers in the Midwest and Mexico, who correctly saw California's 450-mile-long Central Valley as the next farming mecca. The migration to California would continue throughout the Depression with the arrival of Okies fleeing the Dust Bowl, depicted so movingly in John Steinbeck's classic novel *The Grapes of Wrath*.

Florida, in addition to being so much closer to the populous cities of the East, had the advantage of being warmer than California. Its southernmost tip was six hundred miles farther south than San Diego. Florida also quickly earned a reputation as being naughtier and more fun than its rival. Over time, it would claim to offer more activities to more types of people. Kenneth Roberts's description of the Florida migrants in motion gives a flavor of the diversity of people heading south:

> *Of those who traveled in the great trek, the majority seemed to be made up of young men between the ages of twenty-five and forty. Also, however, there were young women traveling alone . . . couples traveling alone with expensive luggage; couples traveling with a half dozen children and next to no luggage; elderly men traveling alone; mothers traveling with two or three children climbing over the steering wheel and making faces out of the rear windows at those behind them; elderly ladies driving closed machines in solitary grandeur; fourteen- or fifteen-year-old boys crammed into wheezing, panting wrecks of automobiles and intimidating all adjacent sections of the procession by their erratic steering; ladies in frills and furbelows; ladies in flannel shirts and broad-beamed knickerbockers; men in caps and torn sweaters; men in derbies and stiff collars and chamois gloves; men in sombreros; decent-looking people; wild-looking people; worried-looking people; and people who looked hard enough to lunch on tenpenny nail sandwiches and hollow-tile pie.*

Social and cultural attitudes were changing in the wake of the Great War. Old ideas of behavior and morality were molting away. The new, more lax attitudes, which had begun to emerge well before the war, now gained prominence, driven in part by the faster pace of life, reactions to rapid industrialization, relief at the war's end, and disillusionment with much of the war's outcome. Two milestone pieces of legislation went into effect at the outset of the decade that epitomized this change. The first was passage of the Volstead Act in January 1920, prohibiting the sale of alcohol; the second was the ratification of Nineteenth Amendment in August 1920, giving women the right to vote.

The accompanying liberalizing of values (in spite of the unpopular "noble experiment" of Prohibition, as President Herbert Hoover once referred to it) led to higher hemlines and the once improbable sight of women smoking cigarettes in public. In the realm of the arts, "modernism" took a firmer hold, rejecting traditional modes of thought and expression in favor of experimentation and innovation in both form and subject matter. Also, for the first time, sports heroes and movie stars became bona fide celebrities. Dixieland jazz rose in popularity, displacing ragtime music. In the party-like atmosphere of the nightclubs and the speakeasies, everyone danced the Charleston; others went to the movies, silent until the premier of *The Jazz Singer* in October 1927; at home, they listened to the radio or played mahjong or tried their hand at crossword puzzles, another new craze. F. Scott Fitzgerald wrote about the flapper generation in the pages of the *Saturday Evening Post*; Ernest Hemingway documented the woes of the "lost" war generation in his short stories and novels; and Sinclair Lewis satirized small-minded small-town life in works such as *Main Street*, *Babbitt*, and *Arrowsmith*. The hero of *Babbitt*, appropriately, was a realtor, "nimble in the calling of selling houses for more than people could afford to pay." In 1930 Lewis would become the first American writer to win the Nobel Prize for Literature. As historian Bruce Catton observed some fifty years later, "All the old rules seemed to be vanishing in the twenties. In exchange came a strange new world both gaudy and sad."

But no development was more significant than the changing attitudes toward the use of money. As the new live-in-the-moment spirit took hold, perhaps a natural response to the recent dour war years, Americans began to spend and borrow more freely than ever before. To do so, they used installment credit.

Also known as hire purchase, installment credit was not entirely new—and consumer credit itself dated back to antiquity. In reality, according to Lendol Calder, an expert on the history of consumer credit, overindebtedness was a headache for the Pilgrims, the colonial planters, and nineteenth-century farmers: "A river of red ink," he writes, "runs through American history." However, up until the 1920s, installment credit had been used primarily for the sale of pianos, and, to a lesser extent, furniture and sewing machines. Installment credit required fixed payments in regular intervals over a certain period of time. This differed from the more typical *demand obligations*, where the loan often had mandatory redemption obligations attached. It was different, too, from *single payment loans*, or the home mortgages of the day, which required a lump sum or a balloon payment at the end of the term of the loan.

In the twenties, installment credit would launch a vast consumer consumption boom. It fueled the purchases of mechanical refrigerators, which were a huge technological leap forward from the icebox, as well as dishwashers, electric washing machines, kitchen ranges, stoves, pop-up toasters, oil burners and automatic furnaces, roofing, insulation, vacuum cleaners, and radios, most of which emerged as viable new technologies in the 1920s. The first commercial radio broadcast was the presidential election returns on November 2, 1920, from Westinghouse's radio station KDKA in East Pittsburgh. Ten years later, half the households in the United States would own a radio. All of these appliances were offered under installment credit terms to the growing number of middle-class Americans, many of whom were feeling flush after the war years. The availability of such credit allowed consumers to buy items today that they would normally need to wait and save to pay for. This created a onetime-only front-end-loading of consumer consumption. No one seemed concerned at the time that it might subtract from consumption levels a few years down the road.

Not surprisingly, the use and popularity of home mortgages soared, too, in this looser financial climate. However, most home mortgages required high down payments on the property—30 percent was standard— and their terms were short: five to seven years. When that term ended, they needed to be refinanced or repaid. (Today's ubiquitous thirty-year mortgage was an innovation of the mid-1930s, established by the newly created Federal Housing Administration in 1934 as part of President Franklin D. Roosevelt's New Deal legislation to help lift the country out of the Great Depression.) As credit restrictions eased throughout the 1920s, many home owners, or aspiring home buyers, layered on second and third mortgages. Many midwestern farmers did the same, but, in many cases, out of financial necessity or in order to buy more land to make up for dwindling profits from crop sales, or to buy farm machinery that would increase productivity, even if such productivity only added to the world's growing surplus of commodities.

From 1919 to 1929, both forms of personal debt—mortgages and installment credit—soared. The volume of home mortgages more than tripled, and the amount of outstanding installment debt more than doubled. Other kinds of credit also became widely available, such as that offered through credit finance companies and department stores.

Concurrent with the arrival of this new consumption-driven economy, advertising came into its own. Glossy magazine ads, radio spots, and outdoor billboard advertising played on various human anxieties, peddling new products and offering new cures if the reader or listener wanted to look right, feel right, or keep up with his or her neighbors. As the migrants to Florida traveled south, they passed billboards on the roadsides, all large enough to attract attention and be read quickly. In memorable slogans, they touted approaching attractions, motor courts or tent camps, and staples such as orange juice, southern barbecue, fireworks, or popular products like Burma Shave, a brushless shaving cream introduced in 1925 that used humorous verses spread across a succession of billboards to tout its virtues.

The layering of store credit and installment debt for cars and kitchen appliances on top of mortgage debt for the home would create a precarious balance for many households, requiring hard work, planning, and disciplined spending simply to meet the family's outstanding loan obligations. Often it left little room for errors in budgeting and added dangerously to a family's financial exposure. If the economy soured and the breadwinner lost his job, the family risked losing everything.

For the moment, Americans didn't care. Their love affair with the automobile, in particular, was now in full force. Cars were everywhere, in all makes and models, including those rumble-seated makes soon to disappear, such as Essex, Franklin, Jordan, Kissel, Marmon, Maxwell, Peerless, Pierce-Arrow, Oakland, and Stutz. By 1924, Henry Ford had driven down the cost of his Model T to $265 from $900 in 1919, reducing it to less than the cost of a team of horses. In its last year of production, 1927, the Model T roadster still sold for $265; the coupe, for $290. That year, a new Buick cost $650; a Chevrolet, $490. Gasoline was 15 cents per gallon. The horse population, incidentally, was now in steep decline. In New York City, horse numbers had dropped from 128,000 to 56,000 in the decade between 1910 and 1920. Other cities saw similar declines, putting further pressure on the prospects of the farmers who grew the grain to feed them.

The automobile was so indispensable to its owner that it invariably became the very last thing that he or she would part with when the family finances went awry. This was especially true if he or she had bought the motor car on credit—and by 1926, 75 percent of all car buyers had done so. To allow the car to be repossessed meant forfeiting whatever payments the buyer had already made under the installment plan.

It wasn't long before the car began to have its own profound effects on the wider culture, especially social conventions. The car allowed young people to easily escape the direct supervision of their parents, and that led inevitably to increased promiscuity, in the backseat and elsewhere. Although this impact was difficult to measure, there was little doubt that the car had contributed mightily to the new, more relaxed sexual mores of the era.

The spread of the automobile, the growth of the suburbs, the popular new forms of credit, and the blossoming consumer culture all combined to shape the first fully articulated conception of the American Dream, although the term itself was not actually coined until 1931 by historian James Truslow Adams in his book *The Epic of America.* He worded it as follows: "The American Dream is that dream of a land in which life should be better and richer and fuller for everyone, with opportunity for each according to ability or achievement." For many, that dream expressed itself in more explicitly materialistic terms: every American should have a car, a home, a vacation, and a chance at greater wealth. By the early 1920s, if you were looking for somewhere to achieve that dream, where better than in Florida, where the winter weather was sublime, the resort lifestyle unfettered, jobs plentiful, and property values on the rise?

Despite Kenneth Roberts's fanciful reporting, the diverse group of migrants heading south to the Sunshine State weren't all upstanding citizens in pursuit of the American Dream. The loose money and even looser morals were open invitations to criminals. Florida during the decade would attract more than its share of con artists and swindlers, such as Charles Ponzi, and murderous gangsters like Al Capone, as we shall see. Only bootlegging alcohol would match land fraud as a favored criminal pastime in the years to follow.

Nor was the new American Dream attainable for everyone. A close reading of Roberts's description above reveals some notable omissions among the hordes of people traveling south. His list makes no mention of black Americans, or any people of color, unless one makes a few broad assumptions about those men he spotted wearing sombreros.

In fact, blacks were migrating in the opposite direction: from southern states to major industrial cities in the North and the West, where the First World War, in particular, had created good jobs for many unskilled or semiskilled workers. The so-called Great Migration of some six million people between 1916 and 1970 was well under way by the early 1920s. It was driven by factors other than the lure of economic opportunity, although the prospects for sharecroppers, along with those of most farmers, were drastically diminished in the wake of the war.

The black community had other compelling reasons for leaving the American South. Chief among them was the abysmal treatment they received at the hands of local authorities across the southern states, as insidious notions of white supremacy spread during the 1920s, bolstering the ranks of the Ku Klux Klan. Blacks throughout the South were denied access to public parks, hotels, schools, beaches, golf courses, swimming pools, and water fountains. Florida was no exception to this harsh climate of intolerance. An avowed racist governor named Sidney Catts, who served from 1917 to 1921, actually encouraged antiblack violence and racial terrorism. Florida would boast the shameful distinction of leading the nation in the ratio of lynchings per capita, with some forty-five recorded cases during the decade. Daily life for blacks in the state was perilous even if they were prosperous enough to afford an automobile. The African American newspaper the *Florida Sentinel* issued an advisory to blacks traveling around the state by car in a 1925 article titled "Warning to Negro Tourists":

Those who have automobiles want to exercise more caution when driving over the state. The small villages and towns are still far from civilized and at every opportunity give their savagery full play. The Negro who drives a Ford gets by no better than one who drives a Lincoln. Every one must pay a toll for driving through these small white settlements. You don't have to speed. If you roll along at the rate of four miles an hour, if you happen to be the least colored, it is sufficient reason to hold you up and take a batch of your cold cash, and on top of that be rough-necked by a man whose nickel-faced badge is his only protection against the charge of highway robbery.

If you want to get abused, be thoughtless enough to get short of gas near one of these village filling-stations. You are likely as not to be arrested on a charge of car stealing and be detained in jail without even the chance of getting a hearing within a week.

The little country court is worse than the speed cop, so there you are. The country judge and speed cop must depend on those they victimize for their support....

Don't take a chance against a backwoods cop and trial court.

Don't leave your city unless you are certain you have enough gas to carry you to the next city.

Don't stop at the village filling-stations.

Don't buy sodas, cigars, or lunches along the path of your trip.

Don't be hard-headed and get the experience of thousands of your fellow autoists who are just as careful to observe the law as you.

Such stern warnings did not prevent autoless black migrant farmworkers from entering the state seasonally to pick crops. Others, joined by large numbers of emigrating Bahamians, continued going into the construction trade to help build the resort hotels and the skyscrapers of Miami and to lay out subdivisions across the state, much as they had done since the era of Henry Flagler. But throughout the 1920s, the black community, which comprised roughly half the population of Florida at the outset of the decade, would remain largely on the periphery of the great land boom story, participating as laborers but unable to benefit from the wild appreciation in land values to follow. And many of these black workers would eventually join the migration northward looking to better their lives—and as a quiet form of protest against their brutal mistreatment under segregation.

En route to Florida, comfortable hotel accommodations could be found in any significant city. For those travelers determined to keep to the highway, the need for cheap accommodations was met through a variety of new venues. Tent camps were one of these.

By the 1920s, tent camping had become a popular feature of automobiling, especially for low-income owners of Model Ts, also known as flivvers or Tin Lizzies, which were open to the elements in the early models. To accommodate the craze, tent camps popped up along roadsides around the country. Here drivers could pull in, park, and pitch or rent a tent for the night. Tent camps would be superseded in the middle of the decade by tourist cabins and motor courts, which in turn would morph into today's motels (an appellation that derives from the contraction of *motor* and *hotel*). Initially the cabins were tiny, simple, even primitive in nature because the owners feared guests would make off with the bedsheets and towels. Most had a separate larger cabin nearby that provided a communal toilet and shower. Many motor courts prohibited locals from frequenting the cabins in an effort to reduce their use for sexual assignations and prostitution—the so-called bounce-on-the-bed trade. More frugal travelers, many of whom were farmers on the off-season or industrial workers on vacation, simply parked on the side of the road and dined off the canned food that they brought with them—earning them the nickname "tin-canners."

On arrival in Florida, local tent camps awaited the migrants, offering longer-term rentals and cheap vacation accommodations. Like RV camps today, these camps shoved guests into close proximity and created a festive, if chaotic, environment. In spite of, or perhaps because of, their openly communal nature, the tent camps were enormously popular. One traveler recalled arriving to spend the night at a tent camp set up in a grove of pecan trees on the edge of a cotton farm in North Carolina. Some fourteen cars were already parked there, bearing license plates from states around the nation, with more arriving every moment, loaded with weary passengers. Around a campfire, stories were swapped in an air of excitement and anticipation. The group consisted of schoolteachers, engineers, lawyers, doctors, salesmen, small business owners, and a disproportionate number of carpenters and bricklayers, who all professed to have sold everything they owned to buy a car and enough camping gear and provisions to get them to Florida. They would admit to their business failures, to their desire to start over in Florida, to being curious about what they would find in the Sunshine State. Not one admitted to their common purpose, which was to get rich through Florida land speculation.

A real estate broker in St. Petersburg named Walter P. Fuller capitalized on the presence of a crowded municipal tent camp near him to make his first big financial score, which in turn, he believed, kicked off the land boom around St. Petersburg in 1921. Most of the guests at his local tent camp were vacationing factory workers from the North, whose pockets, he surmised, must be bulging with unspent wages earned during the war years. He planted two signs directly across the street from the tent camp that read, "For Good Low-Priced Lots in This Vicinity . . . See Fuller." Then he sent his partner, Francis Burklew, to wander through the camp one Sunday morning, posing as an ordinary camper, explaining who Fuller was and proclaiming what a terrific bargain his nearby lots presented. Meanwhile, over at the empty acreage that Fuller had been commissioned to sell, he erected a stake on each of the 326 lots and tacked a manila envelope to each stake that gave the lot number and block number and read: "Bring me this envelope and $50, and the lot is yours for $____. Balance payable $10 a month." By midmorning the following Friday, he had sold every lot, and without spending a nickel on newspaper advertising, commissions, or showing expenses. Not only that, every single contract would be paid in full by his buyers. Fuller spent the rest of the summer flipping lots for a handful of the original sellers, often selling them new and better lots in turn, a process known in the trade as reloading.

After the delays caused by World War I and the ensuing postwar recession, the migrants began arriving in growing numbers. The Florida newspapers, the *Miami Herald* prominent among them, began to report that the land boom looked to be real at last. As the Miami journalist J. Kenneth Ballinger wrote soon afterward, "The most spectacular real estate boom of modern times was getting ready to sprinkle its heedless millions over the state of Florida."

8

A WRITER'S EDUCATION

Nowhere in Florida would the change during the decade be more dramatic or more lunatic than it was in Miami. Perfectly situated to report on the events was the leading newspaper, the *Miami Herald*. The *Herald*, at the time Marjory Douglas began her job there as the society editor, had a tiny staff of three reporters and a handful of circulation executives and ad salesmen who occupied a two-story downtown building on Miami Avenue. She was given her own desk in the city room, which occupied most of the second floor.

Marjory took her seat there excited, if apprehensive, and determined not to disappoint her father. Frank Stoneman worked at a large oblong table in a private office at the far end of this open room. At one point a few years after she arrived, the classified ad desk would be occupied by an aspiring young actor named Joseph Cotten, who went on to fame in Hollywood, starring in such classics as *Citizen Kane* and *The Magnificent Ambersons*. "Besides being one of the handsomest young men I'd ever seen, he was awfully nice," Douglas recalled.

Since Miami boasted a population of only roughly ten thousand in 1915, there were few social engagements to cover other than the infrequent comings and goings of celebrities and state dignitaries. To earn her keep, she did other general assignments, including filling in for her father on the editorial page when he was on vacation. The job would give Douglas an excellent understanding of how the city and state functioned and the key local issues of the day. At first, she didn't always satisfy her father's rigorous journalistic standards—"I sent you out to do a story," he admonished her, "and you come back with three sunsets and an editorial"—but she soon learned her craft and became thoroughly absorbed in the work. From the outset, she seemed keenly attuned to the Florida environment, writing early on about the state's disappearing Caribbean and Dade County pines, which she admired for their "sunny resinous breath."

"Can you see a pine tree?" she asked in one column. "If you can, you're lucky. They are going fast. And every day, somebody cuts down a few more to make a new subdivision that, without them, will be as raw and ugly as plain dirt without trees can be."

Through her job, Marjory met a handful of locals her age, and together they rented a beach house for two weeks during her first summer in Miami. "We lived in bathing suits and ran up and down the beach—there was nobody but us," she recalled. "We spent our evenings in the moonlight. . . . We'd swim and light fires, cook on the beach, then get up early the next morning to swim again." Soon to be successfully divorced, she enjoyed a summer romance with a reporter for the rival newspaper the *Miami Metropolis*. The affair ended when he enlisted with the American Ambulance Service and departed for France in late 1916.

A few months later, her father sent Marjory to report on a story about the first Florida woman to enlist in the new US Naval Reserve Force. She found herself raising her hand and volunteering. An awkward phone call to her father followed. "Look, I got the story about the first woman to enlist," she informed him. "It turned out to be me."

But after a year of mind-numbing secretarial work at the navy headquarters at the foot of Flagler Street, Douglas quit to find something better. Determined to serve overseas, she joined the Red Cross in the summer of 1918, enlisting in a department called Civilian Relief, which had an office in Paris. When the cannons went off along the Seine on November 11, signifying that the war had ended, she joined in the celebrations and the marches along the Place de la Concorde and the Rue de Rivoli. Marjory stayed on in France for another year, traveling around Europe and writing stories about the Red Cross clinics that were being turned over to the local authorities.

When she returned to Miami in January 1920, her father offered her the position of assistant editor, hoping to groom her to succeed him one day. She began writing a column of her own called "The Galley," which gave her an opportunity to opine on local and national affairs. In one, she wrote: "Is it any wonder that south Florida, this new Florida, is young and hopeful and confident? The tired ways of the old countries and of the north have no meaning for us, who are conscious of the banner of a great new belief."

Douglas's own beliefs—and political opinions—had begun to take shape. Even before the war, she had joined Mrs. William Jennings Bryan, the wife of the famed orator and three-time failed presidential candidate, and two other prominent women (wives of former Florida governors) on a trip to Tallahassee to speak to the Florida Legislature on the subject of ratifying the women's suffrage amendment. The women's impassioned pleas were pointedly ignored by the legislators, a group of men she would later dismiss as "wool-hat boys in the red hills beyond the Suwannee." She was not wrong to be dismissive: Florida would be the last state in the union to ratify the suffrage amendment to the Constitution.

Her positions became those of an enlightened urban progressive. She championed women's suffrage, social equality, and foreign trade. She deplored Prohibition, and she was generally critical of politics and politicians: "There are two sound arguments against politics. The first is that they keep so many men running who were obviously built to walk, and the second is that they are politics."

Other causes now caught her attention. When she read about a young North Dakota man who, after being arrested for vagrancy, was whipped to death in a Florida labor camp, Douglas responded by writing a ballad about the incident that appeared at the head of her newspaper column. The poem, "Martin Tabert of North Dakota Is Walking Florida Now," conveyed her shock and outrage: "The other convicts, they stood around him, / When the length of the black strap cracked and found him." The poem was reprinted widely and helped to galvanize public opinion against corporal punishment in the labor camps. At one point, it was read before the state legislature.

At around this time, an influential local woman named Jessica Water-man Seymour encouraged Douglas to focus even more on regional issues in her column. Specifically, she suggested Douglas support a local proposal to create an Everglades National Park. This idea was the pet project of an eccentric, down-on-his-luck landscape architect named Ernest F. Coe, im-mediately recognizable around Miami in his frayed seersucker suit and bow tie. Connecticut born and Yale educated, Coe was willing to tirelessly bore the locals with endless talk about the need for the new park, which earned him the nickname "Pappa of the Everglades." At one point, he succeeded in persuading Carl Fisher to allow a fund-raiser to be thrown at his Nauti-lus Hotel. Douglas joined Coe's park committee and began to explore the Everglades on her own and with friends—as much as one *could* explore an area that in most places was six inches underwater and inaccessible.

Early one morning, after driving out to the edge of the great swamp to see the sunrise, she witnessed a sight that she would remember for the rest of her life: the nuptial flight of the white ibis. The great wheel of white birds rose overhead and then swung around in a giant circle, only to have a second wheel lift off the ground just as the first group landed. It was the start of the ibis breeding season—and the sight marked the beginning of Douglas's passion for Florida's birds. She began to drive out to Royal Palm Park to watch the abundant shorebirds. "You could stand on the old roadway and look back toward a little bridge and see white ibis and wood stork sitting on the railings. . . . In Ten Thousand islands at the edge of the Everglades, I saw great flocks of birds, amazing flights of 30,000 to 40,000 in one swoop, either coming from the sandy coast to their rookeries or going from the rookeries to the sandy coasts where there weren't any pred-ators." Florida's shorebirds were a revelation to her. Douglas had always loved wildlife and animals, and would boast at age ninety-six that she re-membered every animal that she had ever encountered in the wild—as well as every house cat that she had ever met. It wasn't long before she was an avid birder.

At about this time, Marjory fell in with a group of naturalists who lived in Coconut Grove on the outskirts of Miami. They called themselves the Florida Society of Natural History, and they met every few weeks to read and discuss scientific papers they were writing about the unique characteristics of the area's flora and fauna. Their leader was the botanist and plant explorer David Fairchild, a former US Department of Agriculture bureaucrat who had created the agency's Office of Seed and Plant Introduction. An advocate of gathering the world cultivars and dispersing them to new regions of the earth to spur the growth of agricultural industries, he and his department were largely responsible for introducing more than two hundred thousand new plants and crops into the United States, including, notably, such staples today as the Meyer lemon, the date palm, the Calimyrna fig, durum wheat, and certain varieties of soybeans, mangos, and avocados. His efforts would have the secondary effect of enriching the cuisine of this and other countries, making him, in the words of his biographer, Amanda Harris, "the patron saint of foodies." It was Fairchild's idea to plant the Yoshino cherry trees along Washington, DC's Speedway (a section of Independence Avenue) and Tidal Basin.

Another regional issue began to preoccupy Douglas: the condition of blacks in South Florida. A New Englander at heart, she detested what she saw. "I had no sympathy with the old white southern attitude. To me, slavery was the greatest crime ever committed, which we are still suffering to expiate." Visiting Miami's Colored Town, she was appalled to discover that there was no running water and no toilets. The outdoor privies were set up so close to the public well that it wasn't long before the well water became contaminated. She was revolted by the filth. At her father's suggestion, she began a milk fund, which she promoted in her column. It would be the first charity in Miami not run by a church. Douglas realized quickly that the fund was not enough; the black community needed more than milk. It needed legal aid, family counseling, job training, and low-cost loans. She began to advocate for each of these services in her newspaper column, to the dismay of her father and the growing enmity of the newspaper's publisher, Frank Shutts, both of whom, as leaders of the community and virtual founders of the town, took a number of her criticisms personally.

As the *Herald* grew in size and importance, the demands of Douglas's job escalated and with them, the pressures. People were eager to meet her and to use her column to espouse the issues they believed in. She was becoming a Miami celebrity.

She seems to have decided at about this time that she would not remarry, in part because she had never wanted children and had always cared more about books than anything else. Marjory concluded she was not the marrying kind. "I didn't want a normal family life, I wanted my own life in my own way," she reflected. "I was too interested in writing editorials and in writing my column." She began to delve deeper into Florida as a landscape, into its geography, into its social and natural history, reading in depth and exploring the surrounding areas on foot. She continued to socialize, to dance at the hotels, and to swim on Miami Beach whenever she could, but her relations with men never again went any further: "I didn't have any sex life. Sex ended with my marriage." She thought sex a good thing and a healthy thing, and she admitted to having enjoyed it during her marriage, but that time in her life was over. Decades later, she would write, "So I haven't had any sex since before 1915, and I've done very well without it, thank you. It hasn't been any great loss. People don't seem to realize that the energy that goes into sex, all the emotion that surrounds it, can be well deployed in other ways."

But after three years of writing a daily column and helping to edit the newspaper, the pressures of the job began to wear on her. She faced increasing criticism from the publisher Shutts, who chafed at her outspoken progressive and reformist views. He didn't like her, and she didn't like him. This put her father, Frank Stoneman, in an increasingly awkward position, and, for the first time, she found herself at odds with him. "It was hard to tell people of his generation, who'd founded the city, that a helping hand was necessary, or that improving the lives of the disadvantaged would improve the lives of everyone else," she would recall. "To them, it was all a matter of making money and getting rich, then worrying about the rest later." They were particularly sensitive to the issue of local race relations, which was off-limits for most southern newspapers. Douglas's father was sympathetic to the plight of southern blacks but abided by this prohibition so as not to alarm tourists or hurt the local economy. The growing demands of the work aside, Marjory wasn't sure she was making a difference. As she told an interviewer fifty years later, "My feeble pickings and scoldings only irritated people."

Eventually the demands of the job began to affect her to where she grew anxious, exhausted, and had trouble sleeping. Late one night in early 1923, she left her father's house clad in her nightgown, "unhinged a little," and wandered up and down the streets of the Miami neighborhood of Spring Garden until morning, talking to herself, unconscious of where she was or who she was. Douglas had suffered her first nervous breakdown. The doctor told her she had something called nerve fatigue and that she was under too much pressure. He recommended she consider a change of job or venue.

To recover from her breakdown, Marjory took refuge in her bedroom in her father's house, a corner room that overlooked a section of the Miami River that was still remarkably undisturbed, lined with webs of mangroves and alive with seabirds. From her open window, she could watch small boats coming and going and the silent squadrons of brown pelicans as they flew low over the water. Often the air was filled with the liquid chirps and trills of a nearby cardinal. On a rock at the water's edge, an iridescent anhinga, or snake bird, would perch with its wet wings held outstretched to dry as though it were crucified, while nearby a tall, white great egret stood motionless, like a slim porcelain vase. Occasionally she caught a glimpse of a gray hippo-like manatee, soon to become rare, as it wallowed and grazed on sea grass in the shallows. At dusk, the black, double-crested cormorant hurried back to its roost, its long neck extended in flight. Then out of the darkness would come the chorus of insects and tree frogs that made the night even noisier than the day.

It would have been unthinkable to her at the time that in her lifetime all of those mangrove thickets would be gone, replaced by condominium towers and tall office buildings, and the river itself crisscrossed with concrete bridges, roads, and highways.

Douglas spent her days resting and reading. She began to think hard about what other forms of writing she might do to make a living if she were to leave the *Miami Herald*. "I hadn't been a good employee. I hadn't liked regular hours. I hadn't liked being told what to do or working for other people.... I wanted to be an individual rather than an employee or a female. I mean, I didn't mind being an employee or a female, but I'd rather be an individual."

With more time to reflect, Douglas began to question the direction her life had taken. How far, she asked herself, had she really come since her arrival in Florida? Intellectually, she had come a considerable distance, to the point where she had gained confidence in her ideas and in her ability to express them. She also had learned a great deal about the subtropical landscape of Florida and the political and economic issues facing Miami and the state. But in terms of her career and her personal finances, she realized that she had accomplished much less. If the goal was independence—financial independence, an independence of ideas, and independence from men, including her father's strong influence—then she still had work to do. She was thirty-four years old, still living under her father's roof, and still working for the newspaper he had founded.

Marjory resolved to open a new chapter in her life. She would begin a career as a freelance writer and, perhaps, as an author of fiction, one focused primarily on Florida subjects. If she could succeed at this, then she might one day achieve yet another dream—a very American dream shared by countless others who had emigrated to Florida: to have a small house that she could call her own. In July 1923 she took the doctor's advice and quit the *Herald*.

9

TRAIL BLAZERS

*When Marjory Douglas first began to explore the Everglades, in the pro-*cess developing her passion for birding, she would drive down a forty-mile unfinished section of a road that dead-ended deep in the Everglades. The unfinished road, known as the Tamiami Trail, was originally planned as the last leg of the Dixie Highway, a section that would bridge Tampa and Miami by traversing the Everglades at a point roughly parallel with Miami. Carl Fisher and the road's other proponents believed it would be a boon to land development, as well as an attraction and convenience for tourists traveling around the state. For years, it had been the holy grail of Florida road building, championed by newspapers on both coasts.

The story behind the road's construction is notable as a cautionary tale because road and land development so often go hand in hand and in turn have impacts on the environment: too often to the detriment of the environment; sometimes to the detriment of the development; and occasionally both, as we shall see in the larger story of the land boom.

The road's construction began in 1916. After a promising start, with spurs of highway extending toward each other from opposite coasts, the project stalled, with neither county able to procure the funds to complete it. Then, in early April 1923, a group of Tampa businessmen dreamed up a promotional stunt to rekindle interest in the project. Twenty-three men in nine automobiles led by two Miccosukee Indian guides decided to traverse the Everglades along the projected route, still made up mostly of old Indian trails and rough lanes known as "Wish to God" roads—short for "Wish to

God I had taken another road!" The convoy included seven Model T Fords, a brand-new Elcar limousine, and one Overland commissary truck. None of the men had any significant experience as woodsmen. Nor were they likely to have read the cautionary report written in 1892 by Alonzo Church, the compass man on a three-week expedition to explore the Everglades: "My advice is to urge every discontented man to take a trip through the Everglades. A day's journey in slimy, decaying vegetable matter which coats and permeates everything it touches, and no water with which to wash it off, will be good for him. . . . It is enough to make a man swear to be content ever afterward with a board for a bed and a clean shirt once a week."

Auto magnate Henry Ford and the inventor Thomas Edison gave the departing caravan a bottle of grape juice to be presented to William Jennings Bryan upon arrival in Miami. The convoy set off with much fanfare, but almost immediately the cars became mired in saw grass and mud. They had to be dragged to higher ground by a Cletrac caterpillar-type tractor sent in after them. The 3,200-pound Elcar became stuck so frequently that it finally had to turn back. The Overland stripped its gears and was soon abandoned. One of the Model Ts lost its front spring, but a new spring was miraculously fashioned out of the limb of a cypress sapling. Sections of the road would need to be built out of sawed logs, while others had to be shoveled into shape.

The Everglades proved to be a far more varied landscape than the Trail Blazers had anticipated. The waist-high saw grass soon changed to dense cypress forests with their distinctive raised cypress hills, or domes. Farther on, the convoy encountered mangrove swamps and tree islands known as hammocks, populated with oak and pine and palmetto that in turn were home to air plants, exotic orchids, lizards, red-belly turtles, and two-inch-long liguus tree snails in spiraling rainbow-colored shells. Long stretches of terrain—marl prairies—were flat for as far as the eye could see and absolutely still, with no activity on the surface of the tea-colored water other than the buzzing of dragonflies and damselflies or the slow movements of the wading plume birds: herons, egrets, ibises, flamingos, and spoonbills. Occasionally, the same birds could be seen passing overhead in languid flight. Under the water's surface, the Everglades seethed with fish, shrimp, aquatic insects, and crustaceans, all of which provided food for the shore-birds and other animals. Bullfrogs and pig frogs were abundant, too, some weighing as much as two pounds. Years later, with the advent of airboats, the frogs would be harvested by "froggers" at night wearing flashlights on their hats and armed with long, four-pronged spears called gigs. One hundred and fifty pounds of frogs' legs would be considered a good night's catch. Also hunted for their skins and their meat were the American alligators and their cousins the lighter-skinned and more secretive American crocodiles—the males of both species occasionally reaching up to fifteen feet in length.

The flat expanse of wetland was vaster than the men had expected, extending endlessly, monotonously, under an open sky, all of it apparently untouched by any humans before them. As they moved through this strange, soggy wilderness, they could just barely detect that the water was moving slowly over the giant limestone shelf underfoot that dropped, imperceptibly, to the south at a very gradual incline of an inch per mile. On warm, humid days, huge, puffy cumulus clouds would form high overhead, as the Everglades created its own weather and eventually its own torrential bursts of gray rain.

After a week in "the Glades," the party ran out of food and from then on had to survive on deer, cattail roots, and swamp cabbage, supplemented with fish, frogs' legs, and the occasional wild turkey. The men endured afternoon tropical downpours, but to their surprise, mosquitos were not a problem; most of the group was able to sleep out in the open at night. They encountered only one alligator, which launched itself off a bank like a canoe and then sank as though scuttled. They spotted just a single rattlesnake, but water moccasins were another matter. They came across dozens of them and, memorably, a slippery, writhing mass of the reptiles. Their Miccosukee guides showed them how to move among the snakes without alarming them. Despite exaggerated press reports that the party had become hopelessly lost, the men—unharmed, albeit hungry and exhausted—eventually arrived in Miami to a greeting fit for conquering heroes. Although fuel levels had run low, all seven Model Ts and the Cletrac miraculously completed the crossing, a credit to the Ford's durability.

The expedition, a trip that could be made on foot in less than a week, had taken nineteen days to complete. The bottle of grape juice could not be delivered; it had been consumed along the way.

By one estimate, the stunt generated thirty-five thousand columns of publicity in newspapers across the United States and in Europe. That PR helped the construction project win the support of the Florida Legislature, and a month later, a west coast developer named Barron Collier stepped forward to help make the building of the road happen.

Collier was a high school dropout from Memphis who held a virtual monopoly on all of the advertising posted on the nation's trolley cars. He had purchased 1.25 million acres of land in southwestern Florida, making him the largest individual landholder in the state. His main focus was on developing the new city of Everglades, south of Naples, potentially a major beneficiary of a new road to Miami. He offered to fund the continuation of the project, guaranteeing a $350,000 loan. In return for this largesse, the state agreed to carve a new county out of the existing Lee County and to name it Collier County in honor of the tycoon.

Collier may well have become the nation's first billionaire, based on his vast Florida acreage. In most land developments, an acre is divided into five lots, and in Florida at that time, individual lots were selling for thousands of dollars apiece, and those along the coast, for tens of thousands— all of them appreciating rapidly in value. Of course, many of the Collier acres had not been divided yet into lots. Many were coastal acres, but others lay deep in the swamps of the Everglades and were worth next to nothing. Still, there is a very real possibility that by 1925, Collier's net worth had reached more than $1 billion based on the soaring market value of his landholdings. This assumes that he had not heavily leveraged the property—in other words, that he had purchased all the land outright for cash and had not subsequently used it for collateral for loans, both of which appear to have been the case. He also owned the trolley car advertising business, newspapers, banks, hotels, a telephone company, a construction company, and a steamship line. It is likely that any debt held by Collier was more than offset by the value of these cash-generating businesses. It is known that by 1926, his various enterprises were throwing off

$5 million in profits a year and thus could easily have been worth an additional $100 million. By contrast, John D. Rockefeller's net worth likely peaked at $900 million in 1913. Henry Ford's net worth is not thought to have reached $1 billion until late 1925. Admittedly, if Barron Collier became the country's first billionaire, he didn't remain so for long, and Henry Ford's fortune would quickly eclipse his.

The construction of the Tamiami Trail throughout the 1920s would be a remarkable road building achievement—not quite on a par with Flagler's railroad to the sea, but a great accomplishment nevertheless, and one that took four years longer to complete. Surveyors and their assistants known as rodmen cleared a path through saw grass that grew taller than nine feet in places, often working up to their armpits in swamp water. They laid out the centerline of the road with stakes and prepared the way for the drillers who followed behind with oxcarts hauling the dynamite. One advance was a mobile pneumatic rig that could drill 250 nine-foot-deep holes a day into the limestone—equivalent to the work of thirty men armed with sledgehammers. Fifty holes were drilled for each roadway shot, spread out over a section eighteen feet wide and some sixty feet long. Pipes were then inserted into the holes before the dynamite setters lowered the sticks of explosive into them. Two or three shots could be fired each day. It would require three and a half million sticks of dynamite to complete the project. Amazingly, the only significant accident involving dynamite occurred when lightning struck a tin-roofed shed where the explosive was stored. The blast flattened surrounding buildings, and two men in a garage one hundred yards away were killed instantly.

Steam shovels and dredges followed behind the dynamiters to scoop up the aggregate and pile it onto the roadbed, creating a canal on one side as they proceeded at the pace of 150 feet per day. The Bay City Dredge Works company had devised a walking dredge a few years before that allowed the machine to be winched aloft onto a second pair of stowed swiveling feet. The frame of the dredge could then be slid forward and lowered before moving the feet forward to repeat the process. Rolling bunkhouses hauled along the nascent road by oxen, believed to be the first mobile homes in Florida, provided housing for the work crews.

Speculation began immediately on the largely wet and once worthless land on either side of the road and canal. One Miami realtor, Henry Sprague, touted his 140 acres at $68 per acre in a 1924 advertisement: "Wake up—act and buy Tamiami Trail frontage—buy NOW—prices along the Trail are not going down. . . . I would like to buy it myself, but as I cannot handle it, I am offering it for a quick sale. . . . This tract should double in value long before it is paid for. If you want this—better bring your check book."

In 1926 the state of Florida took over the project from Collier and saw it through to completion. The contractors were able to take advantage of an unusual form of state aid: the convict leasing program, which made road gangs of prison inmates available to do the hard work at remarkably low wages. Although the program of convict leasing at the state level had ended in 1923 following the death of young Martin Tabert, the subject of Marjory Douglas's poem, counties were allowed to continue using prison labor. A 1921 Federal Highway Act did not forbid the use of convict labor as long as it was under the jurisdiction and supervision of the state highway department.

A convict camp for the Tamiami Trail was constructed in May 1926. There the mostly black prisoners in their distinctive striped uniforms were set to work finishing the road. Although the convict system was less deadly than it had been decades earlier during Henry Flagler's era, prisoners still endured miserable conditions. They were supervised by fellow inmates known as convict trustees, who would shoot any convict who attempted to escape—and were rewarded with a possible pardon if they did so; a practice that invited abuse. In light of the horrendous working conditions, it's hardly surprising that desperate convicts would attempt to escape. During the exceptionally hot, humid summer of 1927, five convicts led by a murderer named Will Brown, nicknamed the Tampa Kid, jumped and disarmed a guard at a camp south of Naples. They escaped in a dump truck, which ran out of gas almost instantly. They leapt out and stopped a passing car, which also ran out of gas, forcing them to commandeer a second car. They abandoned that car north of the Caloosahatchee River, hoping to hike through the woods to the nearest railroad bridge. The enormous manhunt organized to track them down left other crews undermanned, which prompted eight convicts in another camp to overpower another guard. But a single night in the buggy, often impassable swamps of the Everglades would be enough for the already hungry and exhausted second group of escapees. They turned themselves in the following morning.

Meanwhile, the Tampa Kid's gang reached the railroad tracks and managed to stop in turn a gas-powered maintenance cart and then a larger so-called speeder car, on which they proceeded north past Fort Myers as far as Arcadia. There a sheriff's posse led by bloodhounds tracked them into the woods, surrounded them, and killed three of the five men in a shootout, including the Tampa Kid.

A formal ceremonial opening commemorated the Tamiami Trail's completion in 1928, but by that time, the land boom was effectively over. In all, it had taken thirteen years and $8 million to build the road. And while the trail succeeded in opening up commerce between two of the state's largest cities, it would create an environmental disaster in the process. The road was effectively, if inadvertently, a dike—perhaps the longest dike ever constructed in the United States. Although culverts were installed in various places, the road largely blocked the natural course of water and created a barrier between the upper and lower Glades.

As soon became clear, the Everglades was more than just a gigantic stagnant swamp. It was a sort of freshwater river through grass, ninety miles wide, that spilled out from Lake Okeechobee and its watershed and ran southward to create a unique—and wholly misunderstood—landscape and ecosystem. The Everglades was also the major aquifer for all of southern Florida. By tampering with it, diverting it, and canaling it, the state eventually caused its own water shortages. And by blocking the slow and steady flow of shallow water over the limestone, vast acreage south of the trail began to dry up, inviting brush fires, invasive species, and the catastrophic loss of native flora and fauna.

The seemingly savvy group of naturalists whom Marjory Douglas had befriended failed to foresee the effect the new road would have on Florida's hydrology. Even the botanist David Fairchild delighted in the fact that the Tamiami Trail provided him easier access to remote parts of the Everglades to collect new plant specimens. Douglas herself initially saw the road as a symbol of economic progress. She wrote two poems for her *Miami Herald* column that extolled its virtues. She felt similarly about the spread of agriculture into the fertile Everglades land just below Lake Okeechobee, writing in one of her columns, "the wealth of south Florida . . . lies in the black muck of the Everglades, and the inevitable development of this country." Years later, she would ruefully admit her mistakes, lamenting, "What a liar I turned out to be." Even her father, Frank Stoneman, endorsed the road in editorials for the *Herald*, although he had staunchly opposed, at times, the building of canals and the diverting of the Everglades' rivers, and argued correctly that most of the canal work was not based on sound scientific study.

There was really only one foresighted naturalist in the Coconut Grove group who vehemently opposed the project from the outset. His name was Charles Torrey Simpson, and he was one of the more memorable characters of the era. An entirely self-taught naturalist with little more than a high school education, Simpson would build up a remarkable collection of ten thousand mollusk shells and write a couple of books on Florida natural history. He alone seems to have understood the impact the trail and the canals would have on the Everglades: "I feel that no more complete botch has been made of any project within the lifetime of any of my readers." He was concerned that the road would invite logging and oil exploration and that lowered water levels exposed the mud to the air, thereby degrading it.

The reality was far worse than Simpson had imagined.

The Tamiami Trail roadbed itself became one long killing field for wildlife. Recalled one local scientist, Taylor R. Alexander, who witnessed what happened, "Huge numbers of crayfish, lubber grasshopper, frogs, turtles, snakes, marsh rabbits, otters, and wading birds were hit—sometimes making the road slippery and the stench obnoxious." A dozen years later, the full effects of the reduced water flow had taken hold. "I watched as successive fires of the drought-stricken mid-40s altered the overdrained 'Glades, and created dense smoke all over South Florida," Alexander recalled. "I witnessed the area south of the Tamiami Trail in the vicinity of

Krome Avenue change from saw grass and tree islands eventually to willow with the consumption of the former muck soil—much of it burned down to the rock surface."

By the time David Fairchild and the others admitted their mistake and confessed to how poorly they had understood the effects that the new road would have, the damage was done. As Simpson wrote in a book published late in his life, "If things go on here as they have done in the past few years, this can only end in the destruction of all that is lovely and of value that nature has bestowed on us."

For Douglas, by now a budding environmentalist, the loss of so much of the Everglades was deeply personal. Her emerging militant love for the Glades would now be put the test. She would move well beyond the development-centric and pro-business views of her father and men like Frank Shutts and Florida's real estate kings. Florida wasn't all about making money. There were repercussions to that strategy; the damage from it, she saw now, could be drastic and lasting.

Not until 2000 did the US Congress approve a Comprehensive Everglades Recovery Plan (CERP) to "restore, preserve, and protect" the remains of the Everglades ecosystem. By then, even more damage had been done. The primary goal of the legislation was to provide better flood protection and to safeguard the region's freshwater supply. But the hope was also to address the pollution in Lake Okeechobee, to remove the canals that had displaced sections of the Kissimmee River, and to mitigate the damage caused by the two main roads that traversed the Glades. (A second and even bigger road known as Alligator Alley, now a section of Interstate 75, was built across the Everglades in 1968.) By then, of course, the animal population had been decimated, Lake Okeechobee had been repeatedly polluted, and half the landmass of the Everglades had been lost to urban and agricultural sprawl. The naturalist and herpetologist Thomas Barbour, who grew up visiting his grandparents in Eau Gallie in the 1890s, summarized the problem when he wrote in his 1944 book on Florida, *That Vanishing Eden*, "it was an easy state for man to ruin, and he has ruined it with ruthless efficiency."

At the time of its completion, the Tamiami Trail also had an immediate impact on the resident Seminole and Miccosukee Indians, who had lived and fished and hunted in the Everglades since being driven down into the area by the US military during the Second Seminole War between 1835 and 1842. The road, in concert with the canals and the encroachment of "civilization," had altered the tribes' way of life. By economic necessity, most were forced to work on local farms or ranches or to rely on the tourism trade to survive. A number of them—there were five hundred or so Seminoles in total—moved their villages to the road's edge and turned these into local attractions that sold dolls, baskets, trinkets, and other souvenirs to tourists. Clad in their traditional garb, they themselves became Florida attractions.

Putting aside this environmental and cultural damage, in hindsight it is clear that even Charles Torrey Simpson, who correctly predicted disaster for the Everglades, did not foresee the lasting damage that the gigantic construction boom of the twenties would do the broader economy—and not just locally, but nationally, too, when Florida's great land boom finally unraveled.

10

HABITUAL INTEMPERANCE

*The Tamiami Trail successfully linked the two coasts of Florida. But be-*cause the road was not completed until 1928, it did little to fuel the fever-ish real estate boom beyond driving up the value of all the adjacent land. As it turned out, the broader land boom would do just fine without the road's help. Carl Fisher, for one, at his end of the trail, didn't need the road to see his Miami Beach development succeed spectacularly.

As Miami Beach sales picked up in the early 1920s, Fisher became a whirling dervish of activity. He built more hotels, realizing that they were the best way to generate leads for land sales, although he strictly forbade his salesmen from pestering his guests. That didn't stop the salesmen of other real estate companies from loitering in the lobbies and in the bar areas. In 1923 Fisher opened the Star Yacht Club and hired as its manager Georges Everard, who had owned Maxim's in Paris and managed New York's Plaza Hotel. The club became the epicenter of the Miami Beach deep-sea fishing community. Fisher astutely exploited the appeal of the sport, described as "an ideal sport for affluent, out-of-shape businessmen." From comfortable chairs, these men could enjoy food, drink, and cigars while the crew drove the boat and baited their hooks.

Fisher enjoyed the sport himself, but his real objective was to sell more real estate. He began to use his connections with the automobile industry to drum up leads, writing letters directly to CEOs, sending them promo-tional booklets and descriptions of houses, and pitching them shamelessly on the virtues of Miami Beach. For instance, he wrote the president of the

Packard Motor Car Company, who had been hunting moose in the Maine woods, to urge that "after you come home and finally recuperate from the croup, lumbago, and pneumonia, that you get on a train and come down to Miami and get some real fun and some real sunshine." The auto men responded in kind, pitching him on the latest virtues of their cars: "sweetest little thing you ever saw—strictly high class . . . full of pep and a delight to the eye."

No matter how busy he was, Fisher found time to enjoy himself. Boat racing quickly replaced automobile racing as his favored adrenaline fix. In one five-hour race from Miami Beach to Key West against the Detroit sportsman and lumberman Charles W. Kotcher, Fisher, in the *Raven*, beat his friend by a mere two boat lengths. Polo, too, continued to obsess Fisher. He lured entire teams to the Beach to perform before local crowds, and despite his own erratic riding skills, soon bought an expensive string of polo ponies. Although his strokes lacked form, he played tennis, too, "with reckless enthusiasm."

His cussing was legendary. One friend, monitoring a bridge game that Fisher participated in, transcribed the endless succession of oaths that spilled from his lips as he played his cards: "GOD DAMN****Christ. . . . Christ's Sake***** God Damn! What-the-Hell****CHRIST!!!! DIRTY LITTLE GOD DAMN—WHAT-THE-HELL!! (Ditto). . . . Jesus Christ!!! SON-of-a-BITCH!!! . . . . CHRIST ALMIGHTY!!! . . . For the Love of God. . . . DAMNED SLIK—DAMNED CARD SYSTEM. . . . GOD DAMN**** . . . and so on into the night!" And yet Fisher's friends adored him. As far as they were concerned, cussing was part of his charm.

He could be temperamental, too, in person as well as in his correspondence, and often had to apologize for his outbursts. "After this, you mustn't pay so much attention to my hot temper and cussing spells," he wrote in one letter to the lawyer and newspaper publisher Frank Shutts. Fisher's outburst had followed a negative story about Miami Beach that appeared in the *Miami Herald*. Shutts, not unresponsive, had promptly fired the reporter.

Fisher was especially vexed when he tried to take a houseguest on a tour of Villa Vizcaya's gardens but forgot to bring along the entry pass that

James Deering had personally presented to him. The guard at the gate re-fused to admit them. Fisher insisted that Deering be contacted directly. A half hour later, word came back that Mr. Deering was not at home. Furious at this snub, Fisher wrote Deering a letter. "I happen to know that you were at home and resent very much the treatment I received. . . . Such being the case, I cannot accept any future invitations from you. . . . I can at least save myself future annoyance by not opening myself to a reoccurrence of such a miserably unpleasant thing." Deering apologized and blamed the incident on a miscommunication with a servant. The two men, who were the un-likeliest of friends, quickly patched up their disagreement.

Many of Carl's friendships, however, proved to be deep and enduring. "Of all the friendships I ever formed, none has been any more appreciated than yours," wrote William T. Anderson, the publisher of the *Macon Telegraph*, and a close drinking and fishing companion. "The greatest treasure is that human relation which permits one to be honest and natural and loyal and devoted—free of scheming, design, ulterior purpose. Such has been ours."

As real estate sales improved, Fisher pulled off a succession of brilliant pub-licity coups that raised the national awareness of Miami Beach and helped fuel Florida's growing popularity. His first PR triumph came in late 1920, when US president-elect Warren Harding arrived in the Miami area on a pleasure cruise in the months before his inauguration. Harding had cruised down the inland waterway on New Jersey senator Joseph S. Frelinghuysen's ninety-foot yacht, the *Victoria*. Fisher beat the Miami and Dade County dignitaries to the pier to greet the yacht and promptly whisked Harding off in one of his speedboats to Miami Beach and a penthouse at the Fla-mingo Hotel for a poker game and a bottle of Scotch. Fisher also arranged to have a cottage at the Flamingo available for Harding's personal use.

For the next few days, Fisher kept Harding royally entertained with rounds of golf on his Miami Beach courses. On one of two fishing trips, Harding hooked and landed a sailfish. The president-elect even took a swim at the Roman Pools, which the newspapers recorded faithfully. Perhaps more significantly, Harding also visited Fisher's private club, the

Cocolobo Cay Club on Coco Lobo Key, where he signed the guest register. According to historian Stuart B. McIver, two other guests signing the
guest register that day were future secretary of the interior Albert Bacon
Fall and oilman Edward L. Doheny—two of the men most responsible for
what would become the most sensational scandal of the Harding administration and the one that may well have ruined the twenty-ninth president's
health, leading to his death in office from heart failure in August 1923:
the Teapot Dome scandal. It is entirely possible that the scheme for the
corrupt sale of oil leases in Wyoming and California was hatched that day.
At the end of his holiday, Harding reciprocated by plugging Fisher's resort
in a press release: "Because of the attractiveness of Miami Beach, I hope
to come here again. This beach is wonderful. It is developing like magic."

Fisher had been lobbying for Harding to stop at Miami Beach for
weeks before his arrival. Aware of the married president-elect's reputation
as a ladies' man, Fisher sent his exceptionally attractive secretary, Ann Rossiter, with whom Fisher was having an affair, to Harding's home in Marion,
Ohio, to extend an invitation in person. Somewhat to Rossiter's surprise,
she was ushered straight in to see Harding in his study. She was able to
telegraph back to Fisher that there she had achieved her objective. "This
personal call, personal touch, or whatever you want to call it, may not be
without results," she wrote.

At one point during Harding's visit, Fisher arranged to have Rosie, the
small elephant that he owned, caddy for the president elect, carrying his
golf clubs down one of the Miami Beach fairways. "I am certain I am going
to get a million dollars' worth of advertising out of that elephant," Fisher
boasted, and he was correct. Photos of the stunt appeared in newspapers
nationwide. The reporter covering the Harding visit for the *Miami Herald* was none other than Marjory Stoneman Douglas. By the end of the
incoming chief executive's stay, Miami Beach was on the national map and
lodged firmly in the public's consciousness.

Then one day, possibly as early as the winter of 1920, Fisher's wife,
Jane, appeared at the Roman Pools wearing a newfangled, form-fitting,
stocking-free bathing costume. An avid swimmer, she was eager to learn
the newest racing stroke, the Australian crawl, and found the swim attire

of the day too constricting. The sight of her in the body-hugging swimsuit created a furor in Miami Beach and led a local minister to excoriate her in his Sunday sermon as "a symbol of the brazenness of the modern woman." Although Jane was in tears over the scandal, Fisher told her to keep her head up and insisted that she continue to wear the swimsuit. "I don't see why in hell a woman with a damn pretty figure hasn't a right to show it," he remarked. The public agreed, and within weeks, a new style of bathing costume had taken hold in Miami Beach.

Although the anecdote is charming, it is a stretch to attribute the arrival of the concept of "the bathing beauty" entirely to Jane Fisher. A beauty contest is known to have taken place on Rehoboth Beach in Delaware as early as 1880. As Mark S. Foster notes in *Castles in the Sand: The Life and Times of Carl Graham Fisher*, the head of Miami's Chamber of Commerce, a man named Everett Sewell, had started bathing beauty contests in Miami sometime in 1920, the same year that the first Queen of New York City's five beaches was chosen. The first national beauty contest took place in Atlantic City, New Jersey, in September 1921 and soon morphed into the annual Miss America Pageant. But regardless of who actually created the bathing beauty fad, Fisher had the vision to seize on it. "By God, Jane, you've started something!" he exclaimed. "Why, damn it, I've been trying for months to think up an idea for advertising the Beach nationally. We'll get the prettiest girls we can find and put them in the goddamnest tightest and shortest bathing suits and no stockings or swimming shoes either. We'll have their pictures taken and send them all over the goddamn country as 'the Bathing Beauties of Miami Beach.' "

Fisher's publicist, Steve Hannagan, whom he had hired away from the *Indianapolis Star*, worked the photos into advertisements that he then placed in northern newspapers throughout the decade, describing the ladies as "cheesecake," a label that stuck. Before long, enormous billboards featuring Miami's famous bathing beauties rose above Times Square in the dead of winter. "It's June in Miami Beach," read one, or "Miami Beach: Where Summer Spends the Winter," or "Turalura Lipschits and Her Twin Sister Tondalaya Are in Miami Beach Enjoying Seventy-eight-Degree Sunshine on December 21st!" Reflecting the era's more lax social mores, the ads introduced sex appeal to the idea of a Florida vacation. All of a sudden, it was not just the investment potential that was drawing tourists to Florida. Of course land sales, as a first derivative, did handsomely. In Miami Beach, they climbed from $6 million in 1923 to $23 million in 1925.

Fisher's vision for Miami Beach was coming to fruition. Writes Miami Beach historian Polly Redford, "Everything he touched turned to gold. His investments made fortunes for his friends, his associates, his salesmen, sycophants and drinking companions, male and female, who clung to him like suckerfish for a free ride, free drinks, and scraps of his good fortune."

To celebrate his success, Fisher organized his most elaborate boat race to date. He ordered ten identical eighteen-foot Purdy runabouts to be built, and he then recruited to Miami Beach eleven of the country's best auto drivers to pilot the boats in six heats. The prize money: $7,000. "It was the Indianapolis 500 on water," wrote Redford. Louis Chevrolet beat Tommy Milton for the top prize.

By now, Fisher owned a veritable fleet of boats, most of them built for him by famed boat builder Ned Purdy. They included *Baby Shadow*; *Shadow F*, a 72-foot Ultra-Express cruiser; and the *Shadow K*, a Purdy diesel yacht. The yacht, with its crew of sixteen, was 150 feet in length, 25 feet in beam, 7½ feet in draft. The lounge featured a coal-burning fireplace; the upper deck boasted a mechanical horse that simulated, for exercise, a horseback ride in a park.

Even as he began to realize his dreams, Fisher's daily life remained frantic and chaotic. The record keeping at his office was sloppy at best and reflected a lifelong disdain for accountants. He simply spent what he felt he needed to, often without weighing the consequences, and he was always more interested in building up the business than in posting maximum profits. As his success grew, so did his impatience. Fisher was stopped repeatedly for speeding. When a judge fined him $50 for one infraction, he impudently handed him a $100 bill instead and remarked, "Better keep this. I'll probably be arrested again before I get home."

Marjory Douglas, at this point working as a freelance writer, recalled stopping by the Fisher offices to meet with him about writing publicity for his Miami Beach development. He kept her waiting in the reception area for nearly two hours until she grew furious and left. It was callous treatment for which she never forgave him. "He was too pretentious and wanted everything his way, and I could never have worked with him," she recalled. She knew Jane Fisher better but didn't like her much either: "She tried to be a little snobbish but didn't succeed very well."

Fisher's home life remained as unsettled as his work life. Unable to relax at meals in restaurants, he often insisted that all three dishes he ordered be served at once so that he wouldn't be left "fuming between courses." He owned four dogs, including a gigantic Irish wolfhound that was "nine feet nine inches from tail to nose." He also owned a camel and a polo pony named Jerry that he often rode to his various building sites on the island. Then, of course, there were the elephants. Rosie, who, according to Fisher, was as "kind and gentle as a Newfoundland dog," would ferry children around Miami Beach when not posing for photographs or helping the workers pull mangrove roots from the ground on the various construction sites.

Fisher's other elephant, Carl II, was less compliant. When the pachyderm arrived as a gift from Ed Ballard, a friend with an interest in the Ringling Bros. Circus, Fisher took the animal out of its stall to show him off to friends. "He knocked me down and ran off," Fisher wrote to a friend, "and when I grabbed hold of him by the tail to stop him, he hit me a jolt with his trunk and almost broke my ribs. Then I grabbed him by the trunk, and he locked his trunk around my arm, and if you think that a three-year-old elephant has no particular strength in his trunk, you should let him wrap it around your leg or arm and give you a yank. Anyway, I am all black and blue."

Not all of the pets were domesticated. For example, a macaw lived in a coconut grove at the side of the new Fisher house. Jane could lure the gorgeous bird out of the palm trees with treats: "He would come down the trunk walking 'hand over hand' like a sailor and put up his beak for me to kiss."

The Shadows, an enormous house with a coffered living room ceiling, had a staff of twenty and grocery bills that soon topped $1,000 a month. Houseguests came and went, including close pals such as the humorist

Will Rogers and the Indiana-born poet James Whitcomb Riley. Carl regularly invited dozens home for dinner on a whim. Jane recalled, "Seven o'clock, and the table would be set with the orange-tree dishes and the orange-pattern silver, and any number of people—people I had never seen before—would come pouring into the Shadows. Carl himself might not even know their names." In the middle of dinner, he would excuse himself and retire to his room, leaving Jane to do the bulk of the entertaining. At the end of the evening, she would find him upstairs, sitting upright in bed eating peanuts or chewing tobacco and reading pirate novels by Rafael Sabatini, with a spittoon at one side of the bed and his favorite dog, Rowdy, on the other. Hanging on the wall above the headboard were the painted portraits of his two heroes, Napoléon I and Abraham Lincoln.

Fisher's soaring success apparently added immeasurably to his sex appeal. One letter in his correspondence file from this period gives a flavor of his sudden popularity with the ladies: "Name time, place, and your drink, and I'll be there. One of your playmates, Betty."

Thanks largely to Fisher's ballyhoo, both Miami and Miami Beach were now nationally known as vacation destinations. Even the rich, who had once favored Palm Beach, were arriving in droves. William H. Luden, of the cough drop company, built a house on South Bayshore Drive. William K. Vanderbilt arrived in his $3 million yacht, *Alva*, which he soon traded to Carl Fisher in exchange for the seven acres of the private island known today as Fisher Island. (The *Alva* would be the grandest of the twenty-six motor yachts Carl would own over the years.) Senator T. Coleman du Pont, a former head of the giant chemical concern, appeared regularly as a visitor to the Royal Palm Hotel, as did Alfred I. du Pont, Coleman's wealthy cousin. J. C. Penney, founder of the department store chain, arrived in 1923, and so did the leaders of the so-called gasoline aristocracy, among them William C. Durant, a onetime cigar salesman who cofounded General Motors. Harvey S. Firestone, founder of the tire empire, built himself an especially grand Georgian-style mansion. Others arriving included: Roy D. Chapin, founder of the Hudson Motor Car Company; Harry Stutz, founder of Stutz Motor Company; Albert Champion, inventor of the porcelain Champion spark plug; Frank J. Seiberling, cofounder of the Goodyear Tire & Rubber Company and founder of the Seiberling Rubber Company; as well as Henry Ford's only child, Edsel, the president of the Ford Motor Company.

By late 1925, the nascent city of Miami Beach had grown to 858 homes, 178 apartment buildings, 56 hotels, 308 shops and offices, 4 polo fields, 3 golf courses, and a couple of schools, churches, and movie theaters. In Jane's words: "The dream city was at last complete.... It was all Carl had said it would be. It was paradise risen from swampland." Carl Fisher, the onetime bicycle racer from Indianapolis, was worth $76 million, equivalent to $1.1 billion in today's money.

He had successfully injected the brand names of Miami and Miami Beach into the bloodstream of the American public at a time when the populace was extremely receptive to new intoxicants and to a whole new idea of what a resort and resort life might be like; he had made Florida's resorts the locus of one big party in the sun. Due in no small part to Carl Fisher's ballyhoo, the Roaring Twenties were under way. It would be remembered as an era of unbridled fun, new dances, new ways of dressing and behaving, new art movements and new ideas, and overnight fads from mahjong to crossword puzzles and vitamins. Carl Fisher seemed a Floridian embodiment of all the decade would come to stand for: wild extravagance, kicking up your heels, flouting Prohibition, and getting rich quick.

Meanwhile, at the opposite end of the Tamiami Trail, in Tampa, a local boy was working hard to duplicate what Carl Fisher had achieved on Miami Beach. David P. Davis was the son of a Jacksonville engineer who had worked for a variety of steamships and ferries that plied the waters on both coasts of Florida. Barely five feet tall, with fine, pointed facial features, D.P., as he called himself, developed an early reputation as a loudmouth and, in the words of one contemporary, "a compulsive braggart." He was a high school dropout, although later in life he would falsely claim to have a degree from the University of Florida. Growing up, Davis worked variously as a newsboy, a soda jerk, a salesman in a hardware store, and a bookkeeper for a cigar factory before heading to Panama to work on the construction of the Panama Canal. After a brief stint in real estate in New York City, in 1914 he moved to Jacksonville, where he worked as a shoe salesman and then for a film distribution company.

Married for the first time in 1915, Davis soon had a son. A few years later, however, he was widowed when his wife died after giving birth to their second child. During World War I, he operated a ferry line and managed a canteen at a Jacksonville military camp. After the war, in 1919, he moved to Miami, where he made a tiny investment in an early and successful development called Shadowlawn. Davis rolled his profits into a sequence of small subdivisions that he developed on his own.

He was particularly taken with Fisher's use of dredgers to haul sand from the seabed to convert sandbars into brand-new islands or new waterfront property that could be sold for a premium. In fact, it was while studying Fisher's dredge-and-fill projects and man-made islands that he was reminded of the mud flats and two deserted islands in Tampa Bay at the mouth of the Hillsborough River: Big Grassy Key and Little Grassy Key, which were being used as a Boy Scout camping area. D.P. and his brothers, as children, had rowed out to the flats to net fish and stone crabs.

Tampa was ready for a grand development. Its economy had suffered after the war with the closure of two large shipyards that employed over five thousand locals. Then a labor strike by cigar workers laid off another ten thousand in 1920, and a damaging hurricane followed in 1921. But with the recent arrival of tourists and land speculators, business in the area had picked up considerably.

In January 1924, using the money he had made in Miami, Davis moved back to Tampa and set about acquiring the two islands in Hillsborough Bay. Securing Little Grassy Key, which was privately owned, was simple enough, and cost him $150,000, but Big Grassy and its surrounding tidal mudflats belonged to the city of Tampa. To cultivate some goodwill and the requisite backing for the project, he invited prominent local attorneys and businessmen to join his realty company, D. P. Davis Properties, as officers or directors. With a little persistence, he was also able to secure the support of local politicians. He did this by striking a deal where he agreed to pay the city $200,000 in the form of a surety bond (a legally binding three-way financial agreement), half of which would be forgiven by the city as the development progressed. The proviso was that Davis would be required to build a bridge to the islands, to add seawalls and "fill" to the former mudflats, and then to deed back to the city some fifty-five acres on the Big Grassy Island in the form of a public park.

He set to work. He signed a $2 million contract with a local dredging firm to remove nine million cubic yards of sand from Hillsborough Bay, dumping all of it onto what was soon a single 875-acre development eight feet above sea level and surrounded by a concrete bulkhead. Less than a month later, on October 4, 1924, even before he had completed a temporary version of the bridge, Davis began selling his first lots, most of which were still on land that was submerged and yet to be dredged out of the bay. Buyers, most of them speculators, waited in line for more than forty hours outside the D. P. Davis Properties office in order to buy lots selling at an average cost of $5,610. All three hundred sold in less than three hours. Nine days later, he repeated the feat with his Bay Circle Section, at a slightly higher price. From then on, Davis spaced out the sales over two-week periods, a tactic that allowed him to capture the rapid appreciation in property values. He anticipated that Davis Islands would cost $30 million to fully build out with structures for a variety of incomes, lifestyles, and interests. It would be, in Davis's words, "Florida's supreme $30 million development."

Other developers would adopt similar dredge-and-fill strategies around Florida inspired by Fisher's example, most notably Charles Rhodes at Fort Lauderdale, William McAdoo near St. Petersburg, and John Ringling of the Ringling Bros. Circus on the keys across from Sarasota. Rhodes took the idea the furthest by dredging parallel canals and piling the muck and sand between them to build peninsulas in a soon-to-be popular technique he termed "finger-islanding."

In Tampa, Davis blitzed the local and national newspapers and magazines with advertisements. One such ad assured potential investors that "Success a-plenty will be attained here, fortunes a-many will be made here—not in a long term of years but within a time that practically reduces it to months!" He commissioned a book and a glossy brochure to be authored by the celebrated author Kenneth Roberts touting Davis Islands and the durability of the Florida boom. One brochure read: "Not alone the thrill of tropical moonlights stealing through the leaves of swaying palm trees and dancing about like diamonds on the bosom of the bay, but a veritable Venice at one's home-door for those who live on Davis Islands."

As a publicity stunt, Davis paid Olympic swimmer Helen Wainwright $10,000 to swim around Davis Islands. Next, he brought in tennis professionals and hosted a tournament on the islands. He even gave away free golf lessons with touring pros such as Johnny Farrell and Bobby Cruickshank. He sponsored airplane barnstorming exhibitions and speedboat races— and, like Carl Fisher, entered his own boat in the races. Hydroplanes took potential customers aloft for flights over the islands. Like George Merrick, he purchased a fleet of buses, boldly painted with the D. P. Davis Properties logo across each side and driven by guides dressed in suits and straw boaters. The idea was to lure potential buyers into Tampa from as far away as Orlando and Miami.

Later that same year, Davis, who was thirty-nine and feeling especially cocky, boasted that he was going to get married again—and not to just any woman but to whoever was crowned the queen of Gasparilla the next year. The Gasparilla Pirate Festival was Tampa's version of a Mardi Gras celebration. Somewhat improbably, Davis managed to do exactly as he had promised. The lucky woman was twenty-two-year-old Elizabeth Nelson. Her parents, after meeting the arrogant Davis, were adamantly opposed to the marriage, but the couple went ahead with the wedding. Less than a week after the honeymoon, they quietly divorced. According to one story, Davis slipped the divorce papers in among some other documents related to D. P. Davis Properties that required his wife's signature, and she signed them unwittingly. Then, inexplicably, less than two months later, the couple reversed themselves and remarried.

Their second marriage was no better than the first. Apparently, Davis still carried a torch for an old girlfriend named Lucille Zehring, who would soon become his mistress. Zehring was alleged to have been one of Mack Sennett's celebrated "Bathing Beauties," a group that appeared in the producer-director's silent films of the day and included future stars such as Carole Lombard and Gloria Swanson. After D. P. Davis's untimely demise, his widow would say bitterly, "All I ever got from that marriage was a fur coat and some dishes." The same remark might as well have been made by the wives of Carl Fisher and George Merrick, whose heady career success seemed to lead inexorably to marital infidelity and, in Fisher's case, to constant philandering.

The four leading Florida developers had surprisingly little interaction with one another, but the publicity they generated, each in his own signature style, drove the others to higher feats of showmanship and promotion in order to compete. All four men began to blur the truth and to employ more and more hyperbole in order to sell their dream of wealth, glamour, sex, and fun—a dream they themselves now subscribed to wholly.

Three of them—Fisher, Merrick, and Davis—had one other failing in common: they were prone to what the judge in the Davis divorce proceedings labeled "habitual intemperance." As the decade progressed, each developed a serious drinking problem. (Addison Mizner's vice was food.) Prohibition made little difference in their drinking habits. In fact, if there was any place during the Prohibition years where the Volstead Act was laxly enforced, it was in Florida. In most of the state, the act was not enforced at all. The better hotels at the various resorts served spirits openly, knowing well that the governor and the local authorities would not stop them—not if it boosted the economy and drew more visitors to Florida, which it did, in droves. The developers, of course, couldn't openly promote this fact in light of the Volstead Act and its watchful adherents. They relied instead on word of mouth—the most potent form of advertising. And here, too, they succeeded admirably. For many visitors, a Florida vacation promised easy access to booze, adding immeasurably to the state's allure.

But for all its pervasiveness, alcohol was not the primary stimulant of Florida's boom. What really intoxicated the revelers in the Sunshine State throughout the decade—the tourists as well as the speculators, but above all, the developers themselves—was not the promise of sex or liquor but insatiable greed.

3

TROPICAL FEVER

11

MIZNERLAND

On a clear spring morning in 1922, a young Englishman named Alex Waugh was walking down the Rue Royale in the heart of Paris when he heard someone call out, "Hey, Waugh!" A portly, towering figure was waving and hurrying toward him. It was Addison Mizner. "What in the hell are you doing here?" Mizner asked before continuing on with a litany of "choice multilingual profanity." Waugh, who was familiar with Mizner's expletive-laced harangues, laughed and explained that he was just passing through Paris and planned to leave the next day for London. Mizner corrected him: "Like hell you are. You meet me on the Madrid Express tomorrow morning. We are going on a buying trip through Spain. I'm paying you one hundred a week plus your expenses. And you'll earn every cent."

Waugh was an aspiring antiques dealer and interior decorator. He was unrelated to the best-selling British author Alec Waugh (brother of author Evelyn), with whom he was often confused. A veteran of World War I, he had inhaled mustard gas and endured the lice, rats, trench fever, and stench of chloride of lime in the watery foxholes of France before suffering a serious leg wound in the Battle of the Somme. His was a long and difficult recuperation, but at least he had survived—so many of his friends had not. The prior winter, a sympathetic wealthy American friend named Joe Ritter had invited him to Palm Beach in the hopes that the warm weather would help him to recover fully. Ritter not only paid for his sea passage to New York and onward to Palm Beach by train but also offered him a lovely room for the winter in his house overlooking Lake Worth. Ritter then opened a checking account in Waugh's name, depositing enough money to cover daily expenses. Waugh, who could still vividly feel the weight of his metal helmet on his head and the cold and wet of his army boots, recalled arriving at Ritter's house at the end of the long journey and being overwhelmed when he learned of the scope of his host's generosity: "I sat on the bed and wept."

At a dinner party thrown in honor of the visiting novelist and lecturer Hugh Walpole and the actress Marie Dressler at El Mirasol, the grand new Mizner-designed home of Eva and Edward Stotesbury, Waugh met the architect for the first time. "I had never met a man who could so clothe the dry and dull bones of the past with living flesh and movement. He made one see the breastplate of the warring knight, the streaming sweat, the wounds sustained in battle." But almost immediately, Waugh earned the ire of the celebrated raconteur by having the audacity to interrupt one of Mizner's elaborate stories to interject a correct date. The following morning, Mizner telephoned him to admit his mistake and to apologize for being so boorish about it. The two men met for lunch and bonded over a shared love of antique pewter.

By the spring of 1922, Mizner was the most celebrated architect in Palm Beach. As the journalist Ida Tarbell put it, "Calls for houses flowed upon him." The wedding of Eva Stotesbury's glamorous and beautiful daughter Louise Cromwell Brooks to the distinguished military veteran Brigadier General Douglas MacArthur had taken place at El Mirasol in February. Attended by Palm Beach's high and mighty, the event led to a flurry of new commissions. With four big houses to build and furnish that summer, Mizner had more work than he could handle, and he needed help. "Linen, silver, glass, furniture, curtains, rugs—we were to locate and purchase everything," recalled Waugh, who agreed to join Mizner's grand shopping expedition. "We bought tiles, wrought iron staircases, wooden chairs, fine brocades, china, and crystal by the boxful. Everything had to be shipped via New York; every invoice had to be paid; individual pieces needed tags marked for intended houses." The trip would be a crash course for Waugh in Spanish antiques. His job was to tag the individual pieces and keep all the records. The trip lasted most of the summer and took them through Seville, Burgos, Ávila, Salamanca, Granada, and Madrid. "All doors seemed to open to Addison; and for me never more memorably than when we were allowed entry to the Alhambra and the Generalife in Granada in the evenings, when tourists were not permitted." On one remarkable occasion, they sat alone in the moonlight beside the lion fountain in the Court of the Lions at the heart of the Alhambra, savoring the filigreed splendor of the *sebka* decoration (the interlacing grids unique to Islamic design) and the marble columned arches of the arcades. Everywhere they went, they were greeted warmly, including by a madame nicknamed Carmencita, who ran Spain's most famous brothel in the backstreets of Seville. Once, in Madrid, the king of Spain showed up unannounced at their hotel room. Mizner greeted him warmly, clapping him on the back and exclaiming, "You old son of a bitch!"

Back in Palm Beach, Waugh was persuaded to stay and run Mizner's new antique shop, Antigua Shops, the latest addition to the architect's burgeoning collection of stores, potteries, and factories that manufactured and peddled antique and reproduction furnishings, stonework, and floor and roof tiles for Mizner's clients and for the other local architects who were now obliged to work in the Mediterranean Revival style. At around this time, Mizner also recruited Italian ironmongers who could take the odd scraps of metal gates, gratings, and light fixtures that he had shipped back from Spain and recast them into complete and functioning replicas.

Enormous Mediterranean-style Mizner houses were rising up and down the barrier island of Palm Beach, displacing swamp, jungle, and sand. These were physical manifestations of the enormously profitable national economic expansion that was now under way. They were evidence, too, of the new primacy of the American economy on the global stage following World War I—the superiority of the country's industrial capacity and the popularity of the consumer products it was now delivering to the world. But in Palm Beach, not all of the houses were built with "new" money. In fact, many of the homes were built for the families whose names were now synonymous with fortunes made in oil (Warden, Satterwhite), steel (Phipps), meatpacking (Munn), banking (Biddle, Shearson,), retailing (Rasmussen, Wanamaker), or textiles (Wood). Many of these families would soon be related by marriage. Their new houses had romantic Spanish names such as Casa Bendita, built for John S. Phipps, which included a marvelous swimming pool under a covered loggia; Casa Florencia, for Dr. Preston Pope Satterwhite and his wife, Florence, featuring a gorgeous Gothic dining room; La Guerida, for Rodman Wanamaker II, a house that later served as President John F. Kennedy's Winter White House; Villa Flora, for Edward Shearson, another house blessed with a lovely cloister; Casa Nana for National Tea Company founder George Rasmussen; La Fontana, for George Luke Mesker; and, of course, El Mirasol, for the Stotesburys. There were also the more prosaically named Warden house, for William G. Warden, chairman of Pittsburgh Coal Company, and the Towers for woolen mill owner William M. Wood.

Mizner's biggest commission during this period was the enormous home he built for Joshua S. Cosden, an Oklahoma oil baron known as "the prince of petroleum." The house, called Playa Riente (Laughing Beach), was a spectacular waterfront Venetian Gothic palace. Although commissioned for $300,000, overruns took the cost up to $500,000 ($7.3 million in today's money). The great hall stood out as one of Mizner's most marvelous rooms: sixty feet long, two stories high, with a rib-vaulted ceiling held up by giant columns that twisted like licorice sticks, and a magnificent double stone staircase at the far end.

In all, some eighty houses would be built to Mizner designs during the 1920s. He eventually constructed additions on twelve of them; other architects added to eighteen more. Mizner's preference was always for clients such as Paris Singer, who hired him in the spring and then left him alone with complete control over a project. He professed to envy any doctor who could "chloroform his patient and do as he likes."

Visitors to the Mizner houses noticed first their special air of mystery, romance, and whimsy. This effect had little to do with their size, although many of them were very grand indeed. They often looked, inside and out, like movie sets for an old Spanish palace or Venetian palazzo, the key formal elements teased out for dramatic effect. But they also stood on their own as exceptional works of architecture, which is to say that they were aesthetically pleasing to look at—all the more so if you examined them closely: their impact deepened by a fine sense of proportion and by creative contrasts and blends of textures and massing. Simple flat wall surfaces, for example, contrasted with the elaborate carved or cast doorway arches and the fireplace surrounds. Mizner took real joy in the interplay of these Old World elements and in the use of color; his particular shade of blue and yellow became a signature trait.

The result was that to the layperson as well as to the architectural aficionado, these were fascinating buildings, fun to explore, exciting to experience room by room. As one visitor to Palm Beach noted, "One longs to explore every building of Mr. Mizner's, to probe its hidden secrets; one feels certain that even the most innocent looking of his panels conceals darkened galleries and winding stairs."

The art historian Christina Orr-Cahall cites four key ingredients to Mizner's distinctive style: "his total knowledge of Spanish architecture, his highly developed sense of color and proportion, his complete understanding of the wants of the wealthy, and his fine imagination."

None of this happened by accident. Mizner left behind detailed architectural drawings of the houses he designed. He complemented these with evocative watercolors intended to give the overall impression that he hoped to achieve with each project. And he left behind a remarkable collection of scrapbooks that he assembled over the years—twenty-seven in all, each one nearly two hundred pages long. These are compilations of the ideas and concepts that would inform his work throughout his career. Filled with postcards, photographs, pages torn from magazines, and his own sketches and annotations, they record his reactions to the architectural elements found in the monuments and churches of Europe and Latin America. They also show how deeply immersed—and versed—he was in his work. The titles of the scrapbooks alone give an indication of how focused Mizner was on detail: *Moorish and Near East*; *Byzantine-Romanesque*; *Aztec-Primitive*; and *English Gothic*. Other scrapbooks are devoted to topics such as ceilings, murals, paneling, doors, and cloisters. His biographer Caroline Seebohm rightly describes them as "the visual autobiography of an architect."

Despite Mizner's lack of a formal degree, he was superbly trained as an architect, having studied under Willis Polk in addition to working for and with Stanford White. His time at Spain's University of Salamanca, as well as in Guatemala and other parts of Latin America, had been well spent studying the local architecture. By the time he arrived in Palm Beach, he had nearly twenty-five years of experience designing houses. Mizner subscribed to the leading architectural periodicals of the day, and his library boasted an impressive collection of books on architecture.

And yet despite the thoroughness, seriousness, and soundness of his work, perhaps because he was a bona fide resort swell, the image of him as a dilettante architect would outlive him. Rumors spread in the ensuing years that Mizner was cavalier about his designs; that he would happily sketch a design for a client in the sand on their private beach, or that he would often forget to add such fundamental elements as a staircase—an example of what came to be known as a "Mizner miss." The historical record belies any notion of such slipshod work. In public, he might have been flamboyant, impulsive, and reckless at times, but his work was always sober, thoughtful, and imaginative—in fact, much more like the private side of the man himself.

The fact that Mizner usually insisted on having carte blanche to personally decorate the ground floor of each house helps to explain their overall visual impact. He filled them with heavy, dark oak furniture, giant urns, gilt chandeliers, iron grillwork, and tapestries of the period. Admittedly, not all of the furnishings were original, and he went to some trouble to distress furniture or to give a flight of stairs the worn look of antiquity. And because Mizner was not just the architect but also the de facto general contractor, landscape architect, and interior decorator, he was able to erect his enormous buildings and their patios and orange courts in a short period of time—many of them in eight months or less.

By the time Alex Waugh joined Mizner's team, Addison was not the sole architect in Palm Beach. Most of the others (and there were as many as seventeen by the end of the decade) also worked proficiently in the Mediterranean Revival style. For example, Joseph Urban designed the Bath & Tennis Club, referred to as the B&T, in 1926. A talented architect, he was also a set designer for various operas and the Ziegfeld Follies. The socialite Marjorie Merriweather Post, heir to the Postum Cereal Company fortune, the country's wealthiest woman of her day and the wife of stockbroker E. F. Hutton, also hired Urban to finish her gargantuan home, Mar-a-Lago, a stone's throw from the B&T. The costliest house of the era, it was completed for $8 million (equivalent to $113.6 million in current dollars). Today the massive structure, owned by President Donald Trump, is operated as a private club. It was Urban who gave Mar-a-Lago its potpourri of architectural styles and decorating motifs: a Dutch room featuring antique delft tiles, a Venetian room with chandeliers from Murano, Italy, a Versailles master bedroom, an English guest bedroom all with the requisite antiques. To operate it properly, Mrs. Hutton hired a staff of sixty that swelled to eighty during the high season; fourteen of those were responsible for security alone.

Another well-known architect, Maurice Fatio, a debonair Swiss who arrived from New York in 1923, would design some two hundred buildings, most in the Mediterranean Revival style. He soon became Mizner's greatest competitor for the commissions of Palm Beach's superwealthy, although the two men remained friendly. Like Mizner, Fatio had the social polish to woo an upper-crust clientele. Fatio, twenty-five years old when he arrived (like so many others), vividly described Palm Beach in a letter he wrote home to his parents in Geneva:

> *I had scarcely left the train, after two and half days on the tracks, when I was assailed with invitations. Bachelors are a great rarity here, and it suffices to have two solid feet and know how to dance to be accepted immediately! I have never led a more intense life. One gets up at 10 o'clock to play tennis; at noon one bathes at a splendid beach where thousands of people assemble to dive into a tepid sea (the water is really warm and the sun burning). Then luncheon with friends; golf in the afternoon, then a tea dance which one leaves just in time to change for dinner, and the day ends with magnificent balls in private homes which are veritable palaces.*

Two other fine architects, Marion Sims Wyeth, who arrived in 1919, and John L. Volk, who came there in 1924, also worked in the Mediterranean Revival style.

By 1923, Mizner's design studio and headquarters were situated in a building along an arcade that the architect was constructing just off Worth Avenue, directly across the street from the Everglades Club. Via Mizner and its neighboring street Via Parigi (named after Paris Singer) soon offered up a charming collection of shops, alleyways, and courtyards along a paseo that evoked the backstreets of a Spanish village. Welcoming guests to the district was an old friend of Addison's named Wendell Weed, who one day had turned up destitute on Mizner's doorstep. Addison put him to work as the doorman to the shopping district, clothing him in a dark jacket, white cotton trousers, a scarlet cummerbund, and a matching fez, and equipping him with a large golf umbrella to protect shoppers from passing rain showers as they walked to and from their cars. Wendell soon became a popular fixture in the area, opening doors and helping people in and out of their vehicles. It was here in the shop on Via Mizner that Alex Waugh went to work selling Spanish antiques and replicas, his plummy British accent lending a classy upscale tone to the proceedings.

A short time after his return to Palm Beach, Waugh befriended Mizner's nephew Horace Chase Jr., who managed Mizner's pottery business known as Los Manos Potteries. Horace had joined Canada's Royal Flying Corps during the First World War, where he learned to fly airplanes and became the corps's middleweight boxing champion. He was charming, brash, and free-spirited—described by his uncle Addison as "the best-natured slob I ever saw." Horace's first acquisition upon arriving in Palm Beach a few years earlier had been a war-relic Curtiss "Jenny" biplane, which, according to Waugh, he flew "with self-destructive abandon." When Waugh had trouble finding a place of his own in Palm Beach, Chase invited the Englishman to share a shack with him on the beach. "Built by some six-thumbed Crusoe, it was a rickety lopsided affair that hardly held together. The floor was unmatched boards, with no real foundation. We had a couple of beds, a few tables and chairs, and a vintage kerosene stove that was temperamental beyond belief." Out back was a ramshackle privy. At home, they cast off their work clothes and lived in shorts and T-shirts. It was an idyllic, sunburned, and barefoot life. They awoke each morning to the cries of the gulls, the sea practically lapping at their doorstep.

The shack was situated on a stretch of beach that rumrunners used to bring their contraband ashore at night. "If one wished to witness the transportation of illicit alcohol, it was only necessary to stand quietly with a lighted cigarette held straight down one's right leg and say nothing," Waugh recalled. The bootleggers rewarded the two friends for their complicity and discretion with a sack of bottles left hidden for them in the shrubbery. In June and July giant green sea turtles shuffled out of the water at two or three in the morning to lay their eggs in the sand.

The bachelors Waugh and Chase roomed together off and on for the next five years, eventually moving into an abandoned two-tiered houseboat that Horace bought with the some of the proceeds from the sale of a stretch of beachfront property in the Bahamas—it later became the celebrated Paradise Beach in Nassau. A photograph from the period shows the two men together on Horace's sailboat. The blond and preppy-looking Horace is seated at the helm, navigating, while the dark-haired Waugh, who resembles a young Clark Gable, sprawls in front of him, leaning up against his friend's leg while lighting a briar pipe.

In the summers, they traveled Europe with other friends, looking for fun and adventure, taking advantage of the exceptionally attractive postwar exchange rate between the dollar and the French franc. They spent a good deal of time drinking at the Ritz Bar in Paris, where the barman, Frank Meier, later the author of *The Artistry of Mixing Drinks*, became their friend and confidant. One night, while carousing in Montmarte, Horace and a girlfriend witnessed F. Scott and Zelda Fitzgerald drunkenly smash the large glass door to a local bar. To prevent them from being arrested, Horace hustled the couple into a taxi and whisked them away to safety, ignoring their entreaties that they *wanted* to be arrested. On another occasion, on a visit to the luxury hotel Villa d'Este on Italy's Lake Como, Horace accepted a bet at the bar that he could swim the lake's three-mile width—and did so the following morning despite the water's frigid temperature. In Venice, to save money, the two friends rented a small bath cabin at the Lido beach in lieu of a hotel room and slept at night on the sand.

Alex Waugh would befriend other members of the Mizner clan, including Horace's older sister Ysabel, a quick-witted favorite of Addison's who was a frequent visitor to Palm Beach. A nonstop talker, she liked to refer to herself in mock self-aggrandizement as America's Foremost Beauty or, even less modestly, as the *Venus de Milo*. She and the writer Anita Loos, who was shortly to publish the best seller *Gentlemen Prefer Blondes*, were fast friends. Another frequent guest was Pop Chase, Horace and Ysabel's father, whose California vineyard, Stags' Leap, in Napa Valley, had been closed due to Prohibition. In short, Alex Waugh had landed squarely in the middle of what he came to call Miznerland.

Some historians have intimated that Waugh had a romantic relationship with Addison Mizner. The presumption is that Waugh was gay, given that he became an antiquarian who never married; however, the historical record is less clear. For instance, Waugh reported that he had a series of "fabulous dates" with the daughters of Palm Beach dowagers who were led to believe that he was the best-selling author Alec Waugh. And Alex went into antiques only because his uncle was in the trade and offered him a job. Addison Mizner's sexuality is similarly ambiguous, because, if he was gay, which he likely was, he appears not to have acted on this fact—hardly surprising given the strictures of the era and how the stigma of homosexuality might have tarnished his professional reputation. He did surround himself with a succession of attractive and urbane young men, some gay, some not.

In his memoirs, Addison claims that when he was still in his thirties and working for Willis Polk in San Francisco, he had fallen in love with an heiress named Bertha Dolber, the only daughter of a San Francisco lumber and real estate magnate. She led him to believe that she would marry him if he could find a way to make a respectable living. Determined to do so, he attempted to launch a business importing high-end coffees from Guatemala. He was in the old colonial city of Antigua to line up his suppliers when a telegram reached him that Bertha was dead. She had leapt out a high window of the old Waldorf-Astoria Hotel in New York, disconsolate after the death of her father, with whom, Mizner now learned, she had been inordinately close. The record suggests that Mizner never again pursued an overtly romantic relationship with a woman, although in 1923 he seems to have been smitten with a debutante from the Main Line suburbs of Philadelphia named Peggy Thayer, who was a close friend of his client and confidante Nell Cosden, wife of oilman Joshua Cosden. "The two lasting loves of my life have always been animals and trees," he once remarked.

The antiques business that Alex Waugh began to manage, Antigua Shops (later called La Puerta), was one of Mizner's few consistently profitable businesses outside of his architectural practice. Waugh was given plenty of autonomy to run it, especially since Addison was so busy orchestrating the design and construction of houses for his clients. During the day, the architect drove from project to project in a dilapidated Mack truck, its cabin stripped down to a pair of bucket seats and a steering wheel. "It was one of the sights of Palm Beach to see him belting up the road, his shirttails flapping in the breeze. Clinging to his collar for dear life, and loving it, would be his monkey, Johnnie Brown," Waugh recalled. Mizner's two Chow Chows, Ching and Shadow, usually occupied the seat beside him.

Only at his regular afternoons at home did the architect let himself relax. Through the cocktail hour, he held court upstairs in the spacious second floor of the building he called Villa Mizner, completed in 1924. He could be found there, in the Gothic living room, seated, according to Waugh, with "patriarchal dignity" in a large throne-like chair that could accommodate his growing bulk—by the mid-1920s, he weighed nearly three hundred pounds. Here friends and acquaintances gathered to exchange gossip and trade quips or just to listen to Addison talk about the wanderings and adventures of his remarkable youth. "From this vantage point, he functioned not only as a monarch but as his own court jester," the writer Anita Loos recalled. One guest remembered seeing Jerome Kern, by then a renowned composer for theater and film, doing handstands in the Mizner living room. The songwriter Irving Berlin and his soon-to-be second wife, the Comstock Lode heiress Ellin Mackay, were often in attendance, too. It was said that Berlin, like Kern, had written a couple of his popular songs at Addison's piano. Perhaps one was "Lazy," which Berlin was known to have written around this time in Palm Beach.

Many of Palm Beach's wealthiest citizens would show up for cocktail hour at Villa Mizner. One particular favorite of Addison's was a young woman named Alice DeLamar, who was a good friend of his nephew Horace Chase and described by the press as America's "most interesting heiress." DeLamar was the only child of a remarkable onetime Martha's Vineyard sea captain named Joseph Raphael DeLamar, who, in succession, ran a successful ocean salvage operation, built a mining fortune in Colorado, Idaho, and Nevada, and then added considerably to his wealth with a successful third career on Wall Street. At twenty-three, she was the beneficiary to $10 million of her father's $30 million estate; the rest was left to a handful of universities. After graduating from the Spence School in Manhattan, she had befriended and, for all practical purposes, been adopted by the great connoisseur and historian of Italian Renaissance art Bernard Berenson and his wife, Mary, who once described their protégée as "all angles and resentments and revolts." DeLamar adored Addison like a benevolent uncle.

Another Mizner favorite was the beautiful New York debutante Marjorie Oelrichs, also known as "Bubbles," who later married bandleader Eddy Duchin. A third was Evalyn Walsh McLean, whom Mizner had known in Newport, Rhode Island, in the years before she was married. The sole heir to a Colorado gold mining fortune, she was now the owner of the 45-carat Hope Diamond, a $187,000 gift from her husband, Edward McLean, publisher-owner of the *Washington Post*. In Palm Beach, she was known to appear at charity benefits so bedecked in diamonds and rubies that, according to Addison, she looked "like a hail storm splattered with blood."

Anita Loos, also a part of the group, liked to tell an apocryphal story of how Evalyn once had a large radio delivered to the architect as a token of her esteem. Her chauffeur carried the box upstairs to Mizner's apartment. Addison's butler and valet, Arthur Bedford, plugged it in only to discover that it didn't operate properly. "Ultimately a repairman discovered that the works had been jammed by the Hope Diamond, which Evalyn had thoughtlessly dropped into its bowels for safekeeping," Loos alleged. Mizner liked to tell the same story but dismissed the idea that the big gem jamming up the radio was the Hope Diamond. If it had been, he claimed, he would have had the means to take an early retirement: "just my luck, or I might be living in Central China now."

Alcohol was not needed to fuel Addison Mizner's wit. He restricted his alcohol consumption to a single rum cocktail in the evening and a drink with dinner. His real addiction was food. As his nephew Horace once remarked, "Addison's idea of a square meal is to sit a foot away from the table and eat until he touches."

Mizner also had a voracious appetite for socializing. In February 1920 he and four other socially prominent single young men who called themselves the Cocoanuts organized a strictly-by-invitation masquerade ball that had decadent elements of a Venetian carnival. Mizner himself transformed the ballroom of the Palm Beach Country Club into a jungle. Men showed up dressed as women; women as men. Others arrived dressed as Turkish sultans, Arab sheiks, Venetian ladies, and various Punchinellos, Pierrots, and Pierrettes. One fabulously wealthy heiress came dressed as a peasant, another as a Seminole, and all posed in tableaux vivants to be photographed. The celebrated Palm Beach debutantes and society beauties were in attendance: Peggy Thayer, Alice DeLamar, Marjorie Oerlichs, Mia Frelinghuysen, Cordelia Duke, and the three Pierson sisters. Ford Dabney's Syncopated Orchestra, an all-black orchestra that played for Florenz Ziegfeld Jr. in his *Midnight Frolics* production at the New Amsterdam Theatre's roof garden theater, provided the music. Before parties, after parties, and breakfast parties kept the revelers cavorting through the night and into the morning hours. The next year, Ziegfeld brought his cast of Follies to the ball, and the showgirls, "glorifying the American girl," performed a kick line onstage before joining the increasingly unbridled and inebriated throng on the dance floor. The debauched Cocoanuts Ball quickly became a popular annual event among the younger set.

Villa Mizner was the true social epicenter of Miznerland, and at, first, Alex Waugh mistook it for a kind of amusement park; only with time did he realize that the place was more of a menagerie. In addition to the two Chows and the popular capuchin monkey Johnnie Brown, Mizner owned two macaws (one scarlet; the other, blue and gold) and the occasional raccoon. All of these animals vied for the architect's attention. The monkey was especially unruly and had a knack for snatching women's pocketbooks and absconding with them, scampering up the bookcases or into the rafters and onto the chandeliers, to Mizner's concealed amusement. When Waugh first encountered Johnnie Brown in Addison's apartment, the monkey jumped from a bookcase onto Waugh's shoulder, nipped his ear, and then bounced from his shoulder to Mizner's, where it buried itself down the front of the architect's blazer. Eventually Waugh came to see the monkey, whom he later befriended, as "more like a familiar spirit than an animal." A few years later, Mizner added a kinkajou named Nettie.

The most exotic mammal to reside at Villa Mizner at that time, by far, was Addison's rakish and debauched brother Wilson, who was four years Addison's junior and their mother's favorite. Wilson arrived in Florida in 1922, impoverished and ill, after a doting Addison rescued him from a New York hospital and brought him to Palm Beach to help him recover his health. In his memoirs about his Florida experiences, Alex Waugh describes Wilson emerging from the back of the Mizner apartment looking dissolute and wearing a short nightshirt: "Wilson Mizner peered at me through sunken, menacing eyes. A two-day beard did little to improve his appearance. 'My Gawd,' he rasped in sepulchral tones, 'a goddam Limey.' Then he disappeared down the hall."

Wilson had led an even more colorful life than Addison, a life that frequently skirted or broke the law. He had joined Addison and two other older brothers in the Klondike gold rush but spent most of his time there gambling or devising badger schemes: contriving to put married men in sexually compromising situations in order to then extort money from them. Perhaps most famously, he had run crooked card games on cruise ships, along the way becoming an expert in scams and petty larceny. A decade or so earlier, Wilson had coauthored a pair of successful Broadway productions—*The Deep Purple* (1910) and *The Greyhound* (1912)—so-called crook plays based on his extensive firsthand experience at various confidence games. For a time, he had also managed the career of two-time middleweight boxing champion Stanley Ketchel, also known as the Michigan Assassin. In Manhattan, Wilson once managed Broadway's notoriously seedy Hotel Rand, which became famous for the list of house rules he posted in the lobby. They included: "Guests must carry out their own dead" and "No opium smoking in the elevators."

By all accounts, Wilson made a striking first impression. Recalled Addison's friend Alice DeLamar: "I can see him as though it were yesterday, leaning over the iron balcony of the house where he lived on Worth Avenue, in bare feet and a preposterous wrinkled nightshirt that hung to his hairy knees, a four-day growth of unshaven beard adorning his chin, and obviously nurturing a hangover." Wilson was undeniably, even proudly, louche. "He had a criminal look that convicted him at once," Addison once observed, with ample justification. As Wilson himself admitted: "All my life, I have seen or heard of people being arrested for things that I always do." He meant, of course, swindling people, taking illegal drugs (opium, cocaine, and marijuana), and fixing prizefights. Later in life, living in Hollywood, he would form a close friendship with comedic actor W. C. Fields, who confessed to a similarly checkered past. As Wilson remarked, "We share in common the blight of having been born in eternal jeopardy. Neither of us is afraid—just expectant." His other pals in New York had included the gunslinger turned sportswriter Bat Masterson, the acclaimed short story writers O. Henry (William Sydney Porter) and Damon Runyon, and the shady financier Diamond Jim Brady and his longtime girlfriend, the actress and singer Lillian Russell.

Anita Loos was instantly smitten with Wilson after being introduced to him by Addison shortly after Wilson's arrival in Florida. She vividly recalled her first impression: "Wilson was a badly preserved giant of fifty-one. His massive shoulders had begun to sag; his brown hair was flecked with gray, and Time, the silent old bugler, had started to sound the retreat on his hairline. But his head was leonine and looked as rugged as if it were hacked from granite. His expressions were enlivened by a sort of superhuman awareness. . . . To my youthful eyes, everything about that aging reprobate was exciting: the aura of his reckless past; the challenge of his being a highly unsuitable companion; his air of tranquil assurance, which, as a rule, exists only in men of genius." The two soon became an item, although Loos at the time was married to the actor and silent film director John Emerson.

Wilson's wit was even sharper than Addison's. He was especially adept at coining pointed aphorisms and snappy bon mots, many of which eventually found their way into plays and films of the day. These included: "The best way to keep your friends is never to give them away." "Most hard-boiled people are half-baked." "All the sleep I need is another five minutes." "I hate careless flattery, the kind that exhausts you in your effort to believe it." "A fellow who is always declaring he's no fool usually has his suspicions." "Easy street is a blind alley."

While many of these seem arch and dated today, there is no question that Wilson could be genuinely funny. One time at a Hollywood restaurant, a tiresome film producer sat down uninvited in a booth Wilson was sharing with W. C. Fields. Wilson turned to the actor and remarked casually, "Gangrene sets in." He once described Hollywood as "a trip through a sewer in a glass-bottomed boat." Of one Palm Beach contractor, he would remark, "He's so crooked, he'd steal two left shoes." Years later, while scriptwriting in Hollywood, he would get credit for providing James Cagney, William Powell, and Clark Gable with some of their best tough-guy lines. For the 1936 film *San Francisco,* coscripted by Anita Loos and Robert Hopkins, the protagonist Blackie Norton, played by Gable, was based on Wilson Mizner.

Addison understood that introducing his notorious brother to his high society clientele was bound to be a delicate proposition. When one Palm Beach hostess encouraged him to bring along Wilson to one of her soirees, he felt obliged to caution her, "I warn you, he will probably put his moccasins on the piano, and he isn't house broken." It didn't take Wilson long to prove him correct. At one cocktail party, he examined a canapé being passed and observed in a loud voice, "Those anchovies died of convulsion in a septic tank." At a party at Eva Stotesbury's house, the famous hostess derided the bad taste of the day and remarked how one hardly knew what to expect next. Wilson could not let such snobbery pass uncontested: "How right you are, dear lady! Why, I never set foot outside my own home without the illusion that I am up to my ass in vulgarity." Eva Stotesbury recoiled in indignation. From then, on Wilson was excused from Addison's regular social events—and kept at a safe distance from the Stotesburys.

But Wilson seems to have pulled himself together shortly after his arrival in Palm Beach. He instantly, and opportunistically, recognized the wealthy enclave as "the pecuniary heaven." Determined to exploit it, he disappeared for two weeks and successfully freed himself from an addiction to morphine by going cold turkey. He then set about trying to make himself useful as an assistant to his now famous brother. As Addison surely knew, Wilson's shady background made him a poor choice to be a close business associate. But the architect made light of this, confiding to friends: "The son of a bitch would shoot me just to make book on which way I'd fall."

It is arguable how interested Wilson actually was in advancing his celebrated brother's career. From the outset, he seems to have been more on the lookout for a quick score. He gambled at Colonel Bradley's Casino, and Anita Loos recalled seeing him propped up in his bed one day counting "bales of greenbacks," his share of the spoils for serving as a shill at the gambling den the night before.

The first outside project that he explored with Addison in mid-1924 was a scheme for the two of them to buy and develop a mile of coastline south of Palm Beach near what is today Boynton Beach. The development was to be called Mizner Mile. Neither of them knew a thing about real estate speculation. But Addison went along, ponying up most of the money.

The parcel had one serious limitation: the main road ran too close to the shore to allow room for building beachfront houses. Wilson's idea, which he attempted to implement one night without any local authorization, was to dig up the road and move it a quarter of a mile inland. This maneuver, however, put the bypass on land owned by a settlement of Finnish farmers, who did not take well to the sudden encroachment or to their loss of access to the beach. The following morning, Wilson, still dressed in white tie and a silk top hat from the prior night's revelry, desperately tried to adjudicate a melee that broke out between the farmers and the road workers on their bulldozers. The brothers found themselves entangled in litigation and were soon forced to abandon the project.

This early fiasco should have been a clear warning sign to Addison that he shouldn't involve Wilson too intimately in his business affairs, let alone make him his partner, and yet he chose to ignore the omen. As he tried to explain later, he was more than just deeply loyal to his brother; he genuinely loved him. "Wilson," he once remarked, "has always been my chief weakness and dreaded menace." Only time would demonstrate that Wilson could be far more than a mere menace, but by then Addison would have risked—and lost—everything.

For his part, Wilson wasn't ready to give up on the prospect of a big Florida score. The answer, in his mind, was not to retreat after the botched Mizner Mile project, but to double down. The brothers would try their hand at land development again, only this time they would do it properly. They would bring in outside partners; the wealthiest and most prestigious people the two of them could find. With the considerable backing of this group, and aided by Addison's growing national reputation, the odds of success would tilt firmly in their favor, or so they believed.

12

WEIGALL WHOOPS IT UP

Wilson Mizner was hardly alone in hoping for a big Florida payday. Word was out that money could be made fast in Florida real estate. Newspapers across the country were filled with tales of quick windfalls in the Sunshine State. All one needed, it seemed, was a thirst for adventure and transportation to Florida. The story of George Cusack Jr., who had made $500,000 in four weeks, caught the attention of a visiting twenty-four-year-old London-based journalist named Theyre Hamilton Weigall. In the window of a real estate office near his Manhattan hotel, Weigall read the Cusack story with keen interest and concluded that George Cusack Jr. was "practically half-witted"—at least judging from his photograph—and that if Cusack could make a fortune in Florida real estate, so could he.

Two days later, Weigall boarded a train for Florida. He arrived in Miami in August 1925, possessing "exactly twenty dollars in the world." On his first night in the city, he checked into a hotel that he couldn't afford and walked across the causeway to Miami Beach, where he lay on the cool grass in the fragrant darkness, looking back at the city lights across the bay and listening to the strains of a dance orchestra from a nearby hotel and the distant thumping of the surf, convinced that he had arrived in a tropical Shangri-la.

The next morning, he went looking for a job. Failing to find newspaper work, he tried his hand at selling yacht club memberships. The only one he sold over the next few days was to a retired Scotland Yard detective who took pity on him. He then spent an exhausting day as a dockworker, unloading cargo at the Miami piers. At last, Weigall landed the kind of job to which he was ideally suited: writing press releases for George Merrick's Coral Gables development. On his first morning at work, he was told to borrow one of the company's Tin Lizzies to better acquaint himself with the layout of the burgeoning development. Driving through the newly emerging City Beautiful Movement neighborhood, he was amazed: "Everywhere there were dazzling colors—white walls, striped awnings, red roofs, brilliant greenery, and the intense blue of the Florida sky."

The remarkable publicity machine that he had joined, based out of the Coral Gables Administration Building, was, in effect, a private news organization. Here a double shift of reporters drafted press releases and news articles that ran in local and national papers, all of them extolling the virtues of Coral Gables. Weigall's job consisted of authoring "great manifestos" that announced new building schemes or the launch of additional sections of the giant development. He also interviewed prominent visitors to the area, writing up accounts of local activities that could then be reprinted virtually word for word in newspapers such as the *Miami Herald*. Invitations were extended on a daily basis to every sports, musical, and theatrical celebrity the publicists could think of in hopes of luring them to Coral Gables, where the celebrities would then expound on the wonders of Merrick's marvelous new city. Propaganda poured forth from the publicity department, "most of it extremely subtle and indirect, [that] had about it something that was almost terrifying," Weigall recalled. By now, the Coral Gables Corporation was spending $2 million annually on this publicity.

An additional $2 million was spent on advertising. The advertising department occupied a special building across the street from the administration building, and, according to Weigall, was presided over by "a fiery-eyed young genius who apparently never slept, never laughed, never stopped working for a moment, and was perpetually in a state of nerves bordering on insanity." Weigall thought many of the advertisements crude and at times blatantly misleading, especially the billboards and the posters: "The majority of these depicted an entirely mythical city, with gleaming spires and glistening domes making up an idealized blend of Moscow and Oxford, with the exception that they were invariably rising out of a tropical paradise in which lovely ladies and marvelously dressed gallants disported themselves under the palm trees."

The scope of the Coral Gables ad campaigns in 1925 and 1926 was breathtaking: twenty national magazines carried full-page ads or double-page spreads, many of them in full color, reaching a combined circulation of more than eleven million readers. An additional one hundred newspapers carried Coral Gables ads targeted at another six million readers. In all, some ninety-eight million images of Coral Cables passed before the American public during the decade. It was far and away the most elaborate and comprehensive advertising and publicity campaign ever rolled out for a real estate development.

Similar ad copy poured forth from every land company in Florida, creating a virtual Niagara Falls of national publicity, much of it unreliable. Weigall had a hard time believing the public could be so gullible as to accept the preposterous claims and the stylized pictures. And yet, despite his initial skepticism, he soon became caught up in the excitement and missionary-like zeal of the great project, experiencing what he described as a "semireligious enthusiasm." And he began to enjoy himself. "I suppose I was slightly mad," he conceded. "We all were."

Merrick's group had come up with memorable slogans for Coral Gables such as, "Follow the Golden Galleon Where Your Castles in Spain Are Made Real," and "Coral Gables, the Stuff Dreams Are Made Of," and "Coral Gables, Where Tropical Trade Winds Blow." Florida's other developers looked at what Merrick's team had done and then each cobbled together their own variants. For Fort Lauderdale, "The Tropical Wonderland." For Opa-Locka, "The Baghdad of Dade County." For Indrio, "Florida's Newest and Most Beautiful Town." For Haines City, "The Gateway to the Scenic Highlands." For Miami Shores, "America's Mediterranean on Biscayne Bay" and "Moonbeams Across the Bay." For Sebring, "The Orange Blossom City." For Fort Myers, "The City of Palms." For St. Petersburg, "The Sunshine City." For Sarasota, "A City of Glorified Opportunity." And for Cocoa, "The Friendly Land That Loves a Playmate." Some were slightly more obscure. "Yesterday Is Ancient History in St. Petersburg," read one. Or, for Boca Raton, "The Dream City of the Western World."

Not every newly minted publicist mastered the skill. On the west coast, realtor Walter P. Fuller believed he had hit on a terrific tagline when he dreamed up this one for Jungle Terrace and posted it on a billboard: "Jungle Terrace—Where Nature Did Her Best." He realized his error when someone scrawled below, "But look what Man did to it."

Hired flacks toiled to complement the news-driven publicity that Weigall and his colleagues generated. These professional spellbinders came in two types. The first was the celebrity speaker. At Coral Gables, none was more eminent than William Jennings Bryan, the thrice-defeated Democratic nominee for US president. George Merrick paid Bryan a salary of $100,000, half in cash, half in land, to pitch the resort to potential buyers in his most exalted silver-tongued oratory. Memorably, Bryan described Coral Gables as "the only city in the world where you can tell a lie at breakfast that will come true by evening."

The second type of hired flack was the professional writer. In the case of Coral Gables, Merrick hired, for $18,000, the best-selling author Rex Beach to write a book on the development. Beach's sixty-three-page booklet, *The Miracle of Coral Gables*, detailed the virtues of Merrick and his grand vision for Coral Gables, although one local journalist described the book's cover as its chief merit. Beach seemed to relish the challenge of romanticizing the great developer, whom he described as "a dreamer . . . a man who whose eyes made pictures when they were shut; a man who beheld a stately vision and caused it to become a reality. At heart he was a writer, a poet, an artist, but fate with curious perversity decreed that he should write in wood and steel and stone and paint his pictures upon a canvas of spacious fields, cool groves, and smiling waterways."

Weigall discovered one species of promoter he could not countenance: the self-promoter. He encountered more than a few whose sole objective was to find an excuse for publicly lauding their own success. But Weigall believed that George Merrick was not a self-promoter. For one thing, despite hiring flacks, the man did not seem to be aggressively pursuing his own self-aggrandizement. It was Coral Gables that Merrick promoted, not himself. Proof of this was the fact that Merrick didn't grant interviews to the press. To Weigall, who watched him hurry out to his car alone each night, the great developer seemed increasingly isolated in his work, a Gatsby-like figure of considerable fascination and awe. On the one occasion that Weigall actually met Merrick in person, at a reception on the verandah of Merrick's house, Weigall found himself tongue-tied in the presence of a man they all considered "almost a god." Even people who were much closer to Merrick, like head salesman Doc Dammers, spoke of the boss with reverence. "By hell, it certainly needs a tall giraffe to high-hat *that* guy!" he once whispered in earnest to Weigall.

As Coral Gables's reputation and success grew, prospects poured into the community looking to buy houses or empty lots of land. The company's seventy-six vehicles, mostly buses that seated twenty-three passengers each, offered free transport to Coral Gables from various points in the southern states where Merrick had established sales offices. Occasional runs brought busloads more from as far away as New York, Chicago, and San Francisco. The side of each bus, emblazoned with the Coral Gables logo, was a rolling advertisement for the development.

On April 29, 1925, Coral Gables became more than just a suburb of Miami, when the Florida Legislature created via charter a city by that name. The charter stipulated that Merrick himself and his top officers would serve as the city commissioners until the first elections in June 1929. As a result of these maneuvers, Merrick not only headed the organization that was developing the city but also was the de facto head of the city itself, a profound and, under Florida law, illegal conflict of interest that would come back to vex him.

The more real estate the Coral Gables Corporation sold, the more subdivisions and developments Merrick envisioned and launched: the enormous indoor arena he called the Miami Coliseum in Coral Gables; the Tahiti Beach section; the Coral Gables Biltmore Hotel (planned in partnership with Biltmore founder John McEntee Bowman); and in June 1925 the University of Miami, which Merrick announced with great fanfare, pledging $5 million of his own money toward its construction. The master stroke of the gigantic building endeavor was the $100 million deal with American Building Corporation in 1925 to develop twelve to sixteen villages in varying architectural styles such as Florida Pioneer Village,

French Normandy Village, Chinese Village, Dutch South African Village (or Cape Dutch Revival Village), and Italian Village.

Somewhat surprisingly, Coral Gables's mandated loveliness was initially a hindrance to sales, as Merrick himself admitted: "People resented it as a sort of censorship of their good taste." Aware of this fact early on, and aware that he would have to compete against Carl Fisher's talent for ballyhoo and publicity stunts, Merrick had applied his undeniable organizational skills to developing his unsurpassed publicity and marketing department, of which Weigall was now just a tiny component. And it would be marketing where the real strength of the organization lay. It evolved into a giant engine of sales.

Ironically, the enterprise's huge marketing apparatus would also prove to be its Achilles' heel. As it took on the most ambitious lot-selling campaign of any development, its expenses skyrocketed. According to one account, selling, general, and administrative (SG&A) expenses at the Coral Gables Corporation soon ran as high as 55 percent of revenues—and 30 percent would have been excessive. In other words, the very large selling and marketing and associated administrative expenses wiped out the potential profit that could be earned on each lot sold. The Tampa realtor Martin Fuller identified the problem that was emerging by late 1925, when he observed, "The more lots sold, the more insolvent Merrick became." Put simply, the Coral Gables development at the height of the boom had a deeply flawed business model, and Merrick, with no formal financial training, seems not to have understood the trouble that he was brewing.

Much like Henry Flagler, not a great deal is known about Merrick's personal life during this period in his life, unless one extrapolates from an autobiographical unpublished short story that he wrote in 1926 titled "High Olympus," about a successful developer whose marriage is falling apart. What is known is that despite his great financial success—a fortune that was rumored to be fast approaching $100 million but likely was around half that—he had begun drinking too much and cheating on his wife, Eunice. Despite these alleged problems, she stayed with him.

One day around this time, while driving down a deserted road in the Coral Gables development, Weigall spotted Merrick's car pulled over on the side of the road. "A few yards away, Mr. Merrick was standing on a rise; he was quite alone, gazing out over his domains." When Merrick turned, Weigall had a good look at his boss's grim expression and the strange, haunted look in his eyes. It was a look Weigall would not forget.

Weigall was so adept at writing profiles of visiting celebrities that he was soon promoted to penning feature-length articles. Most of these came in response to requests from magazine editors around the country looking for pieces on Coral Gables. He was given a handsome salary, an expense account, the use of a car, and almost complete autonomy to come and go as he pleased. For Weigall, the job also offered red-carpet access into Miami's nightlife. He attended a succession of "vague and enthusiastic functions" where speeches were made and too much alcohol imbibed. He danced until four in the morning to orchestras in spectacular ballrooms of spectacular hotels or in the ballrooms of equally spectacular private homes.

The job grew even more interesting once he befriended the head salesman, Doc Dammers, who began to include him in some of the after-hour events that entertained visiting celebrities and dignitaries. Weigall's phone would ring late at night, and his attendance would be required at impromptu gatherings at a nightclub or casino. One such dignitary was the handsome and unscrupulous politician Jimmy Walker, who was mayor-elect of New York City in late 1925. Accurately described as "flashy and smart-mouth and Broadway smooth" and "as charming a sinner as God's chirping angels ever forgave," the future mayor was fond of speakeasies, chorus girls, and the good life. He had a special obsession with bespoke suits and packed forty-three suitcases of clothes for one trip to Europe. He was right at home in Miami. "I am here for rest and relaxation and to build up my health for the task that awaits me," Walker told the *New York Times* on November 17, 1925. Doc Dammers, who quickly became Walker's drinking companion, described him as "the rooster's boots!"

Accompanied by a police escort on motorcycles, sirens blaring, the Walker entourage careened down the streets as it raced from nightclub to nightclub. On one such trip—to Club Lido on Hibiscus Island—the trio were pursued by a carful of starlets driven by Miss Dorothy Knapp, the reigning Miss Manhattan and runner-up in the 1922 Miss America Pageant, who had recently been proclaimed the most beautiful woman in America. The car that Walker, Dammers, and Weigall rode in screeched around a corner. "It was only by the grace of Heaven that we were not all pitched into the sea," Weigall recalled. But that only seemed to add to the fun, especially to the starlets bringing up the rear: "'We thought you were all killed, surely; but we were having such a bully time we just whooped!'" reported Miss Manhattan as they all climbed out of their cars at the Lido a few moments later.

According to Weigall, there was no adherence to the Volstead Act whatsoever in Miami. It was as though people had simply forgotten about Prohibition. A bottle of whiskey cost $3; a bottle of champagne, $10. Beer sold for $1 a bottle and was considered a luxury. "I should say that during the boom, there must have been more alcohol per head consumed in Florida than in any other country in the world." Weigall drank his share of it.

He continued to attend parties and dances in every conceivable venue. Some nights found him at roadside juke joints where jazz music blared and couples of mixed races jammed onto tiny, crowded dance floors. Those unadorned spaces could not have contrasted more strikingly with the country clubs and their lantern-hung patios where he found himself on other nights, which in turn contrasted with the open-air dance floors on the beach where younger couples danced in their bathing suits at sunset. He danced the Charleston, the fox-trot, and the black bottom dance that originated among African Americans in the rural South, and he watched the flappers perform the provocative and sometimes-banned shimmy dance. He danced to Isham Jones and His Orchestra performing "It Had to Be You" or "I'll See You in My Dreams." And he danced to the Paul Whiteman Orchestra performing "When the Moon Shines on Coral Gables." The girls he danced with wore sheer and revealing dresses that barely reached their knees.

Before long, Weigall became intoxicated by all the excitement, the loose money, and the sparkling nightlife. "I was living now in a wild dream in which it seemed that every desire would be inevitably realized," he recalled. "I had as much money to spend as I could possibly want; and—again like everyone else—I was spending it with no thought for the future and living like an emperor." Amazingly, up until then, Weigall had not succumbed to the land boom he was helping to promote: he had not yet bought any real estate.

However, he would soon give in to the lure of the quick buck, as would so many others. One representative case was Gertrude Matthews Shelby, a writer for *Harper's Monthly* magazine, who came down to Florida to write a story in late 1925, fully aware of all the hype and "inclined to scoff" at what she saw. Determined not to fall prey to Florida's hucksters and promoters, she failed utterly, even ignoring the admonition of a fellow traveler on the boat trip south who cautioned her, "Don't be drawn in. I wish I'd never seen Florida. It's a magnificent state. Money is still to be made. But speculation is hog-wild. People do things they'd never be guilty of at home. I've done them myself. . . . If you enjoy a good night's sleep now, stay out."

But the fever and the excitement on the streets of Miami were infectious. The stories of overnight fortunes were legion, and many of them true. What harm could come from looking, Shelby asked herself. Whisked from development to development by bus, feted with free meals and endless entertainment, she found herself wavering. "Again and again I declared that I had no intention to buy," she reflected, "but nobody let me forget for an instant that I was a prospect."

Shelby finally resolved that she would make a sound, carefully considered investment. Intrigued by the price and description of one lot, she went to take a look. It turned out to be a rock pit. But in Fort Lauderdale, she passed on another that soon sold for $60,000. A week later, it went for $75,000. Two weeks after that, it sold again for $95,000. If she had bought the binder for $2,500, she could conceivably have made $35,000 in less than a month. "Terror of an insecure old age suddenly assumed exaggerated proportions," she reported. "Right then and there, I succumbed to the boom bacillus. I would gamble outright. The illusion of investment vanished."

And Shelby didn't fare too badly. "I gambled. I won. I remained to turn land salesman. Not only with no superiority, but with defiant shame rather than triumph." She made $13,000 in a month flipping properties: "Not much, perhaps, but a lot to a little buyer on a little bet."

Walter P. Fuller, the aforementioned St. Petersburg–based broker, provides another telling example of the boom's virulence. One day he was showing a banker from St. Louis around town when the man began to pepper him with questions about recent sales. Fuller pointed out the northwest corner of Twenty-Second and Central Avenues in Tampa, which had sold recently for $75,000. The banker turned to him.

"Fuller, what can be built on that lot that will earn six percent on the cost of the improvement plus seventy-five thousand dollars?"

"Nothing," the realtor replied.

"Listen, Fuller, don't ever forget this: no piece of land, no place in the world, is worth more than it can earn, developed to its highest and best use."

This was remarkably sage advice based on sound financial principles. But after a full day viewing other properties on the market and the prices that they had sold for, the banker began to moderate his views, impressed no doubt by the proof of soaring values and eye-popping opportunities for making easy money. Finally, the banker remarked, "Fuller, I want to amend that statement I made about the seventy-five-thousand-dollar lot . . . You have some few wonderful spots in this country where a wealthy man can build and enjoy life as he never has before. In the enjoyment of your pleasant conditions, he can get a pleasure that can't be measured in dollars. Real estate of that kind is worth whatever you can get for it. Charge 'em plenty, boy, and the best of luck."

If a banker could be swayed so easily, it is hardly surprising that Weigall would eventually fall victim to the contagion, even though he was privy to the inner workings of the greatest publicity machine of the era. "Looking back on it now," he recalled, "it seems to me incredible that I was able to hold back so long, when I had access to most of the 'good things' that were going and when people all about me were making so much money that they scarcely knew what to do with it next." One day he proposed to a colleague at work that together they spend $4,000 on a three-month option on land in a planned but still unannounced Coral Gables section. The idea was that they would flip their option on the property when news of the section was formally announced and its value had soared to some multiple of what they had paid for it. Importantly, this had to happen in the next ninety days, before their option expired, or they would be on the hook for the balance of the cost—a sum of money they didn't possess.

They discussed the scheme for five minutes over a chocolate milkshake at the drugstore soda fountain across from the Coral Gables Administration Building, "and never were five minutes spent to worse advantage," he recalled with rueful hindsight. A half hour later, they signed the requisite papers, securing the option. The two friends then treated themselves to a lavish lunch at the Casa Loma Hotel, where they toasted their pending good fortune. Their exhilaration would not last. As Weigall observed, "The very moment when I started to invest on my own account was the very moment when things, though not as yet very openly, had begun to go wrong."

13

A HOUSE IN COCONUT GROVE

In Coconut Grove, right next to the manic Coral Gables development, another former journalist was also struggling to make a living in the booming Florida economy. As she recovered from her nervous breakdown over the summer of 1924, Marjory Stoneman Douglas had set about creating a new career for herself as a writer of fiction. The popularity of general interest magazines in the years following World War I opened up lucrative opportunities for authors of articles and short stories. She hoped to be one of them—with a focus on Florida.

For a number of years, Douglas had been contributing one-line aphorisms to the *Smart Set*, a literary magazine then being edited by H. L. Mencken and George Jean Nathan. She sold these for $100 apiece, which in turn helped her to land a literary agent named Robert Thomas Hardy. To her considerable surprise, Hardy was able to sell her first short story, a work she considered inferior, called "The Queen's Amber." He then sold a longer story of hers to the popular pulp magazine *Black Mask* for $600. Hardy suggested that she try writing for the hugely popular *Saturday Evening Post*, a weekly edited brilliantly by the Louisville-born author George Horace Lorimer.

During his thirty-eight-year stint as editor, Lorimer would create a national magazine addressed to the "average" American, publishing articles on a wide range of topics and short stories that were notable for their wholesomeness. As circulation soared into the millions, American writers such as Ernest Hemingway, William Faulkner, F. Scott Fitzgerald,

Agatha Christie, and P. G. Wodehouse began to appear in the *Post*'s pages. The covers, of course, often featured memorable illustrations of everyday American life by Norman Rockwell.

To break into such august literary ranks, Douglas spent hours deconstructing what she believed to be a prototypical Lorimer story. "I decided he generally liked a success story with a noble character tangled up with a little sex and a few cuss words thrown in. A perfect opening for a Lorimer story was something like: 'Hell,' said the duchess, 'take your hand off my knee.'" The story Douglas wrote featured a beauty parlor owner who had once worked as a stewardess on a cruise ship and ran her business using salty nautical language. She confessed in her memoirs, "I hate to admit this, but I might as well make a clean breast of it—the story was called 'At Home on the Marseilles Waves.'" Lorimer bought it. Marjory was particularly pleased with the reaction of her aunt Fanny, who had predicted she would die in a garret if she pursued a writing career instead of a teaching career. "Aunt Fanny was flabbergasted."

In the years that followed, Douglas would publish some eighty short stories, a remarkable forty-two of them in the *Saturday Evening Post* and most of them set in Florida. In virtually all of them, she paid special attention to the natural world—the landscape, the sky, and the tropical vegetation—so much so that she would come to be seen by some readers as a nature writer. She chafed at being pigeonholed. Years later, when Wellesley College presented her with an alumni award for nature writing, she objected, explaining, "I am a similar breed, but not quite the same." Her theme, as she saw it, was to capture people in relation to nature and nature in relation to people. But one fact was indisputable: she had begun to crusade for nature in her short stories.

The *Saturday Evening Post* paid well—$1,200 per story; the equivalent of $17,160 today—enough that she was able to save some money. To supplement this income, she accepted an assignment from her friend George Merrick to write a booklet of prose and photos titled *Coral Gables: America's Finest Suburb, Miami, Florida—An Interpretation by Marjory Stoneman Douglas*. "Any brief glimpse of Coral Gables gives one this splendid stimulating sense of discovery, the exhilarating realization that here at last wisdom and art and craftsmanship have met the age-old problem of how best shall a man live," she wrote. She was not proud of the hackwork she did for Merrick, her fellow erstwhile poet, and admitted later that she was ill-suited to the task.

How to live had become a pressing personal concern for her, too. Her father took it for granted that Marjory would always live with him, but she wanted her independence and said so. She was thirty-four years old and needed her own place. What she wanted most, as she began to suffer from her own version of real estate fever, was a small house. Among other things, Douglas wanted privacy to write, and she wanted to be able to entertain friends without worrying about disturbing her father and stepmother. When a couple she knew named Henry and Bertha Schultz announced that they had bought a large parcel of land in Coconut Grove, she mentioned in passing that she had always wanted to live there. They offered to sell her a lot on Stuart Avenue.

Coconut Grove, one of the oldest communities in southern Florida, held a great deal of appeal for her. First and foremost, she loved the jungled look of it. "Half garden, half community. It was full of exotic fruit trees," she recalled, and it sat on what the naturalists called a native hammock: a raised area suitable for tree and jungle growth. Tropical vines and air plants grew over the limbs of the trees, and winding dirt roads passed under their canopy. The residents themselves were an assortment of Floridians old and new, many sharing a bohemian bent.

Her closest friends included a couple who would become her next-door neighbors in Coconut Grove: Franklin Harris, a retired pianist, and his wife, Alice. They in turn were great friends of the botanist David Fairchild and his wife, Marian, a daughter of Alexander Graham Bell. The Fairchilds owned a large house on a ridge overlooking Biscayne Bay, and the great inventor was a frequent houseguest there. The other Bell daughter, Elsie May, married Gilbert Hovey Grosvenor, the first full-time editor of *National Geographic* and today considered one of the fathers of photojournalism. The Grosvenors, too, owned property in Coconut Grove. David Fairchild's great benefactor, a wealthy, now elderly botanist named Barbour Lathrop, was also a regular visitor to Coconut Grove. Uncle Barbour, as Marjory called him, recognized her unique qualities immediately and insisted on taking her to dinner weekly at the McAllister Hotel whenever he was in town. "Marjory Douglas is a bounding ball of buoyant babyhood," Lathrop wrote to David Fairchild. "I am very fond of that young woman and love the way in which she smilingly faces the world." Douglas also befriended Ruth Bryan Owen, the daughter of William Jennings Bryan, and Marion Denison Whipple Deering, sister-in-law of James Deering, who built Vizcaya.

Conversations among this unconventional group of people were what steered Douglas toward a career as a conservationist. She became part of a community of like-minded writers and scientists who cared passionately about the natural wonders of Florida and who, enlightened by their experiences in government and academia, spoke out in defense of their beliefs. They also believed in the possibilities of activism. Douglas would be joining a veritable cult of conservationists. Eventually she would marry her writing activities to this new mission and find her greatest voice as both an artist and an activist. But before that transformation could happen, she would need to build her own house in Coconut Grove—a laboratory for her ideas, a place of quiet, privacy, and contemplation.

To make it possible for her to buy her plot of land, Douglas, like so many others in the boom, took out a mortgage. When the Schultzes offered to accept a second mortgage on the property so that she would have enough money to build on the lot, she leapt at the chance. "I didn't need much of a house; just a workshop, a place of my own," she recalled. "All I wanted was one big room with living quarters tacked on." She knew an architect named George Hyde, who specialized in building factories. That didn't trouble her because the house she wanted would be a kind of factory—a literary factory—and it could be simple: "stout and sparse."

The single-story bungalow that Hyde designed for her, which still stands in its original location, was half English Tudor and half Mediterranean Revival in style. Wood framed, it had white stucco walls and a mushroom-shaped shingle roof. Inside, the layout was what today would be described as open plan, with the living room opening into the kitchen area. But there would be no dishwasher, no electric stove, and no air conditioner. Nor was there a driveway, because Douglas had never learned how to drive a car, and never would. Her first contractor, whom she had paid in advance, soon went into receivership, taking her money with him. The next contractor built the bungalow in slow and careful increments, proceeding only as her magazine earnings came in. As she saw it, this was the house that the *Saturday Evening Post* built.

All across Florida and up and down both coasts, new residents were sharing in Douglas's experience of building their new homes, often purchased with a mortgage and furnished with furniture and appliances bought on installment credit. Many of these were bungalows even more modest than hers, and many of them were built on a shoestring budget, without the services of an architect. Hers was finally completed, to her enormous satisfaction and excitement, in the fall of 1926, just before she went north to visit her relatives in Taunton, Massachusetts. Finished but unfurnished, it sat unoccupied in her absence.

14

CRIME WAVES

Despite the magnitude of the real estate frenzy across Florida and despite the vast numbers of Americans building new homes there—whether they were as modest as Douglas's Coconut Grove cottage or as grand as the Mizner Palm Beach mansions—the land boom was anything but inclusive. Florida's blacks, in particular, had a difficult time participating in the new prosperity. A rare exception was one of Douglas's fellow residents in Coconut Grove, Ebenezer Woodbury Franklin Stirrup Sr. Born of mixed-race parentage in Eleuthera, the Bahamas, he had emigrated to Florida as a boy, worked as a chauffeur and carpenter for James Deering at Vizcaya, often taking land in payment for his services. He later built Bahamian-style "conch" houses for the black community and became a celebrated local millionaire—an extraordinary accomplishment in an era of profound racial discrimination. It was Stirrup who created the black community in Coconut Grove—the first all-black community in southern Florida—by cutting a route called Evangelist Street (today Charles Avenue) through Florida's jungle. Kebo, as the community was initially called in honor of a mountain in Africa, was composed almost entirely of Bahamians. Today the area is called West Grove.

Coconut Grove was unusual in having a black population that was at least partially integrated into the broader community. The early Bahamians had emigrated to help build and staff the Peacock Inn in the mid-1880s, an establishment erected by the grandparents of Eunice Peacock, the wife of George Merrick. Many of these Bahamians would go on to work for

Merrick in Coral Gables and help to build many of Miami's hotels and sky-scrapers throughout the 1920s. They, along with African Americans of the post-Reconstruction South, provided much of the labor that fueled the boom. Merrick was one of the very few who acknowledged their contribution. "I do not believe any great body of men worked more wholeheartedly at a single job than the men who have been associated with me in building our city," he said at one event, giving fair credit to his black workers.

Miami's black community, Overtown, which was laid out by Julia Tuttle and Henry Flagler in 1896, was west of the railroad tracks between NW Sixth and Twelfth Streets. By the mid-1920s, it was a bustling village containing some thirty stores and a theater called the Lyric, considered one of the most attractive and most successful black-owned theaters in the American South.

To escape the discrimination and rampant racial abuse, blacks in other parts of Florida attempted to establish their own exclusive communities, but these efforts didn't always fare well. Eatonville and Christina, for instance, succeeded in being entirely black-run towns that had their own mayors, city councils, and police chiefs. One of Eatonville's most cele-brated native-born daughters was Zora Neale Hurston, the anthropologist and author of the classic novel *Their Eyes Were Watching God*, which was published in 1937. But another black township, Rosewood, on the Gulf Coast, was the site of an infamous massacre.

The tragedy occurred in January 1923, when a white woman from a neighboring town dubiously claimed that a Rosewood man had attacked her. A large lynch mob set siege to the town, burning homes, churches, and the local school, before hunting down and shooting men, women, and children, some of whom fought back. Although reports differ, at least eight residents were confirmed dead in the slaughter. The town never re-covered. A similar event occurred in Ocoee, Florida, in 1920, when local African Americans showed up at local polling booths, intending to vote. Local whites responded by torching twenty-five homes in the black com-munity and killing as many as thirty people. And in the town of Perry, in 1922, an escaped African American convict who had murdered a white schoolteacher was subsequently burned at the stake by retaliating whites;

they also stormed the black section of the town to burn homes, a church, a school, and the local amusement center.

The rise of the Ku Klux Klan during the decade—both nationally and in Florida—made matters worse for enterprising blacks. Any hopes of transitioning from, say, carpenter to developer, as the onetime Flagler carpenter Dana A. Dorsey had done, had to be weighed carefully against the risk such a move meant for one's personal safety. Despite organizing a Colored Board of Trade in Miami at the turn of the century, African Americans were denied the opportunity to run businesses that served the white community. Few would risk crossing that so-called color line. Dorsey, Miami's first black millionaire, did what he could in light of the restrictions: he created the first hotel for blacks (the Dorsey Hotel), and the first bank (the Negro Savings Bank), as well as a public park open to blacks. He later gave land to the city so that schools for black children could be built. At one point, he owned twenty-one acres on the barrier island today known as Fisher Island, which he sold to Carl Fisher in 1919 for $100,000. By 2018, this had become the wealthiest zip code in the country.

The KKK was an ominous presence. On the night of June 29, 1920, members of the Klan tossed two lit sticks of dynamite into the center of Colored Town in Miami, destroying a pair of buildings and nearly inciting a riot. The perpetrators were never identified. The following year, the KKK organized a major parade down Flagler Street. Other Klan scare parades in Miami and elsewhere were designed to discourage blacks from voting. Black dummies clad in T-shirts that read, "This Nigger Voted," were hung in effigy from telephone poles as a warning. When, in the fall of 1925, the Miami Police Department found itself understaffed because so many of its officers had left the force to become real estate brokers, the Klan offered to step in to ensure law and order, insisting that it had done something similar in St. Petersburg, with salubrious results. The Miami town fathers politely declined the offer. When a crippled white minister from the Bahamas began preaching at Miami's sole black Episcopal church, he was tarred and feathered by the Klan and released on Flagler Street. Although he nearly died as a consequence of his ordeal, neither of the Miami papers reported the incident.

Throughout the decade, segregation became more rigorously applied, which led to a marked deterioration in work and living conditions for blacks in Coconut Grove and in Miami's Overtown. The bigotry, of course, had been there since the arrival of Flagler's railroad and the early construction of Fisher's Miami Beach, but according to Dr. Samuel Hensdale Johnson, Miami's first black radiologist, who grew up there, "As the town developed, the lines were drawn fast. We became hemmed in. Miami really became a hellhole."

The living conditions of the "crackers"—the poor whites who lived in and around the Everglades—were somewhat better than those of the blacks during the boom, but they were still deplorable. Most of the men worked at menial agricultural or construction jobs, and saw few chances for advancement. It is hardly surprising that crime among this cohort began to rise as they saw themselves left behind during the Roaring Twenties. One of the most notorious gangs of the decade was the Ashley gang, headquartered in the Everglades near Gomez, Florida.

In September 1924 their leader, a cracker named John Ashley, led the robbery of the Bank of Pompano. It occurred on a windy afternoon just as the cashier, C. H. Cates, and the teller, T. H. Myers, the only two employees on duty, were preparing to close the tills and lock the safe after an uneventful day of work. Suddenly the bank's front door swung open, and in walked three armed members of the Ashley gang, not bothering to wear masks to disguise their faces.

John Ashley held a tommy gun at the ready. Ray "Shorty" Lynn and Clarence Middleton, both ex-convicts, carried .45-caliber handguns. While Ashley announced the stickup and ordered the two bank employees to raise their arms in the air, Lynn and Middleton pillaged the open vault and the teller's trays, netting $23,000 in cash and securities. Minutes later, the men fled the building and drove out of town in a stolen taxi, their loot wrapped in a bedsheet. Ashley waved the bundle out the window at E. E. "Gene" Hardy, a friend of the Ashley family and the owner of the filling station on the corner. "We got it all, Gene!" he shouted gleefully. The robbers gunned the taxi onto the Dixie Highway and made a successful getaway.

The gang had been the scourge of South Florida law enforcement for thirteen years—ever since John Ashley murdered a trapper named De Soto Tiger for his pelts in 1911 and sold them for $1,200 in Miami. The gang stole cars, robbed stores as well as banks, and hijacked boats loaded with bootleg liquor. Once, they ordered a handful of diamond engagement rings from a jeweler in New York to be paid for cash on delivery in Florida. When the notice arrived that the rings were waiting at the local railroad Express agency, the gang broke into the office at night and stole the shipment.

Ashley himself had been in and out of Raiford Prison on three occasions. Twice he managed to escape—once by fleeing from a work crew and once by bribing a guard. He had lost an eye during a bank heist in Stuart, Florida, when, during the getaway, one of his accomplices fired a shot out of the rear of their car that ricocheted off a window frame into his cheek. One of his four brothers, Bob, had been shot dead while attempting to free John from a Miami jail in 1915, but not before returning fire and killing a policeman. Two other brothers had died mysteriously during a rum-running trip to Grand Bahama Island. Ashley's father, Joe, had been shot to death seven months earlier when a group of police deputies launched a dawn raid on the Ashley tent camp in Gomez. On that occasion, the Ashley family's dog, Old Bob, had spotted the deputies creeping through the tropical underbrush and begun barking, which precipitated a wild shootout in which the dog was killed. John Ashley grabbed his rifle and took cover behind a forked tree from which he could return fire. Detecting movement behind a nearby palmetto, he took careful aim, fired, and a deputy sheriff named Fred Baker fell out of the shrubbery, a bullet through his forehead. "I knew I had killed a man," Ashley told a reporter later. He ran into his father's tent and there found the old man on the bed, dying. He had been shot while tying his shoelaces. "Poor old Dad," Ashley recalled, "he never stood a chance."

Moments later, Ashley's girlfriend, Laura Upthegrove, was hit with buckshot in the thigh and began screaming. In the ensuing chaos, Ashley escaped into the swamp. He managed to elude a manhunt that lasted for two weeks, until he successfully fled the state. He took refuge in California for a few months but now was back in Florida, once again robbing banks and frustrating the police.

Sheriff R. C. "Bob" Baker led the Palm Beach County police force, just as his father had before him. The feud between Ashley and Baker had long ago turned deeply personal. Baker was promising that he would one day wear Ashley's glass eye on his watch chain. Ashley reciprocated the sentiment by leaving behind a rifle bullet at the Pompano bank robbery with instructions for it to be handed over to the sheriff. The message was clear: Ashley had one just like it for the sheriff if he dared to come after him. "This bunch of desperadoes cost me many thousands of dollars and many restless nights, but after they sent me the message with the bullet, I was determined to get them if they stayed in my jurisdiction," said Baker.

A few weeks after the Pompano bank heist, Baker and his deputies nearly caught the gang leaving the St. Lucie inlet on their way to Bimini islands, but Ashley and his cohorts caught wind of the ambush and again managed to elude the sheriff. In Bimini, the gang raided and ransacked a group of waterfront warehouses in retaliation for being sold a stash of three-gallon jugs of rum that turned out to contain nothing but water. They came away with $8,000 in cash.

Finally, on the morning of November 1, 1924, Sheriff Baker learned from an informant that the Ashley gang planned to drive north that night through Fort Pierce on the Dixie Highway. Baker, who had a reelection campaign speech to make that evening, sent three of his deputies to form a roadblock with the help of St. Lucie County sheriff J. R. Merritt, a tobacco-chewing, Stetson-wearing lawman with a well-earned reputation for brutality. At nightfall, the four men blockaded the local bridge using a heavy chain from which they hung a lit red lantern. Then they settled back in their cars to wait.

Spies brought reports to Sheriff Merritt that the gang had been seen in Fort Pierce, where they had stopped for haircuts and then stayed on to shoot pool in a local billiard hall. Merritt and his men waited some more. Then at ten forty-five at night, a black touring car arrived at the bridge and rumbled across until it reached the roadblock, where it was forced to a stop. The four police officers, armed with sawed-off shotguns, quickly surrounded the car. They ordered the four occupants to step out of the vehicle.

One by one, John Ashley, Lynn, Middleton, and Ashley's seventeen-year-old nephew Hanford Mobley emerged from the car with their hands raised. What happened next remains unclear. According to Sheriff Merritt's sketchy report, he returned to his squad car to fetch four pairs of handcuffs, and while he did so, John Ashley allegedly made a move for a hidden pistol. Shotgun fire exploded. Moments later, the four gang members lay dead on the bridge.

But precisely what had precipitated the shooting soon became shrouded in controversy. Two passersby insisted they had seen all four men alive, standing lined up in the headlights of a car, shackled in handcuffs. A worker at W. I. Fee Hardware and Mortuary claimed he had seen the bodies arrive at the morgue that night, "stacked in the car like cordwood," as he described it—and all four wore handcuffs. Had John Ashley actually attempted to escape? Or had he and the others been executed after they were handcuffed, while the sheriff looked away, perhaps in revenge for the death of deputy sheriff Fred Baker? The latter seemed the more likely scenario.

Letters and telegrams of thanks and commendations flowed in to Sheriff Merritt and the other men for solving this nagging public relations problem. One came from George Merrick of Coral Gables, who hinted at future political patronage for the sheriff, "Good boy. After my good friend Bingham of Palm Beach serves the coming term, it's Merritt next." Two local banks sent in checks totaling $325 to be divided among the policemen in appreciation of their services.

It is hardly surprising that the Pompano bank robbery was what galvanized law enforcement and other local authorities into eliminating the Ashley gang. Bank heists were especially bad news for the real estate business. Real estate sales depended on the confidence of consumers in general, and on their confidence in the local banks in particular.

Other kinds of crimes were actually beneficial to the real estate boom. Chief among these was the illicit liquor trade. Widespread rum-running (the illegal importation of various spirits, not just rum) and bootlegging (the sale of liquor home brewed in secret stills) began within weeks of the passage of the Volstead Act. Familiar imported brands of booze such as Caribbean rum, Scotch whisky, and English gin, although more expensive, were always favored over the potentially dangerous home-brewed varieties that were often little more than flavored grain alcohol, and that meant much of the smuggling had to occur across borders. Most illegal liquor entered the United States on the four hundred or so roads that linked America to Canada. But regular shipments also crossed the Great Lakes, the Saint Lawrence River, and by sea from Newfoundland to Boston, or from Bimini, Gun Cay, Grand Bahama Island, and Cuba to Florida and New Orleans. Some of the booze was flown in by plane. To service the bigger markets of New York, Miami, and New Orleans, smugglers formed what came to be called the Rum Rows, or Rum Lines: flotillas of schooners that rendezvoused off the coast, weighed down with cases of top-shelf liquor and barrels of rum. The hooch was then transferred to smaller, faster vessels that could race the booze ashore under cover of darkness. To lure these vessels and their risk-taking smugglers into doing business with them, the ships of the Rum Rows contained onboard brothels and gambling dens for the visiting crews.

In the early years of Prohibition, the business was so entrepreneurial, and there existed so few of the proverbial barriers to entry, that almost anyone with a boat seaworthy enough to make the fifty-mile trip to Bimini could enter the trade. Bootleggers such as Bill McCoy, Gertrude Lythgoe (aka "the Bahama Queen"), Marie Waite ("Spanish Marie"), and James Horace Alderman ("the Gulf Stream Pirate") became household names across the country. Carl Fisher, never averse to a little adventure, did some rum-running himself and had the speedboats to do so. He had a personal account set up in Nassau in his name and kept a standing order for ten cases of Usher's Green Stripe Blended Scotch Whisky on his boat, the *Shadow K*, for any stops the boat might make on the British protectorates of Bimini, Gun Cay, and Grand Bahama Island, where warehouses were set up on the beach to store the stacks of wooden liquor cases bound for Florida. The average annual import of liquor from the United Kingdom into the Bahamas soared from 50,000 gallons before Prohibition to 1.2 million by 1922, most of it bound for Florida.

The business was highly profitable. A case of Scotch acquired for $25 from a Rum Row or on Bimini or Nassau could be sold to a hotel in Miami for $40 or directly to the tourist trade for $100 to $125. Often six quarts were squeezed into a hessian burlap sack full of straw known as a *ham* or *burlock*, which was easy to stack and to unload and would float if thrown overboard—unless rock salt was added to the package, which would cause it to sink temporarily. When the salt dissolved sometime later, the sack of contraband would bob back to the surface.

The Coast Guard, formed in 1915 and since 1919 under the jurisdiction of the Treasury Department, was initially ill-equipped to respond to this burgeoning and wildly profitable trade, all of it unregulated, lawless, and highly dangerous—dangerous because there was always the threat of the illegal booty being hijacked at sea or onshore by gangs such as the Ashley crew. It was also logistically difficult to halt the trade, because as author Kenneth Roberts remarked, "It would be as easy to catch a rumrunner among the Florida Keys as to locate a red ant in the Hippodrome."

However, by the middle of the decade, the Coast Guard began to make inroads against the rumrunners, thanks to an $11 million appropriation by Congress for vessels and equipment, and thanks to the diligence of a newly appointed US assistant attorney general named Mabel Walker Willebrandt, whose department prosecuted some 48,734 Volstead Act cases and won 39,072 convictions. She organized a major offense against rumrunners along the East Coast in May 1925, using a vastly expanded fleet of destroyers, patrol boats, picketboats, cutters, and seaplanes. Eventually she disrupted New York's Rum Row, scattering the fifty or so participating vessels. In a number of cases, the Coast Guard traded gunfire with the smugglers, confiscated their shipments, and sank their vessels.

She then moved the fleet south to attempt to replicate her success off the coast of Florida, using a Coast Guard station set up at Fort Lauderdale as the center of operations. This unpopular initiative, which lasted only

a single season, was denounced by the local press and by the resort hotels, which feared the tourists would flee Florida for the Bahamas or Cuba,
where liquor flowed freely and legally. In response to the beefed-up Coast
Guard presence, the price for running a liquor shipment ashore rose from
$50 to $150; the cost of each case on board soared from $35 to $125.

One day the new anti-rum-running initiative led to a shootout in
the waters directly in front of the Flamingo Hotel when Carl Fisher was
present. A famed bootlegger name E. W. "Red" Shannon, fleeing from a
Coast Guard cutter in his motorboat, was machine-gunned down while
at the wheel of his skiff—and mortally wounded in plain view of a crowd
of astonished hotel guests attending a tea dance. Shannon's bleeding body
was brought ashore at the hotel dock, laid out on a hotel mattress, and
then raced to the local hospital, although not in time to save him. Fisher,
who bought all his hotel liquor from Shannon, was outraged by what he
saw, and when a Miami judge indicted the culpable Coast Guard officers
for manslaughter, Fisher testified against them at the trial. The officers
were acquitted. And yet, despite the stepped-up law enforcement, massive
amounts of booze, and the profits from it, still found their way ashore, and
continued to arrive until Prohibition was finally overturned by Congress
with ratification of the Twenty-first Amendment in December 1933.

Throughout the decade, the profits from liquor sales helped fuel Florida's real estate boom. All of the hotels and restaurants at the nascent clubs
and resorts used alcohol to lure patrons—who could then be sold on the
virtues of owning land in Florida. Invariably, these potential buyers were
reminded in nearly every sales pitch that Florida was one of the few places
in the country where the Volstead Act was largely ignored by the state and
local authorities. And, then, as now, real estate was a favored way to laun-
der illicit profits.

Liquor also financed and propelled Florida's celebrated nightlife. One
example was a supper club and casino called Club Unique (later Cap's
Place) near Pompano Beach, founded late in the decade by retired rumrunners Captain "Cap" Theodore Knight, his wife, Lola, and their colleague Albert Hasis. Built out of a large barge that was purchased for $100,
towed ashore, and retrofitted, the popular restaurant was accessible only

by launch from a small hidden parking lot along the coast. The club served superb food such as turtle steaks, hearts of palm salad made from sabal palm trees, turtle egg pancakes, and various seafood delicacies. A 25-cent private membership bought members the opportunity to play dice games, roulette, poker, and baccarat. The club attracted notables over the years, among them Franklin D. Roosevelt, the Prince of Wales, Winston Churchill, various Rockefellers and Vanderbilts, baseball player Casey Stengel, actress Gloria Swanson, actor Errol Flynn, and mobsters Meyer Lansky and Al Capone.

Nightclubs of all kinds sprang up in every community, many as a way to sell illicit liquor. As was true in New York City, it was difficult to determine accurately the legality of these clubs because, as the summary of one investigation reported, "they shade up into the realm of the respectable cabaret, and they shade down to the prostitution dive, with many on the borderline."

Gambling also flourished in the Sunshine State, immeasurably increasing its allure as a vacation, second-home, or retirement destination. Gambling at clubs and casinos was actually permitted, or at least tolerated, for nonresidents. Illicit gambling naturally gravitated to Miami's racetracks, both the horse track and the dog track (greyhound racing). The game of jai alai, played at the Hialeah Fronton, became a popular betting venue as well. The quick profits made from land sales in turn spurred more gambling and more rum-running, which in turn spurred more land sales, leading to what might be called a *virtueless* cycle. Florida was becoming a trendsetter of the sort that Las Vegas is today: a gaudy, rowdy, gambling mecca where anything goes.

But the proliferation of rum-running and gambling also had its downside. They soon attracted a new and more dangerous criminal element: organized crime. The most high-profile example of this was Al Capone's appearance in Florida and his purchase, late in the decade, of a waterfront property and house on the eighty-two-acre Palm Island, a man-made island off the County Causeway between Miami and Miami Beach. Capone paid $40,000 for the property in 1928 and spent another $100,000 to add a swimming pool, a boathouse, a dock, and furnishings for the house, rumored to have such amenities as gold-plated faucets in the ground-floor powder room. He enclosed the property within high concrete walls and heavy iron gates.

Six feet tall and weighing 240 pounds, the gangster dressed immaculately when he went out on the town, favoring a dark blue double-breasted-suit adorned with a white linen pocket square and a matching polka dot necktie. He wore a gold and diamond studded watch chain that he had a habit of fiddling with, and, on one pinky finger, a four-carat diamond ring in a platinum setting. Frank J. Wilson, the United States Secret Service agent who finally brought him down—by convicting him for tax evasion—recalled Big Al having dark eyes, thick lips, perfect teeth, "a big flabby paw and dainty manicured nails." A six-inch scar from a knife fight in a bar ran down his left cheek. When the mobster pulled out a silk handkerchief, Wilson got a strong whiff of his cologne: lily of the valley.

Capone, whose first job for the Chicago underworld was providing towels for prostitutes at the Four Deuces brothel on the South Side (2222 S. Wabash Avenue), had risen through the ranks of hit men to become ruler of Chicago's largest crime syndicate. By the time Scarface, or Snorky, as he was known to his friends, arrived in Miami, he was estimated to be grossing $75 million a year from illicit liquor sales, gambling, and prostitution and to have a net worth approaching $100 million. He had complete control over the beer business in Chicago, brewed locally, but he also smuggled in hard liquor through Detroit, New York, New Orleans, and Florida. Mobsters like Capone saw Florida rum-running as a lucrative opportunity, and, using fear and intimidation, they eventually appropriated the lion's share of the trade for themselves and extorted 10 percent to 12 percent of the proceeds from any smaller businesses that they didn't control.

Like others in Miami and Miami Beach, Carl Fisher objected to Capone's house purchase on the grounds that the gangster's presence might hurt real estate sales. The irony here was rich: the two cities had earned their notoriety in part for their lack of liquor enforcement—and yet now they were protesting the fact that they had attracted the country's most notorious bootlegger. In fact, Capone's arrival was the natural outgrowth of the loose morals and petty crime the developers had allowed—and even promoted.

A notorious killer, Capone was directly or indirectly responsible for at least two hundred murders during the decade, a figure that includes the seven men he allegedly had machine-gunned to death in a Lincoln Park garage on Saint Valentine's Day and three others he allegedly nearly beat to death with a baseball bat—before ordering their execution. When the city of Miami brought suit against the mobster, claiming his residence was "a harbor for criminals, crooks, gangsters, racketeers, and fugitives from justice," Fisher courageously took the stand and testified against Capone, although this testimony and the lawsuit itself failed to revoke his right to domicile in Miami. Fisher was also behind the arrest of Capone's brother Albert for vagrancy.

Then suddenly Miami Beach ceased its objections to Capone's presence. The mayor at the time, J. N. Lummus, who along with his brother was one of the earliest land owners and developers on the Beach, was an early vocal critic of the gangster's arrival, but now began defending Capone's right to live wherever he wanted. A suspicious local reporter for the *Miami Daily News* discovered that Lummus had been the buyer's agent of record when Capone bought his Palm Island house. When confronted with this awkward fact, Lummus defended his action, insisting that gangster seemed to be a better citizen than a lot of the folks living in the area—a perfect illustration of the corrupting conflicts of interest now rampant across Florida.

Despite the attempts to discourage him, Capone kept his property, which was held in his wife's name. Before long, he owned interests or controlling interests in the Villa Venice nightclub, the Palm Island Club, and the Fleetwood Hangar Room, and was cultivating friendships with other local politicians and the police, much as he had done so effectively in Chicago. Everywhere he went, he left huge tips and smiled broadly for the cameras. Crime, the provenance of small-time hoods and miscreants like the Ashley gang, had become professionalized and institutionalized, no thanks to Florida's loose morals and the laissez-faire attitudes of developers who had put the new paradise on the map.

15

"A PARADE OF PINK ELEPHANTS AND GREEN MONKEYS"

Easy money, whether legal or illegal, fuels every investment boom. One of the most important sources of cash throughout Florida's frenzy was an "accommodative" Federal Reserve. The Fed lowered its key lending rate, the fed funds rate (the rate at which the Fed lends to other banks), from 4.5 percent in 1920 to 3.0 percent in 1922 and then raised it again, but only modestly, to 3.5 percent in 1925. From then on, the central bank let the US economy roar.

As money poured into the state, deposits in Florida banks spiked from $180 million in 1922 to $875 million in 1925. One bank, the Commercial Bank and Trust Company of Miami, saw its deposits jump from $850,000 to more than $15 million in one year. The drain of deposits out of northern banks grew alarming—to them—as the money accompanied the investors south to Florida, at one point streaming into the state at a rate of $37 million a month. The Massachusetts Savings Bank League reported that a hundred thousand accounts in the state had been drawn upon to buy real estate in Florida, taking with them $20 million in deposits. Savannah reported that twenty thousand of its citizens had decamped for Florida, taking their money with them. Banks in a number of states launched advertising campaigns that warned their depositors against investing in the boom. In Ohio, the state legislature passed "blue sky" laws preventing Florida real estate firms from obtaining licenses to operate there and preventing buyers from acquiring Florida land sight unseen, all in an effort to halt the outflow of bank funds.

Money was cheap, and lending standards were lax. In many cases, the bankers, who were often part-time developers as well, were lending to themselves and to their own projects. Politics, too, of course, entered into the equation. From 1921 through 1925, the entire Miami City Commission was made up of local bankers. The mayor of Miami was Edward C. Romfh, president of the First National Bank. The governor of the state during this period was Carey A. Hardee, president of the First National Bank of Live Oak. Hardee was a staunch supporter of the banking fraternity and urged other bankers to play roles in state and national government. In short, the bankers were in charge—and that was not a good thing. The potential, and then the reality, of self-dealing grew exponentially as the decade progressed. As we shall see, the corruption would reach all the way to the office of the vice president of the United States and soon contributed to a cascade of bank failures: 117 in Florida and Georgia in one ten-day period in late 1926. In fact, according to banking historian Raymond B. Vickers, 90 percent of the Florida banks that failed were guilty of self-dealing or outright fraud by insiders. Vickers, who studied bank records from the period that had been sealed for sixty-three years, concluded: "The sad story told by these records is that insiders looted the banks they pledged to protect. They tried to get rich by wildly speculating with depositors' money, and when their schemes failed, so did their banks."

So, one didn't need to belong to the Ashley gang to rob a Florida bank in the 1920s. There were white-collar methods of theft that were equally effective and far less likely to be detected or prosecuted.

Politicians throughout the country would become remarkably accommodating to real estate development and business in general during the decade. At the national level, President Warren Harding died in office on August 2, 1923, while in San Francisco on a California speaking trip, putting Vice President Calvin Coolidge in the White House. Coolidge's subsequent election on November 4, 1924, with a huge Republican majority, further boosted business confidence.

In Florida, John W. Martin, a lawyer and former three-time mayor of Jacksonville, was elected governor on his promise to build more highways, which were a boon to real estate development. But there was also a legitimate need to vastly expand and improve what roads were there. The *Miami Herald* complained that parts of the Dixie Highway "are paved only with good intentions." A few months later, Martin kept his word by firing the two heads of the Florida State Road Department for "incompetency and neglect of duty," informing them that they were "not in sympathy with this administration and its determination to take Florida out of the sand and the mud and put her people on paved highways."

Perhaps the greatest contribution to the boom by Florida's politicians was the change made to Florida's constitution in 1924 that abolished the state's income tax and inheritance tax. Florida was the first state in the nation to do so. The move was designed to tempt wealthy residents of other states to move their domiciles to Florida. It worked: Florida went from being an attractive vacation venue to an alluring tax haven overnight.

Attitudes toward money in a financial boom can be every bit as important as legislation, interest rate levels, and bank lending standards. If money looks easy to make, then it isn't long before everybody wants his or her chance to make it. T. H. Weigall's belated deal at Coral Gables was just one example of literally millions of transactions that took place in Florida by investors from all over the country during 1925, many of them buying their property sight unseen. As Gertrude Matthews Shelby, the writer for *Harper's Monthly*, put it in early 1926: "The smell of money in Florida, which attracts men as the smell of blood attracts a wild animal, became ripe and strong last spring. The whole United States began to catch whiffs of it. Pungent tales of immense quick wealth carried far."

Among those attracted by the smell were various fraudsters, the most notorious of whom was Charles Ponzi, who arrived in September 1925. He had recently served a five-year sentence on federal charges of mail fraud for his infamous pyramid scheme using international reply coupons (IRCs), only to be reconvicted on larceny charges in Massachusetts on his release. Out on bail while he appealed the state conviction, he launched a scam in Florida called the Charpon Land Syndicate. The plan laid out in a slick brochure was the sale of ten million small building lots at a development near Jacksonville. In fact, they were located on worthless swampland sixty-five miles inland.

Ponzi offered twenty-tree tiny lots per acre at $10 apiece ($230 for an entire acre) through the mail, as well as partial interests in the parent company via "unit certificate of indebtedness." To sweeten the offer, he promised investors that they would receive a 200 percent return in just sixty days. Then he sat back and waited to collect the money that soon began to flow in.

The following February, Ponzi was indicted for operating without a license. In April he was convicted for a handful of violations of Florida land statutes. At this point, he faked suicide, shaved his head, grew a mustache, and donned a sailor's cap. Using an alias, he signed on to a Tampa freighter bound for Houston, working as a waiter and dishwasher. Ponzi managed to elude a multistate manhunt until he boastfully revealed his identity to a shipmate, which led to his arrest on board the ship when it stopped at New Orleans. He spent the next seven years in a Massachusetts prison sewing underwear. Released in 1934, he was extradited to his native Italy. Ponzi was unrepentant regarding this and his other schemes, proclaiming that he had given investors "the best show that was ever staged in their territory since the landing of the Pilgrims! It was easily worth fifteen million bucks to watch me put the thing over."

Ponzi was hardly alone in exploiting gullible investors, particularly those from out of state. Similar by-mail schemes were concocted for, among others, Manhattan Estates, which was essentially a deserted turpentine camp in northern Florida, and for a collection of developments called Melbourne Gardens, Melbourne Manor, and Melbourne Heights in Brevard County. The Melbourne sites were located in Everglades muck three miles from the nearest access road.

No one knows how much money rushed into Florida during the boom, in part because real estate firms and their nascent associations kept few records. Much of the funds came from Wall Street investors looking for alternatives to expensive stocks and bonds. The stock market, too, had been performing well, doubling from its low in July 1921, although there was a brief hiccup in November 1925, after which the market resumed an upward trajectory that would see prices more than double again from year-end 1925 to September 1929. For a time, though, Florida was the preferable investment vehicle. You could put your money in stocks, but everyone knew that the market could go down as well as up. Florida real estate could only go up, it seemed.

By the midtwenties, Wall Street was forming syndicates on a near daily basis to pool money for new Florida developments or to take shares in existing ones. But even more money came from small towns and cities around the country, where once prudent citizens suddenly began to buy Florida lots and houses. New England and Ohio saw particularly large and alarming transfers out of their banks. Some estimates put the amount of money flowing into Florida investments at more than $1 billion in 1925 alone, and that number is likely low. Carl Fisher's wife, Jane, may have described the frenzy best: "all Florida was like a mighty vacuum sucking in all the loose money in the world."

Perhaps the surest indication that the boom had reached its speculative-excess stage was the arrival in Miami, St. Petersburg, and elsewhere of the so-called binder (pronounced like cinder) boys. These were a new breed of white-knickers-wearing salesmen, mostly from New York City, who arrived determined to make quick money despite possessing very little capital of their own. They exploited the delays in the state's deed and title recording and transfer system at the swamped county courthouses. They did so by drawing up contracts, or binders, on the purchase of real estate that required as little as a 10 percent down payment and that could be traded before the deeds on the transaction were registered some thirty to ninety days later. Only when a transaction was finally recorded at a courthouse did the larger down payment come due, usually 25 percent of the purchase price with the balance to be paid over a period of one, two, or three years. In the interim weeks before that closing, the binder could be sold and resold, adding fuel to the speculative fires.

The binder boys sold binders on the streets and at the train stations, or swapped them among themselves, creating a new curb market in local real estate. As Mark S. Foster writes in *Castles in the Sand*, "They trafficked in human greed." They were, in effect, trading in options, a highly speculative activity that gave the investor—even one with only a small initial investment—the opportunity to reap massive returns, assuming he bet correctly on the direction of the prices. At this time, there was only one direction to bet on, and that was upward.

The binder boys crammed into the cheaper hotels and rooming houses in Miami and on Miami Beach, sleeping three or four to a room. A binder could trade numerous times—some as many as eight times in a single day—before the deeds associated with them were finally registered. The various obligations associated with each binder clung to the transaction "like ticks to a cow," quipped Miami journalist Kenneth Ballinger. Even the legitimate promoters, who disparaged the binder boys, offered "resale" services for lots bought for a quick profit. And they often hired unlicensed workers, so-called bird dogs, to find leads among the disembarking tourists at the railroad stations and on the streets, and steer them to the offices where expert "closers" could conclude the deal.

Florida lots were being purchased now in real estate offices around the country, from elaborate plat maps and blueprints, by buyers who had never set foot in Florida. The maps and drawings of these burgeoning developments gave the buyers dramatic, enticing—and often fictional—overviews of each project. Subdivisions sold out on their first day of sale. In cities such as Miami, real estate agents were being hired at such a rapid clip that there simply wasn't room for them all. Porches were enclosed, basements cleared, and every square foot of existing floor space was repurposed into sales offices.

One tract bought for $775,000 was parceled up and sold a month later for $1.5 million. Prices per square foot of residential real estate in downtown Miami now rivaled what was paid in the better neighborhoods of Manhattan. Retail rents were even worse: a store brought in an average rental of $30,000 at a time when comparable properties along Broadway in Midtown Manhattan rented for $5,000 or less. The Florida banks by now were routinely, and recklessly, lending to builders or investors as much as 80 percent of the value of the raw land purchased. A bungalow could be built for $7,000 and sold for $20,000 the day it was completed. A leading Miami contractor named John Orr, who was badly overcommitted, turned down new building contracts totaling $5 million in one month toward the end of 1925.

Following suit, the real estate advertisements grew preposterously exaggerated, if not outright fraudulent, in their claims. One billboard proclaimed, "Fifteen-Story Fleetwood Hotel Is Making Money for Investors at Daytona Shores." There was no such hotel, and never would be. Drainage ditches were often depicted as Venetian canals.

All of this real estate advertising, whether hyped or not, was wonderful for the newspaper business. The *Miami Herald* was racking up records for the amount of paid advertising it sold. By November, it had run 34.1 million lines of advertising, easily surpassing (by 3.5 million lines) the record set by the *Detroit News* for all of 1924. By year-end, the newspaper could take credit for publishing an astonishing 674,738 separate classified ads.

When a statewide railroad embargo took hold on October 29, 1925, in response to the overwhelming influx of building materials headed for South Florida, prices of consumer staples soared. The cost of a cup of coffee nearly doubled to 25 cents; a breakfast of two eggs sold for 75 cents. Room rents in boardinghouses and homes spiked to $15 a night ($214 in today's money). The cost of a shave in a barbershop went from 10 cents to 25 cents, while the cost of a haircut rose from 40 cents to 65 cents. Long lines formed at restaurants.

The pandemonium had reached its crescendo. To those paying close attention, one sale in August 1925 should have stood out as a warning. A lot on Miami Beach sold for $7,000 early in the month but was quickly bid up in a series of binder transactions to $50,000. However, the transaction didn't close at that price. The binder owner at that price chose to walk away from his deposit, somewhat shockingly allowing the property to revert to the depositor below, also without being sold, and then to the binder holder below him. At last, a binder holder stepped up and closed the sale, but at a surprisingly low price: $25,000, half of what had been agreed to. This was something new. The first small crack in the giant edifice of the boom had appeared.

There was another disturbing development. In August the Internal Revenue Service declared that federal taxes must be paid on the entire sale price of a property and not just on the actual amount of the sales collected, despite the fact that most contracts allowed for payments for purchases to be made over three or four years. In other words, the full sale price had to be declared as income, not just the first 25 percent, which is what most buyers expected. This new edict had the potential to slam developers and speculators alike when the taxes came due on March 15 of the following year. The new ruling was rescinded within a year, but psychological damage had been done.

At this point, the national media became more openly critical of the rampant speculation in Florida. *Forbes* magazine, in a scolding October 1925 article titled "Even Florida Is Not Fool-Proof," gave one of the sternest warnings: "Florida has made money for those who had money, and is making money for those who have money. But victims of the get-rich-quick mania who are sending money to Florida or going to Florida to buy lots in expectation of reselling them overnight at a dazzling profit will be disappointed. Brains, effort, and foresight have yielded, and are yielding, many fortunes in Florida, but blind speculation is little likely to reap anything but loss and sorrow. Investigate before you invest.... Even the stock market has not boiled as violently as the land boom. Watch your step!" Oscar H. Smith, commissioner of the Minnesota State Board of Immigration, went a step further when he wrote in *Immigration Bulletin* in October, "When this boom busts, which it will just as sure as the sun shines, it will result in a crash the likes of which has never before been experienced in this country."

Even the nation's stand-up comics had picked up on the controversy surrounding the boom and began to feature it in their acts. Milton Berle, for example, quipped, "I just got wonderful news from my real estate agent in Florida. They found land on my property." On December 25 the Marx Brothers' comedy *The Cocoanuts* opened on Broadway, songs and lyrics by none other than the Palm Beach regular Irving Berlin, with a libretto by George S. Kaufman. In one scene, Groucho pitches a group of tourists on Florida real estate: "You can have any kind of a home you want. You can even get stucco. Oh, how you can get stuck-oh!" The play was a hit and four years later was released as a *musical* feature film.

George Merrick responded to the new skepticism by authoring a piece for the *New York Times* that extolled the unique virtues of South Florida and its bright future. "Miami never had a boom and is not having a boom now. The lure of the tropics is a great and a definite thing alone to build upon," he opined. "The Miami area and thence on south to Cape Sable (all of which is tributary to Miami) comprises absolutely the only American tropics, and in that great fact Miami owns and will forever hold a priceless American monopoly."

Addison Mizner, now a presumed authority on the subject, spoke out during a business trip to New York in September 1925: "There is much talk about the Florida 'boom,' but so far as I can see, there is no 'boom.' Land values are mounting steadily, and large fortunes are being made exactly as they have been in Los Angeles and New York. Property bought now will increase in value as improvements are made. There is nothing artificial about it." D. P. Davis echoed his colleagues' optimism, telling a local paper: "I regard the prices at which lots have been and are being sold in the better class of developments as being generally far below actual values. So buy up!"

But famed Washington correspondent Jesse Frederick Essary, president of the Gridiron Club, summed up the emerging problem in an article that appeared in the *New Republic*, also in October, by pointing out that there were five hundred thousand home-site lots for sale or sold between Miami and West Palm Beach alone, and how it would require a population of three million people—the entire population of Chicago—to build houses on them to fill them all. He was dumbfounded: "Where, in the name of high heaven, are they to come from? What are they to do, once they arrive? How are they to make a living, with the Everglades behind them and the Atlantic Ocean in front? How will food and clothing and fuel and the rest of it be transported to them? How will they all get there? These questions can be multiplied indefinitely. There is no answer, except that no such number is coming."

Florida's developers and promoters grew alarmed by the succession of damning articles and by what they termed "northern propaganda." Increasingly concerned that the entire boom would be tarred with this same negative brush, damaging the state and its reputation, to say nothing of its business prospects, a group of them decided to counterpunch, and quickly. They organized a press conference in New York City to dispel all the myths about the boom. The event, called "The Truth About Florida," was held on October 9 at the old and celebrated Waldorf-Astoria Hotel, owned now by Delaware senator T. Coleman du Pont, a former president of the du Pont Chemical Company, who, by no coincidence, was a significant investor in the Florida boom.

Among the thirty luminaries from the Florida delegation was Paris Singer, who had kicked off the great Florida frenzy with his private Everglades Club in Palm Beach. He was now planning a development north of Palm Beach to be called Palm Beach Ocean, which would feature a huge Mizner-designed hotel called the Blue Heron. Also in attendance was John Martin, the governor recently elected on a pro-business and pro-road-building platform; Herman A. Dann, president of the Florida Chamber of Commerce; the developers George Merrick, Barron G. Collier, George Sebring, Joseph Young (of Hollywood-by-the-Sea), and N. B. T. Roney; the bankers G. G. Ware and Joe H. Scales; and the publishers Frank B. Shutts of the *Miami Herald* and John H. Perry of the *Jacksonville Journal*. These were the very men who were most culpable in creating the speculative boom in the first place, a boom that they now insisted didn't exist.

At the press conference, the governor and others vowed to do everything in their power to halt the swindlers and to curb the fraudulent advertising. All they asked for in return was that the national press act responsibly in its reporting and merely tell the truth about what was happening in the state, and, above all, not to simply accept the negative or "bear case"—or what today might be called "fake news"—when it came to Florida's real estate boom.

The journalist Kenneth Ballinger, covering the event for the *Miami Herald*, dutifully listened and took notes as "splendid, convincing speeches" were made. Later, he reported that "Florida today made her appeal for truth in advertising in the very heart of the nation's publishing center, an appeal designed to still the propaganda that is being circulated to the detriment of the state." The irony was not lost on him that it was the propagandists who were the ones now complaining the most vociferously about what they perceived to be negative propaganda. As he observed drolly, "the nation by late 1925 was somewhat cockeyed from trying to follow the kaleidoscopic

[Florida] whirl that looked from a distance not unlike a parade of pink elephants and green monkeys."

Five days later, the *New York Times* weighed in on the event in an editorial entitled "Floridians Getting Uneasy," which picked up on the angst that was evident in the room. The editorial defended "the missioners who assumed the task of uttering timely words of warning," pointing out that while they might not endear themselves to all their fellow citizens, "they will have the approval of the wiser ones among them." Even a few of the delegation, Senator du Pont among them, left the event suspecting that the real estate market in Florida had now peaked. But as Ballinger observed later, "Virtually no one of that Florida delegation would have dreamed the boom in Florida would be as dead as a salted mackerel three months later."

16

PIRATES OF PROMOTION

T. Coleman du Pont, who had retired as president of the E. I. du Pont de Nemours Powder Company in 1915, had just been elected to a second term as a US senator from Delaware when he joined the board of directors of the Mizner Development Company, the company the Mizner brothers set up to develop Boca Raton. He was just the sort of "man of large affairs" that Addison and Wilson Mizner were looking for when they conceived of their new development—a far more ambitious project than the Mizner Mile project in Boynton Beach that had failed so spectacularly. Gregarious, loud, and often silly, Coly, as he was known, had a fondness for horseplay, practical jokes, and slapstick. He subjected his friends to loaded cigars ("an exploding cigar convulsed him in a frenzy of knee slapping," according to Wilson Mizner's biographer John Burke), matchsticks that went off like sparklers, dribbling highball glasses, electrified chairs, water pistols, and a plaster bulldog that emitted mechanical growls and whose eyes glowed in the dark. Wilson Mizner sized up Coleman du Pont as the kind of easy mark that he would have targeted for one of his badger schemes and disparaged him to friends as "a screwball; a peasant who got lucky and made the most of his family connections." But this time Wilson badly misread his quarry.

At six foot four, Kentucky-born Coly du Pont was a superb athlete who in his youth could run the hundred-yard dash in just over ten seconds. At Urbana University in Ohio, he captained the varsity football and baseball teams and stroked the college crew. His first job—after transferring to and graduating from the Massachusetts Institute of Technology—had been driving a mule cart underground in a du Pont coal mine in Central City, Kentucky. Superbly trained in business by his uncle Fred du Pont and two of Fred's lieutenants, Coleman took over managing Fred's collection of mining companies, steel mills, and street railways at age twenty-nine. His particular strength was combining companies or putting them on a firmer financial footing and then selling them off. When he was thirty-nine, he and two of his cousins bought out the shareholders of E. I. du Pont de Nemours and Company, in an early example of a leveraged buyout. With Coleman as president and the controlling shareholder, the company made more than one hundred acquisitions, creating the "Powder Trust," a virtual monopoly in the lucrative manufacture of gunpowder and explosives. Shortly before he retired from the family business, Coly acquired control of the Equitable Life Assurance Society from J. P. Morgan and then built, for $30 million, the forty-story Equitable Trust Building in lower Manhattan, which at that time was the largest office building in the world by floor area (1.2 million square feet). The enormous H-shaped structure cast such a large shadow on the streets below that outrage against it prompted the first zoning legislation in New York City. This legislation incorporated setback principles that gave the next generation of Manhattan skyscrapers their distinctive tiered or stairstep look. Eight years later, in 1924, the US Department of Commerce issued a planning document (the Standard State Zoning Enabling Act) that encouraged states to adopt similar zoning standards nationwide.

By the time the Mizner brothers met him, Coly had made fortunes in coal, steel, street railroads, munitions, real estate, and insurance. He had built a small coal town that became the industry standard for all subsequent towns. He had also assembled a hotel empire, perhaps inspired by Henry Flagler's example, that included New York's original Waldorf-Astoria, the Willard Hotel in Washington, DC, and Philadelphia's Bellevue-Stratford Hotel. In one biographer's accurate assessment, Coleman du Pont possessed "a brain of the first order for matters of corporate reorganization and management." Despite his odd, show-offy manner, he was a bold and decisive business buccaneer, and not the kind of man to ever underestimate.

In short, he was a superb choice for chairman of the Mizner Development Company.

In early 1924, with the botched Mizner Mile project behind them, the Mizner brothers settled on their new Boca Raton project as the one that would bring them wealth, status, and fame. Addison, of course, did not need more fame. He was by now a celebrated architect, known nationally for the collection of houses that he had built in Palm Beach. He'd even made some money. "I have a million dollars put away in government bonds, and you can rest assured that I'll never touch a penny of the principal," he remarked to an old friend. However, for Wilson, Boca Raton represented his best opportunity for the major financial score he'd been chasing his entire shady career. All Wilson needed to do was to persuade his older brother to complete the transition from architect to developer. Eventually Addison agreed that Boca Raton offered the chance to put the capstone on a brilliant career and, perhaps, to create an even more impressive and lasting legacy. As Alex Waugh recalled, "Even Addison became intoxicated with dreams of glory." To friends, the architect confided that he hoped to help out Wilson. He also wanted to build a home for his only other surviving brother, Henry, a retired ordained Episcopal minister who had a wife and daughter, and to leave something to the memory of his beloved mother, Mama Mizner, who'd died in Addison's Long Island home back in 1915. For some time, he had dreamed of building a small cathedral in her honor.

There was one further inducement. At Boca Raton, Addison would have the opportunity to accomplish what his friend Paris Singer had done in Palm Beach: create his own town and reign over it like a potentate. And that, of course, entailed a house of Addison's own, with even more grand accommodations than he currently occupied in Villa Mizner, his mansion overlooking Worth Avenue—and certainly more splendid than Paris Singer's apartment atop the Everglades Club. He envisioned, and painted in watercolor, a $1 million castle practically afloat on the water, with towering turrets and a drawbridge that connected the structure to the mainland. It would also serve as a repository of superb Spanish antiquities that, along with the castle, could be left to the new city of Boca Raton as a museum upon his death. Wilson had his own architectural fantasy: he hoped to build a cabaret on Lake Boca Raton that would be under his direct supervision: the Pirate Ship Cabaret.

Using Addison's now national reputation as an architect and builder, the brothers assembled an impressive group of investors and board members that included (or, in some cases, they simply alleged to include) the celebrated Wall Street stock operator Jesse Livermore; the brothers William K. and Harold Vanderbilt (grandsons of shipping and railroad tycoon Cornelius Vanderbilt); songwriter Irving Berlin; Rodman Wanamaker (son of the founder of the popular Philadelphia department store); Elizabeth Arden of the rapidly expanding cosmetics empire; Clarence Geist, the Chicago utilities magnate; and journalist Herbert Bayard Swope, winner of the first Pulitzer Prize for reporting. To lend a dash of aristocratic cachet, they rounded up as initial investors Alice Heine (Duchess of Richelieu and Dowager Princess of Monaco); Lady Diana Manners (Viscountess Norwich); the Duchess of Sutherland, aka Lady Millicent Hawes, who wrote fiction under the pen name Erskine Gower; and Charles Spencer-Churchill (9th Duke of Marlborough), all of whom were either regular Florida visitors, Florida home owners, or friends of people in the first two categories. T. Coleman du Pont, who planned to build his own grand waterfront home in Boca Raton, was duly elected chairman of the company's board. Addison was appointed president, while Wilson was named secretary and treasurer.

With the initial funds raised, the Mizner Development Corporation purchased sixteen thousand acres that included two miles of waterfront in the coastal farming village of Boca Raton, twenty-eight miles south of Palm Beach. Addison drew up the plans for the enormously ambitious project. It was an all-encompassing town plan, with commercial and industrial areas as well as residential areas. He even platted a subdivision for the homes of black workers in an area across the Hillsboro Canal. The project consisted of an airport, a yacht basin, a Venetian bridge over the Intercoastal Waterway, sixty-one miles of canals, and a section of shops and offices that resembled London's classy Burlington Arcade. Ultimately there would be four golf courses (Palm Beach had "only" three), each one designed by famed golf course architect Donald Ross, plus a polo field, tennis courts, and private beaches "restricted against all intrusion." There were even tentative plans for a $6 million, seven-hundred-room Ritz-Carlton hotel on the ocean. The goal, as Addison articulated it, was "to give Florida and the nation a resort city perfect as study and ideals can make it." Much like George Merrick, Mizner found the City Beautiful Movement approach compelling, his interest dating back to a visit he'd made to the Chicago Columbian Exhibition in 1893. According to Wilson Mizner's biographer John Burke, "Wilson and Addison became almost delirious in their determination to build a new Byzantium washed by the tepid waters of the Gulf Stream."

The centerpiece of the new resort city would be the Boca Raton Inn, soon renamed the Cloister Inn. Addison intended this to be the finest hotel of its kind in the country and his latest architectural marvel. Inside its spacious and grand halls, Irving Berlin would have his own Cabaret. Leading up to the inn would be El Camino Real (the King's Highway), 160 feet to 220 feet wide with a Venetian canal down the middle. The plans also called for thousands of homes priced from $20,000 to $40,000, although some would be as cheap as $7,000, built "for the man of moderate means." While these prices suggest the brothers were targeting the middle class as well as the very wealthiest Americans, the developers knew better than to even mention the term *middle class* in their marketing, recognizing that no one wanted to be considered middle class. Rather, the goal, as Wilson articulated it, was to make the resort sound so upscale that it would demote Palm Beach to little more than the workers' housing for Boca Raton.

To succeed, the brothers believed that it wasn't enough to match what every other developer was doing; they had to top the competition. From the outset, the plan was to make the Cloister Inn the most luxurious small hotel in America, to make Camino Real the grandest promenade, and to make Mama Mizner's cathedral the most ornate small cathedral in the country. Entry into this rarefied community, they insisted, would be granted only to the most exclusive clientele. As their publicist would later whisper, "Get the big snobs, and the little snobs will follow."

Construction began in early 1925 on the Cloister Inn and the all-important administration building to house the architects, engineers, and publicity department. The latter was alleged to be modeled on the Spanish painter El Greco's house in Toledo, as many such Spanish-style buildings were, neatly overlooking the fact that no one knew what El Greco's house had looked like; the house in Toledo so often sourced as the artist's home was actually a museum built in 1911, nearly three hundred years after the painter's death. Work also began on dozens of houses in the Old Floresta and Spanish Village subdivisions.

Initially, Wilson seems to have taken his job seriously, which was something new for him. According to biographer John Burke, "Around the corporate offices, his manner was dynamic, commanding, and occasionally verged on the satirical. He rushed around barking orders at the help. He studied sales charts with a gravity worthy of the Harvard Business School and adopted a manner compatible with that of the chairmanship of United States Steel."

Hoping also to get the best publicity that money could buy, Wilson went out and hired, at $3,000 a week, the celebrated publicist Harry Reichenbach, whom he knew from his Broadway days. Reichenbach was a questionable choice for the assignment. He was known for sensational publicity stunts such as staging phony kidnappings of Hollywood starlets shortly before their movies were released, or for persuading matinee idol Rudolph Valentino to grow a beard, to the consternation of his adoring fans, and then to shave it off, to their relief, a month later. Before the release of a Tarzan film, Reichenbach arranged to have an actor arrested for sharing his hotel room with a caged lion; the actor then professed to the assembled press that it was all because he was such a big fan of Tarzan.

To further help with sales, the brothers recruited their good friend the actress Marie Dressler and dubbed her the "Duchess of Boca Raton."

Wilson, as corporate secretary-treasurer, focused on the marketing and the financial side of the business—neither of which he was qualified to do. Not surprisingly, both would go horribly wrong. It didn't help matters that he actually thought he knew what he was doing, particularly when it came to advertising and sales. There was little question that Wilson could be persuasive—which is to say that he possessed the ability to con people. As Alex Waugh observed, "Wilson could have sold six television sets to a blind man and made him feel grateful for the opportunity to buy." From the outset, Wilson's advertisements ramped up the hyperbole: "The Riviera, Biarritz, Mentone, Nice, Sorrento, the Lido, Egypt, all that charms in each of these finds culmination in Boca Raton. Art assures her ascendancy in the creative genius of Addison Mizner. . . . Boca Raton is Addison Mizner's culminating achievement." Boca Raton was described as no less than the "anteroom of heaven," "the bride of the Gulf Stream," "the sun porch of America," and "the world's most architecturally beautiful playground."

The ballyhoo, first deployed so effectively by Carl Fisher at the outset of the decade, now bordered on the ludicrous. "Every promise of the Mizner Development Corporation is made to be kept. Exaggeration has no place in Boca Raton's lexicon." Nevertheless, on the first day of sales, in May, a stunning $2.1 million worth of lots were sold. On May 4, the deal was finalized for the Ritz-Carlton Investment Corporation to build its oceanfront hotel. When the second section of lots was put up for sale, the feat of $2 million in sales was repeated, with $1 million worth sold in the first twenty minutes. Sales offices were promptly opened in major cities from Chicago to Boston. A De Lux Pullman bus left Miami for Boca Raton at ten every morning so that potential buyers could tour the area. According to some reports, perhaps exaggerated, $25 million worth of lots were sold in the first six months. Shares in the closely held Mizner Development Corporation soared from $100 per share to $1,000 per share, while remaining tracts of land in the surrounding area doubled and tripled in value. Not surprisingly, at the first board meeting, Coleman du Pont thanked the company officers and the management team for their good work, remarking that it met with the board's "unqualified approval." Addison and Wilson were suddenly worth a combined $40 million to $50 million. One can only imagine the brothers' celebratory mood. Addison, in one promotional speech, confessed, "I am happier today than ever before in all of my life."

Encouraged by this early success, perhaps even a little drunk with it,

Wilson and Reichenbach wrote ads that took their hyperbole to fresh heights: "I am the greatest resort in the world. I am Boca Raton, Fla." One advertisement in the *Palm Beach Post* reported that "the owners and controllers of Mizner Development Corporation are a group of very rich men." Their combined wealth, it continued, "probably represents considerably over one-third of the entire wealth of the United States. . . . It is reasonable to suppose that every lot buyer . . . should make quick and large profits." Another ad for the development read: "Social supremacy and financial solidarity are assured to Boca Raton by the wealth and standing, the character and achievement of its proprietary sponsors. These men and women of world-standing in society, finance, and affairs know that the best of democracy is the flower of genuine aristocracy. They therefore invite men and women of substance and standing to participate in their unique undertaking."

It took the board directors a couple of meetings to realize just how outlandish the advertising had become—and how out of line it was with reality. For example, some of the ads made it sound as though Boca Raton was up and running, when, in fact, not even the administration building was complete. The Cloister Inn, the resort's flagship hotel, although going up fast, would not be complete until the following February. But buyers couldn't decipher that from the misleading ads. The implication was that you could sail into the Boca Raton harbor on your yacht and tie up at the resort's ample dock, when in reality the dock was still a small, rickety wood structure that protruded into an unnavigable mangrove swamp.

When Coleman du Pont read the ads touting the financial supremacy of Boca Raton's board of directors and its coterie of distinguished investors, he grew concerned. As he had explained to Addison early on, "I have always, in business, believed in being very, very careful not to make a statement that could not be backed up by facts in every way." Not only did the ads violate this precept, they also exemplified the kind of hyperbole that the "Truth About Florida" delegation to New York had objected to, and that its members had agreed to stop. When Wilson and Reichenbach then went a step further and listed in their ads the actual names of the prominent directors and implied that they were guaranteeing the millions of dollars that would be required to build out the resort town, du Pont's concern escalated. He telegraphed the brothers from New York: "Am deeply chagrined by statement and fearful of outcome of a concern that does business this way." Addison responded with apologies and reassurances.

Nevertheless, the next wave of ads devised by Wilson and Reichenbach was even more inflated, urging buyers of the lots to affix the advertising flyer that they had authored to the purchase contract. The actual language read: "Attach this advertisement to your contract for deed. It becomes a part thereof." The purpose of this scheme was to differentiate the development from more fly-by-night projects and to demonstrate to the buyer just how committed the developers were to their grand plans—to the construction of the Cloister Inn, the Ritz-Carlton hotel, the polo fields, the first two golf courses, and all of the other resort amenities, which in a softer real estate market might prove to be unrealistic or a financial stretch. Whatever Wilson's intention, du Pont and others on the board of directors quickly realized that linking the ad to the purchase contract created an implied obligation and potential personal liability for them, and not without justification: they would be sued as a group for the false advertising in 1929.

Coleman du Pont exploded in dismay and wrote a letter announcing his resignation from the board. The *New York Times* picked up on the story and interviewed Addison Mizner, who attempted to minimize the damage by depicting the disagreement as simply a board personnel matter: "The differences between General du Pont and the directors are solely over the personnel of the directorate. He wanted some men on it and the directors wanted others, whereupon General du Pont resigned." This was accurate as far as it went, but it was far from the full story. The directors that Coleman du Pont happened to be concerned about—and wanted removed from the board—were the two Mizner brothers.

Around this time, someone brought to du Pont's attention an old newspaper article describing Wilson Mizner's conviction for operating a gambling house on Long Island in 1919. What happened next is murky. According to one story, likely fanciful, Wilson responded to the article's re-emergence by producing a document of his own. He visited a local jail and talked a female inmate into writing du Pont a letter that claimed she was about to have his child; Wilson then tried to use the letter as counter-leverage against the financier. While the story may be apocryphal, it wasn't past Wilson to employ such tactics.

Four days later, Jesse Livermore, who chaired the finance committee, and two others, Louis H. Bean and stockbroker Hollyday S. Meeds Jr., also quit the company's board of directors; Matthew C. Brush, president of the insurance company American International Corporation, resigned from the finance committee. In a second letter to the *New York Times*, the men spelled out their displeasure with the current management team: "As we consider it inconsistent with our business experience and personal convictions to be connected with a corporation unless it is under com-petent and reasonable management and we find after several meetings of the board and months of negotiation on our part that we cannot persuade the controlling directors to adopt our views of what is necessary in this respect, we have become obliged to sever our connection with the cor-poration." They went on to explain that they had failed in their efforts to "regularize the affairs and the management of the corporation" and to eliminate the exaggerated publicity that had been propagated by the Mizner brothers.

These resignations were a horrendous public rebuke to Addison and Wilson and a major setback for the Mizner Development Corporation, which, like every other development company, depended heavily on favor-able public perception to attract sales. Wilson and Reichenbach had made a grave error.

The brothers scrambled to replace these prominent directors, signing up W. E. Shappercotter, a railroad baron, to be chairman of the board, but real damage had been done. They also announced that famed Wall Street investment banker Otto Kahn, managing partner of the prominent investment bank Kuhn, Loeb & Co., had made a six-figure investment in the project. Nevertheless, sales, which had begun to slow in the late fall with the railroad embargo and the negative publicity about Florida's boom in the national press, now came to a virtual standstill. The development's prospects promptly collapsed. What had looked like a remarkably sound investment, backed by many of the wealthiest and most prominent people in the country, now looked questionable at best.

In truth, the financing of the Boca Raton project, overseen by Wilson as the corporate treasurer and Anderson Herd as the general manager, had always been shaky. It now devolved into a web of self-dealing and conflicts of interest. From the outset, the Mizners sold stock in the corporation to anyone who could further the project's prospects. Even the publisher of the *Palm Beach Post* owned 1,500 shares and thus could be depended on to keep a steady drumbeat of positive publicity appearing in the paper. According to financial historian Raymond Vickers, the company also sold stock to local bankers in return for large bank loans, creating an array of obvious conflicts. In another instance, the Mizner Development Corporation bought more than 50 percent of the stock in the Palm Beach National Bank, which put the corporation in a position where it could ensure that the bank would guarantee loans and offer mortgages to Boca Raton lot purchasers. D. Lester Williams and Howard P. Smith, the controlling stockholders of the Palm Beach National Bank (and of the Palm Beach Bank and Trust Company), both large stockholders in the Mizner company, now sold their remaining interest in the bank, which they had founded, to a real estate promoter named William A. White, another large shareholder and board member of Mizner Development Corporation. White would become the bank's president despite having no banking experience whatsoever. Joining the bank's board were Congressman George S. Graham and Ward A. Wickwire, both also directors of the Mizner Development Company, and H. Halpine Smith, the manager of Mizner Industries. With the bank effectively under Mizner Development Corporation control, the officers proceeded to lend 200 percent of the bank's capital to the Boca Raton project and to Addison's other businesses (Mizner Industries, Antigua Shops, Los Manos Pottery), thereby placing the bank in grave financial peril.

Addison, Wilson, their nephew Horace Chase, Harry Reichenbach, and Anderson Herd, as well as others, then took out personal loans. Apparently, even the assistant cashier took what he could, stealing cash from the tills and embezzling bank funds before vanishing. The bank's record keeping was lax and sloppy. Its examiner, who hoped to become a banker himself, duly reported the abuses he found but never undertook any strong enforcement actions against the bank. His discretion in this matter, here and at other banks, appears to have been rewarded: he later become president and chairman of a Tampa bank, president of the Florida Bankers Association, and a chairman of the congressional committee of the American Bankers Association.

Addison, who took little or no interest in the financial affairs of the development, which hardly exonerates him, made his share of *operational* missteps. To secure the coquina stone necessary to construct the assortment of Boca Raton buildings, he bought a five-acre quarry on Islamorada Key. That acquisition cost, plus the expense of the machinery to cut and quarry the stone on the scale required for Boca Raton, vastly exceeded the company's budget.

Such missteps aside, an even more fundamental problem existed in the brothers' strategy. Little effort had been made to ensure that the lots' buyers actually intended to build homes at Boca Raton. It soon became clear that the vast majority of the lots sold in 1925 were bought purely for speculative purposes and now could not be resold. When the second installment of the payments came due, few of these payments were forthcoming. Most buyers simply walked away, sacrificing their 10 percent down payments—proof of their lack of confidence in the development's future.

The brothers struggled to save face. On Christmas Eve 1925 they threw a preopening black-tie dinner party in the Salamanca Room at the Cloister Inn, "a truly Lucullan repast," according to the *Palm Beach Post*, replete with "red-coated, gold-braided servitors, responding in French and Spanish to whispered queries." The hotel itself was a triumph, and Addison was delighted when Stanford White's widow, Bessie, who attended, described Addison as "the foremost genius of the age" and the Cloister Inn as "superb." A review of the building in *Arts and Decoration* magazine described it as a "Spanish gem." The brothers succeeded in opening the hotel on February 6, 1926, furnished with Mizner Industries furniture and a few antiques from Addison's personal collection. On that date, the brothers threw a formal opening party and dinner dance to which they invited five hundred members of Palm Beach and European society—a guest list that "rivaled the social registers of two continents," according to the Mizner publicity department. It included such luminaries as the Stotesburys, the Seligmans, the Cosdens, Al Jolson, and the Countess Salm (the Standard Oil heiress and socialite Millicent Rogers), among many others.

On February 19, 1926, Addison Mizner gave an interview to the *Miami Daily News* in which he somewhat bitterly defended the real estate boom and attempted to exude an air of confidence: "Where are these Florida critics we hear so much about? Maybe I haven't seen them because I do not often visit zoos, or menageries. But if any of them are at large without a keeper, let them rave. All they need is a little rope. They will hang themselves."

Having lost his moral compass, he'd begun to sound very much like Wilson.

17

LULL BEFORE THE STORM

Over in Tampa, D. P. Davis was equally adamant that his investors should not be concerned. In October 1925, after selling every lot of his Davis Islands development on the mudflats off Tampa—with sales totaling $18.1 million—Davis announced with great fanfare that he intended to repeat his success at one end of the marshy Anastasia Island across from St. Augustine.

The plans were drawn up for the $60 million Davis Shores project that would feature 1,500 acres of mostly newly dredged prime waterfront property, a yacht club, two golf courses, hotels, and the ubiquitous bathing casino. A mammoth waterfront hotel was planned that featured a Giralda tower. The early ads toted "America's Foremost Watering Place" and urged prospective buyers to "Follow D. P. Davis for Big Quick Real Estate Profits." Most of his sales force simply crossed the state and switched from Davis Islands to Davis Shores, where $16.3 million in lots sold in a few hours on November 14, 1925. The dredges went to work. But other than the bridge over to the island development, known as the Bridge of Lions, which alone cost $1 million, few structures would ever get built. By the spring, sales had begun to slow. Disaster struck in the early summer when Davis Islands investors who should have made their second of three payments on their lots simply walked away from their contracts. Instead of the $4 million in income that Davis had anticipated, he took in a paltry $30,000.

Desperate for cash, he negotiated the sale of 51 percent of Davis Islands, thus ceding control of his Tampa development to a syndicate led by the construction company Stone and Webster, which in turn was owned by seven public utility companies. The deal was announced on August 2 at the Waldorf-Astoria Hotel in Manhattan. Davis immediately posted his 49 percent share in the new entity (Island Investment Company) as collateral for a $250,000 loan that he used to continue construction at Davis Shores. He seems to have believed that the slowdown would be temporary.

By now, Davis's resurrected marriage to his second wife, Elizabeth Nelson, former queen of the Gasparilla carnival, had collapsed for a second time. His brother would insist that D.P. had married Nelson in the first place only to make his mistress, Lucille Zehring, jealous. Meanwhile, Lucille had left her impecunious Hollywood actor husband and moved to New York City, where she shared an apartment with her mother—an apartment most likely paid for by D. P. Davis.

Elizabeth left for Europe around September 5 on the liner *Homeric*, accompanied by her best friend, presumably to vacation for a month and then to establish domicile in Paris for a quickie Paris divorce—a favored method for the wealthy to part ways during those years. As the lawyer Frank Shutts explained to Carl Fisher, whose marriage was in similar trouble, "the French court will grant divorce decrees up on the general proposition that two people do not want to live together anymore." Davis planned to follow his wife to Paris one month later with a small entourage that would include Zehring, her mother, and his lawyer and his publicist (who could help with the divorce and subsequent remarriage), all of them traveling aboard the White Star liner RMS *Majestic*. It would be a fateful journey that would not end well for D. P. Davis or Davis Shores.

In these peak years of the boom, nobody had more fun than Carl Fisher on Miami Beach. His papers now archived at the HistoryMiami Museum contain boxes of photographs of countless boating trips and deep-sea fishing expeditions taken with friends, sales prospects, and celebrities. He continued to try to lure any dignitary visiting Florida to Miami Beach, although he retained a special fondness for auto executives. One telegram, dated March 13, 1926, to a vacationing Henry Ford in Fort Myers, read:

"I'll bet you an inner-tube against a rubber patching outfit that I have a fiddler here that can beat yours Stop Why don't you come over and see this country Stop If the roads are too rough I'll send my boat around for you in the next few days. Carl G. Fisher." In another, to his friend the humorist Will Rogers, he wrote, "Is there anything in rumor that Rogers boom is on the verge of bursting? Understand great mental anguish in some northern banking circles because of enormous number people withdrawing money from banks to go to hear you talk. Persistent propaganda to effect your talk is not worth what people are spending on it. If you are at the end of your rope wire me collect and will send you ticket to Florida."

But the tenor of the boom was changing—and with it the kind of people it attracted. In her memoirs, *Fabulous Hoosier*, Carl's first wife, Jane, captures the surreal nature of the late boom years and how the clientele of their once sleepy resort town had changed: "Pouring into Miami Beach they came, fantastic visitors to a fantastic city. The gold diggers and the sugar daddies, the gigolos, the 'butter and egg men,' the playboys and the gilded heiresses, the professional huntresses, the tired businessmen who never grew tired, the gentlemen who preferred blonds. Miami Beach was the playground of millionaires and the happy hunting ground of predatory women."

Carl Fisher's former partner in Prest-O-Lite, Jim Allison, who had recently built the Miami Aquarium and the Allison Hospital on North Beach, took note of the presence of the binder boys and raised the alarm to Fisher, "Get out while the going is good. Things are going to go sky high and blow the lid off Miami Beach." Fisher suspected that Allison was right. In June 1925, calculating that land was selling at five times its normal value, Fisher walked into his Alton Beach Realty Company office and barked out an order: "Take all our property off the market." This order came to the dismay of his sales force, which had sold $23 million in the first half of the year. However, he didn't retreat from real estate altogether, which would have been the correct decision at the time. Instead, Fisher chose to redeploy his capital elsewhere.

By now, Fisher controlled, one way or another, nearly half of Miami Beach. He was president of three companies: the Alton Beach Realty

Company, the Miami Beach Bayshore Company, and the Peninsula Terminal Company. He had also just built a mile-and-a-quarter board speedway at Fulford-by-the-Sea, a few miles from Miami. In spite of this heavy commitment, he decided to risk it all on a new project in Montauk, at the far end of Long Island. What he had in mind was a project three times the size of what he had done in Miami Beach, spread over nine miles of oceanfront property. To help him, Fisher lined up many of the same partners, including his old friend Jim Allison, Albert Champion of the spark plug company, Howard Coffin, founder of the Hudson Motor Company, and a pair of bankers. He spent $2.5 million to buy nearly ten thousand acres of land. Fully built out, the project was estimated to cost $30 million, but, happily, wouldn't require significant dredging. "At least I won't have to make the land," he quipped to Jane in a letter. What he envisioned was a Tudor-style development: "a city of medieval cottages and thatched roofs, windmills, sheep with shepherds and dogs to herd them." He hoped to bring the entire Miami Beach organization north and duplicate everything he had done in Florida.

Fisher had also launched a smaller forty-five-lot development in Port Washington, Long Island, called Bayview Colony, much closer to New York City, where he built a dock facility, a shipyard for the Purdy Boat Company, and a waterfront summer home for himself.

Carl's close friend John Oliver LaGorce, the National Geographic Society's adman (and later its president), questioned this ambitious new strategy and asked Carl why he felt the need to make more money. Didn't he have enough? Couldn't he just take it easy? Carl answered in a fury, "Damn your soul, who said I'm building Montauk for money? What the hell do I care about money! Miami Beach is finished, and there's nothing left for me to do there but sit around in white pants looking pretty like the rest of you goddamn winter loafers."

Carl Fisher's personal life was becoming problematic. After twelve years of marriage, Jane finally got pregnant and gave birth to the baby boy they'd always wanted. Their joy, however, was short-lived: the child, born after a traumatic delivery, survived only twenty-six days, dying in Jane's arms of pyloric stenosis, a stomach blockage. The loss of their son dealt their marriage a mortal blow, as is not uncommon in such circumstances. "That was the real ending," Jane recalled. "We would never be complete again." Not long afterward, she managed to adopt for them a three-year-old boy named Jackie, but Carl never bonded with the child. At this point, his drinking, always reckless and heavy, took on a more determined and serious complexion. As Jane recalled, "Drinking, he brought into our homes the sort of people that in sober moments he despised. When sober again, he cleared them out with the abhorrence he would show a nest of cockroaches. But the craving always came back, and, with it, Carl's drinking companions." Carl's womanizing grew worse as well.

By 1925, the couple had legally separated, and Jane was living in a villa on the outskirts of Paris along with "a veritable genius of a French cook," an au pair for Jackie, and a chauffeur. She would sit in the back of her Minerva town car clad in a sable coat, with a white camellia corsage pinned to her lapel. "There were entertaining men in Paris ready to kiss the hand, dance, and sympathize with the neglected wife of an American millionaire," she recalled. "Paris appreciated me—La Dame aux Camélias." On one occasion, she spent $86,000 in a shopping spree in a Paris jewelry emporium.

As for Carl, he lived alone now, the boozing and the hard living having caught up with him at last. He wrote Jane a philosophical letter in January 1926, telling her that he didn't blame her for leaving him and that he only wanted to make sure she was happy, although he had a caveat on the subject of happiness: "I don't think you can be happy all the time—excited and on the go. Your nerves will soon snap, as mine have done. Then you will know for the first time the real punishment nature gives for high pressure." He was just fifty-two years old.

When Jane returned later in the year to see if her husband was ready to reconcile, he was not at the passenger terminal to meet her ship in New York. Nor was he at the front door to greet her when she arrived at his house on Long Island. She found him upstairs, bedridden, recuperating from a drinking binge. When she begged him to come away with her for six months of rest and recuperation, he flatly refused. That put to rest any lingering hopes she had of a rapprochement. After a brief conversation, she left. On her way down the stairs, she heard Carl frantically ring his bedside bell, and she passed his valet hurrying up the stairs with a Scotch and soda on a tray.

While she was away in Paris, Carl had sold the Shadows—the house they had built and lived in together—to the local builder N. B. T. Roney without bothering to tell her. He had begun work on a new and grander house that boasted a tall watchtower and a long dock projecting into Biscayne Bay. That winter, back in Florida once again, Jane stopped by the Shadows one afternoon on her way to the beach, determined to take a nostalgic look at the home that she recalled so fondly. Roney had converted it into a gambling club now operated by a pair of gangland figures. She strolled up the palm-lined driveway and past the rosebushes that she herself had planted. At the top of the front steps, she discovered that the verandah had been converted into a cocktail bar. She tried the front door, and when she found that it was unlocked, walked into the house. Slot machines crowded her spacious living room. She walked around and then climbed the front stairs to the second floor, where she paused to peer into Carl's former bedroom. "A roulette wheel was standing where his bed had once stood under the pictures of Lincoln and Napoléon!" The fate of the house seemed to mirror what had happened to all of Florida during the boom. Not long afterward, she informed Carl that she wanted a divorce. To his credit, he would remain a loyal friend and confidant to her for the rest of his life.

Paris Singer was another developer struggling to balance his Florida success and his personal life. Singer seemingly had everything a man could ask for: a new wife, the prestige of ruling the Everglades Club like a personal fiefdom, and a gorgeous cliff-side villa overlooking the water in Cap Ferrat, France, where he could escape Florida's hot summer months. But he was unsatisfied, personally as well as financially. He had married the nurse Joan Bates, but within a year or so, he was cheating on her, which led to loud and public arguments that caused observers to speculate that he still pined for Isadora Duncan. As Addison Mizner commented bemusedly: "What a good slapping in his youth would have done."

Addison's friend Alice DeLamar described the goateed Singer at this point in his life as resembling a Renaissance king. Fittingly, he had hired Sir Oswald Birley, the famous British royal portrait painter, to come to Palm Beach to paint his portrait. Singer even built an artist's studio where Birley could paint the portrait. When the work was finished, Singer had it hung prominently in the Everglades Club. He also was taking flying lessons and, indulging this new hobby, had purchased a pair of Curtiss Seagull wooden flying boats that he kept moored in Lake Worth. His three children from his first marriage visited him periodically in Palm Beach, but as Alice DeLamar observed, "Singer always seemed very bored with all his children, and I think they were all relieved to be away from him. . . . I did not envy them having such a capricious egotist for a father. He could never stand not having his own way about everything."

Singer apparently felt the need to build something bigger and better than the Everglades Club and settled on developing a parcel of land north of Palm Beach that he called, appropriately, Singer Island. It was rumored that he had already spent $20 million of his fortune in six years—pouring most of it into Florida real estate. Nevertheless, he hired his friend Addison to design a large hotel there. The project would be his financial downfall.

By the end of 1925, architecture at the Florida developments was starting to become more diverse, veering away from the Spanish and Mediterranean Revival styles that Mizner had used when he kicked off the boom. Glenn Curtiss, an early aviation innovator who had cashed out of his Curtiss Aeroplane and Motor Company with a $32 million fortune, was developing Opa-Locka. (He had already developed Hialeah, Florida, and the golfing mecca known as Country Club Estates, done in partnership with the Missouri cattleman James Bright.) His new development would feature fanciful Moorish Revival architecture: domes with minarets, crenellated roofs, mosques, wide Moorish archways, and Arabian-inspired decor inspired by the book *Arabian Nights*. George Eugene Sebring, who had made his fortune in pottery and china, developed the town of Sebring, allegedly modeling it on the ancient Egyptian city of Heliopolis.

In fact, for buyers, there was so much variety in the style, construction, and amenities at the various Florida developments that it was becoming difficult to choose among them. The investment opportunities, too, seemed boundless, which, for many people, certainly made shopping a lot more fun. Writer Gertrude Matthews Shelby recalled meeting a young widow on a bus ride to a development who confessed to having invested everything in Florida. "Madly absorbing place. My husband died three weeks ago. I nursed him over a year with cancer. Yet I've actually forgotten I ever had a husband. And I loved him, too, at that!" You could visit the developments on foot, by bus, or by private car. The Shoreland Company, for example, had ten brand-new Cadillac sedans to ferry you about.

If you were serious about doing your due diligence, you certainly didn't want to miss what Joseph Wesley Young, the three-hundred-pound former gold prospector and newspaperman, had created in Hollywood-by-the-Sea and Hollywood Beach. His accomplishments nearly rivaled George Merrick's in scope, and he had a fleet of sixty buses to get you there and show you around. By 1926, he had built more than 2,400 homes, 252 commercial buildings, 9 hotels, 36 apartment buildings, and a black township called Liberia—the entire development encompassing 18,000 acres and 6.5 miles of waterfront and attracting some 18,000 residents. The hub of Young's city was a ten-acre traffic circle. His pink Hollywood Beach Hotel had the world's largest solarium and contained a direct wire connection to Wall Street for those interested in trading stocks. His bathing casino was the state's largest, with 824 dressing rooms and 80 shower baths.

If you wanted something more modest, there was Croissantania, developed by G. Frank Croissant, a Chicago real estate developer who had titled himself America's Greatest Salesman. After a significant success with the 1,200-acre Croissant Park in southwestern Fort Lauderdale, he launched this new development—located just north of the Mizner brothers' development in Boca Raton—in January 1926. The idea was to provide homes for the working man. One of his ads proclaimed: "No one who thinks can blame me for investing here millions of dollars in the development of a Dream City, a City of incomparable beauty and facilities for ideal American family life. But I can tell every man with five hundred dollars, or more, this: you will blame yourself and before very long, if you do not invest in Croissantania's unquestionable destiny.... I can honestly state that if I were starting today, I would put every cent I could get into Croissantania." Lots would be sold, but despite his ballyhoo, not a single building would be constructed there, as the air went out of the real estate bubble.

The other good opportunity for the workingman was the Venice Beach project planned by the Brotherhood of Locomotive Engineers (BLE), the richest labor union in the country at the time. Seeking a lucrative capital investment in Florida for its pension fund, the group bought thirty thousand acres of land for $10 million on the west coast at the precise top of the market, taking honors for the single worst market timing of any project. The development included farm estates, an industrial area, and affordable housing for union retirees. When construction finally petered out a few years later, a decade of lawsuits followed.

An entirely different approach was that taken at Picture City, which was launched in 1925 near what is today Hobe Sound. Here film distributor Lewis J. Selznick, father of future Hollywood producer David O. Selznick, bought two thousand acres, and an option for six thousand more, which a brochure touted dubiously as "the finest land in all of Florida, if not the entire world." He planned a business and residential development that would include a large motion picture studio and a resident movie colony of stars and moguls. But it was all a fantasy. Many lots were sold, but, again, not a single house would be built. No studio was ever erected; just as perplexing, the movie stars and moguls failed to appear.

In St. Petersburg, "Handsome Jack" Taylor, a high-rolling former investment banker married to a du Pont heiress, was building the sprawling Rolyat ("Taylor" spelled backward) Hotel and the surrounding development of Pasadena-on-the-Gulf (now called Pasadena Estates). He, too, launched modestly but soon expanded as he became, according to the realtor Fuller, "a convert of his own preaching." Taylor installed a Gilded Age railroad car at the entry to his development, where he threw tea parties for prospects. He parked his Daimler sedan nearby to convey an aura of impending wealth and splendor.

Buyers on real estate shopping excursions around Florida were sure to hear about N. B. T. Roney and his remarkable accomplishments. In late 1925 Roney embellished his reputation as a financial magician when he bought a stretch of beach for $3 million and sold it a week later for $12 million. In Miami Beach, it was impossible to avoid his commercial buildings and hotels, which housed some two hundred shops of various kinds. One of these, Espanola Way, consisted of eighteen separate buildings; it became the headquarters for Al Capone's gambling operations and, some years later, the spot where the Cuban-born entertainer Desi Arnaz got his start.

When you located a house or a lot that you liked, you were urged to act quickly, and many people did. At the Arch Creek section of Miami Shores, a crowd of buyers stormed the sales office when it opened at eight thirty in the morning and proceeded to throw checks at the salesmen—so many that they had to be collected in barrels. The section sold out in two and a half hours and brought in a record $33.7 million; it was some $11 million oversubscribed. Twelve miles north of Miami, Roney and James M. Cox, former governor of Ohio and owner of the *Miami Daily News*, paid $3 million for Seminole Beach, which they sold to a mob of buyers in six and a half hours for $7.6 million. One Miami broker, John B. Reid, working alone, reportedly sold $2 million worth of parcels in one week—$28 million in today's money.

If you could tear yourself away from these seductive developments, and countless others like them, there was a great deal of fun to be had, both during the day and at night. In Hialeah, on the outskirts of Miami, you could gamble, as mentioned, on horses, greyhounds, or jai alai, the Spanish game where a goatskin ball is hurled around a walled space at remarkable speeds. There was even an amusement park. Hollywood, closer to Fort Lauderdale, offered miniature golf—a new fad—or you could try night golf played on a regulation-sized course using phosphorescent balls. Or how about a daylight round with the new golf sensation Gene Sarazen at the Miami Springs Golf Club? Sarazen, the inventor of the sand wedge, would win seven major championships in the 1920s and 1930s and was the chief rival of Bobby Jones and Walter Hagen.

Or, as the sun set, you could catch the top bands as they performed at the resort hotels or catch acts such as Gilda Gray, the shimmy queen, as she performed her seductive dance on the glass dance floor of the Hollywood Golf and Country Club. Alas, like the land boom itself, she was "beginning to show the despoiling effects of time." Ignacy Jan Paderewski played the piano at the White Temple Methodist Church. You could even hear Rachel Jane Hamilton sing "Carry Me Back to Old Virginny" at the band shell in Royal Palm Park.

Flo Ziegfeld brought his Follies to the Royal Palm Hotel at around this time. And for ten weeks, his show performed at a supper club in Palm Beach called Club de Montmartre. The show featured, among others, the starlet Claire Luce. She and a handful of the other Ziegfeld girls were stopped and reprimanded on the beach by local police for not wearing black stockings with their black bathing costumes. Chicago-born Florenz Ziegfeld Jr. was a character tailor made for Florida in the twenties. Credit for his success was due his first wife, the Polish-born actress Anna Held, who had persuaded him in 1907 to launch a review that would be the American version of the Paris Follies at the Folies Bergère cabaret. It had become a blockbuster success and an annual Broadway event. Notably, it featured an incomparable lineup of American beauties, many of whom Ziegfeld bedded, who paraded onstage, descended staircases, and performed highly synchronized movements in chorus sequences, clad in show-stopping gowns designed by leading fashion designers of the day, such as Erté and Lady Duff-Gordon. A few of the ladies enhanced their reputations by posing for the company's photographer, Alfred Cheney Johnston (including secretly in the nude), who produced lovely stock photos of the extravagantly clad or unclad ladies that made them all the more famous offstage. Many of the women went on to successful Hollywood or theatrical careers, including Paulette Goddard, Marilyn Miller, and Barbara Stanwyck, who remarked about this period in her career, "I just wanted to survive and eat and have a nice coat."

The program also included popular acts of the day such as Will Rogers, W. C. Fields, Eddie Cantor, and Fanny Brice, each of whom had made a small fortune performing for the hit show over the years. Ziegfeld anticipated the signature Florida ballyhoo with his adept use of publicity stunts and saucy rumors about his stars leaked surreptitiously to the press. Hits by Jerome Kern, Irving Berlin, and George Gershwin featured prominently among the production numbers. The extravaganza was in its heyday throughout the twenties. Flo Ziegfeld and his clotheshorse second wife, actress Billie Burke, who would go on to play Glinda the Good Witch of the North in *The Wizard of Oz*, spent much of each winter in Palm Beach, socializing, deep-sea fishing, and squandering their money at Colonel Bradley's Casino, because, according to Burke, "we thought we had all the money in the world." They would lose everything in the stock market crash of '29.

On Miami Beach, Fisher's Flamingo Hotel, with its impressive glass dome and pink flamingo murals painted by ornithologist and illustrator Louis Agassiz Fuertes, was the epicenter of the local social scene, attracting Hollywood stars such as Gloria Swanson, the highest-paid actress of 1925, with earnings of over $1 million. Three years later, she would embark on an affair with Palm Beach millionaire Joseph Kennedy. Among the other guests was the handsome boxer Gene Tunney. He was supposed to be prepping for his first heavyweight title bout against world champion Jack Dempsey but had fallen for fellow hotel guest Mary Garden, who was performing with the visiting Civic Opera Company from Chicago: "Gene was in a state of juvenile adoration over Mary," recalled Jane Fisher. A month later, he would accept a temporary job as sales manager for Hollywood Pines Estates, where he began selling real estate, as other celebrities were doing.

By now, fifty to seventy-five Pullman cars were arriving daily in Miami, releasing hordes of people into a land where hotels sprouted like toadstools. By year-end, there would be more Rolls-Royce and Lincoln cars registered in Florida than in any other state. The soaring stock market itself was now contributing to the land boom, as investors followed the adage that you should make your money on Wall Street and invest it on Main Street.

The Roaring Twenties were in full swing. Open any magazine—*Saturday Evening Post, Harper's, Liberty, Literary Digest*—and you would behold endless articles and short stories about the ubiquitous short-skirted flappers with their bobbed hair and cloche hats. Ellin Mackay, a debutante and Comstock Lode heiress, who was in love with the songwriter Irving Berlin, had just announced, audaciously, in the pages of the popular new magazine the *New Yorker*, that she and her generation "prefer rubbing shoulders in a cabaret to dancing at an exclusive party." Two well-heeled students at the University of Chicago, Nathan Freudenthal Leopold Jr. and Richard Albert Loeb, were in prison for having kidnapped and then bludgeoned to death fourteen-year-old Robert Franks, in pursuit of committing the "perfect crime."

The Teapot Dome scandal, a gas lease kickback scheme of the Harding administration, was still simmering, but without ever implicating Harding's onetime vice president, Calvin Coolidge. Enjoying his first full term as president, Coolidge epitomized what one biographer would call "the genius of the average." Jazz, popularized by iconic figures such as bandleader Duke Ellington, could be heard in clubs and cabarets everywhere and even on the radio. In June, Darwin's theory of evolution had gone on trial—and lost—in the famous Scopes case in Tennessee, where a substitute teacher had violated the Butler Act by teaching human evolution in a state-funded school.

Babe Ruth, the Sultan of Swat, who had won the American League batting title with the New York Yankees the year before, was having an off year in 1925, and was hospitalized with a mysterious "bellyache." Ruth remained the darling of the sports press—and much of the nation—which seemed fixated on the exploits of this humble, big-hearted, fun-loving slugger who had grown up in a reform school and whose favorite trophy was the one he was awarded in a farting contest. Ruth had spent spring training in St. Petersburg griping about being broke (he was the highest-paid player in baseball) and refusing to shag fly balls in the outfield, which abutted an alligator-infested lake. He was witnessed wolfing down six hot dogs in a single sitting and gambling late into the night at the local greyhound track.

The bout of prosperity and exuberance extended to Europe, which had been slow to recover from the stupefying human losses of World War I. At last, its industrial production had recovered to prewar levels. The French would call these years, "les années folles," or "the wild years." No one appeared wilder than the nineteen-year-old US-born dancer and singer Josephine Baker, who had begun performing nearly nude at Paris's Théâtre des Champs Élysées in October. Also in Paris that year, at the International

Exhibition of Modern Decorative and Industrial Arts, a Swiss-French architect named Le Corbusier achieved notoriety by turning the conventional notion of architectural style on its head, denouncing decorative ornamentation and historical homage, such as Addison Mizner espoused, and arguing instead for a new, stark, rectilinear, and industrial aesthetic.

This was also the year that Benito Mussolini of Italy dropped the pretext of being anything other than what he was: a Fascist dictator. A little-known German politician named Adolf Hitler had been released from prison after serving time for a seditious beer-hall putsch in Munich; he was publishing the first volume of a memoir and manifesto called *Mein Kampf*. In May, Britain's chancellor of the exchequer, Winston Churchill, had returned the United Kingdom to the gold bullion standard, effectively tying the hands of central bank policy makers and setting up the country for a downward spiral of deflation. That same month, the British explorer Lieutenant Colonel Percy Fawcett trekked into the Amazon jungle, never to reappear.

On Christmas Day, over at the hastily constructed Coral Gables Athletic Stadium, a football game was under way between the local Coral Gables Collegiate All-Stars and no less a team than the Chicago Bears, featuring no less a player than their sensational rookie running back, Harold "Red" Grange. The Galloping Ghost, they called him. The Bears were on a nineteen-game national tour over two months that would help put the nascent National Football League on the map as a bona fide American spectator sport. Over the course of the barnstorming tour, 350,000 spectators would see Grange play.

At one point, the schedule had Chicago play eight games in twelve days. Perhaps the team was exhausted when it reached Coral Gables on Christmas Day, because the Bears beat the amateur collegians only by the feeble score of 7–0.

The winter season that followed would be a confusing period for the Florida economy. As 1926 dawned, there were more intimations that the tempo of the boom had changed. For one thing, the binder boys were gone—discouraged by the much higher down payments required by developers such as Carl Fisher and by new regulations stipulated by the state's association of realtors. The binder boys would leave behind $8 million worth of unpaid binders. As one journalist wrote, "If they could be viewed as rats leaving a sinking ship, then the plight of the ship was hardly a happy one."

The plight of the *Prinz Valdemar*, by now capsized and blocking the channel in Miami Harbor that January, was not a happy one, either. An object of fury and derision, it prevented entry into the harbor until the end of February, compounding all the problems created by the railroad embargo. Still, the business news was largely favorable. Local papers reported that Tatum Brothers Company, a well-known firm of realtors in Miami, had reported revenues of $65 million for 1925, up from $14 million the year before—and promptly paid out a massive $400,000 in bonuses to its seventy-two salesmen. That fact alone had to bode well for the local economy.

As Florida's real estate kings' businesses stalled—temporarily, they believed—it provided the perfect opportunity to take stock and take some of the risk off the table. And yet, not one of the big developers chose to do so. Instead, they succumbed to the temptation to celebrate their spectacular success by buying new cars and building new homes. As the *New Republic* aptly reported in late January, "We are all practitioners in greater or lesser degree of the new hedonism. We insist on living, if not for pleasure alone, at least a life in which comfort and ease are predominant aspects. . . . The Florida madness is itself sufficient proof that this civilization is still far from having found its equilibrium."

What the Florida developers, their bankers, and the local politicians—and, indeed, the leaders at the national level as well—did not fully comprehend was that the liberal and unfettered approach to capitalism that they espoused was not lifting all boats. Nor was it addressing the underlying fragility of the new industrial economy and the discontent that was arising from the profoundly inequitable distribution of wealth. Instead, this era of fads seemed to be leading inexorably to a succession of financial manias. These were simply fads of a different order that were likely to be temporary, as fads are, and to overshoot and then end in disappointment for everyone, including the onetime winners of the boom.

Florida's real estate kings were by now enormously successful. And yet the greater their success, the harder it was for them to see their success as something separate and distinct from their own labors; to believe that circumstances, even luck, might have played a part in what they had accomplished. In the months ahead, Fisher, Mizner, Merrick, Davis, and even Singer would double down on their current investments by taking on new developments and leveraging themselves to ever-greater heights. Carl Fisher, who had urged caution to his sales force and others, came the closest to altering his policies and his behavior, but even he could not resist the challenge of rolling out his biggest development ever—on Long Island instead of in Florida. His dream was to link his two resorts together by sea, recognizing that a retired, wealthy East Coast elite would very likely, as they do today, enjoy wintering in Palm Beach or Miami and thereafter summering in the Hamptons.

Surely at this point, each of these developers must have asked himself how badly exposed he would be if the economy should falter. But perhaps each reasoned that his personal wealth, even if it was mostly on paper in the form of unrealized capital gains on his real estate holdings, had reached a point where he could weather any turbulence and therefore could afford to take exorbitant chances. What they all overlooked, however—what real estate buyers throughout the country would overlook—was the role that personal debt plays in a downturn and how badly it leverages your losses.

If Florida's real estate kings had bothered to glance back over the prior year, they might have recalled a cautionary event that made headlines. It took place on March 18, 1925, a windy day in Palm Beach: the Breakers Hotel caught fire and, in a matter of hours, burned to the ground. According to one report, a handicapped woman's electric hair curler ignited the fire, which soon raced through the wood structure. Personal property and jewelry losses totaled more than $2 million. Embers from the fire ignited a neighboring hotel, the Palm Beach Hotel, which also burned down. There the personal losses were proportionately higher because so many of their guests were out watching the conflagration at the Breakers and failed to rescue their possessions.

At the nearby house of bank president Louis G. Kaufman, the servants worried about the fire spreading farther. Panicked, they threw valuable art and antiques out the windows, only to have looters make off with the booty. A relieved Jesse Livermore, the Wall Street stock speculator, who was in the midst of his annual stay at the Breakers with his wife and his mother-in-law, blithely reported that their losses of clothing and jewelry would not amount to more than $20,000. One guest who lost all of his clothing, other than the sport coat, white linen knickers, and golf hose that he was wearing at the time, remarked to a reporter, "Nero fiddled while Rome burned. I played golf while the Breakers burned."

The owners of the Breakers, the Florida East Coast Hotel Company, controlled now by the heirs of the late Mary Lily Flagler, quickly announced that they would hire Leonard Schultze of the architectural firm Schultze & Weaver to design an even grander hotel, an Italian palace topped with another Giralda tower. The new hotel, if not 100 percent fireproof, would at least be built to last, which it has. But if nothing else, the fire was confirmation that disaster could strike—often when you least expected it.

Meanwhile, "the dance of the dollars," as journalist Kenneth Ballinger dubbed it, continued, although perhaps not quite so frantically. The heat and humidity of the prior summer was said to have deterred some potential real estate buyers from traveling back to Florida. Others bought into the idea that Florida wasn't quite as fashionable as it had once been. Liners bound for Europe were crowded again with passengers heading abroad instead of south to the Sunshine State. Florida's developers soon calculated that 1926 wouldn't be as strong as 1925, but that didn't mean there wouldn't be sales—and, indeed, there were plenty. The modest decline in prices was attracting buyers who felt they had been priced out of the market the year before. In stock market parlance, the value investors had arrived.

Up in Palm Beach, the pipe-smoking antiquarian Alex Waugh chose this moment—exactly the wrong one—to quit his job running Addison

Mizner's antique shop on Via Mizner to become a real estate broker. He joined Webb Brothers, a group of agents whose probity, he believed, was "in sharp contrast with the fly-by-night organizations." But he would find sales hard to come by.

Over at Coral Gables, as improbable as it seemed, the pace of development had grown even more frantic. Buying in to his own publicity and apparently believing himself to be infallible, Merrick, if anything, accelerated the pace of development, pushing ahead with the Riviera section, "the greatest of all of Coral Gables's fine sections." In January 1926 the $10 million Biltmore Hotel opened with an enormous stag dinner party attended by the leading men of the area, followed by a grand gala ball for which dozens of fur- and jewel-bedecked fashion models were imported from New York City. The new Biltmore was the most expensive of the 481 hotels and apartment complexes built in the Miami vicinity in the prior year alone.

One extraordinary feature of the hotel was the L-shaped swimming pool, allegedly the largest in the world at 23,000 square feet of surface area, some 240 feet long, and 150 feet wide. A handsome young man named Johnny Weissmuller was shortly to be hired as a swimming instructor. He would earn local renown for chasing a young coed naked through the halls of the hotel and later far greater fame as an Olympic swimmer—he won five gold medals—and then world renown as the bare-chested, ululating star of the first Tarzan films.

As part of the opening celebration, famed golfers Bobby Jones, Gene Sarazen, Tommy Armour, and Leo Diegel teed off in an exhibition match to showcase yet another Donald Ross–designed golf course. Just two weeks later, before seven thousand spectators, the cornerstone was set for the University of Miami's first building. Then only days after that, the Tahiti Beach section opened, a man-made South Seas atoll. Tahiti Beach boasted a variation on a plan that Paul Chalfin, James Deering's designer, had originally intended for the grounds of the Vizcaya estate. A canal was under construction that would link Tahiti Beach to the new Biltmore Hotel a couple of miles inland, allowing guests to be ferried back and forth by gondola. The area included one hundred Tahitian bath huts thatched with palmetto, a matching pavilion, and a scallop-shaped band shell, where, before long, Jan Garber and His Orchestra could be heard performing. According to an advertisement in *Collier's* magazine, "Tahiti Beach is destined to take its place with Deauville and the Lido as one of the great watering places of the world."

George Merrick had moved his office from the administration building onto the fifteenth floor of the Biltmore's Giralda tower and into a suite of offices expensively furnished with Spanish antiques. Here he could stand before a twelve-foot-high picture window after concluding a day of meetings and phone calls. Clad immaculately in a linen jacket, white flannels, striped tie, and white bucks, sipping a highball of his favorite rum, Bacardí Carta de Oro, prepared by his valet, Fletcher, Merrick could survey with enormous satisfaction—from what he referred to as his "High Olympus"—his $100 million planned City Beautiful below. The floor beneath him was laid with rare imported tiles, and every massive wood door in the suite of offices had been hand carved. A nearby bedroom had been dubbed the Caruso Room because it featured an ornate iron bed that once belonged to the legendary Italian tenor Enrico Caruso. The bed was a gift to Merrick from his new business partner John McEntee Bowman.

Only five years before, Coral Gables had consisted of nothing but a jungle hammock and a 160-acre citrus grove where a young Merrick had helped his father eke out a living as a farmer. Now the property was recording $4 million in land and building sales each month, and Merrick himself had achieved heroic stature as one of the nation's master builders.

It is difficult to determine at what point all the attention that Merrick was receiving went to his head and began to impair his judgment. What is clearer is that, even as the local market began to roll over, he would choose to ignore the warning signs. And it was during this period that he turned down an $80 million offer (equivalent to $1.14 billion today) for his share of the entire Coral Gables project.

By now, Merrick had six hundred employees and was spending $3 million annually on operating expenses. His company had invested capital of $150 million in the development, although significantly, even ominously, some $60 million to $70 million of that consisted of funds borrowed from twelve different banks and companies that had eagerly lent him money. He was massively leveraged. His attorney and close friend, Clifton Benson, admonished him to slow down, but Merrick willfully chose to ignore him.

Even more revealing were the actions that he took with his newfound wealth. Perhaps in an effort to salvage his marriage—the Merricks had just celebrated their tenth anniversary—George bought Eunice a fifteen-acre estate on Nassau in the Bahamas. Next, he broke ground on the edge of the Biltmore golf course for a new home intended to be "one of the most beautiful residences in the entire South." It would feature separate wings for each of them, six bedrooms, two libraries, a roof garden, a swimming pool, servants' quarters, and a six-car garage.

Even after the *Prinz Valdemar* capsized in Miami Harbor, Merrick pushed ahead with his grand plans. He was by now, as one historian has put it, "captive of his own publicity." His biggest commitment of all was to the new Biscayne Bay section, a $100 million development that would give Coral Gables its first significant access to the waterfront. He had purchased the parcel of land from the brothers Charles and James Deering for a reported $6 million. Developed in partnership with his new friend Bowman, it would feature a casino and an even larger Biltmore Hotel, a yacht basin, and homes in a variety of architectural styles. The new Tahiti Beach would be just the beginning of a South Sea Isles theme that would now run along the coast of Biscayne Bay. No longer just for the middle class, Coral Gables was ready to make its own pitch to the country's wealthiest citizens.

The feverish activity in the Coral Gables Administration Building, one press release following another, one publicity campaign launched in the wake of another, finally took its toll on T. H. Weigall, who toiled writing promotional articles for the Coral Gables publicity department. One morning, only four or five days after he and his business partner made their first foray into Florida real estate by purchasing the option on a chunk of a Coral Gables subdivision, he awoke with a start and an intimation that something was very wrong. "It is very difficult to describe the effect that these dawnings had on me," he recalled, "and at first, in a way, I was more disturbed by my own lack of faith than by any other more material consideration."

He went to work as usual that day and was greeted by another tall stack of papers and press releases announcing the ground-breaking of a new $9 million hotel and medical facility to be called the Towers. "It was to be primarily a resort for those of delicate constitution, and would contain a private chapel, a private theater, a private bathing beach, and a complete hospital wing staffed by trained nurses and resident doctors and surgeons," Weigall remembered. The press release announced that the Towers would "supply every human need for health and happiness . . . within the house and grounds of one magnificent hotel." As he continued to read about the private waterways, the canal system, and the man-made lake, as well as a list of luxuries on offer that seemed to go on for pages, the accumulation of details began to overwhelm him. He began to panic: "I didn't believe any of them."

A few days later, he arranged to meet with his business partner to discuss the option they had bought on a pending subdivision. It transpired that neither of them was as keen on the deal as they had been when they signed the papers and lunched together so lavishly. There were rumors of a delay in the extension being formally announced, which might mean, if they couldn't flip their option in the interim, that they could be on the hook for much more money. A day or so later, the two received an unexpected offer for the option and promptly accepted it, incurring a $500 loss on the transaction. "I then and there joined the up-to-then select few who had failed to make money out of a Florida land deal," Weigall recalled. The very next day, the opening of the extension was launched, causing a gigantic spike in the value of the option that they had just sold.

Convinced that he had been an absolute fool to have let it go, Weigall went out during his lunch break and impulsively bought shares in the $1 million Miami Coliseum Corporation, a development company that was planning to build a 7,200-seat indoor arena, another surefire project that he had just heard about. He promptly spent a large portion of the money that he had saved during his four months of work for George Merrick and

Coral Gables. "It was a completely fatuous move, and even before I had left the building, the reaction had already set in, and I was bitterly regretting it." When he returned to his office, it was to read of yet another announcement, this one about Merrick's latest plan to develop the largest extension yet: the Biscayne section planned with his new partner, John McEntee Bowman. "I felt the whole thing had suddenly crossed the borderline of sanity, and that we were entering into a world where nothing meant anything anymore.... I wrote the announcement myself, but even as I wrote it, it meant nothing to me. The thing was too colossal to bring into focus; the pressure and the excitement which had kept me going during the last four months seemed suddenly to have gone, and I felt we were all madmen."

Two nights later, while swimming alone in the warmish, inky-black water off Miami Beach well after dark, Weigall resolved that he would hand in his resignation and return to London, where he still owned a tiny flat in Kensington. There he would attempt to resurrect his dormant career in journalism. He resigned the following morning, a decision his colleagues greeted with laughter and derision. They simply could not believe that he would do something so rash and foolish. "Ain't you making more cash than you've ever made in your sweet life?" one of the men asked him. He nodded. "Then why th' hell...?" Even the owner of his favorite coffee stand called him a "gazoob," which he took to be a variation on fool. But his mind was made up.

The last thing Weigall did on the very same afternoon that he departed Florida, never to return, was to sell his shares in the Miami Coliseum Corporation to a well-known sports star whom he knew only casually. "I handed over the certificates in advance and made arrangements for the money to be forwarded to me in New York the next day. I never saw or heard from him again, nor did I ever see or hear of his money."

He boarded the sleeper train to New York at the Miami station, climbed up onto his berth, and fell asleep while propped up reading the *Saturday Evening Post*. An hour or so later, Weigall awoke with a start, unsure where he was, and promptly banged his head on the roof of his Pullman bed when he sat up suddenly. Rubbing his head, he pulled back the curtain to look out the window. "There, drawn up to let us pass, their headlights glaring on the trunks of the pine trees, was a little crowd of automobiles southbound toward Miami. They moved off like glow-worms as I watched them and disappeared among the trees; the train roared on, crashing and swaying, toward the icy winds of the North and to the boat that was waiting, even already, to carry me to London."

No one would notice that he was gone. The party simply went on without him, offering up a dizzying array of new events. Chicago's Civic Opera Company, featuring Scottish soprano Mary Garden, who had caught the eye of the boxer Gene Tunney, performed nine separate operas at the Coral Gables Athletic Stadium throughout the winter. The 820,000-gallon Venetian Pool, formerly the quarry from which the stone for Coral Gables houses was cut, was drained for a performance of the new Miami Grand Opera Company. Crowds showed up to attend the first Biltmore Art Show at the new grand hotel. John McEntee Bowman even organized a fox hunt on the grounds. Evening entertainment at the Biltmore featured arias by the famed Russian opera basso Feodor Chaliapin, of New York's Metropolitan Opera. In Miami, at J. S. Bain's real estate office on NE First Avenue potential lot buyers could meet heavyweight boxer Jack Dempsey in person. Or over at the J. C. H. Corporation, you could purchase lots directly from the members of the World Champion Pittsburgh Pirates baseball team.

Lacking the lumber and concrete needed to proceed with construction—due to the rail embargo and the capsizing of the *Prinz Valdemar*—George Merrick was eventually forced to suspend work on individual houses and prioritize the projects that he could finish while building materials were in such short supply. He continued work on hotels like the Anastasia, on the Douglas Entrance, on the shopping area to be known as the Colonnade, and, most important to him personally, on the University of Miami's Merrick Building, named after his pioneering preacher father, Rev. Solomon Merrick, who had arrived in the area with no money in 1899. A few outside investors and builders with their own projects in Coral Gables managed to find enough materials during the embargo to continue construction on their own projects. There were 228 such firms from cities around the country. One of them went so far as to erect his own lumber mill and cement facility. Somehow Merrick soldiered on, still refusing to concede that economic realities had changed. At one point, he even doubled the seating at the new Coral Gables Country Club and brought back Paul Whiteman and His Orchestra to perform at the club's reopening.

But as winter became spring, it became irrefutable that the economic environment had changed for the worse. The *New York Times* described it as "a lull" and opined: "The promised boom has not materialized. Real estate men say a digestive period has set in. Florida, they say, may suffer from a slight attack of colic due to swallowing more than she could really digest. But the attack won't be serious." In downtown Miami, auctions began to take place as a popular way to move lots that were otherwise slow to sell. In late March a midwestern newspaper picked up on a rumor that Merrick had committed suicide, and a reporter telephoned his home to see if the story was true. He was reading in his library when the phone rang, and, according to the *Miami Daily News*, "He was in a very good position to deny it." By summer, with the last of the embargo lifted, the hoped-for pickup in business still had not materialized, and the change in business conditions could no longer be ignored. For one thing, many purchasers of Coral Gables lots were choosing not to make their mortgage or purchase payments. This was a shocking development. Merrick, suddenly feeling squeezed, could not meet his $5 million pledge to the University of Miami and had to offer a package of securities, mortgages, and land contracts that paid interest instead. Ultimately, the costly work on the Merrick Building would be halted and a temporary campus for the new university created at the Anastasia Hotel.

In the face of escalating financial pressure, Merrick sought to show the civic-mindedness that his publicists liked to extol. For example, he gifted the Boy Scouts a piece of property and built them a clubhouse. He converted the third floor of the San Sebastian Apartments into dormitory space for the women who would be attending his new university. He donated land, or steeply discounted its cost, to various religious denominations so that they could build churches in Coral Gables. In a speech to the community at the Coral Gables Country Club in May 1926, he advocated for keeping Coral Gables a community with "a soul."

A thorough reorganization of the business was badly needed, and Merrick managed to negotiate one in July, with the cooperation of his lenders, creating a new entity called Coral Gables Consolidated out of the old Coral Gables Corporation. The refinanced company consisted of seven subsidiary businesses (valued collectively at $75 million) that focused separately on construction, hotels, rapid transit, titles, and sales. It was designed to bring more order, and capital, to an organization whose complexity had become a problem. The sales pitch claimed the new entity—"the Second Phase of Coral Gables' Amazing Development"—now had the ability to be national in scope and could operate on a ten-year time horizon. This would not be the last reconfiguring of the business. In reality, the move served only to camouflage the far deeper problem: an alarming absence of sales.

In July the magazine the *Nation* gave voice to the great unspoken fear. "The Florida boom has collapsed," it wrote. "The world's greatest poker game, played with building lots instead of chips, is over. And the players are now cashing in or paying up."

Not long after this, Walter Fuller, the realtor from St. Petersburg, where real estate sales had yet to slow appreciatively, arrived in Miami with his father, shopping for real estate salesmen to help them launch Jack Taylor's Pasadena Estates. When all of the salesmen who showed up to be interviewed appeared to be from Coral Gables, Fuller and his father drove over to see George Merrick at his palatial office on the fifteenth floor of the Biltmore. "We told Merrick what had happened and assured him we had no plan to raid his selling force. What was the situation? . . . 'I am broke,' he said. 'I have a fine bunch of boys. They are stranded, and you will be doing them and me a favor if you give them jobs. Go ahead and hire them.'" Fuller and his father hired the cream of Merrick's sales force, most of whom were already so strapped financially that the Fullers had to pay their transportation costs to St. Petersburg.

Throughout the summer of 1926, George Merrick tried his best to stay positive and to hide his growing desperation from his wife and colleagues.

Unbeknownst to any of them, he was approaching a state of nervous collapse. Desperate to do something, he wrote a personal invitation to the twenty thousand Coral Gables lot owners, urging them to come see how well the great development was proceeding, suggesting that perhaps now was the time to start building their dream homes. As an inducement, he offered cheap transportation and free tickets to the new University of Miami's homecoming football game in October. This "Come and See" correspondence was the Hail Mary pass for Merrick and Coral Gables. It overlooked the fact that a majority of these lots, too, may have been bought for purely speculative purposes, as they had been elsewhere, their owners having no intention of ever building. The mailing was completed in early September, but the initial response was lukewarm at best.

On September 17, a few days after the last of the envelopes were mailed out, Eunice Peacock Merrick, George's wife, who had only recently been elected president of the Coral Gables Garden Club, drove from her house into downtown Miami for a few routine shopping errands. As she stepped out of a store onto the still-crowded Flagler Street, she noticed that the sky had turned exceptionally dark. "Nobody seemed worried about it," she recalled years later, "but during the night, the wind rose to top speed, and we knew a hurricane had hit."

4

GRAVEYARD OF DREAMS

18

HURRICANES

On the morning of her second marriage, Jane Fisher had breakfast in bed in her Paris hotel room. With the help of the prominent attorney Dudley Field Malone, she had successfully divorced Carl Fisher in a quickie Paris divorce and now planned to wed a Princeton University graduate named Bob Johnson, who was a decade or so her junior. On her breakfast tray was a copy of the *Paris Herald Tribune*. She picked it up and read the alarming headline: "South Florida Wiped Out by Hurricane. Where Miami Beach Was Is Now a Sandy Waste." She understood immediately that much of Carl's fortune would surely have been lost, and that meant that much of her fortune, too, was gone. She leapt out of bed to telegraph Fisher but soon learned that that there was no radio communication with Miami Beach. Later that morning, as she slipped on her blue velvet wedding dress and prepared for the ceremony, it occurred to her that her young fiancé had no money, no career, and no job prospects. It was not an auspicious start to a second marriage.

According to Jane's recollection, Fisher was aboard his yacht, *Shadow K*, halfway between Montauk and Miami Beach when the storm hit. It was there he received the radio message from a staffer that would alter his life: "Miami Beach Total Loss. Entirely Swept Away by Hurricane. Untold Damage."

The hurricane, which began on the night of September 17, 1926, came as a complete surprise to most citizens of South Florida. The morning newspapers in Miami had reported the presence of three tropical storms in the Caribbean, but they buried the story on their back pages. The evening edition of the *Miami Daily News* printed a front-page warning of a storm but noted that the weather bureau predicted it would hit the Bahamas, not Miami. It wasn't until eleven thirty that same night that the city's weather chief, Richard W. Gray, hoisted the red-and-black hurricane flags on the roof of the Miami Weather Bureau Office downtown. His warning came too late.

The full brunt of the storm arrived in the middle of the night. The gusts of wind and rain blew up into a full-throated Category 4 hurricane, based on the Saffir-Simpson scale, with 5 being the most severe. Winds were recorded at speeds of 132 miles per hour. Peak winds may actually have reached 150 miles per hour, which would have been a record wind speed for the time. No one could be sure of its top speed because the storm tore the three-cup anemometer off the roof of Allison Hospital on the morning of September 18 before any readings could be taken. The highest wind ever recorded before the Miami hurricane was 140 miles per hour atop Mount Washington, in New Hampshire, on January 11, 1876.

A railroad porter named Ray Jackson sat in his Pullman car at the Miami station when the storm struck. "The wind blew so hard, it rocked the car like a cradle," he recalled. That was only the beginning. Up and down the streets of Miami and Miami Beach, awnings over windows and doorways were ripped loose along with their poles, which flew like spears through the air. At the Roman Pools, the wind bent the palm trees nearly in half before stripping them of their fronds. The arms of the windmill itself were boxed aside and then broken away. The entire structure was soon so badly damaged that its remains would later be torn down. Farther along the beach, a gust smashed through the famous glass dome of the Flamingo Hotel, raining down shards and exposing the cushy furniture and the flamingo wall murals to repeated onslaughts of rain.

A fresh gust lifted the freight cars parked at Bayshore Drive and Sixth Street and flipped them onto their sides. Elsewhere, telephone poles swayed, then snapped in half; billboards were flattened; entire tent camps of tin-canners simply vanished. Even at those camps that were more sheltered by trees, the wind shredded the canvas tents or lifted them one by one like spinnakers before tearing them free. Five hundred tents were destroyed at Coral Gables. In the gardens of Villa Vizcaya, the heavy statuary was blown from its pedestals. Down at the Meteor Docks, a battery of wind and rain crumpled a row of warehouses. The unfinished seventeen-story Meyer-Kiser building, its girders exposed, shimmied in the wind until eventually the entire building was twisted, its unfinished walls stripped clean, leaving the structure looking as defaced as though it had endured an aerial bombardment. The building would later be condemned and all but the bottom six stories removed.

The devastation extended thirty miles up and down the east coast of Florida. In Buena Vista, the storm punched out the windows on all four stories of the Shackleford Motor Car Company before the weight of rainwater caved in the roof. In Hialeah, virtually every structure—the race track, the jai alai fronton, the motion picture studio, and the local Seminole Indian village, to say nothing of all the flimsily constructed housing built late in the boom—was stripped of its roof, flattened, or wrecked beyond repair. Over in Hollywood, sand swept over cars parked outside the hotels, leaving them looking like vehicles half buried in a snowdrift. The sand filled the lobbies of the hotels—halfway to the ceiling, in one case. The Hollywood Bathing Casino, inundated with water, was nearly completely destroyed. Fisher's new board speedway at Fulford-by-the-Sea was reduced to rubble. The one hundred or so huts along the waterfront at Merrick's new Tahiti Beach were erased from the sand.

One rogue wave washed clear across Miami Beach, depositing enough sand along Collins Avenue to bury every patch of grass. Other waves hoisted up a handful of yachts in Biscayne Bay and deposited them in Royal Palm Park or at the foot of the McAllister and Columbus hotels. Forty-nine other boats of various sizes sank in the bay. The yacht *Nohab*, formerly owned by Germany's Kaiser Wilhelm II, was capsized and half submerged. Another famous yacht, the one-hundred-foot *Fleetwood III*, owned by Commodore J. P. Stoltz, crashed against the stone arch of a causeway before it sank. In the Miami River, where a number of boats had sought refuge, ninety vessels were sunk or battered to pieces against the shoreline. At Fort Lauderdale, the tidal surge heaved the enormous Coast

Guard ship stationed there high up onto the sand, leaving it beached on its side like a dead whale.

The tidal surge would be the highest ever recorded, reaching 11.7 feet above mean sea level on Biscayne Boulevard and estimated at 14 to 15 feet in Coconut Grove, where Marjory Stoneman Douglas's brand-new bungalow stood in the path of the onslaught. Douglas, although visiting relatives in the North at the time of the storm, later wrote a description of the event in her iconic book about the Everglades: "The water of the bay was lifted and blown inland, in streaming sheets of salt, with boats, scows, ships, the *Rose Mahoney*, coconuts, debris of all sorts, up on the highest ridge of the mainland. Miami Beach was isolated in a sea of raving white water."

Leo F. Reardon, a journalist who lived just west of Coral Gables in a house that stood alone on high ground, fully exposed to the elements, was at home with his wife, Deanie, and their two kids, Mark, eight, and Sheila, six, when the storm sent the iron bar of a canvas awning crashing through a bedroom window. He hurriedly moved his family to the other end of the house. More windows blew out, and the power was lost, leaving them in pitch darkness. With the winds now roaring steadily, he decided the safest place to hide would be inside their automobile, which was parked in the garage at the side of the house away from the wind. They had to crawl on their hands and knees to get there. Once the kids were settled inside the car, he threw an old mattress over the top to add further protection. For five hours, the wind blew continuously, tearing down a big pine on the property, and threatening to rip the roof off the house and the garage. At dawn, the wind finally died down. Not realizing that they were now in eye of the storm, Reardon cleared the debris from the driveway and set out in the car to purchase supplies. "The scene of wreckage brought tears to my eyes. Coral Gables' buildings, with a few exceptions, had weathered the terrific blast, but the beautiful foliage was laid low. Light and telephone wires were strewn about in reckless abandon. The ground was covered with green grapefruit." He managed to buy a few groceries at a local store before realizing that the wind was picking up again. Sensing that the storm was still far from over, he sped home in a panic.

According to a salesman for the American Bakeries Company named Kirby Jones, another eyewitness to the events, it was the lull in the eye of the storm that caused so many of the ensuing casualties. "Hundreds of persons, believing the storm was over, started for work. . . . Thousands of homes were ripped from their foundations, and the air was filled with flying timbers." The wind now blew from the opposite direction, he said, "like a hundred steamer whistles blowing at once."

Back in his house, Riordan steered his family into the laundry room at the opposite end of the house from the garage, which was now facing the brunt of the storm. He put the two kids into the two large slate washbasins and covered them with pillows. He and his wife crouched nearby. Through the empty window frames, they could see the tall Australian pines in the backyard writhing in the wind. "The air was streaked with garbage cans, automobile tops, dog houses, furniture, and parts of buildings," he recalled. "We could barely see the ground because of the rain, which was being driven in white stinging sheets. The force of the wind inside the house shattered the glass of the kitchen door like the report of a gun above the roar and peppered our backs."

The swollen waters of Lake Okeechobee, driven by the wind, burst through a levee and swamped the town of Moore Haven under fourteen feet of water, drowning 150 residents. This may have been one of two such events author Zora Neale Hurston had in mind when she wrote her famous description of a Florida hurricane in her classic 1937 novel *Their Eyes Were Watching God*:

> *Ten feet higher and as far as they could see the muttering wall advanced before the braced-up waters like a road crusher on a cosmic scale. The monstropolous beast had left his bed. The two hundred miles an hour wind had loosed his chains. He seized hold of his dikes and ran forward until he met the quarters; uprooted them like grass and rushed on after his supposed-to-be conquerors, rolling the dikes, rolling the houses, rolling the people in the houses along with other timbers. The sea was walking the earth with a heavy heel.*

Four hours later, the Riordan family emerged from the remains of their ruined, windowless home, stunned, exhausted, and traumatized. They packed a few belongings into the back of their car and headed for Miami's Everglades Hotel, where they hoped to take refuge. They passed entire roofs that had been torn off buildings and were sitting intact blocks away from their original structures. "Whole sides of apartment blocks had been torn away, disclosing seminaked men and women moving dazedly about the ruins of their homes. Houses, stores, and shops lay sprawled," Riordan recalled. The few people on the streets of Miami were either weeping or laughing hysterically.

The governor declared martial law, the National Guard was deployed, and traffic was banned from the streets so that the damage could be properly assessed and the massive amounts of debris cleared. The Red Cross calculated that 373 people had died (150 of those in Moore Haven), 6,381 had been injured, and 17,884 families had been left homeless. Overlooked in these tallies were the hundreds of dead black farmworkers who were never counted because, to the authorities, they had never much mattered.

It would prove to be the most expensive catastrophe in the history of the United States since the earthquake and fire in San Francisco in 1906. The cost was estimated as high as $500 million ($6.9 billion in today's money). In fact, it remains, in today's dollars, one of the more expensive hurricanes to hit US shores. Building loss in Miami alone was estimated at $20 million, with 2,000 homes lost and 3,000 damaged; in Fort Lauderdale, 1,200 homes were destroyed and 3,600 damaged; in Hollywood, 1,000 were lost and 2,000 damaged. All the boats moored or docked along the Miami waterfront were sunk or severely impaired, except for two: a yacht called *Adventure II* and the giant barkentine *Prinz Valdemar* still floated nonchalantly in the harbor.

In some respects, the loss of property was not as dire as the newspapers indicated initially. Miami Beach was not a sandy wasteland, as reported; most of the buildings were damaged but still standing. However, the damage *was* far worse than the great developers would be willing to admit. Denial was their reflexive response to the tragedy. George Merrick, for example, released a statement on behalf of his colleagues and his corporation that read, in part: "The damage done by the hurricane in other parts of the Greater Miami district, as well as in Coral Gables, has been greatly exaggerated, and it is proper that a correct and authorized statement of this damage should be furnished to the people of America so that no erroneous impression will be created. There will be no future change in the future plans of Coral Gables."

The habit of hype was deeply ingrained. "When will Florida come back?" Doc Dammers asked rhetorically before answering his own question: "Florida never went, and it doesn't have to come back." Ed Romfh, Miami's mayor, tried to echo this optimistic tone in a press release. "I want to give positive assurance that our friends will find Miami this winter the same enjoyable, hospitable, comfortable vacation city it has always been," he insisted—and then elaborated: "I predict that Miami will make a world record in coming back." John McEntee Bowman, founder of the Biltmore chain of hotels, declared that "out of the ruins of the old will arise a bigger and stronger city that will attract tourists as never before." These remarks, and others like them, would prove premature. And by laboring so strenuously—and cravenly—to minimize the damage done to Florida's image in the national press, these men severely hampered the Red Cross's ability to raise the necessary funds to treat the vast number of injured and homeless.

The repair work began immediately: roofs were restored, sand removed, docks and bulkheads rebuilt. Carl Fisher issued a statement that read: "[T]he order to rebuild supersedes all others." Up went new telephone poles and power lines. By the time the winter season arrived, Miami and Miami Beach were ready to resume business, if in a chastened and cautious state. South Florida appeared to be on a slow path to recovery from the storm. But despite the developers' optimistic projections, the good times failed to return.

One genuinely helpful result in the wake of the storm was a concerted effort on the part of Miami authorities to address the nearly complete absence of building codes, zoning, and inspection requirements in the city. John J. Farrey, the new chief building, plumbing, and electrical inspector for Miami Beach, developed the first hurricane code and the model for coastal building codes in the United States. It would come to be called the Miami Standard and was widely adopted by cities around the country.

Marjory Stoneman Douglas's brand-new bungalow sat six and a half feet above sea level, not high enough, as she read in the Massachusetts papers, to withstand the hurricane's fourteen-foot surge. Her father, who was in Jacksonville during the storm, hurried back to inspect his house, which survived intact, and then went on to inspect hers. Once the telephone lines were restored, the two spoke. He described how her windows were blown out and some shingles were missing. Various debris had gathered inside the bungalow, but it remained structurally sound. There were water stains on the outside walls but, amazingly, none on the inside. A few weeks later, Douglas's insurance company offered to pay her $250 for the damage. It cost her $50 to replace the windows and the shingles, which meant that she had money left over to put in wood flooring that she had been unable to afford. "To me, the hurricane of '26 had done more good than harm," she recalled. Marjory quickly furnished the house with hand-me-downs, and began to fill it with bookcases and books.

The storm left a deep impression on her, and she would later write a book on hurricanes. They touched on one of her central literary themes: how mankind repeatedly misjudged nature—both the impact man was having on it, and the impact that nature could have on man.

In the prior decade, she had found her calling and her voice as a writer, and now she had what she needed most: her own abode. The house, her "workshop," would remain enormously important to her. Douglas loved it as though it were her own child. "The house was a great influence on my life," she would recall later, "and so important that I often think of it more than the other things I was doing during those years." It was an appropriate symbol of what she had achieved—and of her own highly valued and hard-won independence. It would provide her with the privacy, peace of mind, and intellectual freedom she needed, and became a source of contentment that allowed her to pursue her best work in the years ahead. "With no dependents, a well-oiled typewriter and decent health, you can live indefinitely, so to speak, on your own fat," she once remarked. What followed would be a remarkably productive writing career followed by a life as a conservation activist.

The more inland location of Merrick's Coral Gables and its relatively stringent building codes helped to protect it from the storm's worst ravages. Not a single life was lost there. Still, wood structures were flattened, windows shattered, palm trees toppled, and plantings destroyed. The *Miami Riviera*, the local newspaper and the house organ of the development company, began to publish a "Hurricane Extra" that sought to provide reassurance and keep the residents informed about the reconstruction work. A concerted effort was made to tamp down any negative publicity. Merrick continued to insist that Coral Gables would come back stronger and better than ever. He announced the first annual "Progress Week" celebration that would highlight all that had been accomplished over the prior five years and promote special events such as a circus and a parade. On October 15 the University of Miami opened in the unfinished Anastasia Hotel with seven hundred students enrolled. It would be nicknamed "the Cardboard College," in honor of the cardboard walls erected to create the classrooms.

Seeking to avert a financial disaster, the commissioners of the recently incorporated city of Coral Gables, governed by Merrick and his men, voted to float a thirty-year municipal bond issue of $4.5 million paying interest of 6 percent. The bond issue would allow the city to purchase key assets from George Merrick and his Coral Gables Consolidated to ensure that they were completed, or so it was argued. Given Merrick's obvious financial interest in the outcome, the bond program was controversial. Another smaller bond issue was floated to allow the city to pay for the cost of street and sidewalk improvements—improvements that the corporation (owned by Merrick) had promised its lot buyers that the company itself would fund. In all, four such bond issues were floated by Coral Gables to pay for the assets or obligations of Merrick's corporation. Years later, these questionable bond issuances would lead to an investigation by the Securities and Exchange Commission (SEC), the regulatory body set up to monitor the financial markets and prosecute security law violations. Merrick would defend himself by insisting that he was pouring all of his profits into the city of Coral Gables and that the bond program was the only way to raise the necessary money to stabilize the development. But few residents knew or understood the full details of these deals or how much desperation they signaled.

Plunging ahead, George launched new publicity and ad campaigns to promote the city, including one of his most elaborate brochures, called *Coral Gables Today*. What the public didn't know was that by mid-November 1926, Merrick had suffered a devastating nervous breakdown, perhaps exacerbated by the questionable financial actions he had undertaken to try to save his business. By now, his heavy drinking had begun to alarm his closest friends and colleagues. He entered the Washington Sanitarium and Hospital in Takoma Park, Maryland, complaining of "extreme fatigue, sleep deprivation, and problems from abscessed teeth." Privately, he admitted to feeling like "poor Humpty Dumpty," not only broken but also defeated.

Despite Merrick's optimistic public assertions, the real estate business in Coral Gables and elsewhere in Florida failed to improve. In fact, it was getting worse, and George Merrick had begun a humiliating fall from grace, the likes of which few people can ever fully recover from. The fall began gradually and escalated as one disappointment was heaped on another. As he ran out of money, he halted work on virtually all of the projects. Without new financing, the entire development looked doomed to failure. The *Miami Riviera*, naturally, continued to defend him: "We are with him to a man, in all his efforts on our behalf. We wish he were here [for Progress Week]. Since he can't be here, let us cheer him on with the knowledge that we are trying to further his ideals while we glory in his achievement. Let us take a moment to salute George E. Merrick—who works for all of us." Despite the hollowness of this cheerleading, residents of the community continued to back him, although their support was beginning to wane.

Merrick spent months trying to refinance the development without success—at one point, he spent four and a half months in New York, negotiating with reluctant bankers. Finally, in February 1928 he launched what he called the Comprehensive Refinancing Plan. The idea was to exchange the existing obligations, some $65 million in debt, for a mix of longer-term mortgages and preferred and common stock in a new corporation, with

George and his associates remaining the majority owners and the general managers. The annual budget of Coral Gables Consolidated, which had shrunk from $3 million in the boom years to $1 million in October 1927, would be cut to a mere $250,000 in October 1928.

But before the details of the new plan could be finalized, Merrick faced an insurrection from a group of residents calling itself the Citizens League of Coral Gables, which demanded a special election of commissioners. The members were determined to remove Merrick and his associates from power before the 1929 deadline stipulated in the city's charter. For the first time, Merrick faced a direct and very personal attack. "Merrick rode to the top of the crest of the boom and ran his shoestring up to a seventy-five-million-dollar paper profit and left most of us the pleasure of riding down on the wave," remarked Vincent D. Wyman, a future mayor of the city, at an opposition rally at the Coral Gables Grammar School. "Merrick built Coral Gables for businesses purposes only, and his advertising and sales methods have put a halo of hokum about his head."

When the vote finally came, every commissioner except Merrick was voted out of office, and his reelection was a pyrrhic victory at best. The new commissioners immediately demanded an audit of the city's finances. At the very next board meeting, the new members voted to expel him from his position as a city commissioner. Their action proved to be something of a moot point. The banks soon seized control of Coral Gables Consolidated and replaced the entire management team. Merrick was allowed to stay on, but only in a largely ceremonial position. In a subsequent move, he would be required to relinquish all equity in the enterprise that he had founded. Depressed, ill again, and drinking heavily, he would be hospitalized for a second nervous breakdown. This hospitalization, in Atlanta, marked the formal end of Merrick's career as a developer, although he was not yet ready to concede defeat.

Unlike George Merrick's stairstep decline to career oblivion, D. P. Davis's career—and life—came to a sudden and alarming halt. His Davis Shores development in St. Augustine had been spared the hurricane that ravaged southern Florida, but he must have known by September 1926 that the negative publicity from the storm, on top of the already waning sales, would badly damage, if not ruin, his business. On September 23, less than a week after the storm, he attended the heavyweight boxing title match in Philadelphia between defending champ Jack Dempsey and challenger Gene Tunney in the company of George, his ten-year-old son from his first marriage. The underdog Tunney won in a ten-round unanimous decision. Father and son bet $1 on the outcome; Davis backed Tunney. "That may have been the last dollar he earned," wrote one biographer.

On Saturday, October 9, Davis boarded Star Line ocean liner *Majestic*, the largest ship afloat, for the five-day sail to Paris. His entourage included his son, his twenty-six-year-old mistress, Lucille Zehring, her mother, his lawyer, his publicist, and his publicist's wife, and a friend named Raymond Schindler, who was a celebrated private detective. Davis presumably intended not just to divorce Elizabeth Nelson in a quickie Paris divorce but also to marry Lucille on the same trip. It is likely he planned to use Schindler to testify in the divorce proceedings and his public relations team to publicize the new wedding.

Despite the elaborate preparations, the voyage ended in disaster. Four days later, very early in the morning, the captain of the *Majestic* wired ashore that Davis had disappeared overboard at around five o'clock. The ship circled for an hour attempting to find the missing passenger, but Davis's body was never recovered. Newspapers reported that a steward outside his stateroom had overheard Davis and Lucille arguing, and Davis saying that he "could go either way"—that he could jump overboard, or not, and that he didn't really care which. Those were the last words ever heard from the boastful D. P. Davis.

Controversy has surrounded his death ever since. Did he commit suicide? Had he accidentally fallen overboard? Or was he the victim of foul play—was he pushed? His mistress claimed, improbably, that he was showing off by sitting astride the porthole and that he was blown overboard, and she insisted that he hadn't been drinking. Few believed her. Brochure photographs of the *Majestic*'s staterooms show windows far too small for anyone to sit in easily, although Davis, a small man, could conceivably have climbed through one if he was determined to jump overboard. But he seems not to have known yet the full dimensions of the grave financial peril he faced at Davis Shores. And why would he commit suicide if he were shortly to divorce one wife and happily marry the next one? As part of the inquest, the authorities interviewed the steward and found his story about an overheard lovers' quarrel to be credible.

Only eight months after Davis's death, Lucille married a Neapolitan duke named Fabio Carafa d'Andria, hardly the behavior of a grieving mistress and fiancée. Their marriage lasted only two years, although she continued to call herself Duchess Carafa d'Andria years later, despite the Duke's protestations. The last record of her whereabouts is a 1940 census record that shows her and her sister working as waitresses in a hotel coffee shop in Chicago.

The Mizner brothers had lost control of their company even before the Miami hurricane hit, although the public didn't know it. A cash flow squeeze in May 1926 caused unpaid contractors to file claims against the company, which in turn forced a hasty reorganization. By July, the company was controlled by Chicago's Central Equities Corporation, which in turn was controlled by financier Rufus Dawes and his brothers Behman, Henry, and Charles. At the time, Charles happened to be vice president of the United States in the Coolidge administration. Perhaps even more impressively, he was a recent corecipient of the Nobel Peace Prize for his Dawes Plan, which eased the reparations Germany was required to pay in the aftermath of World War I—a plan that, among other things, helped to shore up the German currency.

The Dawes brothers had secured a 51 percent controlling interest in the enterprise by promising $1.5 million in new capital. In actuality, they advanced only $151,113 and promptly demoted Addison to head of architectural development, a figurehead position given that there would be no further development. Wilson Mizner and Harry Reichenbach were both fired. The actress Marie Dressler, who had helped head up sales as the so-called Duchess of Boca Raton, appears to have quit her job. She had come to deeply regret her involvement in the project. "I accepted as gospel what I was told about the value of land down there," she recalled in her memoirs. "Almost beside myself with distress, I did what I could to straighten things out. This experience was one of the most humiliating of my life."

In keeping with their vulture style of investing, the Dawes brothers now looted the company by mortgaging the undeveloped acreage of the property, placing liens on the equipment, automobiles, and furniture of Mizner Development Corporation, and by taking possession of all of the purchase contracts on the sold lots. They then removed the cash. Burdened with debts, its assets depleted, the corporation was left to fend for itself in bankruptcy court. Specifically, 173 creditors were left holding the tab for approximately $4.2 million in debts and contractors' claims. Three years later, these creditors would receive one-tenth of a cent for every dollar owed them.

Meanwhile, the Palm Beach National Bank, which had provided the Mizner company with much of its financing and held $25,000 of its promissory notes, began to teeter as its book of mortgage loans—many of them to Boca Raton lot owners—went sour. The Federal Reserve Bank of Atlanta stepped in to supplement the bank's reserves, but by June 29, 1926, the bank was forced to shut its doors. This early bank failure in Florida can be viewed as a tipping point—the moment when bank failures went from being an irregular and rural phenomenon to a smoldering threat to the national economy.

The devalued real estate assets of the Mizner Development Corporation would eventually be sold out of bankruptcy in November 1927 to an attorney acting on behalf of an anonymous buyer who spent $76,350 plus the assumption of $7 million in mortgage debt. The buyer turned out to be Clarence Geist, a utilities magnate who had been an original member of the board of directors of Mizner Development and a former partner of the Dawes brothers in various midwestern gas and electric enterprises. As an insider, he knew what he was buying. According to one rumor, Geist had been blackballed at the Everglades Club in Palm Beach when he applied there for membership and was looking to exact revenge by creating a social club to directly compete with it. The rumor is almost certainly false: Geist owned a house designed by Marion Sims Wyeth on the grounds of the Everglades Club, where he appears to have been a member in good standing. The truth was that Geist hoped to replicate in Florida the success he had achieved with the Seaview Golf Club near Atlantic City. In the following years, he would spend more than $8 million to fulfill much of Addison's vision for the Cloister Inn, hiring the architectural firm of Schultze & Weaver to do a redesign that vastly expanded the hotel to more than four hundred rooms. Membership in the new club cost an extravagant $5,000 annually. Despite the Great Depression, the Boca Raton Club emerged as one of the finest and most private winter resorts in the country, and one especially favored by the fabulously wealthy, very much as Addison Mizner had intended it to be.

The year 1927 proved to be a calamitous one for the beleaguered architect. Exhausted and humiliated by his failure, his weight soared to well over three hundred pounds, and he fell ill with pneumonia. Bedridden, his recovery would be a slow one. In March the Cocoanuts Ball, the annual bacchanal that Addison had helped to found, went on without him at the Oasis Club, but then, as a reflection of the changed times, the event was suspended—for the next three decades.

As the year progressed, Addison began to lose the pets and the people to whom he was closest. The first to go was his beloved monkey Johnnie Brown, who died suddenly in April. With him seemed to die the antic spirit of the boom. Mizner had a small gravestone inscribed and then with due solemnity buried the capuchin's remains in a corner of a Via Mizner courtyard in the presence of Johnnie's closest friends. Among them was Alex Waugh, who had already quit his job at the Antigua Shops to become a realtor. Admitting his mistake, Waugh now resolved to leave Florida altogether. He accepted a job offer from McCreery's, a well-known furniture store in New York City. After only a few months there, he moved to San Francisco to work for Dick Gump at Gump's famed luxury emporium as head of the interior design and decorating department.

Meanwhile, Addison's fun-loving nephew Horace Chase announced that he would be moving permanently to France, where the cost of living was much cheaper. The following year, in September 1928, while flying his World War I Curtiss Jenny up to Baltimore to trade it in for a new Bellanca aircraft, the vintage biplane malfunctioned and nosedived. Horace died tragically along with his copilot in the ensuing crash. The news stunned Addison and the denizens of Miznerland. "A part of each of us died with him," recalled Waugh.

The last of Addison's intimates to leave Palm Beach was his troublesome brother. The threat of pending litigation, as much as economic necessity, may have driven Wilson away. "I never open my door, but a writ blows in," Wilson complained in a letter to the writer Arthur Somers Roche around this time. "When the bell rings, I open the door, automatically stick out my hand, admit being Wilson Mizner, and accept service. I spend my evenings shuffling these fearsome documents and can cut to any complaint." In one court case that followed the collapse of Boca Raton, he was asked in testimony, "Did you tell this man that he could grow nuts on that land?" Wilson's response: "I told him he could *go* nuts on that land."

In the fall, Wilson loaded up the big Packard car that he referred to as his "stone-crusher," and said his good-byes. He left Florida bound for the Ambassador Hotel on Wilshire Boulevard in Los Angeles, where he hoped to launch a new career writing dialogue for Hollywood's newest innovation: the talking picture.

Wilson left behind an older brother who was deeply in debt, in large part due to him. In fact, Wilson had only added to Addison's woes by secretly opening a joint checking account in their names and then overdrawing it. He now left his brother alone to cope with the bulk of their bills and legal headaches. Addison wrote him from Florida asking that he do his part to help—"I am enclosing a list of the bills you owe locally and which throw you into a very unpleasant light and naturally come back to me. . . . If it is possible for you to pay off an account a certain monthly portion of the bills, I think it would be very advisable."

Wilson refused. His callous behavior brings to mind a remark he made during the Boynton Beach "Mizner Mile" trial, when he was asked on the witness stand, "You love your brother, don't you? You have a great affection for him, don't you?" Wilson replied drolly, "I have a vague regard for him."

And yet it is unfair to pigeonhole Wilson simply as a heartless and opportunistic villain. The truth had more gradations of gray. Wilson was a man of surprising compassion, who looked after his friends when they fell on hard times, his own brother being the notable exception. As the *New Yorker* writer Alva Johnston noted, "He used to visit narcotic hospitals to cheer up old pals. He had a real talent for comforting a friend in distress." Alex Waugh, who admitted to being intimidated by Wilson and his sharp tongue, remembered him as "hard in speech, but kind in action." When Waugh, whom Wilson continued to teasingly call "a bloody Limey," fell sick from his old wartime injuries, Wilson arrived at his door to nurse him back to health.

"I suppose it is true enough that his more harebrained schemes were the downfall of Addison and all he had built up," Waugh admitted later. Still, he observed, "There was something at once lovable and terrifying about Wilson, with his gaunt Mephistophelean cast of countenance, his irresistible wisecracks, and incredible stories of misdeeds in which he reveled." Even more to Wilson's credit was an episode in 1930 that occurred when two drunken patrons at the El Cholo, a Mexican restaurant in downtown Los Angeles, taunted the songwriter Irving Berlin, calling him a dirty Jew. An indignant Wilson rose to his friend's aid and confronted the abusers. When one of the drunks took a swing at Wilson, he ducked, grabbed a beer bottle, and smashed it over the fellow's head, instigating a brawl that wrecked the restaurant, according to the recollection of the British society photographer Cecil Beaton, who was present at the melee. In one of her memoirs, Anita Loos aptly described Wilson "as lovable as he was monstrous." Addison, of course, forgave him. He simply could not hold a grudge against his younger brother, whom he described as the "the only one I knew and loved in the world."

Although Addison had lost the Mizner Development Company, he still owned Mizner Industries, with its furniture factory, pottery, and antique business, and Mizner Inc., his architectural practice. But these, too, were now in jeopardy as the demand for his services waned. His most valuable asset remained Villa Mizner on Worth Avenue, the five-story building where he still lived, worked, and entertained. He mortgaged it to raise money to help pay off other bills. As he returned to his Palm Beach architectural practice, which had languished as he focused on the Boca Raton development, Mizner began to accept commissions much farther afield. These included designing a house for his niece Ysabel in Pebble Beach, California, along with a far grander house in Montecito, California, to be called Casa Bienvenida (House of Welcome) for Alfred E. Dieterich, a cofounder of Union Carbide. The Dieterich house would have forty rooms and encompass seventeen thousand square feet.

With his business in the doldrums, Addison's health began to deteriorate alarmingly. Already plagued with ulcers and early-stage heart disease, further adding to his woes were obesity, depression, and recurrent phlebitis. His close friend Alice DeLamar stepped in to try to help. Highly intelligent, well traveled, and cultured, she recognized Addison's Palm Beach houses for what they were: remarkable aesthetic achievements in their own right. She decided to take it upon herself to record and memorialize them in a monograph, mindful that many of these houses might well disappear over time. Secretly, she hoped the monograph would help to rekindle Addison's career. She spared no expense, hiring Frank E. Geisler, a nationally acclaimed portrait and landscape photographer. She accompanied Geisler on many of the photo shoots and built a raised platform on the back of a Ford pickup truck she owned so that Geisler wouldn't need to climb a ladder to photograph the exteriors.

DeLamar then chose the photos of the twenty-eight residences herself, selected Baskerville as the book's typeface, wrote the captions, and persuaded the journalist Ida Tarbell to contribute an introduction. It read in part: "What Mizner had done in Palm Beach was like a revelation to me. You need not ruin the enchantment of Florida by development. You could preserve it all, enhance it, even, if you only knew how—and he knew how." Paris Singer added a short foreword in which he remarked of Mizner's Palm Beach houses that "although inspired by the art of Spain and Italy, they are an order of Architecture of his own which will live in the history of American Architecture when we are gone and forgotten."

In March 1928 the upmarket publisher William Helburn released *Florida Architecture of Addison Mizner*. The work was a triumph, a lovely depiction of and appraisal of Mizner's work. It was also a profound act of friendship. Mizner, spending the summer in California, wrote to thank his benefactor: "My dearest Alice, I have been so ill since *The* Book took shape that I have never made it quite clear how much I appreciated the greatest compliment ever paid a living architect. I should be very conceited about it; but it has had just the opposite effect, for now I will have to do something to justify myself. The house I am doing at Santa Barbara [Dieterich's Casa Bienvenida] is I think my very best. I will send you pictures of it next spring. . . . Always devotedly, Addison."

The monograph led to a brief spike in commissions and two more large and memorable structures: La Ronda, a mammoth Gothic-style private home situated on 249 acres in Bryn Mawr, Pennsylvania, for the heir to a kid leather fortune; and a three-story hotel, the Cloister, on Sea Island, Georgia, for Howard Coffin of the Hudson Motor Car Company and his cousin. Otherwise, few big commissions came Addison's way. In Palm Beach, he was awarded the commission for the Memorial Fountain and Plaza and, to fulfill it, erected an impressive fountain in honor of Henry Flagler and Elisha "Chap" Dimick, Palm Beach's first mayor. Its rearing stone horses paid homage to the marble lions in the fountain of the Court of the Lions at the Alhambra. Despite his poor health, Addison hadn't lost his touch.

In the fall of 1928, another hurricane struck Florida. This one made landfall September 16 and did far more damage in Palm Beach than in Miami, putting to rest any hopes of a bright economic recovery for Florida real estate. The death toll was far higher than the '26 hurricane, because the 130-mile-an-hour wind drove the waters of Lake Okeechobee over its dikes, flooding the settlements of Belle Glade, Canal Point, Chosen, Pakhokee, and South Bay in an area known as the Muck Bowl, and drowning 1,800 to 2,500 mostly black Bahamian and Haitian farmworkers. Many of their bodies were never recovered. Six hundred were buried in a mass grave in West Palm Beach and promptly forgotten. Years later, skeletons were still being discovered miles away, deep in the saw grass of the Everglades. Fifteen thousand people were left homeless, with some five thousand of those living in Red Cross refugee camps. Little help was forthcoming.

When a white National Guard soldier shot and killed an African American World War I veteran with a wife and two children during the recovery efforts, apparently without serious provocation, the soldier was quickly exonerated at the inquest.

A different sort of hurricane still lay in store for the Florida economy as the decade drew to a close: a financial one. The stock market crash that occurred in October 1929 would strike deep into the pocketbooks of Mizner's wealthy Palm Beach clients and friends, including Paris Singer, who never recouped his losses. By now, Singer, too, had drastically overextended himself in Florida real estate. His $25 million Singer Island project situated on the largely inaccessible Palm Beach Inlet north of Palm Beach had stalled in the early development stages, but not before he sank millions into purchasing the land and starting construction on the Mizner-designed Blue Heron Hotel. His backers included such Palm Beach luminaries as Anthony J. Drexel Biddle, E. F. Hutton, the brothers Charles and Gurnee Munn, John Magee, John S. Pillsbury Sr., and George Sloane, most of whom owned Mizner houses in Palm Beach. Initially, Singer planned to connect the island to Palm Beach by means of an "aerial ferry," with a dozen cable cars passing one hundred feet above the water. When that proved unfeasible, he announced a $2 million automobile tunnel dug under Lake Worth to connect Palm Beach with Palm Beach Ocean. In the end, he personally backed a bond offering to pay for a simple bridge. At one point in its construction, he went so far as to pledge the Everglades Club property as collateral.

None of it came to fruition. In April 1927 Singer was charged with fraud. The actual charge was "obtaining money under false pretenses to the amount of $1.5 million." He was arrested at his apartment atop the Everglades Club and escorted from the premises by a Palm Beach deputy sheriff. At the courthouse, he was released on $20,000 bail. Three weeks later, the charges were dropped during a preliminary hearing, but the humiliation and the threat of future litigation caused Singer to pack up and abandon Florida for his Moorish cliff-side villa, which overlooked the Mediterranean in the South of France. His wife, the former nurse Joan Bates, accompanied him, but he was a broken man, his confidence and health shattered by his financial reverses. At one point, Singer quarreled with Mizner over the $75,000 commission for the design of the Blue Heron, and the two stopped speaking to each other, except through their lawyers. After Singer's arrest, however, Addison reached out to his old friend in sympathy, and the two were warmly reconciled. Singer wrote to Mizner, addressing him as "My dearest old Addison," urging him to please consider rejoining the Everglades Club, which Addison had quit in protest during their feud. "It is the one name that has any right to be there, and when you took it off, you gave me one 'right in the jaw'!" Addison replied by telling him to forget about the matter until his return to Palm Beach and added warmly, "I am looking forward to seeing you more than anything else in the world." They were reconciled in time for Singer to write a short introduction to Alice DeLamar's monograph on Mizner's architecture.

According to DeLamar, Paris Singer died suddenly of a heart attack while cruising the Nile River on a houseboat in the winter of 1932, but this was likely not the case. An obituary in the *New York Times* reported that he had died the night of June 24 in a hotel room in London, where he had gone to consult a heart specialist. Joan Bates lived on in seclusion until her death at the Cap Ferrat villa in February 1946. The Everglades Club went into receivership in the mid-1930s. Eventually a group of members who were bondholders in the club bought it for $450,000 in 1936. It had been appraised at $1.5 million in 1927. The dilapidated Blue Heron Hotel, nicknamed "Singer's Folly," remained unfinished and abandoned, a popular roost for seagulls until it was razed in 1940.

Meanwhile, for an already out-of-favor Addison Mizner, the increasingly grim economic realities of the Great Depression were the final blow to his prospects for a career comeback. It didn't help his spirits when, in the spring of 1929, angry investors in the Boca Raton project sued him along with the other officers of the Mizner Development Corporation for inflating the value of Boca Raton real estate. The scandal left his reputation in tatters.

Addison had a single commission in 1930: the lovely coquina stone E. F. Hutton Building, with its inset clock face, that still stands in Palm Beach. It is worth noting that his chief rival in the town, the suddenly popular Maurice Fatio, received a remarkable eight commissions that year in spite of the deteriorating economic climate. The following year, Mizner would complete the design of his last large (eleven thousand square feet) Florida villa, Casa Coe da Sol, for Cincinnati insurance executive William J. Williams, in St. Petersburg. Tastes, too, had changed. Gone was the demand for grand and formal palaces, especially those in Mizner's signature Spanish and Mediterranean Revival style.

19

SPECULATIVE DEMENTIA

Roger W. Babson, one of the era's preeminent stock market authorities and the author of the popular investment column "Be Right with Babson," had been fulsome in his praise of Florida real estate throughout the boom. His own initial investment came in February 1922, when he purchased five acres of an abandoned turpentine plantation from a friend and developer named Frederick S. Ruth for $10,000. Ruth was a Baltimore-born former attorney for the Alabama Power Company who had quit his job to develop a couple hundred acres of bare land that his family owned near Lake Wales. The resulting private golf resort was named Mountain Lake.

Babson and his wife, Grace, who loved Florida for its bright sunshine, temperate climate, and easy living conditions, built themselves a comfortable house at Mountain Lake and then, near the peak of the boom, added another four hundred acres to their Florida holdings. Even more significantly, Babson loaded up his personal portfolio with Florida municipal bonds that offered handsome yields of 6 percent to 8 percent, free from state or federal income tax. The state of Florida did not issue any public debt, thanks to a constitutional provision prohibiting it, but the state's various cities and municipalities did. In fact, Florida municipal debt had grown from $110 million in 1922 to $600 million in 1929. But by 1927, these bonds were proving to be singularly poor investments. The issuance situation had been aggravated by a 1923 piece of legislation that allowed municipalities, desirous of building roads and other improvements, to issue liens against the property abutting their incomplete roads, sidewalks, water mains, and sewers, and then to issue bonds against those liens to pay for the improvements—well in advance of the abutting property's development. For all practical purposes, these were not bonds at all but rather speculative futures contracts on pending construction and development. When the buildouts failed to occur, as was now the case across the state, these bonds collapsed in value—as did the more widely accepted and standard issue "general obligation" and "revenue" bonds.

Babson was not alone in his miscalculation. As the realtor Walter P. Fuller noted, only a few people saw the lien-bond combination as the "dynamite" that it was. Meanwhile, St. Petersburg, where Fuller lived, became the most indebted municipality in Florida, boasting very likely the highest public debt per capita in the country, with a bonded indebtedness of $23.7 million. Soon it would become one of the cities hurt the worst in the downturn. But it wouldn't be alone: seven out of every eight of Florida's cities and towns, including St. Petersburg, would default on both the interest and principal of their municipal bonds.

Babson had trouble comprehending his sudden loses. "Five years before these defaults, no banker or bond expert in the United States would have believed that such municipal bond repudiation would have been possible," he noted. After all, reputable municipal bond attorneys in New York had given these bonds creditworthy ratings. Years later, he would blame himself and not the rating agencies: "I bought largely without visiting these Florida cities and seeing for what purposes the money was being spent. If I had done this, I would have seen that most of this money was being spent, at the solicitation of irresponsible real estate promoters and contractors, for the building of asphalt roads through undeveloped property that would not be occupied for fifty years."

The collapse of countless Florida municipalities that followed the plummet in land prices was only the beginning of Florida's problems. When a housing bubble bursts, construction spending and housing naturally start to collapse with it. This would be true not only in Florida but also latterly across the rest of the country: construction spending between 1928 and 1933 plummeted 95 percent; similarly, expenditures on home repairs dropped 90 percent.

When housing construction evaporates, so, too, does the demand for building materials such as lumber and structural steel, leading to layoffs in the lumber and steel industry, which creates financial stress in lumber and steel centers, ultimately affecting the housing market (and wages) in those communities as well. It was exactly this kind of slow contagion that took place across the United States in the months following the end of Florida's gigantic land boom. Recall that real estate values were inflated nationally, not just in Florida. Between 1922 and 1929, the value of new nonfarm housing in the country increased by 49 percent, growing $60.8 billion to $90.6 billion, a remarkable gain of $29.8 billion.

There was vast overbuilding, not just in the suburbs surrounding major metropolitan areas but also within the cities—in co-operative apartments in New York City, for example. When the single biggest demand for building materials—the Florida housing market—simply went away, leaving construction companies and building materials companies around the country overextended, a downward spiral began. Nervous investors pulled back. Apartment construction in the major cities would peak in 1927, but it accounted for only 20 percent of all residential construction; commercial construction fared better because it was better financed, and it actually peaked a few years later. But twenty-four years would pass before spending on residential real estate reached the level it had achieved in 1926.

Nervous banks, locally and then soon nationally, began to curtail their lending, as home owners began to default on their mortgages and as overleveraged Americans who were overexposed to Florida—or real estate elsewhere—began to rethink all their borrowing and spending habits, and not just on real estate but also on consumer goods such as cars, which were hugely important to the economy of the day. Again, Florida was the epicenter of this contraction. As liquidity drained from the Florida banks, they began to modify their lending, pulling in their horns, and looking desperately for ways to raise capital to cover soaring losses, defaults, and bank withdrawals. Many of their loans were unsecured or so-called "signature loans" with no collateral to back them up. Soon many of these banks began to fail.

Some forty local banks and branches of national banks went under in Florida in 1926. A similar number of failures followed over the next two years, with the total rising to fifty-seven in 1929. When the Mizner Development Corporation entered bankruptcy, taking down two Palm Beach banks with it, the contagion spread to other banks in a chain of banks across Florida and Georgia controlled by a pair of freewheeling bankers named Wesley D. Manley and James R. Anthony. Eighty-three banks promptly failed in Georgia when the men were accused of fraud—and the announcement of those failures caused even more banks in Florida to fail. Two banks in Daytona failed in the summer of 1927, reopened, and then failed again in 1928. Eight of the eleven banks in Palm Beach and West Palm Beach eventually went under. In St. Petersburg, all nine went under by 1930, although two new ones sprang up in their place. Fifteen of the eighteen banks in Pinellas County failed.

And yet it could have been worse. At least a dozen banks in the north of the state were saved when Jacksonville banker Bion Hall Barnett, owner the well-capitalized Barnett Bank, stepped in to backstop the runs on neighboring county banks, transferring sums as large as $200,000 at a time to his fellow bankers to help them meet their withdrawals. In Miami, every single local bank went under, with the exception of the First National Bank of Miami run by mayor Ed Romfh. An astute and conservative banker, Romfh alone had sufficient capital reserves on hand at his bank, and low enough leverage on that capital, to halt the bank runs. Still, his deposits shrank from $66.7 million at the height of the boom to a low of $12 million a few years later. More than once, in the midst of a run on his bank, the chubby-cheeked banker with his hair parted down the middle stood on a balcony overlooking the crowded lobby and shouted down to the crowd, "Could I have your attention? I am E. C. Romfh, president of this bank! All of you down there who do not have confidence in me or this bank, I want you to get your money, and I want you to get out of this bank and don't come back!" More often than not, this tactic worked to calm anxious depositors.

Similarly, Alfred du Pont, Coleman's cousin, who had taken a controlling interest in the Florida National Bank of Jacksonville in 1927, had deep enough pockets to forestall a bank run there. In 1929 he deposited $15 million of his own money into his bank to keep it open. He had a vested interest in seeing the bank and the surrounding community survive: he had acquired nine hundred thousand acres in the Florida Panhandle, landholdings that would be the foundation of the du Pont family's enormous St. Joe Paper Company, a paper mill and land development company.

But most Florida banks were not so lucky. The state deposit insurance system did not have risk-adjusted premiums. In fact, the state insurance system had backfired. It had actually encouraged overly risky lending because bankers believed that they were shielded from losses. The truth was that depositors in banks risked losing everything when a bank folded, a terrifying prospect that led to bank runs fueled by mass fear. Federal insurance on bank deposits offered by the Federal Deposit Insurance Corporation (FDIC) would not be created until 1933 as part of the New Deal legislation.

At first, little attention was paid to these regional bank failures, which had grown commonplace in the American heartland without spreading to the cities. The various Federal Reserve banks thought that these failures had more to do with corruption and mismanagement than with any potentially systemic banking failure that might be in the works. They were right about the former; wrong about the latter. In the twelve years leading up to the Great Depression, 12,677 banks failed nationally, an alarming number. Bank failures and their contagion began to reach critical mass when the Bank of Tennessee failed in November 1930, dragging down affiliated banks in Knoxville, Tennessee, and Louisville, Kentucky.

Then, in December, the Bank of the U.S., a cobbled-together commercial banking conglomerate in New York City with sixty branches and 450,000 depositors, was forced to close after a run on the bank depleted its reserves. The bank's books were loaded with bad mortgages and real estate loans to new Manhattan structures such as the San Remo, the Beresford, and the Century apartment buildings.

Banks in Chicago followed suit in June 1932, their books also loaded with bad real estate loans. In all, ten thousand banks holding deposits of more than $6.8 billion (equivalent to $122 billion today) would fail or be suspended across the United States between 1930 and 1933, causing customers in those banks to lose nearly 20 percent of their hard-earned deposits. The earlier bank runs were even more expensive, costing customers 28 percent to 40 percent of their deposits.

Once a deflationary spiral takes hold, it is increasingly difficult to stop; it gathers size and speed as it goes. The shuffling and reallocation of resources in the economy that must take place to restore a proper supply-and-demand balance and thus stabilize prices simply can't occur fast enough in a debt-ridden economy. Net worth is being destroyed too rapidly. Furthermore, the 1920s and early 1930s were a period where laissez-faire economics prevailed and where government intervention was considered anathema to sound monetary policy. Consequently, the institutions and procedures, or checks and balances, were not in place to help moderate an economic downturn. The Federal Reserve, created only in 1913, saw no need to play the role of "lender of last resort" and was not prepared to step in to backstop major banks. That would compound the growing problems; nor was the Fed particularly focused on housing markets.

For every dollar of decline in a home's value, an indebted home owner will rein in his or her spending by an even larger dollar amount, leveraging the negative effects of the downward spiral. Just as home owners overspend when the value of their property seems to be soaring, they will *under*spend as the value of their property shrinks. So it was that, in the late 1920s, Americans stopped buying new cars; then they stopped buying dishwashers, washing machines, sewing machines, and radios. And, of course, the home owners who had mortgages were those who, for the most part, could least afford the losses that ensued. "This is a fundamental feature of debt: it imposes enormous losses on exactly the households that have the least," explain Atif Mian and Amir Sufi in their book *House of Debt.* But that doesn't mean the rest of us don't pay a price. "The problem of levered losses quickly spreads throughout the economy; the sharp pullback in household spending by levered households affects us all," they write. In other words, before long, we are all in the same mess together.

By mid-1927, Roger Babson had concluded that the stock market was overvalued. Aware from his firsthand experience in Florida that the US economy now had a punctured tire, he began to warn his clients to watch out for an impending steep correction in the market. As it happened, he was eighteen months too early.

There were a couple of factors unique to the 1920s stock market that help explain why it didn't react sooner to what was happening to real estate in Florida and around the country, and, instead, persisted in climbing higher. First, as mentioned, it took time for the damage to unfold. For one thing, home owners didn't default on their mortgages the instant their home equity evaporated. Also, the pace of life was slower in the twenties and thirties than it is today—and the stock market was less quick to reflect fundamental change. It simply took time for the decline in real estate values in Florida to spread like an infection across the suburbs and cities in the rest of the country—to places such as Cook County, Illinois, which went bust in 1928, followed by the cities of Skokie, Illinois, and Burbank, California. Even in Washington, DC, not generally thought to be an overheated real estate market during the 1920s, single-family home prices, which had risen 38 percent during the decade, had declined 10 percent from their peak by 1929. In Manhattan, prices had risen 54 percent to their peak in the second quarter of 1926, and were down 28 percent by the second quarter of 1928—although in Manhattan's case, the stock market boom helped those prices to rebound briefly before falling again more precipitously. But across the country, by the end of 1926, housing starts were in a steep, even startling, decline, and residential construction was shortly to follow.

Only gradually was the effect of the real estate downturn reflected in the broader economy, and only then in the sentiment gauges and, finally, in the stock market itself. Economists Carmen M. Reinhart and Kenneth S. Rogoff, in their book *This Time Is Different: Eight Centuries of Financial Folly*, categorize this kind of slow-motion erosion as "the 'slow-burn' spillover" contagion that gradually leads to a collapse. As the late MIT economist Rudiger Dornbusch once noted, "In economics, things take longer to happen than you think they will, and then they happen faster than you thought they could."

Masking what was happening was the fact that very few Florida public companies were listed on the major stock exchanges. In fact, only two stocks of note were actively traded: the FEC (the Flagler railroad), which traded on the New York Stock Exchange, and the Land Company of Florida, a real estate trust that owned railroad "right of way" land, which traded on the less important New York Curb Exchange (later to become the American Stock Exchange). Both stocks declined steeply in concert with the bursting of the land bubble, but they were far too insignificant in their weighting to move the averages. First, the Florida railroad embargo knocked the price of Land Company shares from $90 to $63; then the implosion of the land bubble took the shares down to $20 by February 1926. The shares would hit $5 on Black Tuesday of the Great Crash: October 29, 1929. By 1931, the stock sold for 50 cents and was delisted in May of that year. The stock of Flagler's FEC took a similar nosedive. The company went into receivership in September 1931, although it was eventually resurrected when the Alfred I. du Pont estate, led by Alfred's politically influential brother-in-law, Edward Ball, bought up the bonds and brought the company out of bankruptcy in the mid-1930s.

Also clouding the picture was the fact that, by the late 1920s, the US stock market was in a unique debt-driven bubble of its own. The Dow Jones Industrial Average quadrupled during the decade, driven upward, in part, by the leverage made possible by margin lending, available for the first time to the general public—a general public that had little experience with the risks associated with this kind of leverage. Some $8 billion in margin debt was outstanding by the fall of 1929. Also, supporting the stock market and pushing the Dow 20 percent higher between June and September in 1929 was the fact that stocks were attracting the speculative money that would otherwise have gone into Florida real estate. And many of Florida's losers surely hoped to make up for their losses with compensatory gains on Wall Street. A final factor helping to propel stocks higher was the tax cut passed by Congress in 1925, mostly benefiting the wealthy, which created additional capital to invest in the stock market.

Adding to the false sense of security on Wall Street was a novel investment vehicle known as the investment trust, popularized late in the decade. Investors in these trusts, which were much like closed-end mutual funds today, believed that they were investing in diversified portfolios run by financial professionals. The truth was often otherwise: the trusts were creating even more leverage within the system by purchasing the stock of other trusts, piling risk on top of risk. Most were not listed on the New York Stock Exchange, and thus investors possessed little transparency into what they owned—or what had been paid for what they now owned. Many trusts used debt or preferred stock to leverage their returns.

Utility stocks, too, had emerged as a pocket of intense market focus and speculation. By engaging in elaborate industry consolidations, or roll-ups through acquisitions, these companies were achieving a multiplier effect on their earnings that was highly seductive to shareholders, who in turn rewarded them with unusually high stock valuations. As a class of investments, utilities were only just starting to get the kind of serious scrutiny from Wall Street analysts that they deserved. In fact, critical comments by the Massachusetts Department of Public Utilities about the rates being charged by the Edison Electric Illuminating Company of Boston may have jarred investors in October 1929.

In hindsight, it appears that the broader stock market was in one of those periods where it acted, in investment sage Benjamin Graham's memorable phrase, more like a voting machine than a weighing machine. Normally, of course, the stock market reflects the prospects for corporate earnings and accords those hypothetical earnings some reasonable multiple. But not always. In this occasion, the stock market's movements were no longer bolted to earnings. Money went into stocks simply because stocks were rising and had been rising, reliably, for a number of years. The stock market went up simply because it was going up. It was this feature that led Philip Snowden, chancellor of the exchequer in Britain, to describe the US market as "a perfect orgy of speculation." Strictly speaking, this wasn't true. The market had become expensive but not yet egregiously so. In fact, there continues to be considerable debate among financial historians about just how overextended stock prices were in the late twenties. The Dow Jones Industrial Average was selling at an average price-earnings (P/E) ratio of 24.3 times 1929 earnings (and 20.4 times the median P/E with a range of 11.5 to 65.2), historically a high number, but not an outlandish one.

Markets, of course, overshoot on the way up—as well as on the way down. But there is often a strong bias to the upside when stocks are rising. David Wiedemar, Robert Wiedemar, and Cindy Spitzer aptly describe this as "the Hamptons Effect" in their 2011 book *Aftershock: Protect Yourself and Profit in the Next Global Financial Meltdown*: "Wealthy people, stock-brokers, and asset managers have a deep need to keep believing we don't have any bubbles and to keep investing in the stock market. . . . The bigger your house, the more denial you need to sleep at night." The stock market in the twenties overshot, and it took some time to do so.

Certain stocks were obviously overpriced by the late twenties. Chief among these was Radio Corporation of America (RCA), which, much like a high-flying young technology stock today, paid no dividend and was sell-ing at an exorbitant sixty times its current yearly earnings, despite showing a growth rate only in the high teens. However, RCA was the exception; few stocks were anywhere near that expensive. Many analysts argued that there was a deserved premium on stock prices, justifiable because, at the time, profitability was exceptionally high for corporate America, especially as reflected in the high return on equity (ROE) of the average public com-pany, an important measure of profitability. Similarly, the dividend yield—what stocks paid out in dividends relative to their stock price—of around 4 percent for the Standard & Poor's 500 did not seem outlandish relative to the market's history or relative to the interest rate on the ten-year bond, a key benchmark.

In late 1929 there existed so little obvious evidence that weak earnings and economic collapse lay dead ahead that it is hardly surprising so many stock investors would be blindsided by what occurred. A second famous stock market guru, Irving Fisher, who focused strictly on such economic fundamentals, proclaimed boldly in September 1929, "Stock prices have reached what looks like a permanently high plateau." On October 21, only days before the crash began, he would reiterate his optimistic forecast, tell-ing the *New York Times* that stock prices were low and that he saw no cause for a slump. That forecast is today remembered as perhaps the worst stock market call in history. Others, however, were less sanguine, among them the notorious stock speculator Jesse Livermore, who admitted that he was "short" the market (betting against it) but denied that he was part of a pool preparing to drive the market down.

On September 5, 1929, Roger Babson delivered a very pessimistic speech before the annual meeting of the National Business Council, an event that he had organized. He reiterated his deeply negative view of the stock market. "Sooner or later a crash is coming. . . . Wise are those investors who now reef their sails. . . . there may be a stampede for selling which will exceed anything that the stock exchange has ever witnessed." Babson suggested that what had happened in Florida would now happen on Wall Street. He concluded by predicting "a serious business depression."

That afternoon, almost on cue, the market plunged and the major averages dropped 3 percent in what came to be called the "Babson Break." The market then recovered partially, but what followed was a series of lower highs and lower lows for the next few weeks as new worries arose. The London Stock Exchange, for example, had plummeted on the arrest for fraud of a prominent and flamboyant British investor named Clarence Hatry. Unmistakably, a gradual downtrend had taken hold. Then came the calamity of the two "black" days: Black Thursday, October 24, when the market dropped 9 percent (33 points on the Dow Jones Industrial Average) in a selling panic that saw 12.9 million shares change hands; and the following Black Tuesday, October 29, which was the worst day of all in terms of percentage and volume. On that day, the market dropped 12 percent (30 points on the Dow), and 16.4 million shares were exchanged. Overnight, $14 billion in stock market value evaporated; $30 billion would vanish in the entire crash.

That was just the beginning. The worst declines in the market would not come until later, when the Depression whirled out of control in the early 1930s. Prices would completely collapse from an inflated 381.17 on the Dow Jones Industrial Average on September 3, 1929, to a pathetic 41.22 on July 8, 1933—an 89.2 percent decline from top to bottom.

The market would not fully recover until November 23, 1954, when it finally returned to the September 3, 1929, peak of 381.17. Two examples of what happened to popular individual stocks are worth noting. RCA, the darling of the market and the Apple stock of its day, selling at the aforementioned price-earnings multiple of 60, collapsed in the ensuing years from a high of $114 to a low of $2.50. Anaconda Copper, the target of a "pool" that had manipulated its price for enormous profits, declined from $125 to $4.

In the aftermath, Roger Babson would be credited with one of the best stock market calls of all time. However, he knew the truth and freely admitted to it in his memoirs: he had been early on his initial call. In hindsight, he believed that he had been in too much of a hurry, reflecting, "It is human nature for us all to want to beat the other fellow in our forecasts." But perhaps if the various exogenous factors propping up the market had not been in place, the correction might have come earlier, and Babson's original call might have been spot-on in terms of timing. The fact that it didn't, and the fact that the stock market crash came almost three years after the Florida land bubble burst, has obscured what was really happening in the broader economy ever since. Even today, the popular view is that the crashing of the stock market—and not the puncturing of the Florida land boom—is what triggered the Great Depression.

In this context, it is worth remembering that stock markets rarely cause recessions, let alone depressions, although they can depress consumer sentiment. Economist Milton Friedman was adamant on this point: "Whatever happens in a stock market," he wrote, "it cannot lead to a Great Depression unless it produces or is accompanied by a monetary collapse." Historically, stock market collapses have occurred every thirteen years on average and have rarely lasted more than two and a half years. Housing price collapses are much less frequent, last for twice as long, and result in gross domestic product (GDP) losses that are twice as large. This has led Edward Leamer, an economist at the University of California, Los Angeles, to observe: "Housing *is* the business cycle."

The dollar losses in the 1929 stock market crash were surely greater ($30 billion in the crash; $57 billion between 1929 and 1933) than the total losses in Florida land, which was likely in the low billions, but, importantly, the number of stock market investors was likely far smaller than the number of investors in Florida. There were thought to be only some 1.5 million investors significant enough to have brokerage accounts by 1929.

That number varies, and some estimates put it as low as 1 percent of the population, or 1.2 million, although a far better metric is what percent of the nation's 30 million households owned accounts: 4 percent. Meanwhile, 84 percent of the population is thought to have had no savings at all, so the widespread idea at the time of every American playing the market was far from accurate. By contrast, the highest estimate, which is largely anecdotal, put the number of people who bought Florida real estate at 15 percent of the 120 million population by around 1927, or roughly 18 million people. That figure is surely far too high, given that there were just 30 million households in the United States at the time. But even a tenth of that would be problematic for the American economy.

Hypothetically, if there were some 1.8 million buyers of land who had spent on the order of $5 billion over the decade, they would have paid an average of $2,777 for a lot or the combination of a lot and a house, which seems plausible in light of the fact that the average price of a home across the country at the time was $5,000. Late in the boom, many Florida investors bought only binders, or the options on lots as speculative investments, or simply made initial down payments; their losses in these cases would have been 100 percent if they couldn't or chose not to cough up the rest of the money. Additional money was lost on investments in hotels, golf courses, and on direct investments in real estate development companies, to say nothing of the large amount of "safe" money lost in Florida municipal bonds. So, while it is fair to say that more money was lost in the stock market than in the land boom, those losses were likely not as significant in their impact on the economy as were the earlier losses in Florida. Much of that Florida money was the hard-earned money of America's middle class. Conversely, money in the stock market was primarily money of the wealthy, as the top 5 percent of the country held 90 percent of the wealth, and they were the primary investors and speculators in equities. Seventy-four percent of all dividends went to less than six hundred thousand individuals. Nevertheless, the drawdown of *their* capital, as the margin calls went out after the crash, surely added to the emerging credit crisis, the deflationary spiral, and the plunge in consumer sentiment.

Despite the staggering aggregate losses that occurred during the stock market crash of 1929, most recent economic scholarship has largely decoupled the stock market from the causes of the Great Depression and absolved it of any real blame in triggering the downturn. Again, monetarist economists, in particular, share this view. As the aforementioned Milton Friedman, for instance, once remarked, "The stock market crash in 1929 was a momentous event, but it did not produce the Great Depression, and it was not a major factor in the Depression's severity." In his opinion, the real culprits were (1) the Federal Reserve's overly restrictive monetary policy from 1928 onward (four increases that moved the discount rate—the rate at which the Federal Reserve lends to its member banks—from 3.5 percent to 6 percent) and (2) the credit squeeze that resulted from the failing banks. The economist Paul Samuelson blamed the Depression on "a series of historical accidents" that set up the economy for a stumble, most of them macroeconomic in nature. Both theories have been deemed inadequate by others, such as Charles O. Kindleberger, a Federal Reserve banker, author, and professor of economics at MIT. Kindleberger favored European macroeconomic explanations, emphasized simple financial contagion, and pointed to the role played by the gold standard. (He meant the worldwide run on US gold deposits driven by Britain's surprise abandonment of the gold standard in September 1931; this had the secondary effect of pushing up the value of the dollar and forcing the Federal Reserve to raise interest rates.) Author and economist John Kenneth Galbraith came up with five causes: unequal income distribution, bad corporate structure, bad banking structure, the poor state of the foreign trade balance, and the lousy economic intelligence of the day. Other, more heterodox theories, too elaborate to outline here, have placed the blame on combinations of declining commodity prices, the psychology of panics, the introduction of restrictive international trade tariffs (the Smoot-Hawley Tariff Act of 1930, which slapped protectionist trade tariffs on foreign imports), and misguided wage controls. Roosevelt blamed Hoover; Hoover blamed Roosevelt. The debate continues to this day.

By 1932, unemployment extended to a quarter of the population, leaving them without the means to afford food or shelter. Half the working population worked only part-time—and at reduced wages. US industrial production collapsed by 46 percent. International trade dropped by 50 percent. Crop prices fell by 60 percent. The toll the Great Depression took on people's personal, psychological, and financial well-being was seismic. Every metropolitan area had breadlines and shantytowns, or so-called Hoovervilles, where those displaced by unemployment and evictions were forced to live. A number of recoveries failed for varying reasons, and the downturn lasted an entire decade.

Today there is a growing awareness that the real estate collapse was a major reason for why the Great Depression ran so long and so deep. Like Florida, the country as a whole in the 1930s was awash in near-worthless excess real estate that could not be easily accessed for new development because it was encumbered with liens that had soared in value relative to the depressed value of the property. Much of the nation's real estate was tied up in disputes over title and ownership. The cities and countryside were littered with dilapidated buildings or partially developed infrastructure that could not be easily recycled or repurposed. Just finding the owner was often a problem. These challenges added levels of complexity and cost that most developers wanted nothing to do with, despite the often-desirable locations of the properties. It was estimated that even at the end of the Depression, the United States had as many as twenty million to thirty million abandoned subdivided lots—a number that staggers the imagination given that there were only thirty million occupied units in the entire country in 1946.

I believe that the collapse of the Florida land boom pricked the national real estate bubble of the twenties, causing the initial contraction in the economy to begin. This explanation accommodates both classical monetarist thinking and the competing Keynesian explanations for what happened. In other words, this real estate theory provides an underlying cause for the credit squeeze (all important to the monetarists), while also providing an underlying explanation for the collapse of demand (so central to the Keynesian explanation for what happened). Of course, in an economy as complex as ours, we need to be wary of single, or monocausal, explanations for any event. However, the role played by the collapse of Florida's real estate boom in launching the Great Depression has surely been vastly underappreciated by economists and historians. Perhaps we needed to live through the Great Recession of 2008, where distressed real estate was front and center, to see the historical importance and economic significance of the collapse of the Florida land boom.

The parallels are hard to ignore. In the 2008 calamity, just as in the 1929 calamity, the overleveraging of real estate was the single factor most toxic to the economy and most responsible for the crash. In the 2008 case, the leverage came, as it had in the 1920s, from the introduction of novel financial instruments—subprime mortgages, collateralized debt obligations, and credit default swaps—in concert with lax banking regulation. Here's another parallel: in both cases, a lag occurred before the stock market reflected the new economic realities. In the case of Great Recession, there followed a nearly a two-year delay between the time that real estate—Florida and California housing stock—began to roll over in 2006 and the moment when the stock market eventually collapsed in 2008. In both 1929 and 2008, real estate, not the stock market, was the chief villain in the crisis that followed.

A handful of almost star-aligned factors created the great Florida real estate bubble. These might be summarized as the emergence of a "last-frontier" investment opportunity that was made accessible by the automobile and publicized by potent new methods of advertising to an optimistic population looking for a way to fulfill a newly articulated American Dream. Once that bubble burst, other factors soon played into the chaos of the downturn, including massive policy mistakes at the federal level—perhaps most notably the passage of Smoot-Hawley. It would be wrong to claim there wouldn't have been a Depression had it not been for the Florida boom and bust, but the Sunshine State did provide both the dynamite and the detonator.

The one-off nature of the Florida boom-bust suggests that other investment manias of a different complexion—such as the current one in the contemporary art market and on display each December at the international art fair Art Basel in America at Miami Beach—will be difficult to predict, regulate, or avoid without ending in horrific financial losses. All the more reason to look under the historical hood of these booms to see how they arose, what went wrong, and who or what might be to blame.

One final explanation exists for why, historically, a closer link hasn't been established between the Florida land boom and the wider collapse of the US economy: the paucity of good financial data collected during this era. Missing is a clear estimate of how much investment capital went into Florida. Similarly, there was no adequate measure of housing wealth at the time. As Eugene White, an economist at Rutgers University, notes, "Unfortunately, minimal data at the national level has been collected for financial intermediaries lending on real estate in this period. The most detailed data available is for national banks, but, legally constrained, they lent very little on real estate. Data on state banks, insurance companies, and saving and loans that contributed most to the rapid mortgage growth is extremely limited."

Nor was there anything in the way of a reliable housing price index. What we do know is that the total value of issued home mortgages in the country exploded from $12 billion in 1919 to $43 billion by 1930, and that delinquencies and foreclosures were soaring by the late 1920s. (In 1930, $1 billion had the simple purchasing power equivalent to $15 billion in today's dollars.) Defaults didn't peak until 1933 because most mortgages averaged five to seven years in duration, and did not self-amortize, which meant the holder was faced with a balloon payment at the time of the loan's termination. By then, some 60 percent of all home mortgages in the country were in arrears! This actually makes sense: most of these mortgages had originated in the 1920s at lower interest rates and would be much harder to refinance, assuming that the home owner, having lost his or her entire equity in the home, still had the desire, let alone the wherewithal, to do so. Most didn't.

Not surprisingly, a thousand foreclosures were occurring each day by 1933. The average price of a home, nationwide, had fallen from $5,000 to $3,200, a nominal decline of 36 percent. Real estate loans to developers and development companies, which had emerged as a new asset class, had exploded in the years leading up to the Depression, from $150 million in 1913, to $502 million in 1926, and reaching $5 billion by 1931. Defaults began in 1925 and escalated throughout the remainder of the decade. By 1928, 77 percent of those loans were failing to meet their contracts and were in arrears. In Chicago, an important real estate market for the nation, fully 95 percent would be in default by 1936. Farmers, too, had continued to run up debt on their lands during the decade. Farm mortgages, which had risen from $3.3 billion in 1910 to $6.7 billion in 1920, continued to rise to $9.4 billion by 1925. Apparently, as many as 85 percent of the farms in some states were mortgaged. In fact, the burden of this debt is thought to have exceeded the value of all the rural land in the country during the Great Depression.

Eventually the Federal Housing Administration, founded in 1934, would extend the term (or duration) of home mortgages to twenty and thirty years, helping to lower monthly mortgage payments and reduce default rates. The FHA also increased the size of the loans available (by increasing the loan-to-value ratio), which even further improved the affordability of housing. It also began to insure mortgages against default. This package of reforms stimulated demand for housing and housing construction, and it put unemployed construction workers back to work at last.

Roger Babson held on to his rapidly depreciating Florida property throughout the Depression years and later astutely added to his holdings, eventually owning some two thousand acres in an area he called Babson Park, today the site of Webber International University, which he also founded. But as Babson noted in his memoirs, his friend Frederick S. Ruth of Baltimore, the developer from whom he'd purchased his first Florida property, did not fare nearly so well.

Fred Ruth, once described as "a man of sweeping imagination and vast self-confidence," had hired Frederick Law Olmsted Jr., son of the designer of Manhattan's Central Park and proponent of the City Beautiful Movement, to develop his Mountain Lake subdivision, the residential and citrus-growing settlement that endures today as an exclusive private resort area. Ruth also talked Edward Bok, the retired longtime editor of the popular and progressive *Ladies' Home Journal*, into buying property at Mountain Lake. Bok went on to build the neighboring Bok Tower Gardens and its iconic Bok Tower.

Not content with the notable success of Mountain Lake, Ruth launched other golf club and resort developments, including the Mid Ocean Club in Bermuda; the Whippoorwill Club in Armonk, New York; and the Fishers Island Club on the island off the coast of Connecticut. Overextended and heavily indebted on the Fishers Island project and another one in Florida (Indian River Islands Corporation) when the Depression took hold, Ruth grew desperate and increasingly depressed. At around four o'clock in the afternoon on Friday, April 22, 1932, he checked himself into a suite on the eleventh floor of the new Waldorf-Astoria Hotel on Park Avenue in New York City, carrying a shotgun and a box of shotgun shells in a duffel bag. From there he telephoned his brother Theodore and told him where he was and what he planned to do—before abruptly hanging up. Then he put a note on a table that read, "I can't stand it any longer. I realize that I can't raise the necessary money." In the bathroom, he undressed, climbed into the bathtub, and put the barrel of the shotgun in his mouth. He pulled the trigger with his big toe. He was forty-eight and married with no children. "If he had only been content to rest with that [Mountain Lake development]," Babson wrote, "he would have had a handsome income for the remainder of his life as well as a monument to his efforts. Like so many others, he was not content but plunged into more enterprises. . . . Poor Fred Ruth! I shall always have a soft spot in my heart for him."

20

◆❖◆

THE DEATH OF
BALLYHOO AND HOKUM

In the wake of the boom, abandoned developments striped both Florida coasts and checkerboarded the inland areas, many reduced to bare wasteland. Wilson Mizner, on a rare return visit to Florida a few years after the bust, recalled a memorable drive down the east coast of the state, passing vast, deserted subdivisions, one after another, their ornate stone and stucco gates now sagging or collapsed. He passed paved sidewalks lined with streetlights with nothing to illuminate. Street signs hung drunkenly from their lampposts. Unfinished golf courses, empty country clubs, and half-built casinos seemed little more than empty promises and proof of financial shenanigans.

Henry S. Villard, a journalist for Hearst Newspapers, reported seeing a similar apocalypse, as he wrote in a story for the *Nation*. "Dead subdivisions line the highway, their pompous names half-obliterated on crumbling stucco gates. Lonely white-way lights stand guard over miles of concrete sidewalks, where grass and palmetto take the place of homes that were to be.... Whole sections of outlying subdivisions are composed of unoccupied houses, past which one speeds on broad thoroughfares as if traversing a city in the grip of death."

On the west coast of Florida, the picture was little better. Florida historian John Rothchild, only a boy at the time, recalled walking through scrub pines on the outskirts of St. Petersburg and encountering the ruins of a failed subdivision: "There were rusted fire hydrants, ornate streetlights overgrown with vines, old brick streets half sunk in sandy soil, some railroad tracks, as if the area had been prepared for civilization and then abandoned quickly, as the Maya had abandoned their temples."

Davis Shores, the doomed second act of the drowned developer D. P. Davis, was described at the time as treeless, windswept, and devoid of topsoil. The remnants of his $60 million development, which had once sold a record $16 million worth of lots in a single day at the peak of the boom, would bring in less than $10,000 on the courthouse steps in 1933. Properties that had sold in the tens of thousands now sold for only a few hundred—if they sold at all. The corporate losses combined with the individual losses resulted in incalculable financial ruin. Wilson Mizner colorfully summarized the new status quo:

> *Suddenly there came a general and pathetic discovery that a piece of Florida real estate was no assurance of either wealth or happiness. Slowly the brothers Ballyhoo and Hokum lay back on harsh cots of bankruptcy and died off—or cooled off, as we say. Thousands of desperate paupers, who had just a bit ago seemed successful promoters, began the dismal trek north. In their frantic quest for gold, that seemed almost in their fingers, they had gotten that thing that is so easy to find when seeking something else— experience.*

Wilson may have summed it up perfectly, but he lacked the humility to admit that he, too, was one of those once-successful promoters who were culpable in the fiasco.

In St. Petersburg, the developer Jack Taylor and his wife abandoned the Rolyat Hotel abruptly, firing all the staff, including all of those talented salesmen recruited from George Merrick's Coral Gables late in the boom. He and his wealthy wife drove off in a brand-new Pierce-Arrow motorcar. Exotic parrots were left behind in their aviaries, and a handful of imported monkeys were stranded on a man-made island on a golf course lake. The realtor Walter Fuller took it upon himself to free the parrots. The monkeys rescued themselves. "To my dying day I will remember the silent troop of monkeys on an early foggy morning proceeding single file down the sea-wall of my Boca Ciega Bay home," Fuller recalled. "They ended up in the Jungle [Estates development]; lived there happily several years." Years later, the Rolyat Hotel would become Stetson University College of Law.

By some estimates, 90 percent of the people who invested in the boom lost money. One of those was a good friend of Water Fuller's named Tom Hammond, who had started out as a real estate broker working for Fuller's father. Late in the boom, Hammond sold a parcel of land he owned for more than $1 million and believed that he was set for life. He planned to take his family on a grand tour of Europe and was just waiting to collect the repayment of a note lent to the developer of a project called Moorish Estates. Fuller remembered visiting Hammond in his office. "He was dressed like a movie senator with black ribbon pince-nez. Almost ritzed me out of the office." The payment, of course, never came. "This was early 1926. I knew the boom was over, but obviously Tom didn't." The cruise was canceled. "He would sit and shake his head and mutter, 'I just don't understand it.' And, he didn't."

Where real estate ads had once filled the pages of the Miami newspapers, now it was the list of tax delinquencies: forty-one pages of newsprint in a single issue in 1927.

By 1930, Addison Mizner was so broke that he had to borrow money from friends. Alice DeLamar recalled that his spirit was broken as well. Irving Berlin lent Addison $25,000, with little expectation of getting it back. One former client, Edward E. Moore, the personal secretary and right-hand man to wealthy businessman Joseph P. Kennedy (father of President John F. Kennedy), provided desperately needed assistance during this time, simply as a token of his affection and admiration for the architect, arriving one day with a check for $10,000 that he handed to Addison's secretary, Madena Galloway. "Give that to Addison," he said, "and tell him that it is a present from me." Another client named Edith Rae, who owned Mizner's Lagomar, also stepped forward to provide additional financial support, picking up the bills for groceries and the servants' salaries.

Addison's last known commission was an Art Deco movie theater, restaurant, and hotel complex in Belle Glade in 1932. At this point,

Henry Flagler's first two gigantic Florida hotels around 1890: his flagship Ponce de Leon Hotel and, across the street, his Alcazar, both in St. Augustine. By assembling the Flagler System, an unprecedented collection of resort hotels, railroads, newspapers, land companies, and utilities, the Standard Oil tycoon would orchestrate one of most remarkable second acts in American business history and provide the template for all the resort development that would follow.

The taciturn Flagler at age 74 in 1904, when he was his era's greatest entrepreneur. Despite his extraordinary business acumen, he was unable to smooth out the rollercoaster of his personal life.

The pedicycles known as Palm Beach chariots. Two hundred black chairmen were paid $5 per day to pedal hotel guests around the Flagler hotel properties. Day-to-day racial prohibitions and restrictions along with restrictive covenants on land deeds kept the races apart and prevented blacks from participating in the land boom.

Farm equipment magnate James Deering's 1914 Venetian-style villa, Vizcaya, with its baroque stone barge on Biscayne Bay south of Miami. The estate, which at one point employed 10 percent of the local population, formally introduced the Mediterranean Revival style to Florida and inspired architects like Addison Mizner to think big. "Must we be so grand?" Deering moaned to his designer Paul Chalfin as the cost of the house and its furnishings soared.

Carl Graham Fisher, a onetime news-boy, at the height of his early success as an Indiana auto executive circa 1910. Addicted to speed from an early age, he raced bicycles and early automobiles and founded the Indianapolis Motor Speed-way before betting his entire fortune on the development of Miami Beach.

The new Dixie Highway on the outskirts of Tampa was the last piece of infrastructure needed to spark the massive land boom of the twenties. The dual north-south road, launched in 1915, linked Chicago and Upper Michigan with Tampa and Miami, encompassed 5,786 miles, and took more than a decade to build.

Ubiquitous canal networks like this one, built throughout the twenties and long afterward, altered the natural flow of the Everglades, opening up new land for development but disrupting the natural hydrology and ecology of the Florida environment while doing little to mitigate flooding.

The architect Addison Mizner with members of his menagerie, including his monkey, Johnnie Brown, in the early twenties when he was earning renown for the extraordinary houses he designed and built for the wealthy of Palm Beach. A master craftsman and an inveterate do-it-yourselfer, he knew how to please his clients without pandering to their whims.

Addison Mizner's friend and patron Paris Singer, an heir to the vast Singer Sewing Machine fortune. Together they would recast the look and style of Palm Beach and appoint themselves gate-keepers of the smart set. The goal was nothing less than to make Palm Beach the winter capital of the world.

The Everglades Club overlooking Lake Worth in Palm Beach was Addison Mizner's first major Florida commission (completed in 1919), and the one that established the Spanish Revival style as the prevailing aesthetic of the twenties. Challenged to envision a building for the site, the architect remarked, "It is so beautiful that it ought to be something religious—a nunnery, with a chapel built into the lake."

Marjory Stoneman Douglas in her thirties as a young reporter for the *Miami Herald*. She would fall in love with Florida's birds, build her own bungalow, write the definitive book on the Everglades, and become a formidable advocate for the environment.

George Merrick, the founder of Coral Gables, at right, with his partner, John McEntee Bowman, founder of the Biltmore Hotel chain. The two would partner to construct the Miami Biltmore Hotel in Coral Gables, the centerpiece of Merrick's vast development empire, which made him for a time the nation's most famous— and most revered—land developer.

Developer D. P. Davis followed in Carl Fisher's footsteps and founded, on opposite coasts, Davis Islands and Davis Shores, two of the most promoted land developments of the era. His bizarre disappearance from the ocean liner RMS *Majestic* during a transatlantic crossing in late 1926 remains unexplained.

Davis Islands under construction in Tampa Bay. The dredge churns made of sand and marl and pumped up from the seafloor hardened into bright-white concrete-hard landfill and allowed islands to be pulled from the bays. When the project sold out, Davis doubled down on Davis Shores outside St. Augustine.

The Tamiami Trail Blazers bushwhacking across the Everglades in 1923 in their Model T Fords. The stunt generated 35,000 lines of publicity and the funds to ensure the road's construction. The world's longest dike, it became a killing field for wildlife and had disastrous effects on the great swamp's ecology.

The Seminole and Miccosukee tribes found their cultures under siege as development in and around the Everglades disrupted their traditional way of life. To survive, the tribes turned their villages into local attractions where they could sell trinkets and souvenirs to tourists.

The seventy-room Mizner-designed Playa Riente in Palm Beach, built in 1923 on twenty-seven ocean-to-lake acres for Oklahoma oil baron Joshua Cosden. One of the great artistic artifacts of the Florida boom, it was demolished in 1957.

Addison Mizner's living room in Villa Mizner, where he entertained the likes of Irving Berlin, George Gershwin, and Jerome Kern, as well as members of Palm Beach's high society.

Wilson Mizner, a playwright, wit, con artist, and blackmailer. "[He] has always been my chief weakness and dreaded menace," admitted his brother Addison, who nevertheless partnered with him to develop Boca Raton.

The songwriter Irving Berlin at the Roney-Plaza Casino at Miami Beach, where he wintered in the midtwenties before he eloped with the heiress Ellin Mackay. Around this time he wrote the songs and lyrics to *The Cocoanuts*, the Broadway musical about the Florida land boom that made the Marx Brothers famous.

Party girl Louise Cromwell Brooks, the daughter of the socialite Eva Stotesbury, known as the queen of Palm Beach. Brooks married Brigadier General Douglas MacArthur at the Stotesbury estate El Mirasol in 1922, the second of four marriages that all ended in divorce.

Camping at Six Mile Creek near Tampa in 1925. The migration to Florida in the 1920s exceeded in numbers all previous American migrations and included "tin canners" such as these—the tourists who packed their automobiles with tents and canned food for their road trips to the Sunshine State.

Flagler Street in Miami at the peak of the boom in 1925. "Everybody in Miami was real estate mad," wrote newcomer T. H. Weigall. Salesmen known as binder boys sold contracts on the streets and at the train stations, or swapped them among themselves, creating a new curb market in local real estate.

Shotgun houses in Miami's Colored Town (later called Overtown), where living conditions were squalid. Recalled one resident, "We became hemmed in. Miami really became a hell hole."

Carl Fisher enjoying himself during the Miami Beach years when, according to a local historian, "everything he touched turned to gold." He built hotels, office buildings, houses, golf courses, opened his second race track, organized speedboat races and polo matches, and lavishly entertained the so-called gasoline aristocracy.

Steve Hannagan, Fisher's publicist, popularized what came to be called "cheesecake" with images of bathing beauties on Miami Beach. At left, girls from the Miami High dancing class practice on a palm tree.

Carl Fisher's elephant Rosie serving as a tee for a golfer on Miami Beach in the kind of improbable publicity stunt, or ballyhoo, that made the resort nationally known in the twenties.

The Flamingo Hotel, the social epicenter of Miami Beach, was particularly popular with visiting celebrities. Here astonished guests at a tea dance in February 1926 watched a Coast Guard cutter just offshore chase down and machine-gun to death the famed rumrunner Red Shannon.

Gloria Swanson, a leading film star of the 1920s and a frequent guest at the Flamingo Hotel. It was on a visit to Palm Beach in the winter of 1928 that she began her affair with millionaire Joseph P. Kennedy.

The Coral Gables Biltmore under construction in 1925, one of 481 hotels and apartment complexes built in the Miami region in that year alone. George Merrick's lavish suite of offices on the fifteenth floor of the hotel's Giralda tower included a king-sized bed that once belonged to the Italian tenor Enrico Caruso.

Babe Ruth, Yankee owner Jacob Ruppert, pitcher Bob Shawkey, and Lou Gehrig at the March 1925 spring training camp in St. Petersburg. The highest paid player in baseball and an icon of the Roaring Twenties, Ruth took full advantage of all Florida had to offer, wolfing down six hot dogs in a single sitting and gambling late into the night at the local greyhound track.

An omen ignored: the Breakers Hotel in Palm Beach consumed by fire on March 18, 1925. Recalled one guest: "Nero fiddled while Rome burned. I played golf while the Breakers burned."

Salvage efforts under way on the *Prinz Valdemar*, capsized in Miami Harbor in January 1926. With the harbor blocked, the railroad embargoed, and the roads into Florida jammed, the boom came to a momentary standstill.

Swindler Charles Ponzi, promoter of the Charpon Land Syndicate, sold worthless Florida swampland through the mail. When the scheme was revealed as a fraud, Ponzi fled the state on a Tampa freighter, disguised as a sailor and working as a waiter and dishwasher. He was arrested in New Orleans. This photograph was taken just after his arraignment.

Florida in the twenties attracted its share of gangsters, including the dapper Chicago psychopath Al Capone, who arrived in Miami in 1928 to buy a waterfront mansion and seize control of Florida's profitable bootlegging and gambling rackets.

Palm Beach habitués: Broadway impresario Florenz Ziegfeld Jr. with his second wife, actress Billie Burke, who would play Glinda, the Good Witch of the North in *The Wizard of Oz*, posing for *Vanity Fair* in 1926. "We thought we had all the money in the world," she recalled. They would lose it all in the Great Crash of 1929.

The Miami hurricane of September 1926 arrived with little warning, bringing winds that approached 150 miles per hour and a tidal surge of fifteen feet. The storm claimed 373 lives, injured 6,381, and left 17,884 families homeless. Estimates put the total cost of the damages as high as $500 million, equivalent to $7.1 billion today.

Once the site of Alligator Joe's Jungle Trail, Worth Avenue with its Addison Mizner–designed arcade remains Palm Beach's premier shopping address. The boom over, the architect lived on with the remnants of his menagerie in the five-story Villa Mizner, at center—his spirit and his health broken—until his death in 1933.

96-year-old Marjory Stoneman Douglas at home in Coconut Grove in April 1986, with a halo over her head. "She was not just a pioneer of the environmental movement," eulogized Florida governor Lawton Chiles when she died at age 108, "she was a prophet, calling out to us to save the planet for our children and our grandchildren."

Addison went to the trouble of becoming certified as an architect in Florida, perhaps hoping to do more work in California, which would have recognized his Florida architectural license. But no such commissions were forthcoming.

During these years, he dictated the first volume of his memoirs to his secretary, Madena, and managed to get them published in September 1932. *The Many Mizners* recounts his adventures up until the year 1915. It received several good reviews and then was quickly forgotten. As Alice DeLamar noted, his "inimitable style of talking" did not translate to the page; perhaps that was a reflection of his state of mind at the time. "All the flavor was lacking. The real picture of the warm personality of the man was just not there in the book." A second volume was started but never completed.

In Hollywood, studio head Jack Warner had hired Wilson Mizner to add tough-guy dialogue to the scripts for the gangster films written for James Cagney and Edward G. Robinson. Wilson soon had a desk and chair in the script department on the Warner Bros. lot. He happily contributed to the scripts he was assigned to work on but generally let others do most of the writing. Wilson admitted freely that he had never possessed Addison's work ethic: "I hate work like the Lord hates Saint Louis." He is credited with coming up with the concept and contributing much of the dialogue for William Powell's film *One Way Passage*, although Robert Lord was given credit for the actual screenplay, which won the Academy Award for Best Story in 1933. He added dialogue to Cagney's *Hard to Handle* and *20,000 Years in Sing Sing*, a film, starring Spencer Tracy and Bette Davis, about the famous prison warden Lewis E. Lawes. Wilson also had a cameo role in the first film adaptation of Anita Loos's *Gentlemen Prefer Blondes*, released in 1928.

Soon after arriving in Hollywood, he launched the Brown Derby restaurant—later a chain of restaurants—in partnership with Jack Warner and Herbert Somborn, a former husband of Gloria Swanson. The restaurant, which was conveniently located directly across the street from the Ambassador Hotel, where Wilson lived, occupied a brown stucco building constructed in the shape of a giant bowler hat. It quickly became popular with vaudevillians and Hollywood celebrities of the day such as Charlie

Chaplin, Douglas Fairbanks, Darryl Zanuck, and, of course, Wilson's close friend W. C. Fields. Although he was under contract to Warner Bros., Wilson seems to have spent most of his time in booth number fifty at the Brown Derby, where he continued to burnish his reputation as a raconteur and enjoy the restaurant's popular sirloin steaks. He soon reconnected with a pair of old girlfriends, Anita Loos, who by now was a Hollywood scriptwriter, and a woman named Florence Atkinson, to whom Wilson had pretended to be married at one point during his Palm Beach years—before she eloped with one of Addison's handsome assistants.

Addison began to make an annual summer pilgrimage to California to be closer to his relatives, especially to his beloved niece Ysabel, who had married and settled in Pebble Beach in June 1930. In 1928, when Addison still had some cash, he had bought a ranch near Carmel, California, for $15,000, paid for in part with a loan against his architectural practice, Addison Mizner Inc. Now he began to use the property in the summer, building a cottage for himself and toiling in the garden. However, it wasn't long before he could no longer afford the upkeep and reluctantly signed over the property to Ysabel. While in California, he would drive down to visit Wilson in Los Angeles. Once, the two were photographed at the Del Monte Racetrack. When the photo of Addison ran in the local newspaper, the caption under it read, "Mr. Addison Mizner is the brother of Wilson Mizner, the wit." Wilson mailed the clipping to his brother in Florida after amending the remark: "This should put you in your place."

The brothers kept up their repartee, largely by mail. Wilson complained of hearing loss, and Addison replied, "What do you care? You've heard it all." On another occasion, Wilson, while working on the script for *Merry Wives of Reno*, learned that Addison had suffered another heart attack and telegraphed him: "Stop dying. Am trying to write a comedy." Addison's response: "Am going to get well. The comedy goes on." When Wilson was made an honorary member of the Los Angeles Police Department as part of a prank organized by his Hollywood friends, Addison wired him by way of congratulations: "Thank God Mama is Dead."

Although only in their midfifties, the two brothers were now in failing health. Both tried to make light of it. Wilson, for example, referred to death as "the final mild guffaw at life." In March 1928 Wilson suffered *his* first heart attack and collapsed in the lobby of the Ambassador Hotel. Three years later, he collapsed there a second time after returning in an open car from a party at Tallulah Bankhead's house. This time the diagnosis was bronchial pneumonia. "I haven't breathed since '86 anyhow, so what difference did pneumonia make to me?" he quipped. The former hobo and boxer Jim Tully, one of the first reporters to cover the Hollywood scene and thus "the most-hated man in Hollywood," recalled Wilson as looking prematurely aged, "like an immense leprechaun who must laugh at the world that deserved tears." Wilson had largely recovered by the time Addison visited him in December 1932, but it would be their last visit together. During that stay, it was Addison's turn to fall ill, from what he described to Ysabel as "culinary thrombosis," his jokey take on *coronary sclerosis*.

Addison drove himself back to Florida by way of the Baker Hotel in Mineral Wells, Texas, where he hoped to stop and avail himself of its popular mineral springs. But by the time he arrived at the resort, he was too weakened and too sick to use the facilities. As soon as he could, he continued the journey, driving through horrific winter weather, his Chow named Ching perched in the seat beside him. He eventually made it home to Palm Beach, where he suffered a series of heart attacks that weakened him further.

Throughout these ordeals, he somehow retained his sense of humor and his bonhomie. Although Addison was alone most of the time and ate all of his meals by himself, he still held court in the living room of Villa Mizner in the late afternoons, seated in his enormous Papa Mizner armchair, a tiny monkey named Nettie sticking its head out of his waistcoat. But he could no longer rise from the chair without the help of his valet Arthur Bedford, who remained devotedly in his employ. Friends stopped by to see Addison as they had in the past, but it was far quieter in Villa Mizner than it had been just a few years earlier. If the guests stayed to play cards, it was hearts, not bridge—and, according to one fellow player, Mrs. H. Halpine Smith, whose husband managed Mizner's factory, Addison cheated like mad.

The sixty-year-old architect's heart failed at cocktail hour on Sunday, February 5, 1933. Although he had insisted that he did not want a funeral service of any kind, his secretary, Madena Galloway, disregarded this request and arranged for a memorial service to take place at Villa Mizner on February 9. Despite a rain shower that day, a large crowd showed up to pay their respects, a crowd that included Palm Beach's social elite as well as the workmen from his factories. Characteristically, Wilson did not attend. A prayer was read, followed by some poetry (Keats, Tennyson, and Shelley), and, finally, the great American baritone John Charles Thomas sang a requiem. Addison's old friend Eva Stotesbury (Queen Eva), the first client to commission a Mizner private residence in Palm Beach, quietly pinned a bouquet of orange blossoms to his big, empty chair.

Addison's body was cremated, and his ashes were placed in a blue jar and shipped off to San Franciso, where Ysabel buried them in Cypress Lawn cemetery in Colma. The only money he had left at the time of his death was $200 worth of traveler's checks. The total value of his possessions came to $2,604, but his debts were more than $200,000. The tally included the heavily mortgaged Villa Mizner, his silver and china, an assortment of yet-to-be appraised Spanish antiques that included his collection of crucifixes, and the Via Mizner shops, although, collectively, they were not worth the value of the various mortgages that encumbered them ($180,000). Four months after the architect's death, Mizner Industries, along with Addison Mizner Inc., declared bankruptcy. Loyal to his friends (and to his brother) to a fault, Addison had managed to keep the umbrella-wielding Wendell Weed employed until the businesses finally went under.

Wilson outlived Addison by a mere two months. In late February he suffered a heart attack on the Warner Bros. studio lot. At his insistence, he was carried back to his room at the Ambassador Hotel instead of to a local hospital. He knew he was dying. When asked if he wanted a priest to administer the last sacrament, he replied, "I want a priest, a rabbi, and a Protestant minister. I want to hedge my bets." He confided to another friend, "I don't expect too much. You can't be a rascal for forty years and then cop a plea at the last minute. God keeps better books than that." He eventually died on the night of April 3, 1933.

Wilson's remains were also cremated. There is some dispute as to whether or not his ashes were buried beside Addison's at Cypress Lawn or whether, according to the terms of his will, they were tossed to the wind from the deck of San Francisco's Golden Gate Bridge.

Shortly after Addison Mizner's death, the attacks on his architecture began, accusing him of a deploying a bastardized mix of Renaissance styles and excess theatricality. The most scathing of these came from Frank G. Lopez, an editor of *Progressive Architecture*, who mocked Mizner as a "slight architectural talent" and "a shady 'architect'" who simply copied Latin precedents with "appalling" results, in a review that was disdainfully headlined "We Were Having Some People in for Cocktails." Although this critique is now widely discredited, architectural trends would need to move through Modernism, with its stripped-down Bauhaus aesthetic, before a fair appreciation of Mizner's work could reemerge. And yet, even when his work was most out of favor, Addison retained his champions— and Frank Lloyd Wright was one of them. "Many architects have imagination, but only Mizner had the courage to let his out of the cage," he once remarked. Another was Ada Louise Huxtable, architectural critic of the *New York Times*. In 1977 she wrote of his houses: "These are expert plans . . . and their spaces work superbly as architecture; even empty, their functional and decorative logic give extreme visual and sensual pleasure." Recent appraisals, such as Stephen Perkins and James Caughman, in their elegant coffee-table book *Addison Mizner: The Architect Whose Genius Defined Palm Beach*, make the case for Mizner's enduring importance as one of the nation's finest architects, irrespective of the period.

21

"I USED TO MAKE DREAMS COME TRUE"

Jane Fisher was correct about the impact the 1926 hurricane would have on Carl Fisher's personal—post-divorce—wealth. Virtually overnight, the value of his Miami Beach real estate holdings shrank by a third, from an estimated $30 million to $20 million. On top of that, he had to spend $1 million in cash to repair his hotels and various commercial buildings that had been damaged by the storm, although insurance covered a portion of the cost. But this was just the beginning of his troubles.

These new financial pressures didn't stop him from remarrying. His second wife, Margaret Collier, was the former secretary and mistress who had taken over from Ann Rossiter after she left the company to marry a clergyman. Like Fisher, Margaret drank too much. The couple quarreled, and, within a few years, they were living apart. Her health was fragile, and, at one point, she moved into the St. Regis Hotel in New York City for a five-month stay under the aegis of an expensive quack doctor who claimed he could cure her of her thyroid problems. Despite the strains, inside and outside their union, the couple managed to stay married. Usually, Margaret would live on Long Island when Fisher was in Florida, or vice versa. She had been shrewd enough to get him to sign a generous prenuptial agreement that paid out over time, although Fisher would die with some $80,000 still owing on it.

Under growing financial pressure, Fisher was plagued by back problems that frequently left him bedridden. Adding to his lifelong vision problems, he was struck in the face by a tennis ball during a match and lost the vision in one eye. The fifteen to twenty-five cigars he had smoked each day for the prior fifteen years—the smoke from them wafting into his face—hadn't helped the vision in his remaining eye. By now, he was borderline diabetic as well.

He traveled back and forth between Miami and Montauk, struggling to hold his crumbling empire together. In his spare time, Carl continued to launch new schemes, some of them promising, such as a trailer called an Aerocar, which he attempted to develop in partnership with the aviator and developer Glenn Curtiss. This elaborately kitted out camper trailer could be towed behind a car and was something of a precursor to the now iconic Airstream. Other schemes involved a neon and electric sign business, an improved design for ice cube trays, an improved diesel engine, skid-proof soles or treads for shoes or tires made of sand and rubber, and something aptly named the Solar Operating Refrigerating System, which may well have been ahead of its time. These projects sapped his energy and attention, and not one of them came to fruition. Fisher did help to organize a couple of new boating clubs, and a new private fishing club called the Caribbean Club on Key Largo, where the membership was limited to one hundred anglers.

Ultimately, however, it was the Montauk project that dragged him under. Fisher and his investors had already invested $2.5 million to purchase the land and another $6 million to erect the two-hundred-room Montauk Manor Hotel, the obligatory administration building (seven stories high), a golf course, docks, polo fields—all of this just in time for the stock market crash in October 1929. Undaunted, Carl attempted to talk, cajole, and force the project through to completion, much as he had done at Miami Beach in the early days.

His appeals to the banks, railroads, and those already financially exposed to the project and not eager to see it fail, eventually did bring in new loans, and Carl, who had already sunk $3 million of his own money into the project, used the stock of his other companies to guarantee more loans that collectively ensured construction could continue. To raise additional cash, he sold his controlling interest in the Indianapolis Speedway to Eddie

Rickenbacker, the World War I flying ace and later the head of Eastern Air Lines, for $673,000.

The Fisher ballyhoo was still there, although lacking its earlier novelty and effectiveness. Proclaimed one brochure: "When your thoughts bend northward to lands of ever-changing seasons, another Carl G. Fisher creation beckons to you from the easternmost tip of Long Island, New York. There beautiful Montauk Manor of early English Tudor-design, surveys nine hundred acres of playground between the waters of the Atlantic and Long Island Sound. The many forms of outdoor recreation are eclipsed by incomparable deep-sea fishing."

This time the lots did not sell. His target buyers—wealthy New Yorkers—were among those most hurt by the Wall Street crash. As Fisher biographer Carl Hungness observed: "Carl Fisher was trying to sell bicycles to people who didn't have legs." A later effort to sell the entire complex to a corporation or to a developer such as William L. Wrigley Jr., who was building out Catalina Island off the coast of Los Angeles, came to nothing. By 1930, Carl was struggling to sell off his other assets as fast as he could.

One of those was his beloved new and very grand waterfront mansion overlooking Biscayne Bay. In November 1930 he wrote a letter to Edsel Ford, the only son of the motor magnate, offering to sell the property to him at a very reasonable price. Ford politely declined, which prompted Fisher to write a follow-up, insisting that Edsel at least take a look at the property. Ford refused again. Carl never succeeded in selling the house, eventually losing it to foreclosure.

Shortly afterward, he wrote Jane a letter in which he insisted he wouldn't miss the place. "I wouldn't have another big house if you gave it to me. The houses that I gave Margaret have turned out to be lemons— nothing but expenses—cannot either rent them or sell them, nothing but work and worry with big houses." He repeated that complaint to a friend: "Hell, it was too far for me to walk to the front door." Next on his list was his Charles Marion Russell painting *Battle of the Forty-Fives*, which once had been appraised at $35,000 and always hung in pride of place over the fireplace at the Shadows. He wrote to his old friend Will Rogers, who was living comfortably in Beverly Hills, "I am as hard up as the devil for cash! We are having a very poor season here and not making any sales. Do you know somebody among your friends who will buy 'Smoke [*sic*] of the Forty-Fives'? You would do me a favor if you could dig around and find me a buyer." The yachts, the cars, the homes were sold off one by one. His elephants were donated to zoos.

By 1932, in the depths of Great Depression, the room rates at his remaining hotels dropped from $40 per night, once the highest on Miami Beach, to $5.49, down from $8.72 per night just the year before. He was out of cash and paying his workers with property deeds instead of money. He also traded lots on Miami Beach for services on his commercial properties. That strategy worked until the loans on those businesses came due in late 1932, at which point Fisher was forced to default on the interest payments and could no longer pay his property taxes. Lenders foreclosed on his properties: the polo fields, the LaGorce golf course, his remaining hotels (the Boulevard, the King Cole, the Nautilus, and the Flamingo), and finally his remaining lots on Lincoln Road.

That was also the year that the Montauk Beach Development Company defaulted on its $3.7 million in outstanding loans. Fisher's holding company, the Carl G. Fisher Company, which at one point held twenty of his other businesses, followed the Montauk company into bankruptcy court in 1934. A year later, Carl Fisher had no choice but to declare personal bankruptcy.

Understandably, he grew angry and quarrelsome. "The poison seeping into his once vital body drove him into outbursts that made him lash out against whoever might be nearest to him in such moments," Jane recalled. "Added to this anguish was the humiliation of failure." He spent a portion of the summer of 1935 in a cottage on the deserted Montauk development, attempting to do the maintenance work himself. "I have blisters from a rake but bought a new scythe blade and have to cut weeds," he wrote in a letter to his wife, Margaret. "Paint floor on porch tomorrow." In another letter to her, he expressed his loneliness in his characteristically candid fashion: "I want to go south and sleep with you and have your god damn coed [dog] fart on me once more. Show that to your folks! Love, Skipper."

He was forced to fire his loyal valet William Galloway, who had worked for him for more than thirty years. Instead of doing it gracefully, Fisher allegedly accused him of spending too much money on a watermelon; amazingly, the men remained good friends, because as Galloway remarked to Jane, it was impossible not to love the man. In Galloway's place, Fisher hired a local kid to help him carry groceries, do errands, and give him his daily insulin injections. Despite a worsening case of cirrhosis of the liver, he ignored the entreaties of his doctors and friends to stop drinking. Fisher no longer cared what they thought and made no effort to stop.

He proceeded to drink himself to death: a glass of Scotch with breakfast, a case of beer in the afternoon, and a bottle of Scotch each night, which he would polish off in bed while reading mysteries or long histories of Elizabethan England. "As to the Depression, do you know of anyone it did not leave an imprint on?" he wrote to his friend and fellow auto racer Claude Mercer. "I myself lost about twenty-five million, but am still able to eat, up to this evening." He was grossly understating his losses.

Sometime in late 1938 or early 1939, a lawyer from Indianapolis named Walter Dennis Myers spotted Fisher, a former client, loitering near a park bench on Lincoln Avenue in Miami Beach. He pulled his car over to the curb and climbed out to talk to him. When asked how he was doing, the ruined developer replied, "I can tell you in a few words. The bottom dropped out of the sea. New York and Long Island took everything I had. I'm a beggar—dead broke, no family to fall back on. Yes, the bottom dropped out of the sea, and I went with it. You know, I promoted Miami Beach here. The grateful people got up a purse, five hundred dollars a month for me. That's what I live on. I used to make dreams come true. Can't do it anymore. I'm only a beggar now. The end can't be far away."

During Fisher's final months, he underwent a series of grim medical procedures, which, as he summarized in a letter to his close friend the race-car driver Barney Oldfield, required the doctors to bore a hole in his stomach to let out up to eighteen pounds of excess fluid, a symptom of cirrhosis of the liver. He urged his friend to come visit but apologized for being unable to put him up in the Flamingo Hotel, because he no longer owned it.

The two old friends exchanged warm letters over the next few months. Oldfield was trying to write his memoirs, and Fisher wanted him to be sure to mention in the book how Oldfield had set a speed record in Indianapolis after a few glasses of Veuve Clicquot champagne. "Of course, if you have tried to dodge the fact that you were drunk a good deal of the time, or at least in a hilarious mood a good part of the time, you not only fly in the face of Providence, but you spit in the eye of a great many of your friends, who, if they weren't pretty tight at the time, were just getting over being tight, or were making preparations to be tight later on in the day."

As was true for all three of Florida's surviving real estate kings, Fisher's friendships had weathered the Depression far better than his fortune had, and ultimately these friendships meant more to him than money. Letters arrived from other old friends, many of them having suffered terrible financial reversals in the Depression and asking for financial assistance. Fisher wrote back dutifully, apologizing that he no longer had the funds to help them.

Finally, on July 15, 1939, he was rushed to St. Francis Hospital in North Beach, where he died a few hours later from a gastric hemorrhage. Carl Fisher was sixty-five years old. His estate, which was left to his widow, Margaret, was appraised at some $40,000 when probated. It included some near-worthless shares in the Carl Fisher Corporation, the reorganized remnants of an empire once worth $76 million ($1.1 billion today).

Three days after Fisher's death, an outdoor memorial service was held on Miami Beach on the lawn in front of the library and arts center. The nearby city hall closed early in honor of the developer, and the flags along the island flew at half-staff. Two hundred people turned up to hear John Oliver LaGorce, associate editor of *National Geographic* and Fisher's close friend, deliver the eulogy. Fisher lay in an open casket, improbably clad in a tuxedo and wearing his horn-rimmed glasses. LaGorce sketched the details of Fisher's remarkable career in Indiana and Florida before commenting, "Carl Graham Fisher was but human and therefore not perfect, which made him the more beloved by those who understood him." A nearby rivet gun sounded taps for the developer. The Reverend Jay Wabeke gave the benediction, after which the active pallbearers clad in white, Barney Oldfield among them, then lifted the casket and carried it to the hearse. His widow, Margaret, who had been in Montauk when he died but arrived in time for the memorial service, took her seat in the car behind the hearse, where she was seen placing a hand over her eyes "as if to shut out the scene and hold back the tears," according to the *Miami Herald*. The funeral cortege then proceeded down Dade Boulevard and over the Venetian Causeway to Miami's Woodlawn Park Cemetery, led by a dozen Miami and Miami Beach policemen on motorcycles. Jane Fisher, who was in upstate New York at the time of her ex-husband's death, arrived too late for the funeral. Two years later, the city of Miami Beach erected a bronze and stone monument in Fisher's honor. It featured a bust of him wearing one of his floppy hats. The inscription read: "Carl Graham Fisher: He carved a great city from a jungle."

After George Merrick lost control of his Coral Gables development company, he reentered the real estate business through a new sales and marketing entity called George E. Merrick Coral Gables Company. As the Great Depression took hold, however, even this would wither away. He watched as the capstone of his Coral Gables development, the Biltmore Hotel, faltered financially and foreclosed in October 1929. Bondholders would pay $1.75 million for a property that had cost Merrick and John McEntee Bowman $10 million to build four years earlier. A year later, it would be sold again for $2 million to an investor group that included former governor of New York and former Democratic presidential candidate Al Smith. Merrick was asked to vacate his sumptuous suite of offices in the hotel's Giralda tower.

Determined to rebuild his business and salvage his reputation, Merrick teamed up with his younger brother, Richard, then just twenty-seven years old, to launch a chain of middle-class vacation, fishing, and retirement communities around Florida and the Caribbean. It would be called Caribee Colony. The prototype would be built on twenty acres of land on Lower Matecumbe Key, land that George had bought as a gift for his Peacock in-laws some years earlier. The pilot colony, with its Samoan huts and "South Seas enchantment," opened in January 1931, only to be largely destroyed by a fire a few months later, ruining its prospects and any hope of expanding the concept into a chain of properties. Two months later, angry investors in the Coral Gables development had Merrick arrested for embezzlement and grand larceny, requiring him to post bail to avoid serving jail time. It would be a year before he was acquitted of the charges.

At this point, Merrick was so financially constrained that a bank foreclosed on his house in Coral Gables and then auctioned it off on the Miami courthouse steps. He and Eunice were forced to move in with her mother until they could find a more modest home of their own. And yet somehow their marriage survived these ordeals. Meanwhile, his troubles were starting to take a physical toll. "His hair is white, and the recent years have not dealt kindly with him, but the great frame which was hardened on the rocky groves of his father has not drooped," one local journalist wrote. "He, like his city, has had to change his sights a little, but he's still there on the firing line."

The spiral continued downward. In December 1932 Merrick's proudest legacy, the University of Miami, went bankrupt. A year and a half later, Henry Doherty, the wealthy founder of Cities Service Corporation, an oil conglomerate, bought it out of receivership. Not one to overlook an obvious opportunity, Merrick tried to interest Doherty (who by then also owned the Biltmore) in yet another new development, this one called Biscayneland, that would purchase and subdivide one hundred thousand acres of South Dade farmland, creating a "Country City" mix of small farms and factories. The idea was to sell five-acre lots for $500 each and create a community of two hundred thousand people. This, too, never got off the ground. When Franklin Roosevelt announced the New Deal, Merrick reformulated his Biscayneland concept into something he called Country Coral Gables, offering subsistence, or low-income, housing for Miamians. He attempted to get the US Interior Department to fund it. When the funding fell through, he tried to launch it on his own, bootstrapping the sales and marketing. He also pursued a plan to develop waterfront land on Grand Bahama Island, hoping to attract middle-class buyers from the United Kingdom and Canada as well as the United States. But nothing worked. By now, the Coral Gables Administration Building, where T. H. Weigall had toiled at the peak of the boom, had been sold for a pittance and converted into a gas station.

Early in the fall of 1935, yet another hurricane struck—the so-called Labor Day Hurricane, which made landfall in the Florida Keys. It peeled away the trestles and tracks of the Florida East Coast Railway that Flagler had built at such human and financial cost. A rescue train sent to retrieve World War I veterans who were working on the construction of the Overseas Highway that ran parallel to Flagler's train tracks arrived too late to be of help and was washed off its tracks in the storm. The Long Key Fishing Camp and the veterans' camps on Windley Key and Lower Matecumbe Key were obliterated by a storm surge of eighteen to twenty feet, drowning 260 of the workers housed there. George and Eunice had leased their property on Lower Matecumbe Key to a husband and wife who were running it as a guest camp. The couple and twenty-four of their guests died in the storm. In all, 488 people lost their lives across the Keys. George went down to volunteer his services and to survey the damage to his property. He helped to load the dead bodies onto a railroad car for the trip back to the mainland. Flagler's great railroad to the sea, the oil tycoon's costliest and most ambitious Florida venture, would never be rebuilt and now seemed little more than a wasteful folly.

Two weeks after that storm, Merrick was subpoenaed to testify in Washington, DC, in a federal investigation into Florida's widespread municipal bond defaults and city bankruptcies. By the mid-1930s, some twenty-six cities and towns in the state had defaulted on the interest or principal payments due on their municipal bonds. One of these municipalities was Coral Gables. Heading the investigation for the Securities and Exchange Commission was a brilliant lawyer and former Yale law professor named William O. Douglas, assisted by his ablest former pupil at Yale, Abe Fortas, and two other more junior attorneys. Both Douglas and Fortas would go on to become associate justices of the US Supreme Court.

Of particular interest, and the first focus of the commission's investigation, was the $4.5 million municipal bond issue that the city of Coral Gables (led by Merrick) floated to purchase the Coral Gables Corporation assets in 1927. That bond offering, one of four that totaled over $7.3 million, entailed an obvious, even profound, conflict of interest, as the investigators pointed out. Merrick and his top lieutenants owned all of Coral Gables Inc., the seller of the assets; in fact, Merrick personally owned 80 percent of the enterprise. At the same time, Merrick and his four top lieutenants made up the entire body of the governing commissioners of the city of Coral Gables, the buyer of the assets. So they were in essence selling to themselves. Many of the details of this deal were damning, such as the price the city paid for the Merrick assets. Buildings such as the fire station, the ambulance house, and the city hall, which had cost Merrick only $34,234 to build, were sold to the city in 1927 for $150,000. By 1930, they would be appraised at only $11,500, and presumably declined in value from there as the Depression deepened. The syndicate that sold the bonds to pay for these acquisitions, led by Century Trust Company, took a 25 percent to 30 percent discount on the face value of the bonds before reselling them to the public, a huge commission. To smooth the deal over with the local community, Merrick admitted to paying, through his corporation, $30,000 to the Miami city attorney John W. Watson Jr. in the form of a house worth $25,000 and an additional $5,000 in cash, payments that looked an awful lot like bribes. Commissioner William O. Douglas described these financial maneuvers, mockingly, as "a curious situation." The payments looked especially curious as they were over and above the $7,500 that the city of Coral Gables paid Watson to "validate" the deal.

Similarly, a remarkably large $750,000 was paid to promote the bond issue, with $600,000 of that being pocketed by the owner of the Century Trust Company. The other $150,000 included money to motivate the salesmen and to ensure the broad support of a so-called Citizens Committee of 100, of which Merrick was also a member. That committee had voted in favor of issuing the bond and then promptly voted again in favor of buying the Merrick assets with the proceeds. As the *New York Times* reported, "It was the contention of counsel for the commission that in all four bond issues, Mr. Merrick and his associates were buying and selling securities, using their official position with the city as a trading post and the organized citizenry as a method of 'unloading properties with which the corporation was stuck.'" The investigators estimated that Merrick personally profited on that one bond deal alone to the tune of $1.4 million. One investigating commissioner characterized the method as loan-sharking; it surely was fraud.

Despite excellent legal representation over the years and his own considerable background in the law, Merrick professed to the committee to be ignorant of the Florida statute that expressly prohibited him from serving simultaneously as both a city official and the leader of a private enterprise. Luckily for Merrick, the statute of limitations for pursuing criminal fraud cases had passed by the time the Securities and Exchange Commission began examining these bond deals. This was precisely the kind of financial malfeasance that had led to the creation of the SEC, with its oversight role, the year before.

It must have been a startling revelation for the worshipful fans of George Merrick to discover that their hero had done something crooked—and not just once, but four times. The debt that he had saddled Coral Gables with would not be paid off until 1961.

The magnitude of the collapse at Coral Gables was laid bare in Merrick's testimony to the commission. In all, he had bought and subdivided ten thousand acres into 24,741 lots that he hoped to fill in five years with 250,000 people. However, by 1930, only 1,812 lots had been built on; the population of Coral Gables stood at 5,697. The scale of the development, so many of its lots now near worthless, looked hopelessly optimistic in hindsight.

Throughout the darkest years of the Great Depression, Merrick operated a tiny real estate business called George Merrick Inc., working out of a small office furnished with the few remaining decent rugs and antiques that he and Eunice still owned. The two of them, with no children to raise, worked side by side in close partnership, laboring hard to expand the business, adding offices and hiring salesmen whenever they could afford to. Throughout the decade, they struggled financially, often pursued by creditors. His best friend, the lawyer Clifton Benson, who lent him money during this period, again advised him to slow down: "It grieves me at times to see you work so hard with no apparent results. You make life hard for yourself." He predicted "disaster upon disaster" unless Merrick changed his behavior. The letter struck Merrick to the quick, and for a few months, he refused to speak to his old friend. Benson eventually apologized, and the two patched up their friendship. Merrick, however, continued to ignore the lawyer's advice and refused to slow down.

George was appointed by Florida's governor to Dade County's first planning board in 1935 and was quickly elected its chair. The commission reviewed and promoted various Works Progress Administration (WPA) efforts to improve roads, schools, community centers, and general infrastructure, matters he cared about deeply. In this new capacity, he actively supported the creation of the Everglades National Park that Ernest Coe and Marjory Stoneman Douglas were championing, although it would be years before it was approved—in 1947—and then not for its scenic appeal but rather for its ecological value.

Merrick finally managed to quit drinking and joined the Christian Science church, to which Eunice belonged. For a short time, his life and career looked to be on the rebound. He was appointed to a Dade County zoning commission, where he promoted a broad zoning plan for the county that would mirror what he had once done at Coral Gables. The plan passed into law only to be quickly repealed by a powerful coalition of developers, attorneys, realtors, and property owners who, predictably, viewed it as too restrictive. He resigned in protest. In 1940 he cofounded the Historical Association of Southern Florida and served as its first president.

Despite the couple's hard work throughout the Depression years, the Merricks' real estate brokerage business ultimately foundered. By 1939, they were back down to two offices and struggling to pay their telephone and electric bills. In a letter to his friend Benson, George apologized for being unable to pay him back a loan and worried aloud that if he didn't get a few breaks soon, he would be forced to close up shop. He admitted that he had no money to service his debts, which included his mother's burial expenses. He had to borrow from his mother-in-law simply to have enough to eat and to pay for his gasoline. "I am wearing a pair of shoes with the bottom on the ground for the last few weeks, so you can tell your friends that George Merrick's feet are on the ground at last." He made little secret of the fact that he considered himself a failure.

Desperate for financial security, George applied for the job of postmaster of Miami, a civil service position that paid $7,000 a year and offered a lifetime pension after retirement. He passed the requisite civil service exam, lobbied his congressman for the job, and allegedly orchestrated a thousand letters to be written on his behalf. When he failed the physical because of his weight and blood pressure, he managed to lose twenty-two pounds; he passed the exam on his second try. He received the requisite Senate and White House confirmation on June 1, 1940.

The job requirements were complicated by the outbreak of World War II the following year and would prove stressful and grueling for him, often requiring ten-hour work days. Soon he began to feel poorly and complained to Eunice that he was having trouble sleeping. A little over a year after his appointment, Merrick was hospitalized. The local papers carried front-page stories about his deteriorating condition. Distraught, aware that he was dying, he needed Eunice at his side to calm him. He died there of a heart attack six days later, in the early morning hours of March 26, 1942, at age fifty-five. The value of his estate at the time of his death: less than $400.

The obituaries praised all that he had accomplished at Coral Gables in the years before the Depression and made no mention of his now-forgotten double-dealing and his conspiracy to defraud the community. Fred W. Hosea, a Miami city commissioner, described him bombastically as "the greatest developer this country has ever known." Frank Shutts, the prominent Miami lawyer, told one reporter, "He lost his money, but he never lost his soul," an assertion that was debatable. The banker and former mayor of Miami, E. C. Romfh, recalled, "I remember George when, as a barefoot boy, he used to peddle vegetables. I watched his climb from the lowest to the top-most rungs of the ladder of success. The beautiful city of Coral Gables is a lasting memorial to his name." Merrick's funeral took place at the Mission-style Plymouth Congregational Church in Coconut Grove, which was built on land that he had donated. Six of his colleagues at the post office were his pallbearers.

Eunice struggled to keep the Merrick real estate office running after George's death. Two years later, in 1944, she married a family friend, Army Lieutenant Colonel Ralph H. Sartor, at which point she closed the office and moved to Panama, where her new husband worked for the Panama Canal Commission. The marriage was a mistake. She divorced Sartor in 1949, complaining that he had treated her like a housekeeper and servant rather than a wife, assuming "a domineering attitude" soon after their marriage began. She moved back to Coral Gables and changed her name back to Mrs. George Merrick. Eunice lived to be ninety-three and died there in 1989.

Jane Fisher did not survive as long as her respected Coral Gables counterpart. Her marriage to Bob Johnson failed within a few years, as did her two subsequent marriages, one to a Christian Science healer, the other to a Portuguese businessman. "Life was just too dull. It was too humdrum. You see, living with Carl Fisher was like living in a circus: there was something going on—something exciting going on—every minute of the day. Sometimes it was very good; sometimes it was very bad. Still, it was living. It was excitement, aliveness, that I never found again." She, too, changed her name back to that of her first and most famous husband. For a time, she wrote a society column for a local newspaper, published a memoir, and taught backgammon on Miami Beach to supplement her modest Social Security income. She felt guilty over the squalid death that Carl had endured, and wrote in her memoirs, *Fabulous Hoosier*, "How did we fail him, that he died sick of soul and discouraged?"

Her financial circumstances worsened as the years went by. At one point, she had traded the last of her Lincoln Road land for a small apartment hotel, which she soon lost to foreclosure. She was down to $3 in her purse and had to borrow from friends. She lived out her final days alone in a small, dilapidated cottage on Miami Beach's Sheridan Avenue in the company of a cat named Puddy Cat and a high-strung Italian greyhound named Pizza, playing a lot of backgammon despite her worsening arthritis. All the same, she was a good sport about her reduced circumstances. Late in her life, over lunch at the local Howard Johnson's, she insisted to local historian Polly Redford that she had no regrets: "I wouldn't change any of it. Not one little bit. You see, I've had it all." Florida's first "bathing beauty" and Paris's "La Dame aux Camélias" would die of a heart attack at age seventy-four in December 1968.

22

A LEGACY OF GREED AND FOLLY

*From one viewpoint, the Florida land boom is a familiar story of middle-*aged men, behaving badly—financially, maritally, and, all too often, morally—in a manner that seems especially unsurprising today. Each of Florida's real estate barons let his ego be warped by the adulation of the crowd, by his susceptibility to greed and ambition, or by his new-found status, wealth, and power. Jane Fisher seemed especially puzzled by Carl's unquenchable drive, which the others shared, and she questioned if this wasn't the very trait that had propelled him to ruin: "Was it thirst for power? Was it that hungry urge for greater achievement that would drive Carl Fisher, like his favorite character, Napoléon, on to his doom? Forever that dynamic driving force, that never-ending desire to conquer ruthlessly! Always there was the dream to do something bigger." While not solely to blame for the real estate crash and its dire economic consequences, these men surely should share in culpability for the era's great missteps.

Why was it that not one of them was able to pull back, step away from his business, or refuse the opportunities for ever greater wealth and glory as they arose? Perhaps it simply wasn't in their DNA to take the necessary precautions or to reduce their risk-taking impulses. Carl Fisher, it should be noted, insisted that money wasn't his chief motivation and that he simply needed something to do. He claimed that his real motive was "just to see steam shovels throwing dirt and buildings going up." There is something childlike about this level of aspiration—and it is shared by every youngster who has ever peered, mesmerized, into the marvels and mysteries of a large construction site.

In what seems like the cruel denouement to a dark Grimm Brothers' fairy tale, not one of Florida's four real estate kings survived the boom with either his fortune or his health intact. One drank himself to death, one ate himself to death, one worked himself to death, and one most probably committed suicide on a desperate, drunken dare.

Part of the trauma these men suffered—the deeply personal nature of it—surely had something to do with the propensity we have to form strong connections and attachments to the land or the house we own, in a way we don't with our other assets. Consequently, the loss of a beloved piece of property—or even a business, if the owner has built it—inflicts more than a mere financial blow; it imparts a deep and searing psychological wound and a loss of identity. Anyone who has surrendered a treasured family home knows this feeling all too well. It is surely one aspect of what makes the bursting of a property bubble and its aftermath so emotionally devastating to those caught in its maelstrom.

Offsetting such losses for each of these unstoppable men, and for many other participants in the boom, were the friendships that they made or maintained during the raucous decade. Their wealth and fame may have proved fleeting, but their friendships, tested and tempered by their professional and financial failures, endured to enrich their lives.

The great Florida land boom left several important legacies; chief among these were the vibrant cities, most notably Palm Beach, Miami, and Miami Beach, which would rebound in the decades to follow and emerge as proper metropolises. Florida would endure more booms and busts in the years to come, most notably in the 1950s, driven by the first generation of Social Security retirees; again in the 1980s, when condominium towers first came into vogue; and then once more, in early 2000s, when real estate boomed across the country thanks to the spread and securitization of subprime mortgages. Today the Miami *urban* area is home to 5.5 million people, the fourth-largest such urban area in the country.

As a prime gateway to Central and South America and a melting pot of American, South American, Latin American, and Caribbean nationalities, cultures, and cuisines, it remains one of the nation's fastest-growing regions. Real estate development continues apace with ever more condominium towers under construction around the state. The reckless growth calls to mind a recent remark by the naturalist David Attenborough, "We have a finite environment—the planet. Anyone who thinks that you can have infinite growth in a finite environment is either a madman or an economist."

Fortunately, in the wake of the great boom came a reaction against the kind of unrestrained development that the real estate kings had championed. The realization dawned that deep incursions into the Everglades and rampant and unconstrained development at its perimeter that occurred during the twenties simply could not continue. The decimation of the great swamp, one of the world's most remarkable ecosystems and its largest freshwater marsh—specifically, the loss of over half its landmass—was proving disastrous for the ecology of South Florida, for its plant and animal species, and for the freshwater aquifer that was so vital to all future economic development. Indeed, the loss had led directly to the water shortages that occur regularly today.

Much of the evolution in the collective consciousness came from the leadership of committed environmentalists such as Arthur R. Marshall Jr., Joe Browder, Nathaniel Reed, Marjorie Harris Carr, Helen Morrison, and, of course, Marjory Stoneman Douglas. Environmental advocates such as these successfully halted a number of ill-considered ventures in the Everglades and elsewhere, such as, in 1971, the Cross Florida Barge Canal, intended to create a waterway from Jacksonville to Yankeetown. Douglas herself played a pivotal role in halting the construction of a jetport in the Big Cypress Swamp section of the Everglades in 1970 by organizing a grassroots group called Friends of the Everglades that successfully lobbied against the project. Today it counts some five thousand members. Over the years, her pleas were heard, and her writings and activism often helped to change hearts and minds and then prompt regulatory change, although not always immediately or without a tough fight against pro-development forces. Douglas had come of age during the great Florida land boom and could speak with authority to the damage it had done.

Although Douglas never remarried, she lived happily and productively in her Coconut Grove bungalow for the rest of her long life. In all of her work, she showed an interest and awareness of the natural world, influenced no doubt by the passions of the naturalists and environmentalists who surrounded her and befriended her in Coconut Grove.

By the 1940s she possessed the confidence in her writing to take on longer pieces of work. In fact, she had begun her first novel when Hervey Allen, the author of the historical novel *Anthony Adverse*, came by to visit her in 1942. He was then editor of the new Rivers of America series being published by Rinehart & Company. He asked her if she would be willing to write a book on the Miami River, which she had studied so closely from the bedroom window in her father's house. She accepted the commission but quickly realized there was a larger story to be told: the story of the Everglades, out of which the Miami River flowed. It would take her four and a half years to research and write her most important book, *The Everglades: The River of Grass*, which was published in 1947 to instant acclaim. She dedicated the book to the memory of her father, "who gave me Florida." Part Florida history and part environmental inquiry, the book concluded with a call for action to save what remained of the Everglades, which, she poignantly noted, were dying—and, at the time, burning: "The endless acres of saw grass, brown as an enormous shadow where rain and lake water had once flowed, rustled dry. The birds flew high above them, the ibis, the egret, the heron beating steadily southward along drying watercourses to the last brackish pools. Fires that one night glittered along a narrow horizon the next day, before a racing wind, flashed crackling and roaring across the grassy world and flamed up in rolling columns of yellow smoke like pillars of dirty clouds."

Her book helped to launch a twenty-year flowering of natural history writing that would largely define the genre by emphasizing the spiritual and aesthetic value of the wilderness as well as the high drama of its ecology. The classics that followed included among others, Aldo Leopold's *A Sand County Almanac* (1949), Rachel Carson's *The Sea Around Us* (1951) and *Silent Spring* (1962), Wallace Stegner's "Wilderness Letter" (1960), Farley Mowat's *Never Cry Wolf* (1963), and Edward Abbey's *Desert Solitaire* (1968).

Although her book redefined the public's conception of the Everglades from a worthless expanse of swamp to a precious and irreplaceable waterway, Douglas rejected the idea that, somehow, through the book, she had "saved" them. "They're not saved yet," she would remind her audiences. And she continued to deplore the fact that the government—local, state, and federal—failed to fully understand the natural mechanics of the great waterway and its importance to the greater Florida ecosystem.

The great developers, two of whom she had known personally, would be dead before Douglas found her true calling, but she had already learned from their mistakes: from their often reckless and shortsighted disregard for the environment, from their failure to see how humankind was inextricably tied to nature, and from their fallibility in the face of greed and the corrupting effects of wealth and power. Like her father, she wasn't opposed to land development per se, or, for that matter, to economic progress and jobs and social justice and equality. But she adamantly opposed the destruction of the wellspring of all Florida life: the Everglades and its water. Her writings and ideas were never a foil to the doings of the real estate kings of the twenties but rather the chief counterbalance to what these men had accomplished.

The sugar-growing interests and the cattle ranchers soon displaced the development community and their captive politicians as her chief opponents, especially after the fertilizers and pollutants from the growers and the manure from the cattle began to spill into Lake Okeechobee and from there into the Everglades. She took on these special interests as best she could by lecturing, by lobbying, by attempting to push legislation through the Florida State Legislature, and by challenging the policies of the federal government. It was hard work and never particularly fun, but she refused to give up. In the decades that followed, Douglas would appear in countless Florida lecture halls and classrooms, "a squat little woman in a wide-brimmed hat." She would slap a map of the South Florida Water Conservation District onto a blackboard and proceed to explain the hydrology of the Everglades and the urgency of preserving them. "I'll talk about the Everglades at the drop of a hat. Whoever wants me to talk, I'll come over and tell about the necessity of preserving the Everglades. Sometimes I tell them more than they want to know," she admitted.

By finding her path as a writer and discovering her activism, Douglas seemed to resolve any outstanding internal conflicts. She experienced a third psychotic episode shortly after her beloved father died in 1941, but that would be the final such occurrence. From then on, her mental and physical health were robust. She continued to go dancing whenever she could and for years continued to swim in the ocean at least three times a week. Her deep and varied friendships, with neighbors and fellow environmentalists, sustained her throughout the decades, and a succession of cats kept her company. One in particular was an outgoing calico named Emily, whom she adored. She was heartbroken when Emily caught and ate a poisonous lizard. She found the cat alive but half paralyzed. "There was nothing to do but take her to the vet and have her killed, because she couldn't live like that. It was very sorrowful indeed."

Also sorrowful was the loss of the supercolonies of birds that she had so admired, which once numbered in the tens of thousands. Between 1930 and 1989, in the Central and Southern Everglades, 85 percent of the nesting areas would be removed, resulting in a similar decline in bird numbers. The white ibis population, which Douglas had admired for its wheeling nuptial flight, saw its population drop from 100,000 nesting pairs to 6,250 pairs by 1989.

In her final years, slowed by age and the loss of her eyesight, restricting herself to a glass of sherry or two ounces of Scotch whisky per day, she worked on a biography of the British novelist W. H. Hudson, whom she considered to be the world's first environmentalist and a writer who belonged in the distinguished company of Henry David Thoreau, John Burroughs, and John Muir. The book remained unfinished and unpublished.

The author John Rothchild, who helped her to write her memoirs when she was in her nineties, recalled taking Douglas to dinner late in her life. "In her floppy hats and dark glasses, she looked like Igor Stravinsky at the Easter parade," he recalled. "In spite of her age and her physical limitations, she could scare the bejesus out of reporters, politicians, bureaucrats, developers, lobbyists, and polluters."

A conservation award was named in her honor, as were several schools and parks. Florida governor Lawton Chiles celebrated Douglas's legacy by observing, "Marjory was the first voice to really wake a lot of us up to what we were doing to our quality of life. She was not just a pioneer of the environmental movement, she was a prophet, calling out to us to save the environment for our children and our grandchildren." In 1993, when she was 103 years old, President Bill Clinton awarded her the nation's highest civilian honor, the Presidential Medal of Freedom, for her efforts to preserve and restore the Everglades. She lived to be 108 before succumbing to a gentle death, far outliving the four great developers who had been her contemporaries. Her ashes were scattered in the Everglades.

Her bungalow survives today as a national historic landmark and a significant artifact of the twenties boom. It sits back from the road in a wooded section of Coconut Grove, a patch of small grass in front of the simple frame structure that still has no driveway. The inside, too, is much as she left it, very modestly furnished, no stove, no dishwasher—a moving memorial to a courageous and enterprising author and activist who explained to the world that Florida's land—and, by extrapolation, all of our land—was unique for reasons other than its vast real estate development potential.

Today, thanks to Douglas, nothing as ill-conceived as the Tamiami Trail will ever go unchallenged again. Steps have been taken to mitigate the ecological damage done by that notorious road by lifting portions of it onto bridges that allow the advance of freshwater to resume. It isn't enough, but it is a start. In one notable environmental achievement, large stretches of the Kissimmee River, once straightened and channelized by the US Army Corps of Engineers, have been restored to their original meandering routes through their natural floodplains. But battles over land use and environmental exploitation are sure to continue. As environmental historian Michael Grunwald notes, "The South Florida ecosystem still provides outstanding habitat for greed and folly."

Another important legacy of the Florida boom is the collection of architectural masterpieces built by Addison Mizner in Palm Beach and Boca Raton, still considered among the supreme artistic achievements of the 1920s. In recent years, some have sold for tens of millions of dollars and have been owned by notables such as the Kennedy family, John Lennon and Yoko Ono, and thriller writer James Patterson. Miami Beach during the 1930s would enrich its own architectural heritage with a succession of Art Deco buildings at South Beach that remain standing to this day, but otherwise little attention has been paid to the architectural aesthetic in the years since. The City Beautiful Movement in Florida that Merrick and Mizner championed had died a sudden death with the collapse of the boom. Frank Lloyd Wright looked at the new construction in Miami in the 1950s and bemoaned the architectural tastes of that era's developers: "They have no feeling, no richness, no sense of that region. Why don't you do something here that belongs? You have something in Miami that belongs to Miami. It has character. It has charm." Merrick and Mizner would have agreed.

The manic-depressive story of the great Florida land boom also endures as a business yarn about capitalism run amok—or, for that matter, capitalism in a muck. It is a yarn from which a few pertinent business lessons can be drawn. One such lesson is how excess household debt leverages the damage in an economic downturn—and thus how important it is that such debt levels, whether held by consumers or on the balance sheets of banks, be monitored closely and mitigated aggressively through legislation, Federal Reserve policy, or bank regulation when the levels get too high. Requiring ample cushions of capital to offset potential losses at the big banks is the minimum precaution. Equally important are banking transparency and sound government oversight of lending practices. Without such precautions, we can't detect when excess financial risk is being taken, and we won't know when we are setting up for the next financial calamity. We are also left blind to the insider dealings, conflicts of interest, and insidious greed that so often accompany the flow of easy money. Nor should we forget how quickly corruption occurs when a community's powerful business interests are allowed to co-opt the local or federal government and exploit the banking system for their own ends. Laissez-faire economics have their practical limits. The late Nobel Prize–winning economist Paul Samuelson put it best when he wrote, "Deregulated capitalism is a fragile flower bound to commit suicide."

In many ways, the Florida of the 1920s was a precursor of America one hundred years later. In Florida then, as in the United States at the moment, two affluent coasts were separated by an often impoverished, largely agricultural interior. Inequitable wealth distribution, racial intolerance, xenophobia, and rising nationalism—the KKK being the most blatant manifestation back then—were combined with a dangerous overreliance on laissez-fare economics and a governance structure where bankers and businesspeople wielded inordinate influence on policy. To complete the analogy, the political leadership of the day displayed profound indifference to the fate of the environment and to society's less fortunate. It didn't end well then, which portends a dismal future for us now unless we change course soon.

The parallels between the story of the Florida land boom and the events leading up to the Great Recession remain uncanny as well. In both cases, the leveraging of real estate (and personal balance sheets) led to inevitable collapse. Leverage and real estate create a toxic combination; a better awareness of this toxicity can help us to avoid, in advance, a repeat of such cataclysmic mistakes. As Roger Babson once observed, "The evils of an economic depression cannot be cured during such a depression. The evils of a future depression can, however, be prevented or reduced by taking proper precautions during the preceding era of prosperity."

During the twenties, the state of Florida, as well as the nation as a whole, saw remarkable social, economic, and environmental changes. Florida went from being the last American frontier (until Alaska, which became a state in 1959) and began the rapid transformation from a predominantly agricultural state to a largely urban state driven by a service-based economy. By 1940, fully 55 percent of Floridians lived in cities and towns. Of course, the country as a whole underwent a similar transformation during this period, but Florida did so in fast-forward. Thirteen new counties were created during the decade, in response to the rush to develop land, and by the end of the decade, the state had swelled its population by 50 percent.

Alas, not everybody had participated meaningfully in the good times—such as they were, and while they lasted. Florida's African American citizens, grievously mistreated and discriminated against, felt little benefit from the boom, and left the state in droves throughout the decade. The abominable treatment of blacks across the South during this period (and long before and long afterward), particularly in Florida, which topped all other states in the ratio of lynchings per resident, remains one of the era's, and the nation's, most grotesque and shameful legacies.

A final lesson to be learned from the land boom is how susceptible we are to the seductions of any speculative frenzy. Greed beckons like a powerful intoxicant, easily overwhelming our sounder instincts and better judgment. This was certainly true for Florida's real estate kings, whose seduction by their own wealth and power offers a sobering lesson for the rest of us.

Just how such speculative episodes arrive at their tragic denouement always remains something of a mystery in their aftermath. What exactly is it that causes the final spike of investment frenzy in a boom to stall, to topple, and then to fall? Here the question is: What caused the rise in land prices to hit their peak and then reverse so precipitously? Was it the railroad embargo? Was it Coleman du Pont so vocally quitting the Mizner Development Corporation's board of directors? Was it the tax authorities stepping in to change the way profits on real estate transactions were booked? Was it the massive blow struck by the hurricane of 1926? Was it the negativity of the national press? Was it the sinking of the *Prinz Valdemar*? Or could it have been some combination—or all—of the above factors?

Reflecting back on Florida's epic boom, Walter P. Fuller, the St. Petersburg realtor who lived through it, offered perhaps the best single explanation for what finally brought the great frenzy to its ignominious end:

"As to why the boom stopped, the answer is very simple. We just ran out of suckers. That's all. We got all their money, then started trading with ourselves. . . . Did I say we ran out of suckers? That isn't quite correct. *We* became the suckers—standing down there at the foot of the class. Very simple. Very simple, indeed."

AFTERWORD

In the mid-1970s, nearly fifty years after the collapse of the great Florida land boom, the former antiquarian Alex Waugh found himself back in the United States on a business trip. Some years before, he had left the antiques trade to pursue a career restoring historic houses and inns in the English countryside. He managed to block out time in his travel itinerary for a return visit to Palm Beach. On his first trip to Florida all those decades before, when he was the guest of his friend Joe Ritter and still recovering from the injuries he had sustained at the Battle of the Somme, the journey had taken him two and a half days on a hot and dusty train to reach his destination. Now the trip took a mere two and a half hours on an Eastern Air Lines jet. Silver-haired, Hollywood handsome, and still smoking a pipe, Waugh had become, by his own description, "a distinguished gentleman." In fact, he was so tweedy and quintessentially British in his accent, appearance, and deportment that he had been asked to star in a television commercial endorsing a well-known brand of Scotch whisky.

He was startled by how much Palm Beach had changed. It was no longer the wealthy debutante of Florida resorts. It had grown up into an immaculate and posh little city. Even the palms along Royal Palm Way now towered over the street—like the rows of stately columns that adorn the Greek temples of Paestum and the Acropolis. He visited a number of old haunts and walked barefoot along the beach—the soft, warm sand a happy shock to the soles of his feet. He also saw for the first time, and admired, Mizner's Memorial Fountain, a stone fountain that would have looked right at home in a piazza in Rome. Later in the day, he met for tea with Addison's friend and patron Alice DeLamar. For Waugh, their meeting was "an affecting reunion." The former ingenue, once described by the press as America's "most interesting heiress," and by Mary Berenson as "all angles and resentments and revolts," was elderly now—as was he. Still, he assured her that she had not changed in the least.

DeLamar, whose monograph *Florida Architecture of Addison Mizner* had done so much to preserve the record of Mizner's remarkable work, had pursued a distinguished career as a patron of the arts. Since the 1940s, she had owned the Worth Avenue Gallery, which promoted little-known Florida artists. In the summers, from her home in Weston, Connecticut, she championed and supported New York City's emerging reparatory theater. Over the years, she had befriended such luminaries as Lincoln Kirsten and George Balanchine, founders of the New York City Ballet, the author Laura Ingalls Wilder, and the artist Salvador Dalí.

But even with all her wealth and influence, she had been unable to prevent the loss of many of Mizner's most remarkable masterpieces. The famous residences were steadily disappearing. All of them faced an array of threats and challenges, from wear and tear, to evolving architectural tastes, to the high cost of maintenance and staff. When the financier Edward Stotesbury died in 1938, his widow, Eva, Mizner's client and friend, would discover that her husband's once vast $100 million fortune had been reduced to a few million, thanks to the Depression and, in no small part, to her lavish lifestyle and relentless homebuilding during the twenties. Eva was forced to sell her other properties and subdivide the Palm Beach estate, El Mirasol, Mizner's first great Florida private residence. The house along with its remaining twelve acres were sold to the Phipps family of Pittsburgh after her death in 1946; it was demolished in the mid-1950s.

As Waugh learned, a fresh generation of wealthy home buyers had arrived in Palm Beach in the 1950s, bringing with them different priorities, less formal tastes, and a desire for air-conditioning. The lovely Casa Florencia, built for the Preston Pope Satterwhites, was acquired by John North Willys, a Toledo automaker, whose daughter tore it down simply because "it was too big." The exceptionally grand Playa Riente was razed in 1957 by its ninety-year-old owner, the widow of automaker Horace Dodge, after she failed to sell it or to secure a zoning variance that would have allowed the house to be used as a club or a school. Casa Bendita, John S. Phipps's giant mansion, went before the wrecker's ball in February 1961. The beautifully detailed and appointed La Fontana vanished in May 1968.

The Towers, another formidable Mizner house, was engulfed in tragedy well before its demise—as the site of two separate suicides. The home was built for William M. Wood, a New England textile baron (and brother-in-law of General George S. Patton). Wood took his own life while living there soon after the home's completion, depressed after a series of strokes that had forced him to retire and following the death of a beloved son in a car crash. The house had then gone through a couple of owners before being bought by the financier and railroad executive Robert R. Young and his wife, Anita (sister of the artist Georgia O'Keeffe). It was here each winter that the Youngs entertained the exiled Duke and Duchess of Windsor, who always arrived with a large retinue that included two personal secretaries, two chauffeurs, two lady's maids, a valet, an upstairs maid, a maître d'hôtel, and two dogs. Robert Young, who had a long history of depression, killed himself with a double-barreled shotgun blast to the head in the billiard room in one of the building's two towers in 1958 after suffering steep financial reverses. The Towers was demolished in the summer of 1964 after one last grand dinner and card party attended by the Duke and Duchess.

Many of the original Mizner estates, stretching from the ocean to Lake Worth, were being subdivided; others, like Mizner's Warden house, eventually would be converted into condominiums. Similar fates were befalling many of the grand estates and homes designed by Palm Beach's other prominent architects. And yet it would be a few more years before a group of concerned locals organized the Palm Beach Landmarks Preservation Commission in 1979 to try to protect some of the remaining structures from development or demolition. A charitable foundation with a similar mission, the Preservation Foundation of Palm Beach, would follow a year later.

Miami Beach and its early architecture had fared little better in the intervening years, as Waugh would hear over a second cup of tea. The community, once a popular retirement destination for first-generation immigrant Jews, many of whom had once worked in New York's garment industry, had fallen on hard times. All of the Carl Fisher hotels were gone, and many of the neighborhoods were now seedy. It would be almost a decade before the condominium boom of the eighties ignited yet another Florida land boom and "the Beach" saw its glamor and desirability restored.

Other parts of Florida did better in the seventies. For instance, the arrival in 1971 of Walt Disney World, the sequel to Disneyland in Anaheim, California, gave a significant boost to development in and around Orlando. Boca Raton, with its Mizner-designed club, had flourished and eventually realized much of Mizner's grand vision for the property, under the patriarchal ownership of a succession of wealthy men that included the long-serving CEO of Alcoa, Arthur Vining Davis.

At the conclusion of their visit together, Alice and Alex reminisced about their mutual friends, so many of them, like the Mizner brothers, now departed. Only recently, the last of Addison's generation of Cocoanuts had passed away. He was Chris Dunphy, a Cocoanut since 1922 and an amateur golfer who had partnered at the Seminole Golf Club with presidents from Warren Harding to John F. Kennedy and kept company with celebrity friends such as C. Z. Guest, Bob Hope, and Bing Crosby. The Ball of the Cocoanuts itself had been resurrected as a New Year's Eve event in 1957 and had quickly regained its luster under the sponsorship of a new generation of wealthy men. The traumas of the Great Depression felt like a long time ago. Waugh recounted how, at the depths of the Florida downturn, a man he knew had offered him a Cadillac in return for the cost of a train ticket to New York.

Waugh had heard rumors that DeLamar had turned shy and reclusive in recent years, but he found her instead "as eager and delightful as ever," and came away from their tea exhilarated by her good company. He would never see her again. Some seven years later, at age eighty-eight, while seeking treatment for liver cancer at the South Norwalk hospital near her Connecticut summer home, she would be left standing alone unattended beside an X-ray machine. She slipped, fell, and hit her head, suffering an injury that led to her death. "Sue them!" were her final words to her friend

Alexandra Fatio Taylor (daughter of the architect Maurice Fatio), who had accompanied her to the hospital.

Later that afternoon, Waugh walked alone to Via Mizner and Mizner Alley, site of the antique shop where he had worked for those memorable years in the mid-1920s. Smoking his briar pipe, he strolled through stucco-clad Via Mizner and the adjoining Via Parigi, the paseos where the red-fez and cummerbund-clad Wendell Weed once greeted shoppers with his big golf umbrella. Waugh was impressed by how little this part of Palm Beach had been altered. Directly across the street, occupying a long city block and looking as grand and imposing as ever, was the exclusive Everglades Club, Mizner's first significant commission in Florida and the one that had introduced Spanish Revival–style architecture to Palm Beach and launched the architect's extraordinary career in 1919.

Waugh climbed the flight of green and blue tiled stairs to Villa Mizner and stopped just outside the heavy oak doors to the apartment where Addison had lived during the last decade of his life. Standing there in the shadows, he recalled the eclectic assortment of guests who would show up for the daily soirees, hoping to hear Irving Berlin, Jerome Kern, or George Gershwin perform at the piano and fully expecting to find Addison enthroned in his big Papa Mizner chair, sipping a Jamaican rum cocktail out of a frosted pewter mug as he held court.

A wave of nostalgia washed over Waugh as he remembered his chance encounter with the architect on Rue Royale in Paris in 1922 and the glorious evening the pair spent together during that first trip to Spain, when they sat alone in the moonlight beside the fountain in the Court of the Lions at the Alhambra. Then, looking up at Villa Mizner's five-story Spanish tower, its red mission tile roof framed against a powder blue sky, he recalled how his great friend Horace Chase liked to fly his Curtiss Jenny biplane straight at his uncle Addie's office-tower window, bedeviling the architect and startling the animals in his menagerie—poor Horrie, "carefree, wacky Horrie," who had crashed that plane in 1928 and died in the wreckage.

Shaken by this painful flashback, Waugh tapped out the ashes of his pipe in a slow, meditative fashion. He descended the stairs, pausing once to admire a swath of scarlet bougainvillea draped like bunting over a nearby balcony. Around the corner in a courtyard now crowded with chatting shoppers huddled at cafe tables, he located a small square tombstone planted in a flower bed. He bent over to read the inscription: "Johnnie Brown, The Human Monkey, Died April 30, 1927." Waugh himself had attended the funeral and had planted the leather-leafed sea grape that grew up beside the gravestone and now reached high overhead.

Here he paused for a moment to say a final good-bye to the memory of his many friends and to "marvelous Miznerland." Then he turned, retraced his steps, and walked briskly through a white stucco Spanish-style archway onto a busy Worth Avenue and into the warm and consoling Florida sunshine.

ACKNOWLEDGMENTS

Growing up in the 1950s and 1960s, I spent fourteen consecutive spring breaks in a pink stucco Mizner-style house in Riomar on the outskirts of Vero Beach in the care of my grandmother Ruth Bull Rathbone. It was she who introduced my brothers and me to Florida on periodic road trips to the McKee Jungle Gardens, to Orlando, Palm Beach, Key West, and once, in February 1962, to Cape Canaveral to watch the Atlas rocket launch that carried aloft the astronaut John Glenn, crouched aboard the tiny Mercury *Friendship 7* space capsule, when he became the first American to orbit Earth. Born in 1901, she had lived through the Roaring Twenties, and if she had not become lame from a bout of polio when she was fifteen, she might have been a flapper. Even way back then she seemed the embodiment of another age—a gentler and more generous one.

As part of the research for this book, during the winter of 2018, my wife, Pippa, and I retraced the route of Flagler's FEC railroad from St. Augustine southward, traveling down the east coast of Florida and stopping at various locales mentioned in the book, as well as the pertinent museums, historical societies, stately homes such as Whitehall and Vizcaya, and historic hotels such as the Ponce de León, the Alcazar, the Breakers, and the Biltmore Hotel Miami Coral Gables. We concluded our trip on the outskirts of Miami with an airboat tour of the Everglades. Then in the spring of 2019, we traveled through Seville, Córdoba, and Granada to see firsthand the Seville Cathedral with its Giralda tower, the Alcázar palace, the Mezquite, the Generalife, and the Alhambra in order to better understand the antecedents of Florida's and California's Andalusian architecture, and also for the fun of it.

I am grateful to the following people for their help during the researching of this book: Nick Golubov, Rose Guerrero, Debi Murray, and Jeremy Johnson at the Historical Society of Palm Beach County; Susan Gillis and Patricia Fiorillo at Boca Raton Historical Society; Jennifer Garcon, Jeremy Salloum, and Ashley Trujillo at HistoryMiami Archives & Research Center at the HistoryMiami Museum; Koichi Tasa, Cristina Favretto, and Nicola Hellman-McFarland at the Otto G. Richter Library at the University of Miami in Coral Gables, and Maura Feeney at the Montauk Library. Other useful collections and exhibitions that proved to be of particular value were the exhibit "Creating the Dream: George E. Merrick and His Vision for Coral Gables," curated by Arva Moore Parks at the Coral Gables Museum; Marjory Stoneman Douglas House; the Miami-Dade County Library Florida Collection; Phillip and Patricia Frost Museum of Science in Miami; the Lightner Museum in St. Augustine; and the Flagler Museum in Palm Beach, including its materials published online. Also consulted online were the websites of Florida Memory of the State Library and Archives of Florida; Society of Four Arts (Palm Beach); Proctor Library Archives at Flagler College; St. Augustine Historical Society; Coral Gables Merrick House; the Indiana Historical Society; and numerous useful articles by Florida social historian Augustus Clemmer Mayhew.

A number of friends, family members, and colleagues were generous with their time, support, suggestions, or encouragement during the writing of this book, chief among them: Prior Parker and Maria Canale, Steve and Terri Frenkel, Ethan and Beth Johnson, Chip Fisher, Luke Swetland and Stacey Beyers, Bob and Carolyn Pisano, Margaret Knowlton, Randy and Alana Stone, Ned and Elizabeth Bacon, Peter and Bonnie Smith, Steve Heiden, Dick Wien, John and Olivia Ferriter, Norman Pearlman, Jim Davenport, Alex and Gina Ziegler, George and Besty Kallop, Doug and Martha Lorch, George and Betsy Matthews, Peter and Angela Hames, Winthrop Knowlton and Maxine Groffsky, Samantha Knowlton, Eliza Oursler, Win Knowlton, Oliver and Lisa Knowlton, Peter and Alice Wyman, Michael and Janet Wyman, Tom Wyman, Jr., Lisa Wyman, and my fellow trustees at the Santa Barbara Museum of Natural History. Peggy Dahl provided invaluable assistance in compiling the bibliography and the endnotes, for which I am indebted to her. A handful of talented people at Simon & Schuster played a part in the editing and production of this work: Tzipora Baitch, Hannah Brown, Jonathan Evans, Phil Bashe, Kimberly Goldstein, and Lisa Erwin. A special thank you to Lewelin Polanco for the book's lovely design. I am the fortunate beneficiary of a first-rate literary team comprised of my agent, Jeff Ourvan of the Jennifer Lyons Literary Agency; my editor, Eamon Dolan at Simon & Schuster; and my wife, Pippa, who continues to be my first and most trusted reader and the wellspring of a wide river through which my happiness flows.

BIBLIOGRAPHY

BOOKS

Adam, James Truslow. *The Epic of America.* Boston: Little, Brown, 1931.

Adman, Ray, et al. *Lightner Museum.* St. Augustine, FL: Lightner Museum, 2014.

Admati, Anat, and Martin Hellwig. *The Bankers' New Clothes: What's Wrong with Banking and What to Do About It.* Princeton, NJ: Princeton University Press, 2013, with new preface by authors, 2014.

Ahamed, Liaquat. *Lords of Finance: The Bankers Who Broke the World.* New York: Penguin Books, 2009.

Akin, Edward N. *Flagler: Rockefeller Partner and Florida Baron.* Gainesville: University Press of Florida, 1991. First published 1988 by Kent State University Press (Kent, OH).

Aliber, Robert Z., and Charles P. Kindleberger. *Manias, Panics, and Crashes: A History of Financial Crises.* 7th ed. New York: Palgrave Macmillan, 2015.

Allen, Everett S. *The Black Ships: Rumrunners of Prohibition.* Beverly, MA: Commonwealth Editions, 2015.

Allen, Frederick Lewis. *The Big Change: America Transforms Itself 1900–1950.* New York: Bantam Books, 1961.

———. *Only Yesterday: An Informal History of the 1920s.* New York: Harper Perennial Modern Classics, 2010. First published 1931 by Harper and Row (New York).

Amory, Cleveland. *The Last Resorts.* New York: Harper and Brothers, 1952.

Appleby, Joyce. *The Relentless Revolution: A History of Capitalism.* New York: W. W. Norton, 2010.

Aron, Cindy S. *Working at Play: A History of Vacations in the United States.* New York: Oxford University Press, 1999.

Atif, Mian, and Amir Sufi. *House of Debt: How They (and You) Caused the Great Recession, and How We Can Prevent It from Happening Again.* Chicago: University of Chicago Press, 2015.

Ayers, R. Wayne. *Florida's Grand Hotels from the Gilded Age.* Mount Pleasant, SC: Arcadia, 2005.

Babson, Roger W. *Actions and Reactions: An Autobiography of Roger W. Babson.* New York: Harper and Brothers, 1935.

Bair, Deirdre. *Al Capone: His Life, Legacy, and Legend.* New York: Anchor Books, 2016.

Ballinger, J. Kenneth. *Miami Millions: The Dance of the Dollars in the Great Florida Land Boom of 1925.* Miami, FL: Franklin Press, 1936.

Baltzell, E. Digby. *An American Business Aristocracy.* New York: Collier Books, 1962. First published 1958 as *Philadelphia Gentlemen: The Making of a National Upper Class,* Free Press (New York).

Banner, Lois W. *American Beauty.* Chicago: University of Chicago Press, 1983.

Barbican, James. *The Confessions of a Rum-Runner.* Mystic, CT: Flat Hammock Press, 2007. First published 1928 by William Blackwood and Sons (London).

Barbour, George M. *Florida for Tourists, Invalids, and Settlers.* New York: D. Appleton, 1882.

Barbour, Thomas. *That Vanishing Eden: A Naturalist's Florida.* Boston: Little, Brown, 1945.

Beach, Rex. *The Miracle of Coral Gables.* Coral Gables, FL: Currier and Harford, 1926.

Belasco, Warren James. *Americans on the Road: From Autocamp to Motel, 1910–1945.* Cambridge, MA: MIT Press, 1979.

Bernanke, Ben S. *Essays on the Great Depression.* Princeton, NJ: Princeton University Press, 2000.

Bettmann, Otto L. *The Good Old Days—They Were Terrible!* New York: Random House, 1974.

Betts, Raymond F. *Europe in Retrospect: A Brief History of the Past Two Hundred Years.* Lexington, MA: D. C. Heath, 1979.

Blades, John, ed. *In Memoriam: Henry Morrison Flagler, Born January 2nd, 1830, Died May 20th, 1913.* Facsimile. Henry Morrison Flagler Museum, 2013. First published 1914 for attendees of memorial service.

Boorstin, Daniel J. *The Americans: The Democratic Experience.* New York: Vintage Books, 1974.

Boyd, Valerie. *Wrapped in Rainbows: The Life of Zora Neale Hurston.* New York: A Lisa Drew Book, an imprint of Scribner, 2003.

Bramson, Seth H. *Coral Cables.* Mount Pleasant, SC: Arcadia, 2006.

———. *Florida East Coast Railway.* Mount Pleasant, SC: Arcadia, 2006.

———. *The Greatest Railroad Story Ever Told: Henry Flagler and the Florida East Coast Railway's Key West Extension.* Charleston, SC: History Press, 2011.

———. *Speedway to Sunshine: The Story of the Florida East Coast Railway.* Erin, Ontario: Boston Mills Press, 1984.

———. *Sunshine, Stone Crabs and Cheesecake: The Story of Miami Beach.* Charleston, SC: History Press, 2009.

Brooks, John. *Once in Golconda: A True Drama of Wall Street 1920–1938.* New York: John Wiley and Sons, 1999.

Burke, John. *Rogue's Progress: The Fabulous Adventures of Wilson Mizner.* New York: G. P. Putnam's Sons, 1975.

Calder, Lendol. *Financing the American Dream: A Cultural History of Consumer Credit.* Princeton, NJ: Princeton University Press, 1999.

Carr, William H. A. *The du Ponts of Delaware: A Fantastic Dynasty.* New York: Dodd, Mead, 1964.

Carse, Robert. *Rum Row: The Liquor Fleet That Fueled the Roaring Twenties.* Mystic, CT: Flat Hammock Press, 2007. First published 1959 by Rinehart (New York).

Carson, Cary. *Face Value: The Consumer Revolution and the Colonizing of America.* Charlottesville: University of Virginia Press, 2017.

Chancellor, Edward. *Devil Take the Hindmost: A History of Financial Speculation.* Reissue ed. New York: Plume, 2000.

Chandler, David Leon. *Henry Flagler: The Astonishing Life and Times of the Visionary Robber Baron Who Founded Florida.* New York: Macmillan, 1986.

Chernow, Ron. *Titan: The Life of John D. Rockefeller, Sr.* New York: Random House, 1998.

Cleary, Malinda Lester. "Denman Fink, Dream Coordinator to George Merrick and the Development of Coral Gables, Florida." Master's thesis, University of Miami, 1996.

Cohn, Jan. *Creating America: George Horace Lorimer and the* Saturday Evening Post. Pittsburgh: University of Pittsburgh Press, 1990.

Cragoe, Carol Davidson. *How to Read Buildings: A Crash Course in Architecture.* New York: Herbert Press, 2012.

Curl, Donald W. *The Boca Raton Resort and Club: Mizner's Inn.* Charleston, SC: History Press, 2008.

———. *Mizner's Florida: American Resort Architecture.* Cambridge, MA: MIT Press, 1996.

Curtis, Charlotte. *The Rich and Other Atrocities.* New York: Harper and Row, 1976.

Dalio, Ray. *Principles for Navigating Big Debt Crises*: Westport, CT: Bridgewater, 2018.

Davis, Jack E. *An Everglades Providence: Marjory Stoneman Douglas and the American Environmental Century.* Athens: University of Georgia Press, 2009.

Davis, Jack E., and Raymond Arsenault, eds. *Paradise Lost? The Environmental History of Florida.* Gainesville: University Press of Florida, 2005.

Denby, Elaine. *Grand Hotels, Reality and Illusion: An Architectural and Social History.* London: Reaktion Books, 1998.

Derr, Mark. *Some Kind of Paradise: A Chronicle of Man and Land in Florida.* New York: William Morrow, 1989.

Diamond, Henry L., and Patrick F. Noonan. *Land Use in America.* Washington, DC: Island Press, 1996.

Diamond, Jared. *Collapse: How Societies Choose to Fail or Succeed*. New York: Penguin Books, 2011.

Didion, Joan. *Miami*. New York: Vintage Books, 1998. First published 1987 by Simon & Schuster (New York).

D'Orso, Michael. *Like Judgment Day: The Ruin and Redemption of a Town Called Rosewood*. New York: G. P. Putnam's Sons, 1996.

Douglas, Marjory Stoneman. *Adventures in a Green World: The Story of David Fairchild and Barbour Lathrop*. Coconut Grove, FL: Field Research Projects, 1973.

———. *Coral Gables, Miami Riviera: An Interpretation*, Coral Gables, FL, Coral Gables, 1925.

———. *The Everglades: River of Glass*. Sarasota, FL: Pineapple Press, 2007. First published 1947 by Rinehart and Company (New York).

———. *The Joys of Bird Watching in Florida*. Miami, FL: Hurricane House, 1969.

———. *Voice of the River*. Sarasota, FL: Pineapple Press, 2011.

Drye, Willie. *For Sale—American Paradise: How Our Nation Was Sold an Impossible Dream in Florida*. Guilford, CT: Lyons Press, 2016.

Duncan, Isadora. *My Life*. New York: Liveright, 2013. First published 1927 by Boni and Liveright (New York).

Dunlop, Beth. *Addison Mizner: Architect of Fantasy and Romance*. New York: Rizzoli, 2019.

Dunn, Marvin. *The Beast in Florida: A History of Anti-Black Violence*. Gainesville: University Press of Florida, 2013.

———. *Black Miami in the Twentieth Century*. Gainesville: University Press of Florida, 1997.

Egan, Timothy. *The Worst Hard Time: The Untold Story of Those Who Survived the Great American Dust Bowl*. Boston/New York: A Mariner Book, an imprint of Houghton Mifflin, 2006.

Epperson, Bruce D. *Roads Through the Everglades: The Building of the Ingraham Highway, the Tamiami Trail and Conners Highway, 1914–1931*. Jefferson, NC: McFarland, 2016.

Fairchild, David. *The World Grows Round My Door: The Story of the Kampong, a Home on the Edge of the Tropics*. New York: Charles Scribner's Sons, 1947.

Fisher, Jane. *Fabulous Hoosier: A Story of American Achievement*. Chicago: Harry Coleman, 1953.

Fisher, Jerry M. *The Pacesetter: The Untold Story of Carl G. Fisher*. Fort Bragg, CA: Lost Coast Press, 1998.

Flink, James J. *The Car Culture*. Cambridge, MA: MIT Press, 1976.

Florida "The East Coast": Its Builders, Resources, Industries, Town and City Developments. Miami: *Miami Herald*, 1926. Available on Florida Atlantic University Digital Library. https://fau.digital.flvc.org/islandora/object/fau%3A23332#page/3/mode/2up.

Folsom, Merrill. *Great American Mansions and Their Stories.* Rev. ed. New York: Hastings House, 2008.

Foner, Eric. *The Reader's Companion to American History.* Boston/New York: Houghton Mifflin Harcourt, 1991.

Foster, Mark S. *Castles in the Sand: The Life and Times of Carl Graham Fisher.* Gainesville: University Press of Florida, 2000.

Fox, Charles Donald. *The Truth About Florida.* New York: Charles Renard, 1925.

Frazer, William, and John J. Guthrie Jr. *The Florida Land Boom: Speculation, Money, and the Banks.* Westport, CT: Quorum Books, 1995.

Friedman, Milton, and Anna Jacobson Schwartz, *A Monetary History of the United States, 1867–1960.* Princeton, NJ: Princeton University Press, 1971. Reprint of 1963 edition by Princeton University Press.

Fuller, Walter P. *This Was Florida's Boom.* St. Petersburg, FL, Times, 1954. Reprint from a series in the *St. Petersburg Times.*

Fuss, Claude Moore. *Calvin Coolidge: The Man from Vermont.* Boston: Little, Brown, 1940.

Gaines, Steven. *Fool's Paradise: Players, Poseurs, and the Culture of Excess in South Beach.* New York: Three Rivers Press, 2009.

Galbraith, John Kenneth. *The Great Crash 1929.* Boston/New York: Mariner Books, an imprint of Houghton Mifflin Harcourt, 2009.

———. *A Short History of Financial Euphoria.* New York: Whittle Books, 1993.

Galbraith, John Kenneth, and Nicole Salinger. *Almost Everyone's Guide to Economics.* New York: Penguin Books, 1990. First published 1978 by Houghton Mifflin (Boston).

Gallagher, Dan. *Florida's Great Ocean Railway: Building the Key West Extension.* Sarasota, FL: Pineapple Press, 2003.

Gannon, Michael. *Florida: A Short History.* Rev. ed. Gainesville: University of Florida Press, 2003.

Gellner, Arrol. *Red Tile Style: America's Spanish Revival Architecture.* New York: Viking Studio, 2002.

Gillis, Susan. *Boomtime Boca: Boca Raton in the 1920s.* Mount Pleasant, SC: Arcadia, 2007.

Goldberg, David J. *Discontented America: The United States in the 1920s.* Baltimore, MD: Johns Hopkins University Press, 1999.

Goldsmith, Raymond W. *A Study of Saving in the United States: Introduction; Tables of Annual Estimates of Saving 1897 to 1949.* Vol. 1. New York: Viking Studio, 1969. Reprint of 1955 edition by Princeton University Press (NJ).

———. *A Study of Saving in the United States: Nature and Derivation of Annual Estimates of Saving 1897 to 1949.* Vol. 2. Westport, CT: Greenwood Press, 1969. Reprint of 1955 edition by Princeton University Press (NJ).

Goldsmith, Raymond W., Dorothy S. Brady, and Horst Mendershausen. *A Study of Saving in the United States: Special Studies*. Vol. 3. Westport, CT: Greenwood Press, 1969. Reprint of 1955 edition by Princeton University Press (NJ).

Goodhue, Bertram Grosvenor. *The Architecture and the Gardens of the San Diego Exposition: A Pictorial Survey of the Aesthetic Features of the Panama California International Exposition*. San Francisco, CA: Paul Elder, 1916.

Gordon, John Steele. *An Empire of Wealth: The Epic History of American Economic Power*. New York: HarperCollins, 2004.

Gordon, Robert J. *The Rise and Fall of American Growth: The U.S. Standard of Living Since the Civil War*. Princeton, NJ: Princeton University Press, 2016.

Graham, Thomas. *Flagler's St. Augustine Hotels*. Sarasota, FL: Pineapple Press, 2004.

———. *Mr. Flagler's St. Augustine*. Gainesville: University Press of Florida, 2014.

Grant, James. *The Forgotten Depression, 1921*. New York: Simon & Schuster, 2015.

Grebler, Leo, David M. Blank, and Louis Winnick. *Capital Formation in Residential Real Estate: Trends and Prospects*. Princeton, NJ: Princeton University Press, 1956.

Grunwald, Michael. *The Swamp: The Everglades, Florida, and the Politics of Paradise*. New York: Simon & Schuster, 2006.

Hanna, Alfred Jackson, and Kathryn Abbey Hanna. *Florida's Golden Sands*. Indianapolis, IN: Bobbs-Merrill, 1950.

Harner, Charles E. *Florida's Promoters: The Men Who Made It Big*. Tampa, FL: Trend House, 1973.

Harris, Amanda. *Fruits of Eden: David Fairchild and America's Plant Hunters*. Gainesville: University Press of Florida, 2015.

Hartfield, Edward A. *California's Knight and Golden Horse, Dwight Murphy, Santa Barbara's Renaissance Man*. Santa Barbara, CA: Dwight Murphy Memorial Project, 2007.

Harwood, Kathryn Chapman. *The Lives of Vizcaya*. Miami, FL: Banyan Books, 1985.

Hatton, Hap. *Tropical Splendor: An Architectural History of Florida*. New York: Alfred A. Knopf, 1987.

Haycox, Stephen, *A Warm Past: Travels in Alaska History, Fifty Essays*. Anchorage, AK: Press North, 1988.

Hemenway, Robert E. *Zora Neale Hurston: A Literary Biography*. Champaign: University of Illinois Press, 1977.

Herford, Oliver, Ethel Watts Mumford, and Addison Mizner. *The Cynic's Calendar of Revised Wisdom for 1904*. San Francisco: Paul Elder, 1903.

Higley, Stephen Richard. *Privilege, Power, and Place: The Geography of the American Upper Class*. Lanham, MD: Rowman & Littlefield, 1995.

Hoffstot, Barbara D. *Landmark Architecture of Palm Beach*. Pittsburgh, PA: Ober Park Associates, 1974.

Hungness, Carl. *I Love to Make the Dirt Fly! A Biography of Carl G. Fisher 1874–1939.* Speedway, IN: Carl Hungness, 2015.

Hurston, Zora Neale. *Dust Tracks on a Road.* New York: Harper Perennial Modern Classics, 2006. First published 1942 by J. B. Lippincott (Philadelphia).

———. *Mules and Men.* New York: Harper Perennial Modern Classics, 2008. First published 1935 by J. B. Lippincott (Philadelphia).

———. *Their Eyes Were Watching God.* New York: Harper Perennial Modern Classics, 2006. First published 1937 by J. B. Lippincott (Philadelphia).

Jackson, Kenneth. *Crabgrass Frontier: The Suburbanization of the United States.* New York: Oxford University Press, 1985.

James, Harold. *The End of Globalization: Lessons from the Great Depression.* Cambridge, MA: Harvard University Press, 2001.

James, Henry, *The American Scene.* London: Chapman & Hall, 1907.

James, Marquis. *Alfred I. du Pont: The Family Rebel.* Indianapolis, IN: Bobbs-Merrill, 1941.

Johnson, Stanley, and Phyllis Shapiro. *Once Upon a Time: The Story of Boca Raton.* Miami, FL: Arvida, 1987.

Johnston, Alva. *The Legendary Mizners.* New York: Farrar, Straus and Giroux, 1986. First published 1953 by Farrar, Straus and Giroux (New York).

Jones, Maxine D., and Kevin M. McCarthy. *African Americans in Florida.* Sarasota, FL: Pineapple Press, 1993.

Kearney, Bob, ed. *Mostly Sunny Days: A Miami Herald Salute to South Florida's Heritage.* Miami, FL: *Miami Herald,* 1986.

Kindleberger, Charles P. *The World Depression 1929–1939: 40th Anniversary of a Classic in Economic History.* Berkeley: University of California Press, 2013.

Kite-Powell, Rodney. *History of Davis Islands: David P. Davis and the History of a Landmark Tampa Neighborhood.* Charleston, SC: History Press, 2013.

Klein, Maury. *Rainbow's End: The Crash of 1929.* New York: Oxford University Press, 2001.

Kleinberg, Howard. *Miami Beach: A History.* Miami Beach, FL: Centennial Press, 1994.

Knetsch, Joe. *Florida's Seminole Wars: 1817–1858.* Mount Pleasant, SC: Arcadia, 2003.

Lakoff, Robin Tolmach, and Raquel L. Scherr. *Face Value: The Politics of Beauty.* Abingdon, UK: Routledge and Kegan Paul, 1984.

Lee, David, ed. *The World as Garden: The Life and Writings of David Fairchild.* North Charleston, SC: Createspace, 2013.

Lewis, Michael. *The Big Short: Inside the Doomsday Machine.* New York: W. W. Norton, 2011.

Lewis, Sinclair. *Babbitt.* New York: Harcourt, Brace and Company, 1922.

Limerick, Jeffrey, Nancy Ferguson, and Richard Oliver. *America's Grand Resort Hotels.* New York: Pantheon Books, 1979.

Ling, Sally J. *Run the Rum In: South Florida During Prohibition.* Charleston, SC: History Press, 2007.

Littlefield, Doris Bayley. *Vizcaya.* 2nd ed. Miami, FL: Martori Enterprises, 1983.

Lodge, Thomas E. *The Everglades Handbook: Understanding the Ecosystem.* 3rd ed. Boca Raton, FL: CRC Press, 2010.

Logan, Andy. *The Man Who Robbed the Robber Barons.* New York: Akadine Press, 2001. First published 1965 by W. W. Norton (New York).

Loos, Anita. *A Girl Like I.* New York: Viking Press, 1966.

———. *Kiss Hollywood Good-Bye.* London, UK: W. H. Allen, 1974.

Lowenstein, Roger. *Origins of the Crash: The Great Bubble and Its Undoing.* New York: Penguin Books, 2004.

Lummus, J. N. *The Miracle of Miami Beach: Facts About the Early Days.* Miami, FL: *Miami Post*, 1952.

Lythgoe, Gertrude. *The Bahama Queen: The Autobiography of Gertrude "Cleo" Lythgoe.* Mystic, CT: Flat Hammock Press, 2007.

Mackay, Charles. *Memoirs of Extraordinary Popular Delusions and the Madness of Crowds.* London, UK: Richard Bentley, 1841.

Martin, Sidney Walter. *Florida's Flagler.* Athens: University of Georgia Press, 1949.

———. *Henry Flagler: Visionary of the Gilded Age.* Lake Buena Vista, FL: Tailored Tours Publications, 1998.

Mayer, Martin. *The Bankers.* New York: Weybright and Talley, 1974.

McCarthy, Kevin M., ed. *Nine Florida Stories by Marjory Stoneman Douglas.* Jacksonville: University of North Florida Press, 1990.

McElvaine, Robert S. *The Great Depression: America, 1929–1941.* New York: Three Rivers Press, 2009. First published 1984 by Times Books (New York).

McIver, Stuart B. *Dreamers, Schemers, and Scalawags: The Florida Chronicles.* Vol. 1. Sarasota, FL: Pineapple Press, 2011.

———. *The Greatest Sale on Earth: The Story of the Miami Board of Realtors, 1920–1980.* Miami, FL: E. A. Seemann, 1980.

———. *Murder in the Tropics: The Florida Chronicles.* Vol. 2. Sarasota, FL: Pineapple Press, 2008.

———. *Touched by the Sun: The Florida Chronicles.* Vol. 3. Sarasota, FL: Pineapple Press, 2008.

Mencken, H. L., ed. *Americana.* New York: Alfred A. Knopf, 1925.

Merrick, George E. *Miami and the Story of Its Remarkable Growth: An Interview with George E. Merrick.* Reprint of the March 15, 1925, article in the *New York Times*.

_____. *Song of the Wind on a Southern Shore and Other Poems of Florida*. Coral Gables, FL: City of Coral Gables, 2003. Reprint of the 1920 edition by Four Seas (Boston, MA).

Michener, Edward C. *The Everglades Club: A Retrospective 1919–1985*. Palm Beach, FL: Everglades Club, 1985.

Millas, Aristides J., and Ellen J. Uguccioni. *Coral Gables: Miami Riviera—An Architectural Guide*. Miami, FL: Dade Heritage Trust, 2003.

Mills, C. Wright. *The Power Elite*. New York: Oxford University Press, 1957.

Mizner, Addison. *Florida Architecture of Addison Mizner*. Mineola, NY: Dover Publications, 1992, with introduction by Donald W. Curl. First published 1928 by William Helburn (New York).

_____. *The Many Mizners*. New York: Sears, 1932.

_____. "The Many Mizners." Vol. 2. Unpublished typescript. Palm Beach Historical Society.

Moore, Gary. *Rosewood: The Full Story*. Memphis, TN: Manantial Press, 2015.

Mormino, Gary R. *Land of Sunshine, State of Dreams: A Social History of Modern Florida*. Gainesville: University Press of Florida, 2005.

Mowry, George E., ed. *The Twenties: Fords, Flappers & Fanatics*. Englewood Cliffs, NJ: Prentice-Hall, 1963.

Muir, Helen. *Miami, U.S.A.* Expanded ed. Gainesville: University Press of Florida, 2000.

Murphy-Lupo, Stephanie. *All Aboard! A History of Florida's Railroads*. Guilford, CT: Globe Pequot Press, 2016.

Myers, Gustavus. *History of the Great American Fortunes*. New York: Modern Library, 1964. First published 1909 by Charles H. Kerr (Chicago).

Nash, Charles Edgar. *The Magic of Miami Beach*. Philadelphia, PA: David McKay, 1938.

Nolan, David. *Fifty Feet in Paradise: The Booming of Florida*. New York: Harcourt Brace Jovanovich, 1984.

Nugent, Rolf. *Consumer Credit and Economic Stability*. New York: Russell Sage Foundation, 1939.

Ohr, Tim. *Florida's Fabulous Natural Places*. Mountain View, CA: World Publications, 1999.

Olney, Martha L. *Buy Now Pay Later: Advertising, Credit, and Consumer Durables in the 1920s*. Chapel Hill: University of North Carolina Press, 1991.

Oppel, Frank, and Tony Meisel. *Tales of Old Florida*, Edison, NJ: Castle Books, 1987.

Orr, Christina. *Addison Mizner: Architect of Dreams and Realities (1872–1933)*. West Palm Beach, FL: Norton Gallery of Art, 1977.

O'Sullivan, Maurice, and Jack C. Lane, eds. *The Florida Reader: Visions of Paradise from 1530 to the Present*. Sarasota, FL: Pineapple Press, 2010.

Ow, Jack. *Palm Beach Scandals: An Intimate Guide*. Highland City, FL: Rainbow Books, 1992.

Parker, Randall E. *Reflections on the Great Depression*. Northampton, MA: Edward Elgar, 2002.

Parks, Arva Moore. *The Forgotten Frontier*. Miami, FL: Banyan Books, 1977.

_____. *George Merrick, Son of the South Wind: Visionary Creator of Coral Gables*. Gainesville: University Press of Florida, 2015.

_____. *Miami Memoirs*. Coral Gables, FL: Arva Parks, 1987.

Parks, Arva Moore, and Carolyn Klesper. *Miami: Then and Now*. Revised ed. London, UK: Salamander Books, 2014. First published 2002 by Anova Books (London).

Parks, Pat. *The Railroad That Died at Sea: The Florida East Coast's Key West Extension*. Key West, FL: Ketch and Yawl Press, 1968.

Perkins, Stephen, and James Caughman. *Addison Mizner: The Architect Whose Genius Defined Palm Beach*. Lanham, MD: Rowman & Littlefield, 2018.

Piketty, Thomas. *Why Save the Bankers? And Other Essays on Our Economic and Political Crisis*. Boston/New York: Houghton Mifflin Harcourt, 2016.

Ponzi, Charles. *The Rise of Mr. Ponzi*. Chicago: Inkwell, 2001.

Posner, Gerald. *Miami Babylon: Crime, Wealth, and Power—A Dispatch from the Beach*. New York: Simon & Schuster, 2009.

Pound, Arthur. *The Turning Wheel: The Story of General Motors, Through Twenty-Five Years 1908–1933*. London, UK: Forgotten Books, 2012. First published 1934 by Doubleday, Doran and Company (New York).

Powell, Anthony. *Miscellaneous Verdicts: Writings on Writers 1946–1989*. Chicago: University of Chicago Press, 1992.

Pratt, Theodore. *The Big Bubble: A Novel of the Florida Boom*. New York: Duell, Sloan and Pearce, 1951.

Rabinowitz, Alan. *The Real Estate Gamble: Lessons from 50 Years of Boom and Bust*. New York: AMACOM, 1980.

Reardon, L. F. *The Florida Hurricane and Disaster: 1926*. Coral Gables, FL: Arva Parks, 1986. Reprint of the 1926 edition, Miami Publishing (Miami).

Redford, Polly. *Billion-Dollar Sandbar: A Biography of Miami Beach*. New York: E. P. Dutton, 1970.

Reinhart, Carmen M., and Kenneth S. Rogoff. *This Time Is Different: Eight Centuries of Financial Folly*. Princeton, NJ: Princeton University Press, 2009.

Roberts, Alasdair. *America's First Great Depression: Economic Crisis and Political Disorder After the Panic of 1837*. Ithaca, NY: Cornell University Press, 2012.

Roberts, Cecil. *Adrift in America, or Work and Adventure in the States*. London, UK: Lawrence and Bullen, 1891.

Roberts, Kenneth L. *Florida*. New York : Harper & Brothers, 1926.

Robinson, W. W. *Land in California: The Story of Mission Lands Ranchos, Squatters, Mining Claims, Railroad Grants, Land Scrip, Homesteads*. Berkeley: University of California Press, 1948. First published in the series *The Chronicles of California*.

Rothbard, Murray N. *America's Great Depression*. Hawthorne, CA: BN, 2009.

Rothchild, John. *Up for Grabs: A Trip Through Time and Space in the Sunshine State*. Gainesville: University Press of Florida, 2000.

Rothman, Hal K. *Devil's Bargains: Tourism in the Twentieth-Century American West*. Lawrence: University Press of Kansas, 1998.

Sakolski, A. M. *The Great American Land Bubble: The Amazing Story of Grabbing, Speculations, and Booms from Colonial Days to the Present Time*. Mansfield Centre, CT: Martino, 2011. First published 1932 by Harper and Brothers (New York).

Sammons, Sandra Wallus. *Henry Flagler: Builder of Florida*. Sarasota, FL: Pineapple Press, 2012.

———. *Marjorie Kinnan Rawlings and the Florida Crackers*. Sarasota, FL: Pineapple Press, 2010.

———. *Marjory Stoneman Douglas and the Florida Everglades*. Sarasota, FL: Pineapple Press, 2010.

Scheinkman, José A. *Speculation, Trading, and Bubbles*. New York: Columbia University Press, 2014.

Seebohm, Caroline. *Boca Rococo: How Addison Mizner Invented Florida's Gold Coast*. New York: Random House, 2001.

Sewell, John. *John Sewell's Memoirs and History of Miami, Florida*. Vol. 1. Self-published, Franklin Press, 1933.

Sexton, R. W. *Spanish Influence on American Architecture and Decoration*. New York: Brentano's, 1927.

Showalter, J. Camille, ed. *The Many Mizners: California Clan Extraordinary*. Oakland, CA: Oakland Museum, 1978.

Sierra, Horacio. "Marjory Stoneman Douglas's River of Progress: Modernism, Feminism, Regionalism, and Environmentalism in Her Early Writings." Master's thesis, University of Florida, 2006.

Silvin, Richard Rene. *Villa Mizner: The House That Changed Palm Beach*. West Palm Beach, FL: StarGroup International, 2014.

Simpson, Charles Torrey. *Florida Wild Life: Observations on the Flora and Fauna of the State and the Influence of Climate and Environment on Their Development*. New York: Macmillan, 1932.

———. *Out of Doors in Florida: The Adventures of a Naturalist*. Miami, FL: E. B. Douglas, 1924.

Smiley, Nixon. *Knights of the Fourth Estate: The Story of the Miami Herald*. Miami, FL: E. A. Seemann, 1974.

———. *Yesterday's Miami*. Miami, FL: E. A. Seemann, 1974.

Smith, Patrick D. *A Land Remembered*. Sarasota, FL: Pineapple Press, 1984.

Sobel, Robert. *The Money Manias: The Eras of Great Speculation in America 1770–1970*. Philadelphia, PA: Beard Books, 2000. First published 1973 by Weybright and Talley (New York).

Stager, Claudette, and Martha Carver. *Looking Beyond the Highway: Dixie Roads and Culture*. Knoxville: University of Tennessee Press, 2006.

Standiford, Les. *Last Train to Paradise: Henry Flagler and the Spectacular Rise and Fall of the Railroad That Crossed an Ocean*. New York: Broadway Books, 2002.

Starr, Kevin. *Material Dreams: Southern California Through the 1920s*. New York: Oxford University Press, 1990.

Stevenson, Elizabeth. *Babbits and Bohemians from the Great War to the Great Depression*. New York: Routledge, 2017.

Stockbridge, Frank Parker, and John Holliday Perry. *Florida in the Making*. New York: de Bower, 1926.

Stronge, William B. *The Sunshine Economy: An Economic History of Florida Since the Civil War*. Gainesville: University Press of Florida, 2008.

Stuart, Hix C. *The Notorious Ashley Gang: A Saga of the King and Queen of the Everglades*. Stuart, FL: St. Lucie, 1928.

Sullivan, Edward Dean. *The Fabulous Wilson Mizner*. New York: Henkle, 1935.

Sullivan, Mark. *Our Times: The United States 1900–1925*. Vol. 6, *The Twenties*. New York: Charles Scribner's Sons, 1935.

Sullivan, Maureen. *Hidden History of Everglades City and Points Nearby*. Charleston, SC: History Press, 2010.

Sutter, Paul S., and Christopher Manganiello, eds. *Environmental History and the American South*. Athens: University of Georgia Press, 2009.

Swarup, Bob. *Money Mania: Booms, Panics, and Busts from Ancient Rome to the Great Meltdown*. New York: Bloomsbury Press, 2014.

Taylor, Alexandra Fatio. *Maurice Fatio: Architect*. Palm Beach, FL: A. Fatio, 1992.

Tebeau, Charlton W., and William Marina. *A History of Florida*. 3rd ed. Coral Gables, FL: University of Miami Press, 1999.

Thomas, Dana L. *Lords of the Land: The Triumphs and Scandals of America's Real Estate Barons from Early Times to the Present*. New York: G. P. Putnam's Sons, 1977.

Train, John. *Famous Financial Fiascos*. Burlington, VT: Fraser, 1995.

Turner, Gregg M. *The Florida Land Boom of the 1920s*. Jefferson, NC: McFarland, 2015.

———. *Florida Railroads in the 1920s*. Mount Pleasant, SC: Arcadia, 2005.

———. *A Short History of Florida Railroads*. Mount Pleasant, SC: Arcadia, 2003.

Van de Water, Frederic F. *The Real McCoy*. Mystic, CT: Flat Hammock Press, 2007.

Van Doren, Charles. *A History of Knowledge: Past, Present, and Future*. New York: Ballantine Books, 1991.

Van Dyke, T. S. *Millionaires of a Day: An Inside History of the Great Southern California "Boom."* New York: Fords, Howard and Hulbert, 1892.

Verrill, Alphaeus Hyatt. *Romantic and Historic Florida*. New York: Dodd, Mead, 1935.

Vickers, Raymond B. *Panic in Paradise: Florida's Crash of 1926*. Tuscaloosa: University of Alabama Press, 1994.

Volti, Rudi. *Cars and Culture: The Life Story of a Technology*. Baltimore, MD: Johns Hopkins University Press, 2006. First published 2004 by Greenwood Press (Westport, CT).

Walker, Melissa. *Living on Wilderness Time*. Charlottesville: University of Virginia Press, 2002.

Waters, Harold. *Smugglers of Spirits: Prohibition and the Coast Guard Patrol*. Mystic, CT: Flat Hammock Press, 2007.

Weidman, John. *Road Show*. New York: Theatre Communications Group, 2009.

Weigall, T. H. *Boom in Paradise*. New York: Alfred H. King, 1932.

Weiss, Murray, and Bill Hoffman. *Palm Beach Babylon: Sins, Scams, and Scandals*. New York: Carol, 1992.

Wheeler, Keith. *The Railroaders*. New York: Time-Life Books, 1973.

White, Richard. *Railroaded: The Transcontinentals and the Making of Modern America*. New York: W. W. Norton, 2011.

Wiedemer, David, Robert A. Wiedemer, and Cindy Spitzer. *Aftershock: Protect Yourself and Profit in the Next Global Financial Meltdown*. 3rd ed. Hoboken, NJ: John Wiley and Sons, 2014.

Williams, Ada Coats. *Florida's Ashley Gang*. Hobe Sound, FL: Florida Classics Library, 1996. Reprint of 1983 edition by Florida State Historical Society.

Willoughby, Malcolm F. *Rum War at Sea*. Washington, DC: US Government Printing Office, 1964.

Wilson, Frank J., and Beth Day. *Special Agent: A Quarter Century with the Treasury Department and the Secret Service*. New York: Holt, Rinehart and Winston, 1965.

Wright, E. Lynne. *Florida Disasters: True Stories of Tragedy and Survival*. Guilford, CT: Globe Pequot, 2017.

Wynne, Nick, and Richard Moorhead. *Paradise for Sale: Florida's Booms and Busts*. Charleston, SC: History Press, 2010.

Zuckoff, Mitchell. *Ponzi's Scheme: The True Story of a Financial Legend*. New York: Random House, 2006.

ARTICLES/JOURNALS/WEB/OTHER

Allen, Brooke. "'What to Read and Why' Review: Essential Reading . . . and Less." *Wall Street Journal*, June 28, 2018. www.wsj.com/articles/what-to-read-and-why-review-essential-reading-and-less-1530232860.

Alston, Lee J., Wayne A. Grove, and David C. Wheelock. "Why Do Banks Fail? Evidence from the 1920s." *Explorations in Economic History* 31 (1994): 409–31.

Alvarez, Lizette. "Despite Rising Seas and Bigger Storms, Florida's Land Rush Endures." *New York Times*, September 18, 2017.

Anderson, Caitlin E. "The Forgotten Real Estate Boom of the 1920s." *Bubbles, Panics & Crashes*, Harvard Business School Baker Library/Bloomberg Center online. www.library.hbs.edu/hc/crises/forgotten.html.

"Ashley's Daring Career Is Ended." *Palm Beach (FL) Post*, November 1924.

Baca, Mandy. "Black History in Early Miami." New Tropic. Last modified February 3, 2015. https://thenewtropic.com/black-history-early-miami.

"Baker's Deputies at River Bridge Shoot Down Four." *Palm Beach (FL) Post*, November 1, 1924.

Ban Ki-moon and Francis Suarez. "Miami Battles Rising Seas." *New York Times* online, February 20, 2019.

"Bank of U.S. Closes Doors." *New York Times*, December 12, 1930, 1.

"Barkentine Upsets, Blocks Miami Harbor." *New York Times*, January 11, 1926, 2.

Barr, Colin. "August 9, 2007, The Day the Mortgage Crisis Went Global: A Look at the Problems Exposed by the Events That Day and What Investors, Bankers Have Learned Since Then." *Wall Street Journal*, August 9, 2017. www.wsj.com/articles /aug-9-2007-the-day-the-mortgage-crisis-went-global-1502271004.

Berlage, Frank. "Why Fixing Trade Deficits Is Essential." *Barron's*, January 9, 2017.

Bernstein, Jacob. "We Built This City." *Miami New Times* online, last modified May 3, 2001. www.miaminewtimes.com/news/we-built-this-city-6352885.

Bierman, Harold, Jr. "The 1929 Stock Market Crash." EH.net, last modified March 26, 2008. http://eh.net/encyclopedia/the-1929-stock-market-crash.

———. "The Causes of the 1929 Stock Market Crash: A Speculative Orgy or a New Era?" Questia. www.questia.com/library/3043262/the-causes-of-the-1929-stock -market-crash-a-speculative.

"Black Bottom (dance)." Wikipedia, last modified January 23, 2019. https://en.wikipedia .org/wiki/Black_Bottom_(dance).

Boomhower, Ray. "Carl G. Fisher: The Hoosier Barnum." *Traces of Indiana and Midwestern History* 6, no. 2 (Spring 1994): 24–27. http://images.indianahistory.org /cdm/pageflip/collection/p16797coll39/id/7424/type/compoundobject/file name/print/page/download/start/5/pftype/pdf.

Branch, Michael P. "Our Lady of the Glades: Marjory Stoneman Douglas and *The Everglades: River of Grass.*" *Marjorie Kinnan Rawlings Journal of Florida Literature* 8 (1977).

Brooker, Nathan. "Miami Breach: Property Market Braced for Climate Change." *Financial Times* online, January 4, 2017, 4. https://www.ft.com/content/de73b604 -c12b-11e6-81c2-f57d90f6741a.

Brown, William E., Jr., and Karen Hudson. "Henry Flagler and the Model Land Company." *Tequesta: The Journal of the Historical Association of Southern Florida* 56 (1996): 46–78. http://digitalcollections.fiu.edu/tequesta/files/1996/96_1_03 .pdf.

Bubil, Harold. "Architect Addison Mizner: Villain or Visionary?" *Sarasota (FL) Herald-Tribune* online, January 27, 2008. www.heraldtribune.com/article/LK /20080127/News/605201891/SH.

———. "Crusading Historian Vickers Is Still Battling His Detractors." *Sarasota (FL) Herald-Tribune* online, February 10, 2008.

———. "The Miami Phenomenon: City Draws the World to Florida." *Sarasota (FL) Herald-Tribune* online, December 13, 2015. www.heraldtribune.com/article /LK/20151213/News/605206589/SH.

Capozzi, Joe. "John Lennon's Last Years in Palm Beach." *Palm Beach Post*, November 30, 2017. www.mypalmbeachpost.com/lifestyles/john-lennon-last-years-palm-beach /IsO4csJLM4kxpMXCz8zhKN.

Cardwell, Mark Riley. "Attenborough: Poor Countries Are Just as Concerned About the Environment." *Guardian* (US edition) online, October 16, 2013. www. theguardian.com/environment/2013/oct/16/attenborough-poorer-countries -concerned-environment.

"Carl G. Fisher Rites Conducted on the Beach." *Miami Herald*, July 19, 1939.

Carmel, Urban. "This Is What a Bubble Looks Like: Japan 1989 Edition." *The Fat Pitch* (blog), Blogspot.com, last modified June 24, 2017. http://fat-pitch.blogspot .com/2017/06/this-is-what-bubble-looks-like-japan.html.

Carper, N. Gordon. "Martin Tabert, Martyr of an Era." *Florida Historical Quarterly* 52, no. 2 (October 1973): 115–31.

Carson, Ruby Leach. "Forty Years of Miami Beach." *Tequesta: The Journal of the Historical Association of Southern Florida*, no. 15 (1955): 3–28. http://digitalcollections .fiu.edu/tequesta/files/1955/55_1_01.pdf.

Case, Karl E., John M. Quigley, and Robert J. Shiller. "Comparing Wealth Effects: The Stock Market Vs. the Housing Market." *Advances in Macroeconomics* 5, no. 1 (2005). www.econ.yale.edu/~shiller/pubs/p1181.pdf.

Catton, Bruce. "The Restless Decade." *American Heritage* 16, no. 5 (August 1965): 5.

"Causes of the Great Depression." *Novelguide.com*. www.novelguide.com/reportessay /history/american-history/causes-great-depression.

Colombo, Jesse. "The 1920s Florida Real Estate Bubble." Bubble, last modified June 26, 2012. www.thebubblebubble.com/florida-property-bubble.

Coolidge, Calvin. Address to the American Society of Newspaper Editors. Washington, DC, January 17, 1925. Available at the American Presidency Project. www .presidency.ucsb.edu/documents/address-the-american-society-newspaper-editors -washington-dc.

"Coral Gables Merrick House: The Home of City Founder George Merrick." City of Coral Gables online. http://coralgables.com/index.aspx?page=913.

"Coral Gables Paid Many to Push Loan: Merrick Tells SEC at Inquiry $30,000 Went to Miami's City Attorney." *New York Times*, September 19, 1935.

Covington, James W. "The Story of Davis Islands, 1924–1926." *Sunland Tribune* 4, no. 1 (November 1978). http://scholarcommons.usf.edu/sunlandtribune/vol4/iss1/5.

———. "The Tampa Bay Hotel." *Tequesta: The Journal of the Historical Association of Southern Florida* 1, no. 26 (1966): 3–20.

Cumming, J. Bruce, Jr. "A Brief Florida Real Estate History." Tampa: Appraisal Institute, West Coast Florida Chapter, September 6, 2006. www.mapoftheweek.net/Post/342/floridarealestatehistory.pdf.

Curl, Donald W. "Boca Raton and the Florida Land Boom of the 1920s." *Tequesta: The Journal of the Historical Association of Southern Florida* 1, no. 46 (1986).

Curtis, Mike, "Henry Ford Caused the Great Depression!" *Georgist Journal*, no. 107 (Spring 2007). www.georgistjournal.org/2012/09/21/henry-ford-caused-the-great-depression.

Daugherty, Greg. "Who Was Really the First American Billionaire?" *Money* online, September 26, 2016. http://money.com/money/4480022/first-american-billionaire-dispute/.

Davis, Doris. "The Tamiami Trail—Muck, Mosquitoes, and Motorists: A Photo Essay." National Park Service online. www.nps.gov/bicy/learn/historyculture/upload/History-of-Tamiami-Trail.pdf.

"Death of Ashley Marks the End of Spectacular Bandit Career." *Palm Beach (FL) Post*, November 1924.

De Rugy, Veronique. "1920s Income Tax Cuts Sparked Economic Growth and Raised Federal Revenues." Cato Institute online, March 4, 2003. www.cato.org/publications/commentary/1920s-income-tax-cuts-sparked-economic-growth-raised-federal-revenues.

Dietrich, Emily Perry. "Doc Dammers, Super-Salesman." *Update* 15, no. 3 (August 1988): 3.

Dill, Mark, "Did Carl Fisher Marry a 15 Year Old? (No!!!)." First Super Speedway, last modified January 7, 2010. www.firstsuperspeedway.com/blog/did-carl-fisher-marry-15-year-old-no.

Dougherty, Conor. "Housing Is Already in a Slump. So It (Probably) Can't Cause a Recession." *New York Times*, February 19, 2019. https://www.nytimes.com/2019/02/19/business/economy/housing-recession.html.

Dovell, J. E., and J. G. Richardson. "History of Banking in Florida, 1828–1954." Orlando, FL: Florida Bankers Association online, 1955. https://archive.org/stream/historyofbanking00dove/historyofbanking00dove_djvu.txt.

"Dream World of Advertising." *American Heritage* 16, no. 5 (August 1965), *Special Issue: The Twenties*, 71.

Dreiser, Theodore. "The Florida Scene: Some Meretricious Phrases in the Exploitation of America's Playground." *Vanity Fair*, May 1926, 51.

Edgerton, Giles. "Great Modern Hotels: Their Architecture and Decoration—The Ritz-Carlton Cloister of Boca Raton Florida." *Arts and Decoration*, April 1926, 57.

Engstrand, Iris H. W. "Inspired by Mexico: Architect Bertram Goodhue Introduces Spanish Colonial Revival into Balboa Park." *Journal of San Diego History* 58, nos. 1/2 (Spring 2012): 57.

Essary, J. Frederick. "Have Faith in Florida!" *New Republic* 44 (October 12, 1925).

Fichter, Margaria. "Pioneering Environmentalist Marjory Stoneman Douglas Dies at 108." *Miami Herald*, May 14, 1998.

Field, Alexander James. "The Interwar Housing Cycle in the Light of 2001–2011: A Comparative Historical Approach." Working paper 18796, National Bureau of Economic Research, Cambridge, MA, February 2013. https://nber.org/papers/w18796.

———. "Uncontrolled Land Development and the Duration of the Depression in the United States." *Journal of Economic History* 52, no. 4 (December 1992): 785–805.

"Financier Fortune in Oil Amassed in Industrial Era of 'Rugged Individualism.'" *New York Times*, May 24, 1937.

"Fireproof Hotels in Palm Beach Plan." *New York Times*, March 22, 1925, 5.

"Fisher Says Prices of Stocks Are Low: Quotations Have Not Caught Up with Real Values as Yet, He Declares." *New York Times*, October 22, 1929.

"Flagler Succumbs to Injuries of Fall." *New York Times*, May 21, 1913.

"Flagler Wills Bulk to Widow." *Tropical Sun*, May 29, 1913.

Florida Department of Environmental Protection. "Florida's Mangroves." November 3, 2017. https://floridadep.gov/fco/fco/content/floridas-mangroves.

"Florida Developer Drowned off Liner: D. P. Davis, Passenger on the Majestic to Europe, Is Lost—Details Are Lacking." *New York Times*, October 14, 1926.

"The Florida Madness." *New Republic* 45 (January 27, 1926): 258–59.

"Florida Realizing Dreams of Wealth." *New York Times*, March 22, 1925, 32.

"Floridians Getting Uneasy." *New York Times*, October 14, 1925, 1.

Freeland, Helen C. "George Edgar Merrick." *Tequesta: The Journal of the Historical Association of Southern Florida* 1, no. 2 (August 1942): 1–7.

Frosch, Dan. "The Year Hurricane Harvey Swamped a Neighborhood—and Split a Friendship." *Wall Street Journal* online, August 16, 2018. www.wsj.com/articles/the-year-hurricane-harvey-swamped-a-neighborhoodand-split-a-friendship-1534431323.

"F. S. Ruth Ends Life with Shot in Hotel." *New York Times*, April 23, 1932.

"Gen. Du Pont Resigns from Mizner Concern." *New York Times*, November 25, 1925.

George, Paul S. "Brokers, Binders, and Builders: Greater Miami's Boom of the Mid-1920s." *Florida Historical Quarterly* 65, no. 1 (July 1986): 27–51.

Gjerstad, Steven, and Vernon L. Smith. "From Bubble to Depression?" *Wall Street Journal* online, April 6, 2009. www.wsj.com/articles/SB123897612802791281.

Green, Nancy L., "When Paris Was Reno: American Divorce Tourism in the City of Light, 1920–1927." Arcade, last modified April 13, 2016. http://arcade .stanford.edu/content/when-paris-was-reno-american-divorce-tourism-city-light -1920-1927.

Green, Richard K., and Susan W. Wachter. "The American Mortgage in Historical and International Context." September 21, 2005. https://repository.upenn.edu/ cgi/viewcontent.cgi?referer=https://search.yahoo.com/&httpsredir=1&article =1000&context=penniur_papers.

Grooten, J., and R. E. A. Almond, eds. *Living Planet Report—2018: Aiming Higher.* Gland, Switz. World Wildlife Fund, 2018, 6. http://awsassets.panda.org/downloads /_embargo_30_oct__lpr2018_full_report_spreads_25_10_2018.pdf.

Harris, Melissa. "Steven Levitt Documents Success of 'Freakonomics': Economics Guru Took Unconventional Path to New Film." *Chicago Tribune* online, October 7, 2010. www.chicagotribune.com/business/ct-xpm-2010-10-07-ct-biz-1007-con fidential-levitt-20101007-story.html.

Hilbert, Betsy S. "Marjory Stoneman Douglas and an Antidote to Despair." *Marjorie Kinnan Rawlings Journal of Florida Literature* 8 (1997).

"Hits Coral Gables Acts: SEC Examiner Says Circular on Bonds Was False." *New York Times*, September 18, 1935.

Hodges, James. "Carl G. Fisher Rites Conducted on Beach." *Miami Herald*, July 19, 1939.

Hofheinz, Darrell, "Mizner-Designed Estate of Late A. Alfred Taubman Listed at $58 Million." *Palm Beach Daily News* online, January 2, 2018. www.palmbeachdaily news.com/business/real-estate/mizner-designed-estate-late-alfred-taubman-listed -million/JHO8HRnorAIEtqsr65AneJ.

"How the Slump Looks to Three Experts." *Newsweek*, May 25, 1970.

Huxtable, Ada Louise. "The Maverick Who Created Palm Beach." *New York Times* online, March 20, 1977.

Jacobson, Louis. "Comparing the Great Recession and the Great Depression." PolitiFact, last modified September 19, 2013. www.politifact.com/truth-o-meter/article /2013/sep/19/comparing-great-recession-and-great-depression.

"John Ashley and 3 of His Gang Killed." *Palm Beach (FL) Post*, November 1, 1924.

Jones, Lucy D. "Marjory Stoneman Douglas' House in Coconut Grove," *My Florida History* (blog), Blogspot.com, last modified November 29, 2006. http://myflorida history.blogspot.com/search?updated-max=2006-12-08T19:56:00-05:00& max-results=10&start=350&by-date=false.

Jones, Maxine D. "Documented History of the Incident Which Occurred at Rosewood, Florida, in January 1923." Remembering Rosewood/Rosewood Heritage Foundation. http://rememberingrosewood.org/rosewoodrp.php.

Jordà, Òscar, Moritz Schularick, and Alan M. Taylor. "Leveraged Bubbles." Working paper 21486, National Bureau of Economic Research, Cambridge, MA, August 2015. www.nber.org/papers/w21486.

Kane, Suzzane. "Finding Addison Mizner: His Scrapbook Testimony." Thesis, University of Nebraska, 2014. https://digitalcommons.unl.edu/cgi/viewcontent.cgi?article =1151&context=archthesis.

Kay, Russell. "Tamiami Trail Blazers: A Personal Memoir." *Florida Historical Quarterly* 49, no. 3 (January 1971): 278–87.

Kite-Powell, Rodney. "In Search of David Paul Davis." Master's thesis, University of South Florida, 2003. http://scholarcommons.usf.edu/cgi/viewcontent.cgi?article =2408&context=etd.

———. "Stories and Theories on the Death of D. P. Davis." www.tampapix.com/dpda vis3.htm.

Knickerbocker, Cholly. "Paris Singer and E. Clarence Jones Credited with Reviving Popularity of Costume Parties in Society World." *Palm Beach Post*, February 5, 1928, 20.

Kolbert, Elizabeth. "The Siege of Miami: As Temperatures Climb, So Too, Will Sea Levels." *New Yorker*, December 21 and 28, 2015, 42–50.

Korb, Michael. "The Collier Family Chronicles." https://www.scvpalmbeach.com /collier.

Krugman, Paul. "Samuelson, Friedman, and Monetary Policy." *New York Times* online, December 14, 2009. https://krugman.blogs.nytimes.com/2009/12/14/samuelson -friedman-and-monetary-policy.

Kusisto, Laura, and Arian Campo-Flores. "Rising Sea Levels Reshape Miami's Housing Market." *Wall Street Journal* online, April 20, 2018.

"La Fontana Is No More but Art Gems Survive." *Palm Beach (FL) Post*, May 19, 1968. www.newspapers.com/clip/8859163/1968_may_la_fontana_demolition_1.

La Plante, Leah. "The Sage of Biscayne Bay: Charles Torrey Simpson's Love Affair with South Florida." *Tequesta: The Journal of the Historical Association of Southern Florida* 50 (1995). http://digitalcollections.fiu.edu/tequesta/files/1995/95_1_03.pdf.

Latson, Jennifer. "The Worst Stock Tip in History." *Time* online, last modified September 3, 2014. http://time.com/3207128/stock-market-high-1929.

Laytner, Ron. "Jane Fisher: Lonely Legacy for Miami Beach's First Lady." *Miami Herald*, September 29, 1968.

Leamer, Edward E. "Housing *Is* the Business Cycle." Working paper 13428, National Bureau of Economic Research, Cambridge, MA, September 2007. www.nber.org /papers/w13428.

Lefèvre, Edwin. "Flagler and Florida." *Everybody's Magazine*. Vol. 2. January–June 1910, 168–86.

Lester, Will. "Environmentalist Marjory Stoneman Douglas Dies at 108." *Washington Post* online, May 15, 1998. www.washingtonpost.com/archive/local/1998/05/15 /environmentalist-marjory-stoneman-douglas-dies-at-108/99d2a81d-2141-4dd1 -b8fc-69d4cb0da27b/?utm_term=.d104d656b8ba.

Levy, Paul. "Ritzy Business." *New York Review of Books*, July 19, 2018, 22.

Liposky, Rosalie, E. "Marjory Stoneman Douglas Bibliography." *Marjorie Kinnan Rawlings Journal of Florida Literature* 8 (1997): 55–73.

"Livermore Not in Bear Pool." *New York Times*, October 22, 1929, 24.

Lopez, Frank G. "We Were Having Some People in for Cocktails." *Architectural Record*, July 1953, 46–48.

Luke, Jim. "Banks Failures: The 1920s and the Great Depression." *Econproph* (blog), October 26, 2009. https://econproph.com/2009/10/26/fdic-managing-the-crisis -the-fdic-and-rtc-experience.

Mackay, Ellin. "Why We Go to Cabarets." *New Yorker*, November 28, 1925.

Maeder, Jay. "Inside Mayor Jimmy (Baeu James) Walker's Mighty Downfall." *New York DailyNews*online, August 14, 2017. www.nydailynews.com/new-york/mayor-jimmy -beau-james-walker-mighty-downfall-article-1.792838.

Mayhew, Augustus. "America First: Howard Major at Palm Beach." *New York Social Diary*, last modified January 12, 2017. www.newyorksocialdiary.com/social-history /2017/america-first-howard-major-at-palm-beach.

———. "The Coconuts! A Palm Beach Party History: 1920–2018." *New York Social Diary*, last modified May 23, 2018. www.newyorksocialdiary.com/social-history /2018/the-coconuts-a-palm-beach-party-history-1920-2018.

———. "House of Munn: The Palm Beach Story." *New York Social Diary*, last modified November 24, 2006. www.newyorksocialdiary.com/legacy/socialdiary /2006/11_24_06/socialdiary11_24_06.php.

———. "Oil Swells: The Standard Oil Crowd in Palm Beach." *New York Social Diary*, last modified November 30, 2010. www.newyorksocialdiary.com/social-history /2010/oil-swells-the-standard-oil-crowd-in-palm-beach.

———. "Remaking History: Paris Singer and the Everglades Club, 1918–1932." *New York Social Diary*, last modified November 1, 2013. www.newyorksocialdiary.com /social-history/2013/palm-beach-social-diary.

McCarthy, Kevin M. "How Marjory Stoneman Douglas Crusaded for South Florida in Her Short Stories." *Marjorie Kinnan Rawlings Journal of Florida Literature* 8 (1997): 15–21.

McGoun, Bill. "Paris Singer: Larger Than Life." *Palm Beach (FL) Post*, November 17, 1977.

McIver, Stuart. "Florida's First Boom—And Bust. Real-Estate Fever Swept Across South Florida in the Roaring '20s, Bringing Instant Wealth, and Later Instant

Bankruptcy, to Opportunists Hoping to Make a Quick Killing." *Fort Lauderdale (FL) Sun-Sentinel*, March 10, 1991. http://articles.sun-sentinel.com/1991-03-10/features/9101120716_1_real-estate-binge-real-estate-lake-park.

Meindl, Christopher F. "Frank Stoneman and the Florida Everglades During the Early 20th Century." *Florida Geographer* 29 (1998). http://journals.fcla.edu/flgeog/article/viewFile/78110/75535.

Melling, Ryan. "Transcript of Wealth in the 1920s." Prezi, last modified October 22, 2013. https://prezi.com/-dy2visjjoba/wealth-in-the-1920s.

Melosi, Martin V. "The Automobile Shapes the City." Automobile in American Life and Society, University of Michigan. www.autolife.umd.umich.edu/Environment/E_Casestudy/E_casestudy.htm.

Merrick, George E. "Planning the Greater Miami for Tomorrow." Speech given to Miami Realty Board, May 17, 1937, and Miami Bay Front Park, May 28, 1937. HistoryMiami Museum archives.

Merritt, Mary Lou. "The Land Boom." www.mypubsite.com/customerfiles/7_Floridas RunawayLandBoom.pdf.

Miller, Philip Warren. "Greater Jacksonville's Response to the Florida Land Boom of the 1920s." Master's thesis, University of Florida, 1989.

"Millions of Capital Drawn to Miami." *New York Times*, March 15, 1925.

"More Directors Quit Mizner Firm." *New York Times*, November 29, 1925, 25.

Newman, Bruce. "Off the Deep End: Seduced by the Sparkle of Those Turquoise Waters, America Has Fallen Head over Heels in Love with the Swimming Pool." *Sports Illustrated*, February 14, 1994.

Nicholas, Tom, and Anna Scherbina. "Real Estate Prices During the Roaring Twenties and the Great Depression." *Real Estate Economics* 41, no. 2 (Summer 2013): 278–309. First published November 1, 2012. https://onlinelibrary.wiley.com/doi/abs/10.1111/j.1540-6229.2012.00346.x.

Nikiforuk, Andrew. "The Big Shift Last Time: From Horse Dung to Car Smog." Tyee, last modified March 6, 2013. https://thetyee.ca/News/2013/03/06/Horse-Dung-Big-Shift.

"The 1920s Boom: Frazer, Guthrie and Fractional Reserve Banking." *Sarasota (FL) Herald-Tribune*, February 10, 2008. www.heraldtribune.com/news/20080210/the-1920s-boom-frazer-guthrie-and-fractional-reserve-banking.

Norton, Leslie P. "Who Says This Stock Market Is Overpriced?" *Barron's*, October 14, 2017.

Norton, Simon D. "The Causes of the Banking Crises of the 1920s." *World Financial Review* online, January 4, 2012. www.worldfinancialreview.com/?p=2446.

"Palatial Homes for Shell-Shocked Convalescent Soldiers Built by Singer Nearing Completion." *Palm Beach (FL) Post*, December 22, 1918.

"Paris Singer and Associate Named in Suit." *Palm Beach (FL) Times*, July 1, 1930.

"Paris Singer Arrested in Fraud Charge." *Palm Beach (FL) Times*, April 9, 1927.

"Paris Singer Dead: Son of Inventor." *New York Times*, June 25, 1932, 13.

"Paris Singer's Daughter Announces Engagement." *Palm Beach (FL) Post*, September 25, 1926.

Parton, John William. "The Gold Coast Land Boom in the 1920s." *Broward Legacy* 2, nos. 1/2 (March 1978).

Postel-Vinay, Natacha. "What Caused Chicago Bank Failures in the Great Depression? A Look at the 1920s." Paper, Department of Economic History, London School of Economics, June 2013. http://eh.net/eha/wp-content/uploads/2013/11/Postel -Vinay.pdf.

Plumer, Brad, and Nadja Popovich. "As Climate Changes, Southern States Will Suffer More Than Others." *New York Times* online, June 29, 2017. www.nytimes.com /interactive/2017/06/29/climate/southern-states-worse-climate-effects.html.

"Progress Week." *Miami Herald*, November 27, 1926.

Radhakrishnan, Ramya, "Biography Sheds Light on Coral Gables Founder George Merrick." *Miami Hurricane*, January 28–January 31, 2016, 12.

Reed, Lawrence W. "Great Myths of the Great Depression." Mackinac Center for Public Policy and Foundation for Economic Education, 2011. Working paper first printed in 1981.

"Rex Beach." Wikipedia, last modified May 28, 2019. https://en.wikipedia.org/wiki /Rex_Beach.

Reyes, Jorge. "'When the Groves Begin to Bear . . .': George Merrick and the Founding of Coral Gables." *The Reyes Report* (blog). Blogspot.com, last modified September 23, 2007. http://the-reyes-report.blogspot.com/2007/09/when-groves-begin-to -bear-george.html.

Rich, Nathaniel. "Losing Earth." *New York Times Magazine*, August 5, 2018, 51.

"Robert R. Young Commits Suicide." *New York Times*, January 26, 1958, 1.

Samuelson, Robert J. "Don't Blame Wall Street." Review of *Rainbow's End*, by Maury Klein, and *The End of Globalization*, by Harold James. *New York Times*, December 9, 2001.

———. "Financial Crisis Work of 'Fiendish Monsters.'" *Economist's View*, February 1, 2009. https://economistsview.typepad.com/economistsview/2009/02/paul-samuel son-financial-crisis-work-of-fiendish-monsters.html.

Schofner, Jerrell H. "Postscript to the Martin Tabert Case: Peonage as Usual in the Florida Turpentine Camps." *Florida Historical Quarterly* 60, no. 2 (October 1981): 161–73.

"Seaboard Air Line Railroad." Wikipedia, last modified April 30, 2019. https:// en.wikipedia.org/wiki/Seaboard_Air_Line_Railroad#Warfield_and_the_South _Florida_expansion.

"SEC Holds Bankers Picked Bond Group: Counsel Shows Coral Gables Body Is Trustee for Sellers and Buyers." *New York Times*, September 20, 1935.

"SEC Sifts Profits in Florida's Boom: Head of Coral Gables Defends Developers and Bares High Promotional Costs." *New York Times*, September 17, 1935.

"SEC to Investigate Coral Gables Plan: Inquiry Part of the Work of the Division Studying Activities of Protective Committees." *New York Times*, September 13, 1935.

Semes, Aretta L. "From Rising Sun to Daunting Storm: Miami in Bloom and Bust, a Reminiscence." *Tequesta: The Journal of the Historical Association of Southern Florida* 58 (1998): 91–108.

Sessa, Frank B. "Anti-Florida Propaganda and Counter Measures During the 1920s." *Tequesta: The Journal of the Historical Association of Southern Florida* 21 (Spring 1961): 41–51.

———. "Miami in 1926." *Tequesta: The Journal of the Historical Association of Southern Florida* 16 (1956): 15–36. http://digitalcollections.fiu.edu/tequesta/files/1956/56_1.pdf.

Shelby, Gertrude Mathews. "Florida Frenzy." *Harper's Monthly* 152 (January 1926): 177–86.

"Sheriff Baker and Men Pursue Bandits." *Palm Beach (FL) Post*, October 7, 1924.

"Sheriff's Posse and Ashley Gang Exchange Shots." *Palm Beach (FL) Post*, October 7, 1924.

Shiller, Robert J. "Long-Term Perspectives on the Current Boom in Home Prices." *Economists' Voice* 3, no. 4 (February 2007): 4. www.researchgate.net/publication/24015447_Long-Term_Perspectives_on_the_Current_Boom_in_Home_Prices.

"Singer Hearing Today: Blue Heron Developer Faces Preliminary Before Justice." *Palm Beach (FL) Post*, April 29, 1927.

"Singer Ocean Front Goes at Court Sale." *Palm Beach (FL) Post*, January 7, 1930.

"Singer Project Represents Patriotism of Highest Order." *Palm Beach (FL) Post*, January 16, 1919.

"Singer Spikes Rumor That Gus' Baths Will Close for New Beach: Jordan to Assume Management of Development North of Inlet." *Palm Beach (FL) Times*, June 15, 1925.

"Singer to Have 200 Unit Dairy Herd to Furnish Milk for His Hospital." *Palm Beach (FL) Post*, May 25, 1918.

Sirkin, Gerald. "The Stock Market of 1929 Revisited: A Note." *Business History Review* 49, no. 2 (Summer 1975): 222–31. https://fraser.stlouisfed.org/files/docs/meltzer/sirsto75.pdf.

Sisto, Bénédicte. "Miami's Land Gambling Fever of 1925." *Tequesta: The Journal of the Historical Association of Southern Florida* 59 (1999). http://digitalcollections.fiu.edu/tequesta/files/1999/99_1_03.pdf.

Smiley, Nixon. "Strange House Built by Noted Naturalist in 1905 Still Stands." *Miami Herald*, July 30, 1950.

Snowden, Philip. "Year's Worst Break Hits Stock Market." *New York Times*, October 3, 1929, 1.

Steig, Stacey. "A History of Coral Gables: A Look into the Past." Coral Gables Chamber of Commerce online. https://coralgableschamber.org/a-history-of-coral-gables.

Sun Sentinel Editorial Board. "Sea-Level Rise: The Defining Issue of the Century." *South Florida Sun Sentinel,* May 4, 2018. www.sun-sentinel.com/opinion/editorials /fl-op-editorial-sea-level-rise-attention-needed-20180503-story.html.

Sweedler, Maya. "Florida Fights Giant Algal Bloom in Lake Okeechobee." *Wall Street Journal* online, July 16, 2018. www.wsj.com/articles/florida-fights-giant-algal -bloom-in-lake-okeechobee-1531746000.

Taylor, B. "The Stock Market Crash of 1929." Fundamentalfinance.com. http://stocks .fundamentalfinance.com/stock-market-crash-of-1929.php.

Taylor, Bryan. "The Land Company of Florida and the Florida Real Estate Bubble." Global Financial Data Blog, last modified October 18, 2013. http://gfdblog.com /GFD/Blog/the-land-company-of-florida-and-florida-real-estate-bubble.

Tedford, Kristin. "History Repeats Itself: A Comparison of the Real Estate Booms in the 1920s Versus the 2000s in the City of Miami." Urban Studies Department, University of Miami, Spring 2011. https://urbanstudies.as.miami.edu/_assets /pdf/history-repeats-itself.pdf.

"Tells Great Plans for Coral Gables: Southern Records Broken, Says G. E. Merrick, Owner—Sales Since Jan. $10,000,00." *New York Times*, March 13, 1926.

Timberlake, Richard H. "Money in the 1920s and 1930s." Foundation for Economic Education online, last modified April 1, 1999. https://fee.org/articles/money-in -the-1920s-and-1930s.

Tindall, George B. "The Bubble in the Sun." *American Heritage* 16, no. 5 (August 1965).

Titus, Elizabeth Spaulding. "The Educator and the Heiress." Alice DeLamar blog on westonmagazinegroupdot.com, May 2013. https://alicedelamar.wordpress.com /articles-about-alice-2/the-educator-and-the-heiress.

"Tremendous Building Activities Now Under Way in Palm Beach." *Palm Beach (FL) Post*, April 21, 1919.

"Two Children of Isadora Duncan Die in Accident." *San Francisco Call*, April 20, 1913.

"Unprecedented Building Activity Forecast in City During Year 1919." *Palm Beach (FL) Post*, December 25, 1918.

Van Buren, Lin. "Isaac Merritt Singer, Town of Pittstown." Rootsweb supported by ancestry.com.www.rootsweb.ancestry.com/~nyrensse/bio206.htm.

Vanderblue, Homer B. "The Florida Land Boom." *Journal of Land & Public Utility Economics* 3, no. 2 (May 1927): 113–31.

_____. "The Florida Land Boom," pt. 2. *Journal of Land & Public Utility Economics* 3, no. 3 (August 1927): 252–69.

Walbook, Anton. "Isadora Duncan and Paris Singer." Dark Lane Creative blog, July 3, 2013. https://darklanecreative.com/isadora-duncan-and-paris-singer-2.

Walker, W. M. "Henry Flagler: Empire Builder." *Suniland: The Magazine of Florida*, January 1925.

"Wall Street Crash of 1929." Wikipedia, last modified June 1, 2019. https://en.wikipedia .org/wiki/Wall_Street_Crash_of_1929.

"Watson Scoffs at Testimony." *New York Times*, September 19, 1935.

Waugh, Alex, as told to Robert V. Doyle. "Miznerland." Unpublished typescript, January 1963. Palm Beach Historical Society.

"When Property Becomes a Roof and a Floor Again." *Financial Times Weekend*. July 15–16, 2017, 8.

White, Eugene N. "The Great American Real Estate Bubble of the 1920s: Causes and Consequences." Working paper, Rutgers University, October 2008.

———. "Lessons from the Great American Real Estate Boom and Bust of the 1920s." Working paper 15573, National Bureau of Research, Cambridge, MA, December 2009. www.nber.org/papers/w15573.

"Yard of Bricks & Pagoda," Indianapolis Motor Speedway online. www.indianapolis motorspeedway.com/at-the-track/yard-of-bricks-pagoda/pagoda-history.

MEDIA/THEATER

Allen, Frederick Lewis. *The Lords of Creation*. MP3 Audio, Audible Studios, 2014.

Avrich, Barry. *Blurred Lines: Inside the Art World*. Melbar Entertainment Group, April 23, 2017.

The History of Boca Raton. Boca Raton Historical Society, 2008, DVD.

Interview with Marjory Stoneman Douglas. Videotaped at the Douglas House in Coconut Grove, June 15 and 16, 1983, Everglades Digital Library.

"Mr. Miami Beach." *American Experience*, Season 10, Episode 4. PBS, February 2, 1998.

Water's Journey: Everglades, a production of Fusionspark Media, Inc. http://theever gladesstory.org.

NOTES

INTRODUCTION

xi   *An additional thirty-one ships:* Homer B. Vanderblue, "The Florida Land Boom," pt. 2, *Journal of Land & Public Utility Economics*, 3, no. 3 (August 1927): 258.

xi   *millions of feet, by one estimate:* 45 million feet of lumber is what was reported, but this seems impossibly high. Perhaps it includes all the lumber destined for Florida at this point in the boom. J. Kenneth Ballinger, *Miami Millions: The Dance of the Dollars in the Great Florida Land Boom of 1925*, 138.

xii   *skyscrapers sheathed in scaffolding:* Marjory Stoneman Douglas, *The Everglades: River of Glass*, 338.

xii   *the recently completed: Miami Daily News Building:* Today it is known as the Freedom Tower.

xii   *fifty railcars full of newsprint:* Charlton W. Tebeau, and William Marina, *A History of Florida*, 368.

xii   *modeled on the Giralda tower:* Giralda is Spanish for a turning or rotating girl. The tower on Stanford White's Madison Square Garden took this idea literally by placing a nude eighteen-foot gilded statue of Diana on top.

xii   *the Seville Cathedral:* The world's third largest cathedral, it is also the largest Gothic cathedral. This is where Christopher Columbus is buried. The cathedral and neighboring Alcázar palace are part of a UNESCO World Heritage site.

xiii   *"Everybody in Miami was real estate mad":* T. H. Weigall, *Boom in Paradise*, 50.

xiii   *totaled $103 million:* Paul S. George, "Brokers, Binders, and Builders: Greater Miami's Boom of the Mid-1920s," *Florida Historical Quarterly* 65, no. 1 (July 1986): 42.

xiii   *thousands of railroad cars:* Vanderblue writes that approximately 10,000 cars were waiting to enter the state, but, again, that number seems impossibly high. Vanderblue, "Florida Land Boom," pt. 2, 256n8.

xiii *up from 45 cents:* Mark S. Foster, *Castles in the Sand: The Life and Times of Carl Graham Fisher*, 228.

xiii *1,800 telegraphers went on strike:* Ibid., 229.

xiv *by one estimate, 970 others:* George, "Brokers, Binders, and Builders," 42.

xiv *with names that evoked garden-like settings:* They included such developments as, in alphabetical order: Aiken Park, Alcazar, Alhambra, Altos Del Mar, Andalusia, Arcadia Gardens, Avondale, Azalea Homes, Bay View Estates, Beach Park, Beauclaire Villa, Belle Vista, Belo Basque, Beverly Heights, Carleton Terrace, Casa Mia, Central Miami, Citrus Gardens, Clermont Hill and Lake, Cleveland Heights, Coquina Gables, Cordoba, Coulee Hammock, Country Club Estates, Croissant Park, Croissantania, Daytona Shores, Del Rio, Don Ce-Sar Place, Eagle Crest, East Shenandoah, El Centro, El Jobe-An, Elysian Fields, Euclid Oasis, Everjune Gardens, Fellsmere Estates, Floral Villa, Floranada Club, Florida Beach, Florida Riviera, Forest Hills, Fort Moosa Gardens, Fountain City, Fulford-by-the-Sea, Ganbridge Hub, Gardendale, Granada Terrace, Haven Villa, Hialeah, Hickory Hills, High Point City, Holly Hill Groves, Hollywood-by-the-Sea, Homosassa, Howey-in-the-Hills, Idleyld, Indialantic, Indrio, Interocean City, Jungle Terrace, Kelsey City, Lacarno, Laguna, Lake Forest, Los Gatos, Lauder Del Mar, Longacre Park, Las Olas, Miami Shores, Moorish Estates, Mountain Lakes Estates, Mount Plymouth, Naranja Nook, North Shore, Okeechobee Highlands, Okeechobee Shores, Oldsmar, Opa-Locka, Palma Ceia Park, Palmetto Country Club Estates, Paradise Park, Parkland Estates, Pasadena Estates, Pasadena-on-the-Gulf, Pennent Park, Penny Farms, Pinecrest, Poinciana, Punta Gorda, Ringling Isles, Riomar, Rio Vista Isles, Riviera Gardens, Royal Palm, San Jose Estates, San Marco, Santa Monica Highlands, Santa Rosa, Saratoga Lake, Seminole Beach, Seminole Estates, Silver Bluff Estates, Skyland, Snell Isle, St. John's Manor, Sylvania Heights, Tampa Beach, Temple Terrace Estates, Useppa Island, Venetia, Vermont Heights, Victoria Park, Vilano Beach, Washington Terrace, Waterview Park, West Lake Pasadena, West Plant City, Whitfield Estates, Wyldewood Park.

xiv *the world's largest concentration of golf courses:* Michael Grunwald, afterword, in Douglas, *Everglades*, 393.

xiv *some twenty million lots were for sale:* The estimate was made by Willard A. Barrett in *Barron's* at year-end 1925. He estimated that the lots in 90 percent of the subdivisions would prove worthless and not worth paying the taxes on. Frank B. Sessa, "Anti-Florida Propaganda and Counter Measures During the 1920s," *Tequesta: The Journal of the Historical Association of Southern Florida* 21 (Spring 1961): 50.

xiv *spending more than $1 million per day:* Charles Donald Fox, *The Truth About Florida*, 80.

xiv   *very likely became the nation's first billionaire:* John D. Rockefeller's wealth peaked at $900 million in 1913; Henry Ford became the second billionaire in 1925.

xiv   *"Something is taking place in Florida":* "Florida Realizing Dreams of Wealth," *New York Times*, March 22, 1925, 32, quoted in George, "Brokers, Binders, and Builders," 33.

xv   *the steamer Lakevort:* E. Lynne Wright, *Florida Disasters: True Stories of Tragedy and Survival*, 61.

xvi   *two and a half million:* Kenneth Roberts, *Florida*, 19.

xvi   *"All of America's gold rushes":* Mark Sullivan, *Our Times: The United States 1900–1925*, vol. 6, *The Twenties*, 647.

xvii   *Most cite the stock market crash:* See, for example, John Kenneth Galbraith, *Great Crash 1929*, 169.

xvii   *never received the attention it deserves:* Although there are good biographies of the key players, before this one, few book-length histories of the subject have been published. The closest to being definitive would be David Nolan's *Fifty Feet in Paradise: The Booming of Florida*, which tells the history of Florida from 1819 to the 1980s, and devotes sixty pages to the boom. Nick Wynne and Richard Moorhead's, *Paradise for Sale: Florida's Booms and Busts*, is a short (186 pages) and cursory overview of the era with no notes, bibliography, or index. *The Florida Land Boom of the 1920s* by Gregg M. Turner is a 166-page monograph of the various developments. Willie Drye's *For Sale—American Paradise: How Our Nation Was Sold an Impossible Dream in Florida*, focuses on the two hurricanes of the era and how figures like William Jenning Bryan and journalist Edwin Menninger promoted Florida and the boom. As Philip Warren Miller has written in "Greater Jacksonville's Response to the Florida Land Boom of the 1920s" (master's thesis, University of Florida, 1989), 136: "Despite its historic significance, however, scholars have largely ignored the Florida land boom as a topic for major research. No definitive works on the subject have as yet been written."

xvii   *"the uncrowned kings":* Weigall, *Boom in Paradise*, 210.

xviii *$1.38 billion in today's dollars:* $1 in 1926 is equivalent to 13.8 times 2018 dollars, according to MeasuringWorth.com.

xix   *more than tripled in volume:* Leo Grebler, David M. Blank, and Louis Winnick, *Capital Formation in Residential Real Estate: Trends and Prospects*, 163. Nonfarm Residential Mortgage Debt rose from $9.354 billion in 1920 to $30.176 billion in 1930, inclusive of real estate bonds. Mortgage debt rose at an accelerating rate for the four decades up until 1930 and then declined during the Great Depression.

1
THE PHARAOH OF FLORIDA

4   *The establishment's food, which consisted of canned meats:* David Leon Chandler, *Henry Flagler: The Astonishing Life and Times of the Visionary Robber Baron Who Founded Florida*, 86–88.

4   *the world's largest and most profitable business:* Sidney Walter Martin, *Henry Flagler: Visionary of the Gilded Age*, 67.

5   *$1.1 million in today's dollars:* $1 in 1861 equals $22.50 in 2018, according to MeasuringWorth.com.

5   *doubling their initial investment to $100,000:* In 1870 this partnership became a joint stock company, incorporated under the name Standard Oil Company. The business was capitalized with $1 million (10,000 shares at $100 per share). John D. Rockefeller took 2,667 shares; Stephen V. Harkness subscribed for 1,334; Flagler, Samuel Andrews, and William Rockefeller took 1,333 shares each; the old partnership took 1,000 shares, as did O. B. Jennings, and William Rockefeller's brother-in-law.

6   *"a friendship founded on business":* Martin, *Henry Flagler*, 41.

6   *it was Henry's idea:* It would become a holding company, the Standard Oil Company of New Jersey, in 1899, after trusts were outlawed.

6   *the firm's clever attorney Samuel C. T. Dodd:* Daniel J. Boorstin, *The Americans: The Democratic Experience*, 417.

6   *gave birth to the Standard Oil Trust:* At the time of the trust creation in 1879, there were 35,000 shares outstanding, owned by 37 shareholders. Rockefeller owed 8,984 of the shares; Flagler owned 3,000; Stephen V. Harkness, Flagler's half brother, owned another 2,925, which Flagler controlled; Charles Pratt owned 2,700; O. H. Payne owned 2,637; J. A. Botwich owned 1,872, and Rockefeller's brother William owned 1,600. Flagler's shares were worth $6 million but were about to soar in value. Chandler, *Henry Flagler*, 79.

6   *"No, sir, I wish I'd had the brains":* Edwin Lefèvre, "Flagler and Florida," *Everybody's Magazine* 22, January–June 1910, 183.

6   *"The key to our success":* John D. Rockefeller, quoted in Seth H. Bramson, *The Greatest Railroad Story Ever Told: Henry Flagler and the Florida East Coast Railway's Key West Extension*, 23.

6   *market capitalization of $154 million:* Martin, *Henry Flagler*, 70.

6   *$4.1 billion in today's money:* $1 in 1885 is equivalent to $26.9 in 2018, according to MeasuringWorth.com.

7   *the Sherman Antitrust Act:* "The popular mind is agitated with problems that disturb the social order," said Senator John Sherman as he introduced the bill in a rallying cry that echoes today, "and among them, none is more threatening

than the inequality of condition, of wealth and opportunity that has grown with a single generation out of the concentration of capital into vast combinations to control production and trade and to bring down competition." Gustavus Myers, *History of the Great American Fortunes*, 697.

7   *"I am trying to expose your robbery"*: Martin, *Henry Flagler*, 67.

8   *He rode horseback:* Chandler, *Henry Flagler*, 75.

8   *"now I am pleasing myself"*: Martin, *Henry Flagler* Martin, 91.

8   *"the great watering places of Europe"*: Chandler, *Henry Flagler*, 94.

8   *"I liked the place and the climate"*: Interview with James Morrow, Jacksonville, *Florida News-Herald*, June 20, 1887. According to a Flagler friend named M. M. Belding, Flagler had a cousin who ran a lumber business in Florida, and this cousin may have played a role in interesting Flagler in investing in Florida. Chandler, *Henry Flagler*, 94.

9   *crystal chandeliers of his own design:* Ibid., 92.

9   *Potter Palmer's 1875 Palmer House:* The original Palmer House, built in 1870, was advertised as "the only fireproof hotel in the world," according to Elaine Denby, *Grand Hotels, Reality and Illusion: An Architectural and Social History*, 36. It burned to the ground a year later in the Chicago fire of 1871.

9   *the Newport, Rhode Island, of the South:* Edward N. Akin, *Flagler: Rockefeller Partner and Florida Baron*, 116.

9   *"we didn't know anything about hotels"*: Mark Alan Hewett, Kate Lemos, William Morrison, and Charle D. Warrren, *Carrère and Hastings, Architects*, vol. 1, 61, quoted in Thomas Graham, *Flagler's St. Augustine Hotels*, 62.

10   *Removing his topcoat:* Martin, *Henry Flagler*, 93.

11   *"more pretty girls in it than any hotel"*: *Jacksonville (FL) Times-Union*, March 24, 1891, quoted in Graham, *Flagler's St. Augustine Hotels*, 255.

11   *It wasn't long before neglected palaces:* These were properties such as Grand Hotel Villa Serbelloni (1850) and Grand Hotel Villa d'Este (1873) on Lake Como, to cite two familiar examples. London's luxurious Savoy and Ritz Hotels did not arrive until much later, in 1889 and 1905, respectively.

12   *vacation destinations for those who could afford them:* J. P. Morgan and a handful of investors would begin construction of the Homestead in 1880, the same year that the Hotel Coronado was completed in San Diego. In 1893 the Astor cousins would combine their two luxury hotels, the Waldorf Hotel and the Astoria Hotel, side by side on what is now the site of the Empire State Building, to create the first Waldorf-Astoria.

12   *billionaires owning highly visible resort properties:* Examples include the Sultan of Brunei (the Dorchester in London, Hotel Le Meurice in Paris, and the Beverly Hills Hotel), Ty Warner (San Ysidro Ranch and the Biltmore Four Season in Santa Barbara, and the Four Seasons in New York City), Paul Tudor Jones

(Singita Grumeti Reserves in Tanzania), Dietrich Mateschitz (Laucala Island), Richard Branson (Necker Island, Kasbah Tamadot), or Urs Schwarzenbach (the Dolder Grand in Zurich), to name just a few.

12   *no one ever before had assembled:* Starting in the late 1890s César Ritz would give him a run for his money with hotels in Paris (1898), London (1905), and Madrid (1906), among others.

<h1 style="text-align:center">2</h1>

<h2 style="text-align:center">A RAILROAD GOES TO SEA</h2>

14   *buy up and combine:* He may have been inspired by the approach used by his friend Henry Bradley Plant, a Southern railroad entrepreneur who had made Tampa, on Florida's west coast, the terminus for his railroad. Plant had dredged the port there and was building his own giant resort hotel, the $3 million Tampa Bay Hotel, soon to compete in grandeur and luxury with Flagler's Ponce de León. Plant's railroad empire extended well into Texas; his steamship line ran between Tampa, Key West, and Havana, spurring early development up and down the west coast of Florida.

14   *the more standard sixty-pound rails:* A few years later, he would replace them again with ninety-pound rails.

14   *seized control of two million acres of land:* Les Standiford, *Last Train to Paradise: Henry Flagler and the Spectacular Rise and Fall of the Railroad That Crossed an Ocean*, 58.

14   *a still-substantial 210,000 acres:* Alfred Jackson Hanna and Kathryn Abbey Hanna, *Florida's Golden Sands*, 321.

14   *he founded the Model Land Company:* The Model Land Company would endure well into the 1960s.

14   *at prices that initially ranged from $1.50 to $5.00:* Hanna and Hanna, *Florida's Golden Sands*, 315.

14   *more African American men were hired:* Dan Gallagher, *Florida's Great Ocean Railway: Building the Key West Extension*, 52.

16   *"I have found a veritable paradise":* Standiford, *Last Train to Paradise*, 59.

16   *the world's largest wooden structure:* Martin, *Henry Flagler*, 117.

16   *eventually boasted 1,081 hotel rooms:* Nolan, *Fifty Feet in Paradise*, 130.

16   *a bellboy in every hallway:* Charles E. Harner, *Florida's Promoters: The Men Who Made It Big*, 33.

17   *the Styx:* Flagler did not, as legend has it, burn down the Styx community to facilitate the move.

17   *the only one of the properties Henry Flagler built that survives:* The Casa Marina Hotel in Key West was built in 1920, seven years after Flagler's death.

17   *that number was down to 150,000:* Hanna and Hanna, *Florida's Golden Sands*, 316.

18   *built a large hotel:* Another widow on the opposite coast would replicate Julia
      Tuttle's experience a few years later, in Sarasota: Mrs. Potter Palmer, a Chicago
      socialite. Left an $8 million fortune by her hotelier husband, the builder of
      Chicago's enormous Palmer House, she invested most of her inheritance into
      a variety of Florida ventures, including a land development company, a 6,000-
      acre cattle ranch replete with 3,000 head of cattle, and a 1,300-acre citrus grove.
      Although she knew nothing about any of these businesses when she made the
      investments, she made a success of each of them. Bertha Palmer died of cancer
      at age sixty-nine in 1918, after more than doubling her fortune in Florida to $20
      million, a remarkable achievement.

18   *"If it wasn't for Florida":* Lefèvre, "Flagler and Florida," 184.

19   *the so-called Flagler System:* The Flagler System consisted of the Florida East Coast
      Railway with its Jacksonville-to-Key-West line as well as its inland extensions; the
      Florida East Coast Hotel Company, which included the Ponce de León Hotel,
      Alcazar Hotel, Roman Beach Hotel, Royal Poinciana Hotel, Breakers Hotel,
      Royal Palm Hotel, Continental Hotel, and Colonial Hotel (Nassau); Model
      Land Company, with its four main subsidiaries, Chuluota Land Company, Fort
      Dallas Land Company, Perrine Grand Land Company, and Okeechobee Land
      Company; two utilities, Miami Electric Light Company and West Palm Beach
      Water Company; and four newspapers: the *Florida Times-Union* (in Jackson-
      ville), *Miami Herald* and *Miami Metropolis,* and *St. Augustine Record.*

19   *Flagler remained largely unknown:* As Florida historian Thomas Graham notes in
      his biography, *Flagler's St. Augustine Hotels,* 21, "Flagler also desired to keep his
      entire private life sealed in a 'plain envelope.'"

20   *"my son has not shown for me the filial regard":* See "Certified Copy of Last Will
      and Testament with Codicils thereto of Henry M. Flagler deceased. And Prob-
      able Proceedings Theon Before Hon. M. R. Cooper, County Judge of St. Johns
      County, Florida, The Record Company, St. Augustine," 3. Flagler Papers, Palm
      Beach Historical Society. His son already had an annual dividend income of
      $75,000 from stocks already gifted to him. The bulk of the fortune and empire
      was left to his third wife and widow, Mary Lily Flagler.

20   *she attacked a visiting doctor:* Martin, *Henry Flagler,* 135–47.

20   *"she lost her reason":* "Flagler Succumbs to Injuries of Fall," *New York Times,* May
      21, 1913, 11.

21   *Flagler was able to divorce Alice:* He gave her a divorce settlement of $2.4 million
      in Standard Oil stock that had appreciated to $15 million at the time of her death.

21   *the Gilded Age's most splendid private homes:* Foremost among these were: newspa-
      per magnate William Randolph Hearst's San Simeon (San Luis Obispo County,
      CA), railroad magnate Cornelius Vanderbilt II's the Breakers (Newport, RI),
      his brother George Vanderbilt's the Biltmore (Asheville, NC), his other brother

William K. Vanderbilt's Marble House (Newport, RI), farm equipment kingpin James Deering's Villa Vizcaya (Miami), circus magnate John Ringling's Ca' d'Zan (St. Augustine), art collector Isabella Stewart Gardener's Fenway Court (Boston), chemical magnate Alfred I. du Pont's Nemours (Wilmington, DE), coal baron Edward Julius Berwin's the Elms (Newport, RI), shipping magnate Herman Oelrichs's Rosecliff (Newport, RI), and philanthropist and suffragist Phoebe Hearst's Wyntoon (Siskiyou County, CA). These extraordinary homes all aspired to something in common: "They expressed the social standing of their wealthy owners and America's belief that it had become the most highly evolved culture in Western history." (Source: *Flagler's Florida* tabloid of the Flagler Museum, 27.) Whether America was right to believe this was another matter.

21   *"the Taj Mahal of North America":* Merrill Folsom, *Great American Mansions and Their Stories*, rev., 167.

21   *110 feet wide by 40 feet deep:* Ibid., 171.

21   *Flagler personally oversaw every detail:* In one letter to his decorator, W. P. Stymus Jr. of the prominent furniture and design firm of Pottier & Stymus, he wrote, "I note your recommendation not to have silk curtains in any of the windows on the second floor looking into the corridor. This was not my original idea and I am glad you brought up the subject, for I don't think that the silk would look well. Arrange just to have shades." Even the floor treatments merited comment: "I wrote to you two or three days ago about the hall of Mrs. Flagler's morning parlor. As it is to be a hardwood floor, I think a simple rug, which will show a margin of hardwood on the sides, will be the best way to treat it." Henry M. Flagler to W. P. Stymus Jr., December, 1901, Henry Flagler Papers, Palm Beach Historical Society.

22   *had suffered a nervous breakdown: New York Journal,* quoted in Standiford, *Last Train to Paradise,* 133. According to historian Thomas Graham, Flagler was ill off and on during 1907 for maladies variously attributed to influenza and the shock at the stock market's Panic of 1907. However, the panic did not begin until mid-October.

22   *"Many prices are paid":* Quoted in Chandler, *Henry Flagler,* 256. According to another acquaintance, George Graham Currie, Flagler remarked that successful men have another thing in common: "The envy of their less successful brothers." (Source: "Anecdotes of Local History: An Address to the Members of the Minute Men of the Congregational Church by George Graham Currie," *Palm Beach Post,* January 15, 1924.) In a revealing letter that Flagler dictated to the Reverend Charles S. Stevens on September 4, 1901, from his Mamaroneck home, Flagler remarked, "If it were not for the misery and wretchedness of mankind, I think I might lead a happy life, in spite of all my own sorrows." Henry Flagler to Rev. Charles S. Stevens, September 4, 1901. Flagler Papers, Palm Beach Historical Society.

22   *"Gentlemen, the railroad will go to sea":* Seth H. Bramson, *Florida East Coast Railway,* 21.

22   *The 155 miles of track:* Harner, *Florida's Promoters*, 36.

23   *an armada that included:* The project could not have been contemplated without the very latest construction technology. Steam shovels had been around since the 1830s, but scoop-type dredges were something new, made possible by the proliferation of steel wire, a critical German innovation first used to build European cable car systems. Flagler's dredges, however, needed to be customized. Dredges normally worked off coal and steam, but his were retrofitted to operate on gasoline, because the coal could not be transported efficiently to his remote, floating sites. His dredges needed to be amphibious, too. He had them retrofitted so that a set of wheels could be added when they were brought ashore, enabling them to glide over steel tracks. Diesel engines and caterpillar tracks would not be introduced until the 1930s.

23   *Waterproof cofferdams were constructed:* Giant catamarans would lower these wood structures in pieces onto the limestone ocean floor, but only after the ocean bed had been scraped clean of coral and sand. The walls were then loosely assembled into the shape of an open box, sealed at the bottom using sand bags around the base. Next, pilings, a foot in diameter and made of green wood, were driven deep into the bedrock, both inside and outside the cofferdam—twenty-four for each of the bigger piers. A German concrete that could set under water was then extruded along the bottom of each box, using a device called a *tremie* to create the proper seal. Four days later, when the concrete had set, the water was pumped out of the now tightly sealed structure, creating a dry, watertight walled chamber with pilings jutting out of the top. At this point the real work began. Wood forms that eventually gave each pier its final shape were then lowered into the cofferdam and hammered together. These were then filled with more poured concrete. When the concrete dried, the pilings in the cofferdam were sawed off at the low-tide level; the cofferdams themselves were removed so they could be reused. The next level of forms was then added, and more concrete poured, to create the parts of the pier that showed above the waterline. Steel rods were used to reinforce the concrete and to connect the various sections.

24   *"until the cop scoops them in":* *Times Union*, March 14, 1907, quoted in Gallagher, *Florida's Great Ocean Railway*, 54.

24   *run over by a train:* Gallagher, *Florida's Great Ocean Railway*, 64.

25   *"where desolation existed only twenty-five years ago":* St. Lucie County (FL) Tribune, February 9, 1912, address given January 22, 1912, at Key West by Henry Morrison Flagler, quoted in Chandler, *Henry Flagler*, 257–58.

25   *"I can hear the children singing":* St. Augustine (FL) Record, January 23, 1912, 1, quoted in Thomas Graham, *Flagler's St. Augustine Hotels*, 478.

26   *his railroad never earned back:* Flagler never saw a return on his investment. The company did not pay its first dividend until 1980. Edward N. Akin, *Flagler: Rockefeller Partner and Florida Baron*, 232.

26 *"I was old and blind and deaf"*: Henry Flagler, quoted in Nolan, *Fifty Feet in Paradise*, 144.

26 *He died:* Mary Lily Flagler would be left a fortune in the neighborhood of $100 million (source: Cleveland Amory, *The Last Resorts*, 344). In November 1916 she married an old beau of hers named Robert Worth Bingham, a lawyer in Louisville, Kentucky. Only eight months later, she died suddenly and somewhat mysteriously, at age fifty, leaving him a $5 million bequest that became the basis for the Bingham family's *Courier-Journal* newspaper empire. She left $60 million of her $68 million fortune to her niece Louise Wise Lewis.

26 *fourth largest economy today:* Fourth largest gross state economy after California, Texas, and New York.

26 *"no individual has had a greater or more lasting impact"*: "Henry Morrison Flagler Biography," Henry Morrison Flagler Museum official website.

3
NEW ARRIVALS

27 *"a hotel civilization"*: Alva Johnston, *The Legendary Mizners*, 49. It was not a civilization that he approved of. "Florida is a fearful fraud," Henry James wrote in a letter to a friend, February 24, 1905. Quoted in Leon Edel edition (Indiana University Press, 1988) of *The American Scene*, 479.

27 *"nothing counts but lucre"*: Johnston, *Legendary Mizners*, 48.

27 *their own private railcar:* Many of these private railroad cars were named: the Adios, owned by Harry Payne Whitney; the Roamer, owned by Joshua Cosden; the Sinco, owned by Harry F. Sinclair; and the Westmount, owned by J. Leonard Replogle. See Amory, *Last Resorts*, 350.

27 *"gold-encrusted Pullmans of the New World nobility"*: Johnston, *Legendary Mizners*, 49.

28 *"The customer is always right"*: Management certainly wasn't. We know today that Cesar Ritz and two others embezzled large sums of money from the Savoy in the 1890s while employed there and were fired for their crimes, a scandal not exposed until 1983. See Paul Levy, "Ritzy Business," *New York Review of Books*, July 19, 2018, 22.

29 *a house on Rue Spontini:* Kathryn Chapman Harwood, *The Lives of Vizcaya*, 2.

30 *One schooner brought in 110 tons of marble:* Ibid., 74.

30 *a rate that today is accelerating:* Thomas E. Lodge, *The Everglades Handbook: Understanding the Ecosystem*, 3rd ed., 122.

30 *at least 10 percent of the population:* There was a population of 10,500 in 1913. Harwood, *Lives of Vizcaya*, 8.

31 *$27,000 worth of wine:* Ibid., 74.

31   *Deering could be found seated:* Ibid., 257.

31   *John Singer Sargent's finest watercolors:* John Singer Sargent was a close friend of Charles Deering, who was an important patron of the arts and the older half brother of James Deering. Charles and his second wife lived nearby on an estate at Brickell Point

32   *"like the beaten prodigal son":* Arva Moore Parks, *George Merrick, Son of the South Wind: Visionary Creator of Coral Gables,* 94.

33   *won a literary contest in 1910:* It was printed February 24, 1910. See Jorge Reyes, "'When the Groves Begin to Bear . . . ': George Merrick and the Founding of Coral Gables." See also Helen C. Freeland, "George Edgar Merrick," *Tequesta: The Journal of the Historical Association of Southern Florida* 1, no. 2 (August 1942).

33   *"pithy, wilted stalks":* Quoted in Parks, *George Merrick,* 94.

33   *a chief proponent of the City Beautiful Movement:* The British "Garden Cities" movement founded by Ebenezer Howard shared a similar aesthetic.

33   *housing in a tranquil, parklike setting:* Another example was Shaker Heights, outside Cleveland, designed by the Van Swearing brothers in strictly regulated English and French architectural style. Other examples of the City Beautiful Movement could be found by this time in Chestnut Hill, outside Philadelphia, and in the suburbs of Kansas City, Denver, and Orlando. Tuxedo Park in Orange County, New York, and Roland Park in Baltimore were two others. Many of the ideals of this movement had been spelled out in the writings of Charles Mulford Robinson, an urban planner, who wrote a series of influential newspaper articles on the subject between 1902 and 1904.

34   *the most famous land developer:* Harner, *Florida's Promoters,* 65. Harner claims Merrick was the most famous developer in the world.

34   *"a skeptic and a dissenter":* Marjory Stoneman Douglas, *Voice of the River,* 50.

34   *"no man took me to a dance":* Ibid., 72.

35   *He had failed at a variety of business ventures:* Nixon Smiley, *Knights of the Fourth Estate: The Story of the Miami Herald,* 26.

36   *"schools of mullet jumping":* Douglas, *Voice of the River,* 103.

36   *"this wonderful white tropic light":* Ibid., 31.

36   *"something I had loved and missed":* Ibid.

37   *"He expected a pretty girl":* Ibid., 96.

37   *the newspaper's first female reporter:* Smiley, *Knights of the Fourth Estate,* 47.

38   *he could embroider:* Addison Mizner, *The Many Mizners,* 53.

39   *He worked with Polk:* According to historian Christina Orr, little archival material from this period survived the fires that happened in the wake of the 1906 earthquake. See Christina Orr, *Addison Mizner: Architect of Dreams and Realities (1872–1933),* 10.

39 *cleverly altered proverbs:* Other revised proverbs included: "It's a strong stomach that has no turning," "People who love in glass houses should pull down the blinds," "A fool and his honey are soon mated," "Misery loves company, but company does not reciprocate," "Stays make waist," "Necessity is the mother of contention," "Hell is paved with big pretensions," "Absinthe makes the heart grow fonder," "Be held truthful that your lies may count." Oliver Herford, Ethel Watts Mumford, and Addison Mizner, *The Cynic's Calendar of Revised Wisdom for 1904.*

40 *"I worshipped him":* Mizner, *Many Mizners,* 253.

40 *"the greatest Cathedral looter":* Johnston, *Legendary Mizners,* 13.

40 *A reckless spender:* Isadora Duncan, *My Life,* 218.

41 *"Is-a-bore-when-drunken":* John Burke, *Rogue's Progress: The Fabulous Adventures of Wilson Mizner,* 213.

41 *died in a tragic accident:* "Two Children of Isadora Duncan Die in Accident," *San Francisco Call,* April 20, 1913, 1. The children were Deirdre Duncan Craig, born September 24, 1906, and Patrick Augustus Duncan, born May 1, 1910. They died April 19, 1913.

41 *a chauffeur-driven car that drove off a bridge:* According to one report, the car was stalled on the bridge, and the driver was in front working the crank in an attempt to start it when the vehicle rolled off the bridge.

41 *"I was so indignant":* Duncan, *My Life,* 300.

4
BALLYHOO

43 *"I just like to see the dirt fly":* "Mr. Miami Beach," *American Experience,* PBS; Carl Hungness, *I Love to Make the Dirt Fly! A Biography of Carl G. Fisher, 1874–1939.*

43 *she was twenty-four:* Jane, in her memoirs, *Fabulous Hoosier: A Story of American Achievement,* lopped a few years off her life and claimed falsely to have been fifteen when Fisher married her. See Mark Dill, "Did Carl Fisher Marry a 15 Year Old? (No!!!)," First Super Speedway.

44 *"free of envy, hostility, and frustration":* Advertisement depicted in Hungness, *I Love to Make the Dirt Fly!,* 27.

44 *his self-help philosophy:* "Happiness is the only good, the way to be happy is to make others so and the time and place to be happy is here and now." Hungness, *I Love to Make the Dirt Fly!,* 15.

45 *he removed the engine:* There were four thousand of these manufactured. Only thirty-four survive, according to ibid., 26.

45 *"the giant balloon and its unusual load":* Polly Redford, *Billion-Dollar Sandbar: A Biography of Miami Beach,* 57.

45   *"as though he were on a curbstone"*: Ibid.

46   *"two skunks"*: Hungness, *I Love to Make the Dirt Fly!*, 29.

46   *"was like living at a circus"*: Ray Boomhower, "Carl G. Fisher: The Hoosier Bar-
     num," *Traces of Indiana and Midwestern History* 6, no. 2 (Spring 1994): 24–27.

46   *a novel automobile headlight system:* Fisher talked his friend Jim Allison into put-
     ting up the $10,000 for a two-thirds interest in the business and took a third of it
     as payment for arranging the deal.

47   *"an old soldier, aged about sixty-one years"*: Hungness, *I Love to Make the Dirt Fly!*,
     31–32.

47   *"Let's build it"*: Redford, *Billion-Dollar Sandbar*, 63.

48   *a total of only $11 million:* Howard Kleinberg, *Miami Beach: A History*, 38.

48   *the National Interstate and Defense Highways Act:* Congress authorized the first
     national highway network in 1947.

48   *Perhaps no other advancement:* Eric Foner, *The Reader's Companion to American
     History.*

48   *"more influence on society"*: William Fielding Ogburn, *Machines and Tomorrow's
     World*, Public Affairs Pamphlet Number Five (New York: Public Affairs Com-
     mittee, 1938), 3, quoted in Kenneth Jackson, *Crabgrass Frontier: The Suburban-
     ization of the United States*, 188.

50   *"He wore a bow tie"*: Redford, *Billion-Dollar Sandbar,* 44.

51   *"Mosquitos blackened our clothing"*: Jane Fisher, *Fabulous Hoosier: A Story of
     American Achievement*, 84–85.

51   *"Carl's imagination saw Miami Beach"*: Ibid., 85–86.

51   *"another one will be coiled there"*: J. N. Lummus, *The Miracle of Miami Beach: Facts
     About the Early Days*, 30.

52   *men tucked newspapers into their socks:* From oral history for Junior Lead, August
     26, 1970, in Kleinberg, *Miami Beach*, 46.

52   *the James Clark Company, of Baltimore:* Ibid., 40.

52   *"sand could hold up a Real Estate sign"*: Redford, *Billion-Dollar Sandbar*, 70.

53   *sprigging*: Jane Fisher, *Fabulous Hoosier*, 115.

53   *"other than of the Caucasian Race"*: This was the standard language of the restric-
     tive covenants. Kleinberg, *Miami Beach*, 52.

53   *white tourists arriving with black chauffeurs:* Redford, *Billion-Dollar Sandbar*, 96.

54   *Jewish immigrants from Eastern Europe:* More than two million would arrive be-
     tween 1880 and 1924, the year restrictive immigration quotas were put in place.

54   *a fair person, staunchly unbiased:* For the best discussion of Fisher's "selective"
     anti-Semitism, see Kleinberg, *Miami Beach*, 74–76.

54   *"no sissy furniture a man won't sit on"*: Jane Fisher, *Fabulous Hoosier*, 28.

55   *"May flies in the dome"*: Kenneth L. Roberts, *Florida*, 84.

57   *"I was on the wrong track"*: Harner, *Florida's Promoters*, 63.

57   *"a youthful city of indeterminate social standing"*: Charlotte Curtis, *The Rich and Other Atrocities*, 183.

57   *"not well pleased with their investment"*: Harner, *Florida's Promoters*, 63.

58   *raw land into real estate*: Martin V. Melosi, "The Automobile Shapes the City," *Automobile in American Life and Society;* James J. Flink argues in *The Car Culture*, 41, that the automobile in the two generations following Ford's automation of his factories, "became the most important for change in American civilization."

58   *"a polo club house"*: Redford, *Billion-Dollar Sandbar*, 116.

58   *"they know no fear"*: Chandler, *Henry Flagler*, 264.

5
A SPANISH DREAMSCAPE

62   *"excellent extensions and embellishments"*: Henry James, *The American Scene*, 355, quoted in Anthony Powell, *Miscellaneous Verdicts: Writings on Writers, 1946–1989*, 143.

62   *"trouble"*: Amory, *Last Resorts*, 23.

63   *"a beautiful way of putting things"*: Mizner, *Many Mizners*, 245.

63   *"dares to be impudent"*: Ibid.

64   *"A Moorish tower"*: Quoted in Caroline Seebohm, *Boca Rococo: How Addison Mizner Invented Florida's Gold Coast*, 157.

64   *"a nunnery, with a chapel"*: Addison Mizner, unpublished typescript of his memoirs, vol. 2, quoted in Seebohm, *Boca Rococo*, 157.

64   *"I was in love with Palm Beach"*: Mizner, unpublished typescript, vol. 2, quoted in Donald W. Curl, *Mizner's Florida: American Resort Architecture*, 60.

64   *the Spanish Colonial Revival style*: The Spanish Colonial Revival style was given its American debut at the San Diego Panama-California Exposition in 1915, where the lead architect for the exposition was Bertram Goodhue, best known for his neo-Gothic commissions and, later, for his Nebraska State Capitol building. He often gets the credit for introducing the new Spanish look, but it was his assistant and colleague, Carleton Winslow Sr., who proposed to his boss that the exposition's architectural vernacular be exclusively Spanish colonial in style. The third member of the group was a young architect named Frank Lloyd Wright.

65   *displays of pinnacles, shields, and neoclassical columns*: Such detailing is known as Churrigueresque (named after the Chrurriguera family of architects) and Plateresque ("in the manner of a silversmith").

65   *American Craftsman*: This was a style championed by Edward Bok, the long-serving editor of *Ladies' Home Journal*. His magazine sold designs and specs, at

$5 a set, for precut and prefitted affordable bungalows (purchased and assembled for $1,500 to $5,000), to the magazine's wide readership.

65 *"Northern architecture didn't register":* John Taylor Boyd Jr., "The Florida House: Mr. Addison Mizner, the Architect, Recounts the Birth of the New Florida Architecture at Palm Beach in an Interview," *Arts and Decoration* 32 (January 1930): 37-40, 80, 102, quoted in Orr, *Addison Mizner*, 18.

65 *architects on both coasts:* The style was championed by George Washington Smith in Santa Barbara and Pasadena, and by F. Burrall Hoffman Jr., August Geiger, and Abram Garfield in Palm Beach.

66 *kilns and a sawmill:* Curl, *Mizner's Florida*, 42.

66 *"a master of all the crafts":* Paul Singer introduction to Addison Mizner, *Florida Architecture of Addison Mizner*, xxxi.

67 *Colonel Bradley's Casino:* It featured roulette, hazard, and, starting in 1923, *chemin de fer,* a variation of baccarat. It also featured exceptional food. It was there that the celebrated Swiss chef Conrad Schmitt took credit for inventing green turtle soup. Joseph Kennedy is said to have lamented its closing in 1945 by remarking, "Palm Beach has lost its zipperoo."

68 *"striped shirts, colorful sweaters":* Curl, *Mizner's Florida*, 48.

68 *"It's up to you and me":* Mizner, unpublished typescript, vol. 2, 40; also quoted in Curl, *Mizner's Florida*, 44.

68 *"there were very few knockers":* Ibid., 45.

68 *"you have made me so discontented":* Ibid., 45-46.

69 *"like riding a see-saw":* Mizner, *Many Mizners*, 244.

69 *"I like nice things":* Ibid.

6
MERRICK'S IDEAL CITY

70 *"a balanced city":* Rex Beach, *The Miracle of Coral Gables*, 19.

71 *"I never told anyone my plans":* George B. Tindall, "The Bubble in the Sun," *American Heritage*, 78.

72 *"miss you every minute":* Ibid., 117.

72 *"Am terribly lonesome":* Ibid., 126.

72 *"if only to save my life!":* Ibid., 112.

73 *"Your old Iggie":* Ibid., 129–30.

73 *he did all the driving:* "George E. Merrick Auto Party, May-June 1917," Althea Merrick Collection, HistoryMiami Museum.

73 *"Fruit for lunch":* Ibid.

73 *They wandered the streets:* Parks, *George Merrick*, 133.

73 *"I ripple the fronds":* Ibid., 17.

74	*"none of your good ones":* George Merrick to Marjory S. Douglas, September 28, 1921, Merrick Collection, University of Miami, quoted in Parks, *George Merrick*, 133.

74	*a handful of architects:* They included his cousin H. George Fink, Martin Luther Hampton, Walter De Garmo, Richard Kiehnel, Harold Hastings Mundy, and Lewis D. Brumm. Source: Aristides J. Millas and Ellen J. Uguccioni, *Coral Gables: Miami Riviera—An Architectural Guide*, 15.

75	*buyers from twenty-nine states:* Reyes, "When the Groves Begin to Bear."

75	*"so that there may be no clash":* *Coral Gables Today* (brochure, Merrick Collection, MiamiHistory Museum, 1926).

75	*"real estate counsel":* Ballinger, *Miami Millions*, 22.

75	*"Women more beautiful":* "Progress Week," *Miami Herald*, November 27, 1926.

75	*his purchases quickly exceeded his commission:* Walter P. Fuller, *This Was Florida's Boom*, 21.

75	*"as brilliant a sale manager":* Ibid., 23.

76	*"Standing six feet tall":* Harner, *Florida's Promoters*, 66. He was five feet nine inches tall.

76	*"a truly great man":* Fuller, *This Was Florida's Boom*, 21.

76	*"one of the most remarkable men":* Weigall, *Boom in Paradise*, 116.

76	*"a genius":* Harner, *Florida's Promoters*, 65.

76	*"There was a man":* "Architect Fink Recalls Merrick's Gables Dream," *Miami Herald*, undated, circa March 28, 1942, Merrick Collection, MiamiHistory Museum.

76	*"one of the finest men":* Parks, *George Merrick*, 271.

7
GREAT MIGRATIONS

77	*exceed any of the great land rushes:* California's gold rush attracted some 80,000 to the state in 1849 alone, Oregon's boom attracted 40,000 over a ten-year period. Some 50,000 were involved in the Oklahoma Land Rush of 1889. The other booms attracted even fewer.

77	*2.5 million entered the state:* Roberts, *Florida*, 19.

77	*"myriad of blackbirds":* Gertrude Mathews Shelby, "Florida Frenzy," *Harper's Monthly*, 152, January 1926, 177, reprinted in George E. Mowry, ed., *The Twenties: Fords, Flappers & Fanatics*, 33.

78	*grow at a rate of 883,000 per year:* Jackson, *Crabgrass Frontier*, 175.

78	*the market's saturation point:* According to Robert J. Gordon, *The Rise and Fall of American Growth: The U.S. Standard of Living Since the Civil War*, 162, 297, 317, by 1929 the ratio of motor vehicles to number of households reached 93 percent, up from 29 percent in 1919. But Gordon seems to have taken 1929 registrations as a percent of 1920 households. By my calculation, there were 26 million car registrations in 1930 and 29.9 million households. Incidentally, 78 percent of the world's automobiles were in the United States.

78   *Output per man hours:* Maury Klein, *Rainbow's End: The Crash of 1929*, 84.

78   *the exodus from farm country to urban areas:* Frederick Lewis Allen, *Only Yesterday: An Informal History of the 1920s*, 247, notes that the urban population would increase from 51.4 percent to 57.6 percent of the population during the decade.

79   *Such straw roads:* Claudette Stager and Martha Carver, *Looking Beyond the Highway: Dixie Roads and Culture*, 56.

80   *the 1,500-mile procession:* Roberts, *Florida*, 11–12.

80   *200 miles per day was doable:* Stager and Carver, *Looking Beyond the Highway*, 275.

80   *a rate comparable with Florida's:* US census data at census.gov, 1935 records, Section 2.

81   *"Of those who traveled in the great trek":* Roberts, *Florida*, 12–13.

82   *"nimble in the calling of selling houses":* Sinclair Lewis, *Babbitt*, 2.

82   *"a strange new world both gaudy and sad":* Bruce Catton, "The Restless Decade," *American Heritage* 16, no. 5 (August 1965): 5.

82   *consumer credit itself dated back to antiquity:* Lendol Calder, *Financing the American Dream: A Cultural History of Consumer Credit*, 17.

82   *"A river of red ink":* Ibid., 26.

83   *When that term ended:* Interest rates on these mortgages ranged from 6 percent to 8 percent throughout the decade. See Jackson, *Crabgrass Frontier*, 205.

84   *installment debt more than doubled:* See Rolf Nugent, *Consumer Credit and Economic Stability*, 92, for the doubling of installment credit. The volume of installment credit was $1.375 billion in 1925 and $3 billion in 1929. See "A Story of Savings in the U.S." for mortgage figures. Charles P. Kindleberger, *The World Depression 1929–1939: 40th Anniversary of a Classic in Economic History*, 61.

84   *credit finance companies:* The number of small loan offices around the country that lent cash grew from 600 to 3,500 between 1923 and 1929; their loan balances soared sixfold. General Motors Acceptance Corporation (GMAC), a wholly owned subsidiary of General Motors, launched in 1919, helped auto dealers finance their inventory and lent credit to GM car buyers so that they could purchase new models. Store credit, or so-called open-book credit granting, became a popular method of financing the purchase of not only furniture but also even such staples as apparel. Macy's would be the last major department store to capitulate to this trend, priding itself on its cash only policy, boasting in its slogan that "No one is in debt to Macy's!" It would reluctantly follow suit in October 1939.

84   *makes soon to disappear:* "Dream World of Advertising," *American Heritage* 16, no. 5 (August 1965), *Special Issue: The Twenties*, 71.

85 *15 cents per gallon:* Hungness, *I Love to Make the Dirt Fly!*, 126.

85 *horse numbers had dropped:* Jackson, *Crabgrass Frontier*, 184.

85 *75 percent of all car buyers:* Gordon, *Rise and Fall of American Growth*, 165.

85 *the new, more relaxed sexual mores:* Rudi Volti, *Cars and Culture: The Life Story of a Technology*, 62.

85 *that dream of a land:* James Truslow Adams, *Epic of America*, xii.

86 *lynchings per capita*: Marvin Dunn, *The Beast in Florida: A History of Anti-Black Violence*, 202–6.

87 *"The Negro who drives a Ford"*: Copies of the *Florida Sentinel* no longer exist. This article is quoted in H. L. Mencken, ed., *Americana*, 48–49.

88 *bounce-on-the-bed trade:* Warren James Belasco, *Americans on the Road: From Autocamp to Motel, 1910–1945*, 161.

89 *their common purpose:* C. P. Russell, "The Pneumatic Hegira," *Outlook,* December 9, 1925, 559, described in Mowry, ed., *The Twenties*, 51.

89 *"the lot is yours":* Fuller, *This Was Florida's Boom*, 12.

90 *"to sprinkle its heedless millions":* Ballinger, *Miami Millions*, 5.

8

A WRITER'S EDUCATION

91 *"he was awfully nice":* Douglas, *Voice of the River*, 102.

91 *a population of only roughly ten thousand:* The US Census put the population at 5,000 in 1910. The *Miami Herald* estimated 10,000 in 1915. The Florida Census put it at 15,000. See Jack E. Davis, *An Everglades Providence: Marjory Stoneman Douglas and the American Environmental Century,* 205.

92 *"sunny resinous breath":* Davis, *Everglades Providence,* 323.

92 *"be as raw and ugly as plain dirt":* Ibid., 207.

92 *"We'd swim and light fires":* Douglas, *Voice of the River*, 110.

93 *the suffrage amendment:* The Nineteenth Amendment was ratified on August 18, 1920.

93 *"two sound arguments against politics":* Davis, *Everglades Providence,* 277.

93 *whipped to death:* These whips were call Black Aunties.

93 *The poem was reprinted widely:* Douglas was not alone in publicizing the killing. The *New York World* won the 1924 Pulitzer Prize for its coverage of the incident.

94 *an avid birder:* One of her books was the slim volume *The Joys of Bird Watching in Florida*, published in 1969.

95 *"the patron saint of foodies":* David Lee, "Introduction to David Fairchild's Life in the Garden," in *The World as Garden: The Life and Writings of David Fairchild,* ed. David Lee.

95   *"I had no sympathy"*: Douglas, *Voice of the River*, 165.

96   *"a matter of making money"*: Ibid., 167.

97   *"My feeble pickings"*: *Interview with Marjory Stoneman Douglas,* videotaped at the Douglas House in Coconut Grove, June 15 and 16, 1983, Everglades Digital Library, quoted in Davis, *Everglades Providence*, 279.

97   *Late one night in early 1923*: Douglas, in her memoir, says the year was 1924, but she appears to have been off by a year. She wrote her last column for the *Miami Herald* in July 1923.

97   *"unhinged a little"*: Douglas, *Voice of the River*, 167.

97   *a change of job or venue:* Ibid.

98   *"I'd rather be an individual"*: Ibid., 170.

9
TRAIL BLAZERS

99   *the holy grail of Florida road building:* Smiley, *Knights of the Fourth Estate*, 42.

100   *"enough to make a man swear to be content"*: Quoted in Bruce D. Epperson, *Roads Through the Everglades: The Building of the Ingraham Highway, the Tamiami Trail and Conners Highway, 1914–1931*, 13.

102   *thirty-five thousand columns of publicity:* Russell Kay, "Tamiami Trail Blazers: A Personal Memoir," *Florida Historical Quarterly* 49, no. 3 (January 1971): 278–87.

102   *the largest individual landholder in the state:* In 1881, Hamilton Disston briefly owned four million acres purchased for $1 million. See Harner, *Florida's Promoters*, 16. The St. Joe Company, a paper company founded by the du Pont family interest, which began buying Florida land aggressively during the Depression and through the 1950s, would eventually own over one million acres on the Florida Panhandle.

102   *throwing off $5 million in profits:* They earned $14,000 each day, according to ibid., 58.

103   *John D. Rockefeller's net worth likely peaked at $900 million:* John D. Rockefeller Jr., the oil magnate's son, made a statement in 1921 to the effect that his father's wealth had never reached $1 billion in part because of the charitable bequests he made during his lifetime. "Financier Fortune in Oil Amassed in Industrial Era of 'Rugged Individualism,'" *New York Times*, May 24, 1937. Rockefeller biographer Ron Chernow uses the $900 million number.

103   *saw grass that grew taller than nine feet:* Lodge, *Everglades Handbook*, xxix.

103   *a walking dredge:* Epperson, *Roads Through the Everglades*, 157.

104   *"better bring your check book"*: Harner, *Florida's Promoters*, 59.

105   *a sheriff's posse led by bloodhounds:* Epperson, *Roads Through the Everglades*, 180–81.

105   *invasive species:* Invasive species such as wax myrtle, saltbush, and drahoon holly. Lodge, *Everglades Handbook*, xxx.

106   *"the wealth of south Florida":* Quoted in afterword in ibid., 394.

106   *"What a liar I turned out to be":* Michael Grunwald quotes her in the afterword of ibid., 393.

106   *"no more complete botch":* Charles Torrey Simpson, *Florida Wild Life: Observations on the Flora and Fauna of the State and the Influence of Climate and Environment on Their Development*, 189.

106   *"Huge numbers of crayfish":* Lodge, *Everglades Handbook*, xxix.

107   *"much of it burned down to the rock surface":* Ibid., xxx.

107   *"this can only end in the destruction":* Simpson, *Florida Wild Life*, 193.

107   *"he has ruined it with ruthless efficiency":* Thomas Barbour, *That Vanishing Eden: A Naturalist's Florida*, 3. He also wrote, "America is proud of her magnificent record in road building, but nothing has been so destructive of wild life as our good roads," *That Vanishing Eden*, 73.

108   *five hundred or so Seminoles:* Their numbers have recovered somewhat. Today some two thousand Seminoles live in Florida. The tribe occupies six reservations around the state on which they operate gaming casinos.

10
HABITUAL INTEMPERANCE

109   *"out-of-shape businessmen":* Foster, *Castles in the Sand*, 187.

110   *"you get on a train and come down to Miami":* Fisher to H. E. Talbot Jr., Dayton Wright Airplane Company, Dayton, OH, October 22, 1917, box 1, Automobile Men, Fisher Papers, HistoryMiami Museum.

110   *"sweetest little thing you ever saw":* Alvan Macauley to Carl Fisher, October 17, 1919, box 1, Automobile Men, Fisher Papers, HistoryMiami Museum.

110   *"with reckless enthusiasm":* Foster, *Castles in the Sand*, 181.

110   *"and so on into the night!":* "Cuss Words by Carl Fisher at bridge, Thursday night, October 9," Fisher Papers, box 14, Personality II, 114, HistoryMiami Museum.

110   *"you mustn't pay so much attention":* Carl Fisher to Frank Shutts, January 2, 1920, Fisher Papers, box 14, Personality II, 15, HistoryMiami Museum.

111   *"save myself future annoyance":* Carl Fisher to James Deering, January 24, 1919, Fisher Papers, box 4, Deering Family, 3, HistoryMiami Museum.

111   *"Such has been ours":* William T. Anderson to Carl Fisher, January 7, 1928, Fisher Papers, box 14, Personality II, 102, HistoryMiami Museum.

111   *promptly whisked Harding off:* Developers in Fort Lauderdale executed a similar coup when they used a dredger to block the yacht *Victoria*'s passage down the

waterway and then sent a boat to invite Harding to play a round of golf on the new nine-hole Fort Lauderdale golf course.

112 *oilman Edward L. Doheny:* Edward Doheny was the inspiration for the character of J. Arnold Ross in Upton Sinclair's 1927 novel *Oil!*, which was much later the basis for the movie *There Will Be Blood*, in which Daniel Day Lewis plays a character much like Doheny.

112 *"This beach is wonderful":* Foster, *Castles in the Sand*, 203–4n9.

112 *"personal touch":* Ibid., 203.

112 *"a million dollars' worth of advertising":* Carl Fisher to John Oliver LaGorce, February 7, 1921, box 4, Elephants, 4, HistoryMiami Museum.

113 *"a symbol of the brazenness":* Jane Fisher, *Fabulous Hoosier*, 128.

113 *A beauty contest is known to have taken place:* Lois W. Banner, *American Beauty*, 265.

113 *beauty contests in Miami:* Foster, *Castles in the Sand*, 324n45.

113 *the first Queen of New York City's five beaches:* Banner, *American Beauty*, 265.

113 *" 'the Bathing Beauties of Miami Beach' ":* Jane Fisher, *Fabulous Hoosier*, 129.

113 *"Turalura Lipschits and Her Twin Sister":* Seth H. Bramson, *Sunshine, Stone Crabs and Cheesecake: The Story of Miami Beach*, 139.

114 *$6 million in 1923 to $23 million in 1925:* Redford, *Billion-Dollar Sandbar*, 154.

114 *"His investments made fortunes":* Ibid., 155.

114 *eleven of the country's best auto drivers:* They included Louis Chevrolet, L. L. Corum, Ray Harroun, Harry Hartz, William Knipper, Tommy Milton, Wade Morton, Pete DePaolo, Phil Shafer, Ira Vail, and Jerry Wonderlich. See Hungness, *I Love to Make the Dirt Fly!*, 116.

114 *"Better keep this":* Jane Fisher, *Fabulous Hoosier*, 135.

115 *"I could never have worked with him":* Douglas, *Voice of the River*, 107.

115 *"She tried to be a little snobbish":* Ibid., 107–8.

115 *"fuming between courses":* Jane Fisher, *Fabulous Hoosier*, 134.

115 *"nine feet nine inches":* Ibid., 131.

115 *"kind and gentle as a Newfoundland dog":* Carl Fisher to F. R. Humpge, April 9, 1932, Fisher Papers, HistoryMiami Museum, quoted in Kleinberg, *Miami Beach*, 80, and in Hungness, *I Love to Make the Dirt Fly!*, 103.

115 *"I am all black and blue":* Carl Fisher to John LaGorce, April 11, 1922, box 4, Elephants, 5, HistoryMiami Museum.

115 *"put up his beak for me":* Jane Fisher, *Fabulous Hoosier*, 132.

115 *grocery bills that soon topped $1,000:* Ibid., 132.

116 *people I had never seen before:* Ibid., 134.

116 *"One of your playmates":* Betty Clearman Twichell to Carl Fisher, December 13, 1924, box 16, Women, 21, HistoryMiami Museum.

116 *the twenty-six motor yachts Carl would own:* Jane Fisher, *Fabulous Hoosier*, illustration section.

116   *gasoline aristocracy:* The term seems to have been first coined by historian Polly Redford.

117   *Henry Ford's only child, Edsel:* Foster, *Castles in the Sand,* 211.

117   *Miami Beach had grown to 858 homes:* Redford, *Billion-Dollar Sandbar,* 154.

117   *"It was paradise risen from swampland":* Jane Fisher, *Fabulous Hoosier,* 138.

117   *worth $76 million:* According to Jane Fisher. Redford, *Billion-Dollar Sandbar,* 155.

117   *"a compulsive braggart":* Harner, *Florida's Promoters,* 48.

118   *he was reminded of the mud flats:* A local Tampa realtor named Burts L. Hamner may have had the original idea to develop the islands and may have alerted Davis to the opportunity. Rodney Kite-Powell, *History of Davis Islands: David P. Davis and the History of a Landmark Tampa Neighborhood,* 39.

118   *a damaging hurricane followed:* Tebeau and Marina, *History of Florida,* 368.

118   *using the money he had made in Miami:* James W. Covington, "The Story of Davis Islands 1924–1926," *Sunland Tribune* 4, no. 1 (November 1978): 69. By Covington's estimate, Davis had made $5 million, but this number seems high.

119   *"Florida's Supreme $30 million development":* Kite-Powell, *History of Davis Islands,* 51.

119   *inspired by Fisher's example:* William B. Stronge, *The Sunshine Economy: An Economic History of Florida Since the Civil War,* 95.

119   *"finger-islanding":* Ibid.

119   *"Success a-plenty":* Kite-Powell, *History of Davis Islands,* 46.

120   *"a veritable Venice at one's home-door":* Harner, *Florida's Promoters,* 51.

120   *an old girlfriend named Lucille Zehring:* Their names appear together on the manifest of a ship sailing from Havana to Key West in April 1923. At the time she was married to a Hollywood actor named Llewellyn Zehring, whom she would divorce in February 1925.

120   *Mack Sennett's celebrated "Bathing Beauties":* She does not appear on any of the surviving lists of these women, but press reports repeatedly identified her as one of the group.

121   *"All I ever got from that marriage":* Covington, "Story of Davis Islands," 74.

121   *"habitual intemperance":* Ibid.

11

MIZNERLAND

125   *"Like hell you are":* Alex Waugh, "Miznerland" (unpublished typescript, January 1963, Palm Beach Historical Society).

125   *best-selling British author Alec Waugh:* Friends of Alex passed him off as Alec Waugh to help him get dates. Waugh, "Miznerland" (unpublished typescript).

125 *the Battle of the Somme:* The losses at the Battle of the Somme were staggering: 1.5 million soldiers (on both sides) died in the Somme Offensive, which lasted between July 1 and November 1, 1916.

126 *"I sat on the bed and wept":* Waugh, "Miznerland" (unpublished typescript).

126 *"clothe the dry and dull bones of the past":* Alex Waugh, "Alex in Miznerland," in J. Camille Showalter, ed., *The Many Mizners: California Clan Extraordinary*, 55.

126 *"Calls for houses flowed upon him":* Ida Tarbell in Addison Mizner, *Florida Architecture of Addison Mizner*, introduction.

126 *"We bought tiles":* Waugh, "Miznerland" (unpublished typescript).

127 *"All doors seemed to open to him":* Ibid.

127 *"You old son of a bitch!":* Ibid.

128 *"the prince of petroleum":* Joshua S. Cosden, "Great American Business Leaders of the 20th Century," Leadership Initiative, HBS.edu

128 *additions on twelve of them:* Curl, *Mizner's Florida*, 132.

128 *"chloroform his patient":* Mizner, unpublished typescript, 47–48, quoted in Curl, *Mizner's Florida*, 65.

129 *"One longs to explore every building":* Weigall, *Boom in Paradise*, 220.

129 *"total knowledge of Spanish architecture":* Christina Orr-Cahall, "Addison—From Scrambled Eggs to Tile Roofs," in Showalter, *Many Mizners: California Clan Extraordinary*, 46.

129 *a remarkable collection of scrapbooks:* They are archived today at the Society of Four Arts in Palm Beach but can be viewed online. https://fourarts.bywatersolutions.com/cgi-bin/koha/opac-shelves.pl?op=view&shelfnumber=27&sortfield=title.

129 *"the visual autobiography of an architect":* Seebohm, *Boca Rococo*, 110.

131 *equivalent to $113.6 million in current dollars:* 14.2 times 1926 dollars because the house was built between 1924 and 1927. See Measuringworth.com.

131 *"I have never led a more intense life":* Maurice Fatio to his parents, February 15, 1923, in Alexandra Fatio Taylor, *Maurice Fatio: Architect*.

131 *Marion Sims Wyeth:* Wyeth was the original architect on Mar-a-Lago, according to Hap Hatton, *Tropical Splendor: An Architectural History of Florida*, 158.

132 *"the best-natured slob I ever saw":* Mizner, unpublished typescript, 57.

132 *"with self-destructive abandon":* Showalter, *Many Mizners: California Clan Extraordinary*, 59

132 *"Built by some six-thumbed Crusoe":* Ibid.

133 *"the transportation of illicit alcohol":* Ibid.

134 *America's Foremost Beauty:* Mizner, unpublished typescript, 105.

135 *"The two lasting loves of my life":* Ibid.

135 *"his monkey, Johnnie Brown":* Waugh, "Miznerland" (unpublished typescript).

135 *"patriarchal dignity":* Ibid.

135 *seeing Jerome Kern*: Curl, *Mizner's Florida*, 17.

136 *"most interesting heiress"* "The $10,000,000 Heiress Who Runs Herself," *Washington Times*, December 11, 1921, 3.

136 *"all angles and resentments and revolts"*: Elizabeth Spaulding Titus, "The Educator and the Heiress," Alice DeLamar blog, https://alicedelamar.wordpress.com/articles-about-alice-2/the-educator-and-the-heiress.

136 *the 45-carat Hope Diamond:* Evelyn Walsh McLean also owned a much larger diamond, the 94-carat Star of the East. Today the Hope Diamond is on display at the Smithsonian Institution in Washington, DC.

136 *"like a hail storm splattered with blood"*: Mizner, unpublished typescript, 107.

136 *an apocryphal story:* Anita Loos, *Kiss Hollywood Good-Bye*, 94.

136 *"just my luck"*: Mizner, unpublished typescript, 108.

137 *"Addison's idea of a square meal"*: Quoted in Stephen Perkins and James Caughman, *Addison Mizner: The Architect Whose Genius Defined Palm Beach*, 289.

137 *a popular annual event:* Augustus Mayhew, "The Coconuts! A Palm Beach Party History: 1920–2018," *New York Social Diary*, last modified May 23, 2018.

138 *"more like a familiar spirit than an animal"*: Waugh, "Miznerland" (unpublished typescript).

138 *their mother's favorite:* Mama Mizner referred to Wilson as "Mama's Birdie Boy."

139 *"obviously nurturing a hangover"*: Alice DeLamar to Alva Johnston, March 14, 1948, Palm Beach Historical Society, quoted by Caroline Seebohm in *Boca Rococo*, 204.

139 *"He had a criminal look"*: Showalter, *Many Mizners: California Clan Extraordinary*, 43.

139 *"heard of people being arrested"*: Edward Dean Sullivan, *The Fabulous Wilson Mizner*, 290.

139 *"Neither of us is afraid"*: Ibid.

139 *"only in men of genius"*: Loos, *Kiss Hollywood Good-Bye*, 97.

140 *"Most hard-boiled people"*: Edward Dean Sullivan, *Fabulous Wilson Mizner*, 266–73.

140 *coscripted by Anita Loos:* Loos, *Kiss Hollywood Good-Bye*, 129. Stephen Sondheim would write a musical based on the careers of the two Mizner brothers called *Road Show*.

140 *"he isn't house broken"*: Mizner, *Many Mizners*, 241.

140 *"Those anchovies died"*: Burke, *Rogue's Progress*, 227.

140 *Wilson was excused:* Loos, *Kiss Hollywood Good-Bye*, 97.

141 *"the pecuniary heaven"*: Edward Dean Sullivan, *Fabulous Wilson Mizner*, 304.

141 *"The son of a bitch"*: Loos, *Kiss Hollywood Good-Bye*, 93.

141　*a settlement of Finnish farmers:* Other accounts suggest that the Finns fought to keep the road where it was and protested its removal.

141　*a melee that broke out:* Emilie Keyes, *Palm Beach Post*, December 12, 1924. See also Seebohm, *Boca Rococo*, 211.

142　*"my chief weakness":* Mizner, *Many Mizners*, 235.

12
WEIGALL WHOOPS IT UP

143　*"practically half-witted":* Weigall, *Boom in Paradise*, 18.

143　*"twenty dollars in the world":* Ibid., 31.

144　*"intense blue of the Florida sky":* Ibid., 95.

144　*Administration Building:* Every significant Florida development had an administration building.

144　*"great manifestos":* Weigall, *Boom in Paradise*, 107.

144　*"most of it extremely subtle":* Ibid., 132.

144　*"a fiery-eyed young genius":* Ibid., 131.

144　*"an entirely mythical city":* Ibid., 132.

145　*the most elaborate and comprehensive advertising:* Malinda Lester Cleary, "Denham Fink, Dream Coordinator to George Merrick and the Development of Coral Gables, Florida," (master's thesis, University of Miami, 1996), 88, n56.

145　*"I suppose I was slightly mad":* Weigall, *Boom in Paradise*, 109.

145　*"The Dream City":* Susan Gillis, *Boomtime Boca: Boca Raton in the 1920s*, 76.

146　*silver-tongued oratory:* H. L. Mencken described Bryan as being "born with a roaring voice and it had a trick of inflaming half-wits." Source: Frederick Lewis Allen, *Only Yesterday*, 201.

146　*"tell a lie at breakfast":* Tindall, "The Bubble in the Sun," 109. Bryan's lucrative gig was cut short by the Scopes trial, which took place in July 1925. A devout Protestant, he joined the trial's prosecution team where he testified, somewhat ineptly, on its behalf. He died in his sleep just five days after the verdict—guilty—during a Sunday afternoon nap, allegedly from overeating. It was not lost on the press that the great advocate of temperance didn't practice what he preached when it came to eating.

146　*Beach's sixty-three-page booklet:* Rex Beach, a failed Alaska prospector, became a best-selling novelist with his second book, *The Spoilers*. He was described as being of the "strong men doing hairy deeds" school of literature. Most of his books, according to Alaskan historian Stephen Haycox, are "mercifully forgotten today." See Stephen Haycox, *A Warm Past, Travels in Alaska History, Fifty Essays*, 113, quoted in Wikipedia, "Rex Beach," https://en.wikipedia.org/wiki/Rex_Beach.

146　*the book's cover as its chief merit:* Ballinger, *Miami Millions*, 117.

146 *"At heart he was a writer"*: Beach, *Miracle of Coral Gables*, 11.

147 *a Gatsby-like figure:* F. Scott Fitzgerald's *The Great Gatsby* had been published by Charles Scribner's Sons in April of that year to mixed reviews.

147 *"needs a tall giraffe"*: Weigall, *Boom in Paradise*, 127.

148 *"People resented it"*: Beach, *Miracle of Coral Gables*, 52.

148 *selling, general, and administrative:* Fuller, *This Was Florida's Boom*, 23.

148 *a deeply flawed business model:* He would not be alone in making this mistake. Jack Taylor at Pasadena Estates on Florida's west coast paid 10 percent commissions to his salesmen, 2.5 percent bonuses when they exceeded quota, a 5 percent override to the manager of his sales force, and the occasional 5 percent override on top of that to others involved. His selling costs easily reached 30 percent on lots that were being sold for 33⅓ percent down payments, creating cash-flow problems from the outset.

148 *"High Olympus"*: Parks, *George Merrick*, 383n1.

148 *rumored to be fast approaching $100 million:* Sales in aggregate totaled $150 million before the company went bust. His 80 percent share of the profits and the value of the remaining land accounted for the bulk of his wealth.

149 *his boss's grim facial expression:* Weigall, *Boom in Paradise*, 119.

149 *"as charming a sinner"*: Jay Maeder, "Inside Mayor Jimmy (Baeu James) Walker's Mighty Downfall," *New York Daily News* online, August 14, 2017.

149 *"I am here for rest"*: *New York Times*, November 17, 1925, 3.

149 *"the rooster's boots!"*: Weigall, *Boom in Paradise,* 122.

150 *"by the grace of Heaven"*: Ibid., 172.

150 *"more alcohol per head"*: Ibid., 179.

150 *the Black Bottom:* Harner, *Florida's Promoters*, 69. Perry Bradford's dance instructions read:

> Hop down front then doodle back
> Mooch to your left then mooch to the right
> Hands on your hips and do the mess around,
> Break a leg until you're near the ground
> Now that's the old black bottom dance

151 *"living like an emperor"*: Weigall, *Boom in Paradise*, 182.

151 *"Don't be drawn in"*: Shelby, "Florida Frenzy," in Mowry, ed., *The Twenties*, 35. Also Shelby, "Florida Frenzy," in *Harper's Monthly*, 177.

151 *"I was a prospect"*: Shelby, "Florida Frenzy," *The Twenties*, 36.

151 *"I succumbed to the boom bacillus"*: Ibid., 38.

151 *"I gambled. I won"*: Ibid., 34.

152 *"Charge 'em plenty, boy"*: Fuller, *This Was Florida's Boom*, 60.

152 *"I was able to hold back":* Weigall, *Boom in Paradise*, 233.

153 *"when I started to invest":* Ibid., 234.

13
A HOUSE IN COCONUT GROVE

155 *"'Hell,' said the duchess":* Douglas, *Voice of the River*, 169.

155 *"Aunt Fanny was flabbergasted":* Ibid., 170.

155 *some eighty short stories:* Rosalie Liposky, "Marjory Stoneman Douglas: A Bibliography," *Marjorie Kinnan Rawlings Journal of Florida Literature* 8 (1997): 55–73.

155 *she paid special attention:* Davis, *Everglades Providence*, 322.

155 *"I am a similar breed":* Ibid., 323.

155 *people in relation to nature:* Ibid.

155 *she had begun to crusade:* Kevin M. McCarthy, "How Marjory Stoneman Douglas Crusaded for South Florida in Her Short Stories," *Marjorie Kinnan Rawlings Journal of Florida Literature* 8 (1997): 15–21.

156 *"how best shall a man live":* Marjory Stoneman Douglas, "A Great American City Region," *Coral Gables, Miami Riviera: An Intrepretation*, 6, quoted in Parks, *George Merrick*, 363.

156 *ill-suited to the task:* Interview with Marjory Stoneman Douglas, June 16, 1983. Everglades Digital Library, http://everglades.fiu.edu/two/transcripts/SPC956_5.htm.

156 *she wanted her independence:* Douglas, *Voice of the River*, 171.

156 *"It was full of exotic fruit trees":* Ibid., 171.

157 *"she smilingly faces the world":* Amanda Harris, *Fruits of Eden: David Fairchild and America's Plant Hunters*, 239–40.

157 *"All I wanted":* Douglas, *Voice of the River*, 172.

157 *"stout and sparse":* Ibid.

14
CRIME WAVES

159 *the black community in Coconut Grove:* The black community of Coconut Grove boasted its own cemetery, founded as early as 1913, that exists to this day.

160 *"the men who have been associated with me":* Parks, *George Merrick*, 237.

160 *entirely black-run towns:* The black coastal community of American Beach on the outskirts of Jacksonville was founded in the 1930s by the founders of the Afro-American Life Insurance Company of Jacksonville.

160 *shooting men, women, and children:* Gary Moore, *Rosewood: The Full Story*, 462. Moore lists eight confirmed dead; other reports claimed there were many more.

160   *The town never recovered:* The events closely parallels the Tulsa Massacre of 1921, where the Greenwood section of Tulsa was destroyed and as many as three hundred people were killed.

161   *denied the opportunity:* Marvin Dunn, *Black Miami in the Twentieth Century* (Florida History and Culture), 77.

161   *neither of the Miami papers:* Interview with Marjory Stoneman Douglas, June 16, 1983. Everglades Digital Library, http://everglades.fiu.edu/two/transcripts/SPC956_5.htm

162   *"Miami really became a hell hole":* Dunn, *Black Miami in the Twentieth Century*, 61.

163   *"I knew I had killed a man":* Hix C. Stuart, *The Notorious Ashley Gang: A Saga of the King and Queen of the Everglades*, 53.

163   *"he never stood a chance":* Ibid.

164   *"This bunch of desperadoes":* Ibid., 38.

165   *"stacked in the car":* Ada Coats Williams, *Florida's Ashley Gang*, 36.

165   *"it's Merritt next":* Ibid.

166   *kept a standing order:* Fisher Papers, box 15, Prohibition, 44.

167   *The average annual import:* Tebeau and Marina, *History of Florida*, 375.

167   *A case of Scotch:* Robert Sobel, *The Money Manias: The Eras of Great Speculation in America, 1770–1970*, 280.

167   *"a red ant in the Hippodrome":* Quoted in ibid., 281.

168   *the cost of each case on board soared:* Sally J. Ling, *Run the Rum In: South Florida During Prohibition*, 128.

169   *The club served superb food:* Ibid., 120.

169   *attracted notables:* Ibid., 121.

169   *"many on the borderline":* George E. Worthington, "The Night Clubs of New York," *Survey*, January 1929, 413, quoted in Mowry, ed., *The Twenties*, 109.

170   *gold-plated faucets:* Deirdre Bair, *Al Capone: His Life, Legacy, and Legend*, 116.

170   *"dainty manicured nails":* Frank J. Wilson and Beth Day, *Special Agent: A Quarter Century with the Treasury Department and the Secret Service*, 43.

170   *the Four Deuces brothel:* Ling, *Run the Rum In*, 111.

171   *two hundred murders:* Harvard case study quoted in Bair, *Al Capone*, 74.

171   *"a harbor for criminals":* Helen Muir, *Miami, U.S.A.*, 165.

171   *the buyer's agent of record:* "Capone Deal Involves Lummis," *Miami Daily News*, June 22, 1928.

15
"A PARADE OF PINK ELEPHANTS AND GREEN MONKEYS"

172   *deposits in Florida banks spiked:* Tebeau and Marina, *History of Florida*, 371.

172   *the Commercial Bank and Trust Company:* Fox, *Truth About Florida*, 51.

172   *$37 million a month:* Ibid., 135.

172   *taking with them $20 million:* Tebeau and Marina, *History of Florida*, 370.

172   *twenty thousand of its citizens:* Sessa, "Anti-Florida Propaganda and Counter Measures During the 1920s," 42.

173   *Carey A. Hardee:* Raymond B. Vickers, *Panic in Paradise: Florida's Crash of 1926*, 33.

173   *90 percent of the Florida banks:* Ibid., 5.

173   *"speculating with depositors' money":* Ibid., 6.

173   *his promise to build more highways:* The progressive sympathies of California's Senator Hiram Johnson were off-putting to conservative businessmen and helped make Florida an attractive alternative to the West Coast, according to Sobel, *Money Manias*, 279.

174   *"paved only with good intentions":* Ballinger, *Miami Millions*, 9.

174   *"put her people on paved highways":* Ibid., 100.

174   *"The smell of money in Florida":* Shelby, "Florida Frenzy," *Harper's Monthly*, 177.

174   *for his famous pyramid scheme:* IRCs were discounted international postal coupons, say, from Italy, that could be redeemed to purchase stamps in the United States. Ponzi spotted an arbitrage opportunity, realizing that once redeemed for stamps in America, the stamps could be sold for a profit—for more than the coupon was bought for in Italy. On top of this legitimate arbitrage opportunity, he built a phony pyramid scheme that used the moneys invested from later investors to provide the "returns" for earlier investors.

175   *he faked suicide:* Mitchell Zuckoff, *Ponzi's Scheme: The True Story of a Financial Legend*, 306.

175   *sewing underwear:* Ibid., 307.

175   *"the best show that was ever staged":* Charles Ponzi, *The Rise of Mr. Ponzi*, 150.

175   *money rushed into Florida investments:* Sobel, *Money Manias*, 290.

176   *"a mighty vacuum":* Jane Fisher, *Fabulous Hoosier*, 172.

176   *"They trafficked in human greed":* Foster, *Castles in the Sand*, 214.

177   *"like ticks to a cow":* Ballinger, *Miami Millions*, 98. Walter Greene and the Miami Board of Realtors cracked down on binder speculation in their October meeting with a series of new requirements on timely filings of abstracts and limitations on assignees. See Stuart B. McIver, *The Greatest Sale on Earth: The Story of the Miami Board of Realtors, 1920–1980*, 66.

177   *"resale" services:* Vanderblue, "Florida Land Boom," pt. 2, 120n8.

177   *sold a month later:* Ibid., 124n15.

177   *residential real estate in downtown Miami:* Weigall, *Boom in Paradise*, 41.

177   *Broadway in Midtown Manhattan:* Vanderblue, "Florida Land Boom," pt. 2, 125n16.

177   *routinely, and recklessly, lending to builders:* Weigall, *Boom in Paradise*, 232.

177   *A bungalow could be built:* Ibid.

177   *A leading Miami contractor:* Roberts, *Florida*, 119.

178   *the record set by the* Detroit News*:* Frank B. Sessa, "Miami in 1926," *Tequesta: The Journal of the Historical Association of Southern Florida* 21 (Spring 1961): 22.

178   *674,738 separate classified ads:* Ibid.

178   *the cost of a haircut:* Vanderblue, "Florida Land Boom," pt. 2, 123n13; George, "Brokers, Binders, and Builders," 48.

178   *a surprisingly low price:* McIver, *Greatest Sale on Earth*, 67–68.

179   *the full sale price had to be declared:* The top marginal tax rate had dropped from 58 percent to 54 percent in the early twenties and then to 25 percent in 1925, where it would remain until 1931. This was way down from a top tax rate of 77 percent—on income of more than $1 million—in 1918, at the conclusion of World War I. To get the benefit of the 12.5 percent long-term capital gains tax treatment a piece of property had to be held for two years.

179   *damage had been done:* Tebeau and Marina, *History of Florida*, 371.

179   *"Watch your step!":* "Even Florida Is Not Fool-Proof," *Forbes*, October 1, 1925, quoted in Fox, *Truth About Florida*, 23.

179   *"a crash the likes of which":* Oscar H. Smith, "Terrible Crash Is Sure to Come," *Immigration Bulletin*, October 1925, quoted in Sessa, "Anti-Florida Propaganda and Counter Measures During the 1920s," 44.

179   *"They found land on my property":* Milton Berle, quoted in Gary R. Mormino, *Land of Sunshine, State of Dreams: A Social History of Modern Florida*, 44.

179   *"Miami never had a boom":* "Millions of Capital Drawn to Miami," *New York Times*, March 15, 1925.

180   *"Land values are mounting steadily":* Seebohm, *Boca Rococo*, 219.

180   *"So buy up!":* J. Bruce Cumming Jr., "A Brief Florida Real Estate History," Appraisal Institute, West Coast Florida Chapter, September 6, 2006.

180   *"There is no answer":* J. Frederick Essary, "Have Faith in Florida!" *New Republic* 44 (October 14, 1925). This would likely have appeared on newsstands just before the event at the Waldorf-Astoria on October 9.

180   *"northern propaganda":* Vanderblue, "Florida Land Boom," pt. 2, 259n12.

181   *the old and celebrated Waldorf-Astoria:* The old Waldorf-Astoria would be razed in 1929 to make room for the Empire State Building. The current Waldorf-Astoria on Park Avenue would be completed in 1931.

181   *"splendid, convincing speeches":* Ballinger, *Miami Millions*, 129.

181   *"Florida today made her appeal":* Ibid., 128.

182   *"pink elephants and green monkeys":* Ibid., 129.

182 *"timely words of warning"*: "Floridians Getting Uneasy," *New York Times*, October 14, 1925, 1.

182 *"dead as a salted mackerel"*: Ballinger, *Miami Millions*, 129.

16
PIRATES OF PROMOTION

183 *"an exploding cigar convulsed him"*: Burke, *Rogue's Progress*, 239.

183 *whose eyes glowed in the dark:* Marquis James, *Alfred I. du Pont: The Family Rebel*, 164-165. See also Burke, *Rogue's Progress*, 239.

183 *"a screwball; a peasant"*: Burke, *Rogue's Progress*, 239.

183 *stroked the college crew:* William H. A. Carr, *The du Ponts of Delaware: A Fantastic Dynasty*, 226.

184 *an early example of a leveraged buyout:* The three partners paid $15.36 million in 1902 for a business that was easily worth $24 million. They issued 100,000 shares in a new company and traded 33,600 of these shares, worth $3.36 million, and $12 million in purchase-money notes that payed 4 percent interest, for the outstanding shares of the old company. The three managing partners, Coleman, Pierre, and Alfred, put up only $2,100 in cash. Thirteen years later when Coleman sold his stake it was worth $13.8 million. See Marquis James, *Alfred I. du Pont*, 157, 267.

184 *the largest office building in the world:* The new Equitable Building replaced the original Equitable Building, which had been gutted by fire—a building that itself was historic because, as the first to feature passenger elevators, it was considered, by some, to be the nation's first bona fide skyscraper.

184 *"a brain of the first order"*: Marquis James, *Alfred I. du Pont*, 148.

185 *Boca Raton:* Boca Raton translates to "mouth of the rat" and not "inlet of sharp pointed rocks," as was later suggested. See Curl, *Mizner's Florida*, 217n9.

185 *"I have a million dollars"*: Johnston, *Legendary Mizners*, 224–25.

185 *"intoxicated with dreams of glory"*: Waugh, "Miznerland" (unpublished typescript), chap. 9, 2.

186 *stock operator Jesse Livermore:* Curl, *Mizner's Florida*, 139.

186 *a subdivision for the homes of black workers:* Ibid., 218n20.

186 *London's classy Burlington Arcade:* Ibid., 218n21.

187 *"to give Florida and the nation"*: Perkins and Caughman, *Addison Mizner: The Architect*, 247.

187 *"to build a new Byzantium"*: Burke, *Rogue's Progress*, 228.

187 *"for the man of moderate means"*: "Boca Raton Homes at Under $10,000," *New York Sun*, January 2, 1926, Mizner Collection, Boca Raton Historical Society.

187 *no one wanted to be considered middle class:* Curl, *Mizner's Florida*, 217n17.

187 *"Get the big snobs"*: Quoted in Johnston, *Legendary Mizners*, 212.

188 *"gravity worthy of the Harvard Business School"*: Burke, *Rogue's Progress*, 221.

189 *"six television sets to a blind man"*: Waugh, "Miznerland" (unpublished type-script), ch. 6, 6.

189 *"Addison Mizner's culminating achievement"*: Newspaper advertising that appeared in the *Palm Beach Post* and the *New York Times* in late 1925 and early 1926. Gillis, *Boomtime Boca*, 34.

189 *"the sun porch of America"*: Cumming, "Brief Florida Real Estate History," 11. See also publicity for Boca Raton, Mizner Collection, Boca Raton Historical Society.

189 *"Exaggeration has no place"*: Advertisement for Boca Raton, Mizner Collection, Boca Raton Historical Society.

189 *$25 million worth of lots:* Curl, *Mizner's Florida*, 154.

189 *soared from $100 per share:* Burke, *Rogue's Progress*, 222.

189 *doubled and tripled in value:* Donald W. Curl, "Boca Raton and the Florida Land Boom of the 1920s," *Tequesta: The Journal of the Historical Association of Southern Florida* 1, no. 46 (1986): 24.

189 *"I am happier today"*: *National*, December 1925, 205, quoted in Caroline Seebohm, *Boca Rococo*, 218.

190 *"I am the greatest resort"*: Publicity for Boca Raton, Mizner Collection, Boca Raton Historical Society.

190 *"the flower of genuine aristocracy"*: Advertisement in Turner, *The Florida Land Boom of the 1920s*, 80.

190 *"believed in being very, very careful"*: Nolan, *Fifty Feet in Paradise*, 218.

191 *"Am deeply chagrined"*: Burke, *Rogue's Progress*, 241.

191 *"Attach this advertisement"*: Perkins and Caughman, *Addison Mizner: The Architect*, 257.

191 *potential personal liability:* Coleman du Pont was right about this liability. The lawsuits came in 1929, claiming that du Pont and Livermore and the other board members were complicit in the false advertising for Boca Raton.

191 *"General du Pont resigned"*: "Gen. Du Pont Resigns from Mizner Concern," *New York Times*, November 25, 1925, 10.

192 *"obliged to sever our connection"*: "More Directors Quit Mizner Firm," *New York Times*, November 29, 1925, 25.

193 *an array of obvious conflicts of interest:* Vickers, *Panic in Paradise*, 59–74.

194 *"a truly Lucullan repast"*: *Palm Beach Post*, February 8, 1926, quoted in Curl, "Boca Raton and the Florida Land Boom of the 1920s," 31.

194 *"the foremost genius"*: Ibid.

194 *a "Spanish gem"*: Giles Edgerton, "Great Modern Hotels: Their Architecture and Decoration—The Ritz-Carlton Cloister of Boca Raton Florida," *Arts and Decoration*, April 1926, 57.

195   *such luminaries as the Stotesburys:* "Dinner Dance Opens New Florida Hotel," *New York Times*, February 7, 1926, 24, quoted in Curl, "Boca Raton and the Florida Land Boom of the 1920s," 31.

195   *"All they need is a little rope":* Cumming, "Brief Florida Real Estate History," 12.

17
LULL BEFORE THE STORM

196   *sales totaling $18.1 million:* Tebeau and Marina, *History of Florida*, 369.

196   *A mammoth waterfront hotel:* Nolan, *Fifty Feet in Paradise*, 208.

197   *collateral for a $250,000 loan:* James W. Covington, "The Tampa Bay Hotel," *Tequesta: The Journal of the Historical Association of Southern Florida* 1, no. 26 (1966): 3–20.

197   *"the French court will grant divorce decrees":* Frank Shutts to Carl Fisher, February 24, 1927, Fisher Papers, Historical Museum of South Florida, quoted in Hungness, *I Love to Make the Dirt Fly!*, 124.

198   *"I have a fiddler here":* Carl Fisher telegram to Henry Ford, March 13, 1926, Fisher Papers, box 1, Automobile men, 34, HistoryMiami Museum.

198   *"If you are at the end of your rope":* Carl Fisher to Will Rogers, undated, circa October 1925, Fisher Papers, box 15, Will Rogers, 10. HistoryMiami Museum.

198   *"butter and egg men":* "Butter and egg men" is a term for the *Babbitt*-like small-town businessmen and farmers who spent money ostentatiously in the big cities.

198   *"hunting ground of predatory women":* Jane Fisher, *Fabulous Hoosier*, 169.

198   *"Get out while the going is good":* Ibid., 176.

198   *"Take all our property off the market":* He typically demanded 25 percent down payment and usually offered a 10 percent discount to anyone who paid all cash.

198   *had sold $23 million:* Jane Fisher, *Fabulous Hoosier*, 179.

199   *the same partners:* Ibid., 186.

199   *"make the land":* Ibid.

199   *"city of medieval cottages":* Advertisement for Montauk Manor. Fisher collection, History/Miami Museum.

199   *Bayview Colony:* Lots sold for $8,000 to $10,000 initially but were later steeply discounted.

199   *"you goddamn winter loafers":* Jane Fisher, *Fabulous Hoosier*, 187.

200   *"That was the real ending":* Ibid., 165.

200   *"the craving always came back":* Ibid., 192.

200   *La Dame aux Camélias: La Dame aux Camélias* was a novel by Alexandre Dumas publisher in 1848. Fisher, *Fabulous Hoosier*, 180.

200   *"Your nerves will soon snap":* Jane Fisher, *Fabulous Hoosier*, 181.

201   *a gambling club:* Wynne and Moorhead, *Paradise for Sale*, 163.

201   *"Lincoln and Napoléon!":* Jane Fisher, *Fabulous Hoosier*, 195.

201   *"a good slapping":* Mizner, unpublished typescript, 88.

202   *taking flying lessons:* Alice DeLamar undated letter, 8, Mizner files, Palm Beach Historical Society.

202   *"a capricious egotist":* Ibid.

202   *Arabian-inspired decor:* Turner, *Florida Land Boom*, 38.

203   *"And I loved him":* Ibid., 35.

203   *ten brand-new Cadillac sedans:* Ibid., 69.

203   *some 18,000 residents:* Cumming, "Brief Florida Real Estate History," 15.

204   *"you will blame yourself":* Advertisement for Croissantania in Gillis, *Boomtime Boca*, 92.

204   *a decade of lawsuits:* Cumming, "Brief Florida Real Estate History," 18.

204   *"the entire world":* Tyler Treadway, "Picture City Promised Hollywood Glitz in 1920s in What Is Now Hobe Sound," TCPalm, last modified October 11, 2012.

204   *"a convert of his own preaching":* Fuller, *This Was Florida's Boom*, 24.

205   *sold it a week later:* Sobel, *Money Manias*, 292.

205   *Desi Arnaz:* Turner, *Florida Land Boom*, 32.

205   *$11 million oversubscribed:* Ibid., 70.

205   *in six and a half hours:* Redford, *Billion-Dollar Sandbar*, 161.

206   *the glass dance floor:* Ballinger, *Miami Millions*, 47.

206   *"the despoiling effects of time":* Ibid.

207   *"all the money in the world":* M. M. Cloutier, "Palm Beach History: When Ziegfeld Gave Palm Beach Its Own Follies," *Palm Beach (FL) Daily News*, March 2, 2019.

207   *sales manager for Hollywood Pines:* Ballinger, *Miami Millions*, 142,

207   *more Rolls-Royce and Lincoln cars:* Roger W. Babson, *Actions and Reactions: An Autobiography of Roger W. Babson*, 325.

208   *"rubbing shoulders in a cabaret":* Ellin Mackay, "Why We Go to Cabarets," *New Yorker*, November 28, 1925, 8.

208   *"the genius of the average":* Claude Moore Fuss, *Calvin Coolidge: The Man from Vermont*, 500.

208   *six hot dogs in a single sitting:* Drye, *For Sale*, 87.

208   *"les années folles":* Raymond F. Betts, "Disorder: Europe in the 1920s," *Europe in Retrospect*, Britannica.com.

209   *industrial aesthetic:* Le Corbusier's vision of an ideal or "radiant" city was in stark contrast to that of George Merrick and the other proponents of the City Beautiful Movement. He argued for a utopian city that featured a severe grid of streets and concrete skyscrapers built around a transport node of motorways, a railroad terminal, and an airport—all designed to replace the historic European cities designed around a church or a cathedral.

209   *beat the amateur collegians:* Harner, *Florida's Promoters*, 69.

210   *"rats leaving a sinking ship"*: McIver, *Greatest Sale on Earth*, 68.

210   *bonuses to its seventy-two salesmen:* Ibid., 69.

210   *"The Florida madness"*: "The Florida Madness," *New Republic* 45 (January 27, 1926): 259.

211   *losses totaled more than $2 million:* Ballinger, *Miami Millions*, 60.

212   *"Nero fiddled while Rome burned"*: "Fireproof Hotels in Palm Beach Plan," *New York Times*, March 22, 1925, 5.

212   *"the dance of the dollars"*: From subtitle, Ballinger, *Miami Millions*.

213   *"the fly-by-night organizations"*: Waugh, "Miznerland" (unpublished typescript).

213   *"the greatest of all of Coral Gables fine sections"*: Parks, *George Merrick*, 219.

213   *481 hotels and apartment complexes:* Smiley, *Knights of the Fourth Estate*, 70.

214   *the Biltmore's Giralda tower:* The tower was designed by the architects Schultze & Weaver, who built three other Giralda towers in Florida: one for the Freedom Tower in Miami, initially the headquarters for the *Miami Daily News*, and for the very grand Roney-Plaza Hotel on Miami Beach, and finally for the third iteration of the Breakers Hotel in Palm Beach. Their towers may have been a homage to Madison Square Garden's Giralda tower built by McKim, Mead & White with its weathervane of Diana on top, a building sadly torn down in 1926. Or perhaps their towers were a homage to Christopher Columbus, the onetime Italian wool weaver who departed for the new world from the port of Seville, near the site of the Cathedral of Seville and the original Giralda tower, now a UNESCO World Heritage Site.

214   *"High Olympus"*: 1926 unpublished manuscript, Merrick Collection, University of Miami.

214   *rare imported tiles:* Parks, *George Merrick*, 235.

214   *$4 million in land and building sales:* George, "Brokers, Binders, and Builders," 38.

214   *he turned down an $80 million offer:* Turner, *Florida Land Boom*, 67.

215   *"one of the most beautiful residences"*: Parks, *George Merrick*, 243.

215   *"captive of his own publicity"*: Vickers, *Panic in Paradise*, 19.

216   *"my own lack of faith"*: Weigall, *Boom in Paradise*, 237.

216   *"for health and happiness"*: Millas and Uguccioni, *Coral Gables: Miami Riviera*, 38.

216   *"I didn't believe any of them"*: Weigall, *Boom in Paradise*, 241.

216   *"the up-to-then select few"*: Ibid., 243.

216   *the $1 million Miami Coliseum:* Merrick touted the fact that the structure included an 84,000-pound steel beam that would be used to support the proscenium arch, "the largest piece of steel ever to enter Florida." According to Ballinger in *Miami Millions*, 108, the acoustics and layout were so terrible that the building would require a complete rebuild.

217   *"I was bitterly regretting it":* Weigall, *Boom in Paradise,* 244.

217   *"we were all madmen":* Ibid., 245.

218   *"the train roared on":* Ibid., 255.

218   *he was gone:* T. H. Weigall returned to London, married the daughter of a tea merchant, and joined her family's business. He died of pneumonia in 1935 at age thirty-four leaving behind his wife and two daughters. His account of the Florida boom, *Boom in Paradise,* was published in 1932.

218   *heavyweight boxer Jack Dempsey:* Sessa, "Miami in 1926," 25.

219   *"a slight attack of colic":* Quoted in ibid., 27.

219   *"a very good position to deny it":* Parks, *George Merrick,* 252.

219   *could not meet his $5 million pledge:* Ibid.

220   *a community with "a soul":* Ibid.

220   *"the Second Phase":* Ibid., 255.

220   *"The world's greatest poker game":* Stella Crossley, "Florida Cashes in Her Chips," *Nation,* January 7, 1926, 11, quoted in Tindall, "Bubble in the Sun," 111.

220   *"'Go ahead and hire them'":* Fuller, *This Was Florida's Boom,* 21.

221   *purely speculative purposes:* Harner, *Florida's Promoters,* 70.

221   *"we knew a hurricane had hit":* Kay Murphy, "Merrick's Dream Castles Now Real, but Their Lines Have 'Gone Modern,'" *Miami Herald,* n.d., ca. 1970, Merrick Collection, HistoryMiami Museum.

18

HURRICANES

225   *Dudley Field Malone:* A prominent divorce lawyer, Malone was also a failed candidate for governor of New York in 1920 and co-counsel with Clarence Darrow for the defense in the Scopes Trial. He later became the chief counsel for 20th Century Fox and acted in a number of movies.

225   *"South Florida Wiped Out":* Jane Fisher, *Fabulous Hoosier,* 200.

225   *"Miami Beach Total Loss":* Ibid., 201.

226   *Peak winds:* L. F. Reardon, *The Florida Hurricane and Disaster: 1926,* 110.

226   *"The wind blew so hard":* Sessa, "Miami in 1926," 33.

227   *halfway to the ceiling:* Source is the Wikipedia entry on Hurricane of 1926.

227   *The yacht Nohab:* Jerry M. Fisher, *The Pacesetter: The Untold Story of Carl G. Fisher,* 303.

228   *"a sea of raving white water":* Douglas, *Everglades,* 339.

228   *"covered with green grapefruit":* Reardon, *Florida Hurricane and Disaster,* 8.

229   *"ripped from their foundations":* Sessa, "Miami in 1926," 33.

229   *"a hundred steamer whistles":* Reardon, *Florida Hurricane and Disaster,* 9.

229   *"The force of the wind":* Ibid., 10.

229 *"The sea was walking the earth"*: Zora Neale Hurston, *Their Eyes Were Watching God*, 161. Hurston is not specific as to the year of the storm that she describes in the novel. The 1928 hurricane actually resulted in far larger loss of life, and most of the dead were the black residents of the towns just south and east of Lake Okeechobee.

230 *"shops lay sprawled"*: Reardon, *Florida Hurricane and Disaster*, 11.

230 *17,884 families had been left homeless:* Ibid., 110.

230 *Building loss in Miami alone:* Ballinger, *Miami Millions*, 155–56.

231 *"There will be no future change"*: Reardon, *Florida Hurricane and Disaster*, 109.

231 *"Florida never went"*: Nolan, *Fifty Feet in Paradise*, 222.

231 *"a world record in coming back"*: Reardon, *Florida Hurricane and Disaster*, 112.

231 *"out of the ruins of the old"*: Ibid., 109.

231 *"[T]he order to rebuild"*: Ibid.

232 *"more good than harm"*: Douglas, *Voice of the River*, 173.

232 *"workshop"*: Davis, *Everglades Providence*, 321.

232 *"I often think of it"*: Lucy D. Jones, "Marjory Stoneman Douglas' House in Coconut Grove."

232 *"you can live indefinitely"*: *Miami Herald*, February 15, 1953, quoted in Davis, *Everglades Providence*, 321.

232 *"the Cardboard College"*: Cleary, "Denman Fink, Dream Coordinator to George Merrick and the Development of Coral Gables, Florida," n157.

234 *"extreme fatigue"*: Parks, *George Merrick*, 269.

234 *"poor Humpty Dumpty"*: "Twinkle, Twinkle Little Star," Merrick Collection, University of Miami; Parks, *George Merrick*, 269n27.

234 *"salute George E. Merrick"*: Parks, *George Merrick*, 287.

234 *Comprehensive Refinancing Plan:* Ibid., 291.

235 *"a halo of hokum"*: "Bitter Attack on Present Administration Launched in Citizen League Talks," *Miami Riviera* (Coral Gables, FL), April 20, 1928, quoted in Parks, *George Merrick*, 295.

236 *the heavyweight boxing title match:* The rematch a year later would feature the famous Long Count and would be won, again, by Tunney.

236 *"the last dollar he earned"*: Kite-Powell, *History of Davis Islands*, 91.

236 *Raymond Schindler:* The renowned private eye Raymond Schindler, who was the focus of a three-part profile in the *New Yorker* in 1943, is best remembered today as the sleuth who never solved the 1943 Harry Oakes murder case in Nassau in the Bahamas that tangentially involved the Duke of Windsor. Schindler was present at Davis's first wedding and may well have been brought along to be the best man at Davis's planned second marriage. Fittingly, Schindler never succeeded in dispelling the mystery over the Davis death, either.

237   *an overheard lovers' quarrel:* The best analysis of this mystery is found in Kite-Powell, *History of Davis Islands*, 93–98.

237   *The last record of her whereabouts:* "Stories and Theories on the Death of D. P. Davis," TampaPix.com, https://www.tampapix.com/dpdavis3.htm.

238   *"Almost beside myself with distress":* Quoted in Burke, *Rogue's Progress*, 221.

238   *sold out of bankruptcy:* Vickers, *Panic in Paradise*, 173.

239   *he would spend more than $8 million:* Stanley Johnson and Phyllis Shapiro, *Once Upon a Time: The Story of Boca Raton*, 44.

240   *"died with him":* Showalter, ed., *Many Mizners: California Clan Extraordinary*, 62.

240   *"a writ blows in":* Burke, *Rogue's Progress*, 127.

240   *"shuffling these fearsome documents":* Ibid., 247.

240   *"he could go nuts":* Edward Dean Sullivan, *Fabulous Wilson Mizner*, 305.

240   *the Ambassador Hotel:* The Ambassador Hotel, built in 1921 (and now demolished) was the venue for the glamorous Cocoanut Grove nightclub, which no doubt added to its allure for Wilson. More infamously, it was the place where Robert F. Kennedy was assassinated on June 5, 1968, the night he won the California Democratic presidential primary.

240   *"I am enclosing a list of the bills":* Addison Mizner to Wilson Mizner, July 1, 1927, quoted in Seebohm, *Boca Rococo*, 245.

240   *"I have a vague regard for him":* Burke, *Rogue's Progress*, 245.

241   *"a real talent for comforting":* Johnston, *Legendary Mizners*, 302.

241   *"his gaunt Mephistophelean cast of countenance":* Waugh, "Miznerland" (unpublished typescript), 8.

241   *a brawl that wrecked the restaurant:* Burke, *Rogue's Progress*, 266.

241   *"as lovable as he was monstrous":* Loos, *Kiss Hollywood Good-Bye*, 130.

241   *"the only one I knew and loved":* Seebohm, *Boca Rococo*, 260.

242   *"will live in the history of American Architecture":* Mizner, *Florida Architecture of Addison Mizner*, xxxi.

243   *"the greatest compliment ever paid a living architect":* Addison Mizner to Alice DeLamar, undated, Palm Beach Historical Society, quoted in Donald W. Curl introduction to Mizner, *Florida Architecture of Addison Mizner*, xx.

243   *skeletons were still being discovered:* Tebeau and Marina, *History of Florida*, 372–73.

244   *His backers:* Curl, *Mizner's Florida*, 167.

244   *he went so far as to pledge the Everglades Club:* Edward C. Michener, *The Everglades Club: A Retrospective, 1919–1985*, 30.

244   *"obtaining money under false pretenses":* "Paris Singer Arrested on Fraud Charge," *Palm Beach Times*, April 9, 1927.

244   *his confidence and health shattered:* Michener, *Everglades Club*, 31.

245   *"It is the one name":* Paris Singer to Addison Mizner, November 28, 1927, quoted in Seebohm, *Boca Rococo,* 234.

245   *"I am looking forward to seeing you":* Ibid.

245   *while cruising the Nile:* Alice DeLamar undated letter in Mizner file, 9. Palm Beach Historical Society.

245   *Singer died suddenly of a heart attack:* Although the Associated Press and the *New York Times* reported that he died in London on June 24, 1932, shortly after arriving to consult a heart specialist, it is possible that they were misled and that was the date his remains arrived back in the United Kingdom.

245   *died the night of June 24:* "Paris Singer Dead: Son of Inventor," *New York Times,* June 25, 1932, 13.

245   *appraised at $1.5 million in 1927:* Michener, *Everglades Club,* 32–33.

245   *the suddenly popular Maurice Fatio:* Perkins and Caughman, *Addison Mizner: The Architect,* 292.

246   *Casa Coe da Sol:* Stephen Perkins and James Caughman think the design, a departure for Mizner, may owe more to the input of Mizner's draftsman Byron Simonson than is generally acknowledged. See ibid., 298.

19
SPECULATIVE DEMENTIA

247   *Roger W. Babson:* Roger Babson is best remembered today for founding Babson College, a once all-male private business school in Wellesley, Massachusetts, and Webber College, a once all-female business college in Babson Park, Florida, today known as Webber International University; both are now coed.

247   *Frederick S. Ruth:* Frederick Ruth's family had bought the acreage in the 1880s. The plan for Mountain Lake was based on the Roland Park suburb of Baltimore where Ruth grew up.

247   *loved Florida for its bright sunshine:* Babson, *Actions and Reactions,* 311.

248   *the lien-bond combination:* Fuller, *This Was Florida's Boom,* 63.

248   *the highest public debt per capita:* Ibid.

248   *"no banker or bond expert":* Babson, *Actions and Reactions,* 331.

248   *"I bought largely without visiting":* Ibid.

248   *expenditure on home repairs:* Jackson, *Crabgrass Frontier,* 193.

249   *the value of new nonfarm housing in the country increased by 49 percent:* Alexander James Field, "Uncontrolled Land Development and the Duration of the Depression in the United States," *Journal of Economic History* 52, no. 4 (December 1992): 795.

249   *20 percent of all residential construction:* Ibid., 787.

249   *twenty-four years would pass:* Ibid.

249   *began to rethink all their borrowing:* After the Great Depression, Irving Fisher
      coined the term the "debt-deflation cycle" to describe this phenomenon. The im-
      pact of wage cuts on the indebted household, as Mian and Sufi write, "leads to a vi-
      cious cycle in which indebted households cut spending, which leads firms to reduce
      wages, which leads to higher debt burdens for households, which leads them to cut
      back further." See Atif Mian and Amir Sufi, *House of Debt: How They (and You)
      Caused the Great Recession, and How We Can Prevent It from Happening Again*, 55.

249   *Some forty local banks:* Tebeau and Marina, *History of Florida*, 378.

250   *caused even more banks in Florida to fail:* Vickers, *Panic in Paradise*, 73.

250   *failed again in 1928:* Vanderblue, "Florida Land Boom," pt. 2, 268.

250   *new ones sprang up in their place:* Fuller, *This Was Florida's Boom*, 54.

250   *banker Bion Hall Barnett:* Harner, *Florida's Promoters*, 41.

250   *to a low of $12 million:* Smiley, *Knights of the Fourth Estate*, 94.

250   *"I am E. C. Romfh":* Ibid., 95.

251   *12,677 banks failed:* J. E. Dovell and J. G. Richardson, *History of Banking in Flor-
      ida, 1828–1954*, 128.

251   *bad mortgages and real estate loans:* "Bank of U.S. Closes Doors," *New York Times*,
      December 12, 1930, 1.

251   *Banks in Chicago followed suit:* In one notable case, a real estate developer named
      John Bain, who owned a chain of banks, lent himself $1.75 million to speculate
      in real estate.

251   *to lose nearly 20 percent:* Jim Luke, "Banks Failures: The 1920's and the Great
      Depression," October 26, 2009, EconProph.com.

252   *costing customers 28 percent to 40 percent:* Ibid.

252   *it is increasingly difficult to stop:* Whether the losses that ensue are "real" or "nom-
      inal," they impact the psychology of the average consumer almost equally, espe-
      cially given that everyone's mortgage payments continue to be in nominal terms;
      a loss feels like a loss.

252   *nor was the Fed:* Eugene N. White, "Lessons from the Great American Real Es-
      tate Boom and Bust of the 1920s" (working paper 15573, National Bureau of
      Economic Research, Cambridge, MA, December 2009), 23.

252   *"This is a fundamental feature of debt":* Mian and Sufi, *House of Debt*, 23.

252   House of Debt: Mian and Sufi advocate for "shared responsibility mortgages,"
      ones where the banks share in the risks associated with real estate downturns, as a
      way to help mitigate the damage done to lower-income households.

252   *"The problem of levered losses":* Ibid., 59.

252   *we are all in the same mess:* Ibid.

253   *Even in Washington, DC:* White, "Lessons from the Great American Real Estate
      Boom and Bust of the 1920s," 9.

253   *In Manhattan:* Ibid..

253   *falling again more precipitously:* Tom Nicholas and Anna Scherbina, "Real Estate Prices During the Roaring Twenties and the Great Depression," *Real Estate Economics* 41, no. 2 (Summer 2013): 278–309.

253   *housing starts were in a steep, even startling, decline:* White, "Lessons from the Great American Real Estate Boom and Bust of the 1920s," 6–7, fig. 4-6.

253   *"the 'slow-burn' spillover":* Carmen M. Reinhart and Kenneth S. Rogoff, *This Time Is Different: Eight Centuries of Financial Folly,* 241.

253   *"things take longer to happen":* Quoted in Frank Berlage, "Why Fixing Trade Deficits Is Essential," *Barron's,* January 9, 2017, 25.

254   *the stock sold for 50 cents:* Bryan Taylor, "The Land Co. of Florida and the Florida Real Estate Bubble," Global Financial Data.com blog, last modified October 18, 2013. http://gfdblog.com/GFD/Blog/the-land-company-of-florida-and-florida-real-estate-bubble.

255   *Benjamin Graham's memorable phrase:* "In the short run, the market is a voting machine; in the long run, however, it becomes a weighing machine."—Benjamin Graham.

255   *"a perfect orgy of speculation":* Philip Snowden, "Year's Worst Break Hits Stock Market," *New York Times,* October 3, 1929, 1; *Wall Street Journal,* October 4, 1929, 20.

255   *just how overextended stock prices were:* See, for example, Harold Bierman Jr., "The 1929 Stock Market Crash." EH.net, http://eh.net/encyclopedia/the-1929-stock-market-crash.

255   *The Dow Jones Industrial Average:* The Dow Jones Industrial Average is the unweighted average of thirty of the largest and soundest industrial companies in the United States. Industrial stocks were the major focus of speculation during this period, making this index an important stock market barometer.

255   *historically a high number:* Gerald Sirkin, "The Stock Market of 1929 Revisited: A Note," *Business History Review* 49, no. 2 (Summer 1975): 225, https://fraser.stlouisfed.org/files/docs/meltzer/sirsto75.pdf.

256   *"The bigger your house":* David Wiedemer, Robert A. Wiedemer, and Cindy Spitzer, *Aftershock: Protect Yourself and Profit in the Next Global Financial Meltdown,* 172.

256   *the dividend yield. . . of around 4 percent:* This is an average of the various dividend yields of the stocks in the index. Each is calculated by dividing the dollar value of the stock dividends into their respective stock price. A dividend yield reveals how much a company pays out in dividends relative to its stock price.

256   *did not seem outlandish:* For the last six decades or so the dividend yield has averaged 3.26 percent.

256   *he would reiterate his optimistic forecast:* "Fisher Says Prices of Stocks Are Low: Quotations Have Not Caught Up with Real Values as Yet, He Declares," *New York Times,* October 22, 1929, 24.

256   *the worst stock market call:* Jennifer Latson, "The Worst Stock Tip in History," *Time*, September 3, 2014, http://time.com/3207128/stock-market-high-1929.

256   *the notorious stock speculator Jesse Livermore:* "Livermore Not in Bear Pool," *New York Times*, October 22, 1929, 24.

257   *denied that he was part of a pool:* Despite his windfall in 1929, Jesse Livermore would lose his fortune by 1934 and commit suicide in the cloakroom of the Sherry-Netherland Hotel in Manhattan. Also, with no "uptick rule" in place, as there was later, short sellers could more easily and continuously drive stocks downward without having to wait for an upward tick in the stock price to implement their trades.

257   *On September 5, 1929:* The Dow Jones Industrial Average hit its high of 381.2 on September 3, 1929.

257   *"a serious business depression":* Quoted in Galbraith, *Great Crash 1929,* 85. See also the *Wall Street Journal,* September 6, 1929.

257   *an 89.2 percent decline:* Other indices showed different declines.

258   *the aforementioned price-earnings multiple of 60:* Sirkin, "Stock Market of 1929 Revisited," 226, https://fraser.stlouisfed.org/files/docs/meltzer/sirsto75.pdf.

258   *"to beat the other fellow in our forecasts":* Babson, *Actions and Reactions,* 364.

258   *"it cannot lead to a Great Depression":* Originally in "How the Slump Looks to Three Experts," *Newsweek,* May 25, 1970, 78–79, quoted in Robert S. McElvaine, *The Great Depression: America, 1929–1941,* 48.

258   *gross domestic product (GDP) losses that are twice as large:* "When Bubbles Burst," International Monetary Fund (IMF), *World Economic Outlook,* April 2003, 61.

258   *"Housing is the business cycle":* Edward E. Leamer, "Housing *Is* the Business Cycle" (working paper, National Bureau of Economic Research Working Paper, Cambridge, MA, September 2007).

258   *$57 billion between 1929 and 1933:* For an excellent analysis of the nominal and real wealth effect that takes into effect the 30 percent deflation in these years, see Alexander James Field, "The Interwar Housing Cycle in the Light of 2001–2011: A Comparative Historical Approach" (working paper 18796, National Bureau of Economic Research, Cambridge, MA, February 2013), 23.

258   *smaller than the number of investors in Florida:* John Kenneth Galbraith thought otherwise but does not support his contention. See *Great Crash 1929,* 6–7.

258   *some 1.5 million investors:* Ibid., 78. Galbraith cites a Senate committee report that surveyed member firms of the twenty-nine exchanges to come up with this number.

259   *as low as 1 percent of the population:* We don't know with any certainty how many individuals owned stocks because few surveys were taken at the time. Klein, in *Rainbow's End,* 126, estimates that 15 million owned stock or bonds by end of decade; McElvaine, in *Great Depression,* 4, estimates that 4 million owned stock.

259 *every American playing the market was far from accurate:* Supporting this contention is the idea that only 50,000 margin accounts were added between the end of
1928 and the end of July 1929, the peak period of speculation. Galbraith, *Great
Crash 1929*, 78.

259 *the number of people who bought Florida real estate:* Wilson Mizner was one person who estimated that 15 percent of the population had bought land in Florida.

259 *less than six hundred thousand individuals:* Six hundred thousand accounts received 74 percent of the dividends in 1929, according to McElvaine, *Great Depression*, 43-44.

260 *"it did not produce the Great Depression":* Quoted in Kindleberger, *World Depres-
sion 1929–1939*, 119. Friedman's famous work on the Depression, *A Monetary
History of the United States, 1867–1960*, was coauthored with Anna Jacobson
Schwartz and first published in 1963.

260 *four increases that moved the discount rate:* Murray N. Rothbard, in *America's
Great Depression*, was critical of the Federal Reserve for inflating the money supply by 60 percent from mid 1921 to mid 1928. Commodity and consumer prices,
however, did not reflect this, so others question the Fed's impact.

260 *simple financial contagion:* See Kindleberger, *World Depression 1929–1939*, 20.

260 *Galbraith came up with five causes:* Galbraith, *Great Crash 1929*, 177–84.

260 *The debate continues:* The academic study of the Great Depression is to the field
of economics what the study of *Moby-Dick* is to literary academics—an endless
source of debates, articles, dissertations, and books.

261 *a growing awareness:* Field, "Uncontrolled Land Development and the Duration
of the Depression in the United States."

261 *thirty million abandoned subdivided lots:* National Housing Administration,
Land Assembly, 36–37, quoted in ibid.

261 *thirty million occupied units:* Bureau of the Census, *Historical Statistics*, vol. 2,
series N-238-41, 646.

262 *real estate, not the stock market:* The economist John Kenneth Galbraith, author
of *The Great Crash 1929*, and other works, thought otherwise and minimized its
importance. In his book *A Short History of Financial Euphoria*, 72, he described
the Florida boom merely as "the first manifestation of the speculative mood of
the 1920s." Galbraith also wrote that "While the number of speculators [in Flor-
ida] was almost certainly small compared with the subsequent participation in
the stock market, nearly every community contained a man who was known to
have taken 'quite a beating' in Florida" (*Great Crash 1929*, 6–7). On the relative
numbers involved, he seems simply to have been misinformed.

262 *the current one in the contemporary art market:* See the Barry Avrich documen-
tary *Blurred Lines: Inside the Art World*, Melbar Entertainment Group, April 23,
2017.

262 *difficult to predict, regulate:* Writer and economist John Kenneth Galbraith put it best, writing, "Regulation outlawing financial incredulity or mass euphoria is not a practical possibility." Galbraith, *Short History of Financial Euphoria*, 108.

263 *Missing is a clear estimate:* Sobel, *Money Manias*, 290.

263 *no adequate measure of housing wealth:* There is a further lack of data: National Income and Product Accounts (NIPA), a measure of consumption, has data that only goes back to 1947. One reason there is so little information on home mortgages or real estate prices is that realtors were only just starting to get organized with associations, licenses, and best practices.

263 *Eugene White:* Eugene N. White, "The Great American Real Estate Bubble of the 1920s: Causes and Consequences," October 2008, 33. Eugene White does not go so far as to claim that the collapsing real estate boom brought on the Depression. In his mind it severely weakened the national economy. But he concedes, the boom's "independent effects are difficult to disentangle from the general economic collapse beginning in 1929."

263 *"Data on state banks":* Ibid., 32.

263 *a reliable housing price index:* White, "Lessons from the Great American Real Estate Boom and Bust of the 1920s," 7; see also Caitlin E. Anderson, "The Forgotten Real Estate Boom of the 1920s," *Bubbles, Panics & Crashes, Historical Collections,* Harvard Business School, https://www.library.hbs.edu/hc/crises/intro.html.

263 *equivalent to $15 billion:* This is the real price as measured by the change in Consumer Price Index. A better measure might be relative *income* value, or the value of that money relative to the per capita gross domestic product. The equivalent number then soars to $79.5 billion. See Measuringworth.com for a good discussion of how to calculate relative value. These numbers are 1930 relative to 2018.

263 *some 60 percent of all home mortgages:* Jackson, *Crabgrass Frontier*, 193; see also White, "Lessons from the Great American Real Estate Boom and Bust of the 1920s."

263 *a thousand foreclosures:* Jackson, *Crabgrass Frontier*, 193.

263 *fallen from $5,000 to $3,200:* Ibid.

264 *In Chicago:* White, "Lessons from the Great American Real Estate Boom and Bust of the 1920s."

264 *Farm mortgages:* Kindleberger, *World Depression 1929–1939,* 97.

264 *85 percent of the farms:* Ibid.

264 *exceeded the value of all the rural land:* Galbraith, *Short History of Financial Euphoria,* 68.

264 *"a man of sweeping imagination":* "The Whippoorwill Club's Beginnings," www.whippoorwillclub.org/public/history.

264 *Edward Bok:* In addition to popularizing the mail-order bungalow, Edward Bok is credited with coining the term "living room."

265 *launched other golf club and resort developments:* Most of these golf clubs were planned with golf course designer Seth Raynor.

265 *He pulled the trigger:* "F. S. Ruth Ends Life with Shot in Hotel," *New York Times*, April 23, 1932.

265 *"Poor Fred Ruth!":* Babson, *Actions and Reactions*, 312. The story echoes what happened a generation earlier to Florida developer Hamilton Disston, who was rumored to have committed suicide as a result of his losses.

20
THE DEATH OF BALLYHOO AND HOKUM

266 *Street signs hung:* Edward Dean Sullivan, *Fabulous Wilson Mizner*, 319.

266 *"a city in the grip of death":* Quoted in Frederick Lewis Allen, *Only Yesterday*, 244.

267 *"then abandoned quickly":* John Rothchild, *Up for Grabs: A Trip Through Time and Space in the Sunshine State*, 80.

267 *devoid of topsoil:* Wynne and Moorhead, *Paradise for Sale*, 156.

267 *would bring in less than $10,000:* Cumming, "Brief Florida Real Estate History," 18, www.mapoftheweek.net/Post/342/floridarealestatehistory.pdf.

267 *"In their frantic quest for gold":* Edward Dean Sullivan, *Fabulous Wilson Mizner*, 310.

267 *"the silent troop of monkeys":* Fuller, *This Was Florida's Boom*, 24.

268 *90 percent of the people:* "An estimated 90 percent of those who took part in the boom lost out," according to Hatton, *Tropical Splendor*, 56.

268 *"He would sit and shake":* Fuller, *This Was Florida's Boom*, 28.

268 *forty-one pages of newsprint:* Hatton, *Tropical Splendor*, 56.

268 *his spirit was broken:* Alice DeLamar letter, Mizner file, 11, Palm Beach Historical Society.

268 *"Give that to Addison":* Seebohm, *Boca Rococo*, 253.

268 *additional financial support:* Curl, *Mizner's Florida*, 201.

269 *hoping to do more work in California:* Perkins and Caughman, *Addison Mizner: The Architect*, 293.

269 *"All the flavor was lacking":* Alice DeLamar to Alva Johnston, March 14, 1948, 18, quoted in Seebohm, *Boca Rococo*, 248.

269 *A second volume:* The typescript can be found in both the archives of the Boca Raton Historical Society and the Palm Beach Historical Society.

269 *"I hate work":* Perkins and Caughman, *Addison Mizner: The Architect*, 303.

269 Gentlemen Prefer Blondes: Edward Dean Sullivan, *Fabulous Wilson Mizner*, 321.

270 *"put you in your place":* Seebohm, *Boca Rococo*, 250.

270 *"The comedy goes on":* Johnson, *Legendary Mizners*, 303.

270 *"Thank God Mama is Dead":* Seebohm, *Boca Rococo*, 254.

271 *"the final mild guffaw":* Edward Dean Sullivan, *Fabulous Wilson Mizner*, 323.

271　*"I haven't breathed"*: Seebohm, *Boca Rococo*, 251.

271　*"the most-hated man"*: See Wikipedia, "Jim Tully."

271　*"an immense leprechaun"*: Burke, *Rogue's Progress*, 271.

271　*"culinary thrombosis"*: Seebohm, *Boca Rococo*, 251.

272　*$200 worth of traveler's checks*: Curl, *Mizner's Florida*, 223n40.

272　*his debts*: Ibid..

272　*"You can't be a rascal"*: Burke, *Rogue's Progress*, 278.

273　*"a shady 'architect'"*: Frank G. Lopez, "We Were Having Some People in for Cock-tails," *Architectural Record*, July 1953, 46–48, quoted in Curl, *Mizner's Florida*, 202.

273　*"Many architects have imagination"*: See Tindall, "The Bubble in the Sun," 82. The remark has been widely attributed to Frank Lloyd Wright, but Wright was not uncritical of Mizner's theatricality.

273　*"These are expert plans"*: Ada Louise Huxtable, "The Maverick Who Created Palm Beach," *New York Times,* March 20, 1977, 27.

21
"I USED TO MAKE DREAMS COME TRUE"

274　*he had to spend $1 million*: Redford, *Billion-Dollar Sandbar*, 179.

275　*smoked each day*: Foster, *Castles in the Sand*, 297.

275　*he sold his controlling interest*: Hungness, *I Love to Make the Dirt Fly!*, 126.

275　*"beautiful Montauk Manor"*: Quoted in ibid., 131.

275　*"trying to sell bicycles"*: Ibid., 140.

275　*losing it to foreclosure*: Jane Fisher, *Fabulous Hoosier*, 218.

275　*"I wouldn't have another big house"*: Jerry Fisher, *Pacesetter*, 389.

275　*"it was too far for me to walk"*: Joe McCarthy "The Man Who Invented," *American Heritage, December 1975,* https://www.americanheritage.com/man-who-invented.

275　*He wrote to his old friend*: Fisher sent the same letter to R. F. Garland, in Tulsa.

277　*"find me a buyer"*: Carl Fisher to Will Rogers, February 19, 1932, Fisher Papers, HistoryMiami Museum, box 15, Will Rogers, 29. Rogers had tried to buy the painting years before when it was on sale for $500 in a Chicago art shop, but couldn't afford it at the time. He was amazed to rediscover it years later in Fisher's possession. Fisher refused to sell it to him when Rogers offered him $10,000 for it and instead commissioned a copy of it for him. It seems to have been sold after Fisher's death, for $5,500 in 1948.

277　*once the highest on Miami Beach*: Foster, *Castles in the Sand*, 240.

277　*He was out of cash*: Ibid., 241.

277　*"Added to this anguish"*: Jane Fisher, *Fabulous Hoosier*, 217.

277 *"I have blisters from a rake"*: Foster, *Castles in the Sand*, 273; Carl Fisher to Margaret Fisher, August 1935, Fisher Papers, box 6, Margaret Collier-Correspondence, HistoryMiami Museum.

277 *"Show that to your folks!"*: Carl Fisher to Margaret Collier Fisher, September 11, 1934, Fisher Papers, box 6, Margaret Collier-Correspondence, 1934, 34, HistoryMiami Museum.

278 *impossible not to love the man:* Jane Fisher, *Fabulous Hoosier*, 317.

278 *"lost about twenty-five million"*: Carl Fisher to Claude Mercer, October 5, 1935, Fisher papers, Finances-Personal after Crash, box 5, 45, HistoryMiami Museum.

278 *"I can tell you in a few words"*: Carl Fisher, Indiana Historical Society online, http://www.indianahistory.org/our-collections/library-and-archives/notable-hoosiers/carl-fisher.

279 *"in a hilarious mood"*: Carl Fisher to Barney Oldfield, April 25, 1939, Fisher Papers, box 1, Automobile Men, p. 64.

279 *"Fisher was but human"*: "Carl G. Fisher Rites Conducted on the Beach," *Miami Herald*, July 19, 1939.

280 *"as if to shut out the scene"*: Ibid.

280 *a bronze and stone monument:* The monument is at the corner of Fifitieth Street and Alton Road, Miami Beach.

280 *asked to vacate:* Parks, *George Merrick*, 303.

280 *"South Seas enchantment"*: Ibid., 308.

281 *"he's still there"*: Ballinger, *Miami Millions*, 24.

281 *"Country City"*: Parks, *George Merrick*, 312.

281 *converted into a gas station:* Ibid., 308.

282 *twenty-six cities and towns:* Frederick Lewis Allen, *Only Yesterday*, 245. Although by statute the state of Florida did not itself issue debt during the twenties, the various Florida municipalities had done so, with disastrous results, as Roger Babson knew from costly firsthand experience.

282 *Heading the investigation:* It was called the Protective Committee Commission or Study.

282 *conflict of interest:* Addison Mizner was guilty of a similar conflict of interest when he served as both the developer of Boca Raton and its city planner. William Frazer and John J. Guthrie Jr., *The Florida Land Boom: Speculation, Money, and the Banks,* 125.

283 *"a curious situation"*: "Coral Gables Paid Many to Push Loan: Merrick Tells SEC at Inquiry $30,000 Went to Miami's City Attorney," *New York Times*, September 19, 1935, 37.

283 *buying the Merrick assets:* Ibid.

283 *"using their official position"*: "SEC Sifts Profits in Florida's Boom: Head of Coral Gables Defends Developers and Bares High Promotional Costs," *New York Times,* September 17, 1935, 33.

283 *Merrick personally profited:* In one of the four bond issues, the city of Coral Gables issued the bond, Coral Gables Inc., bought the whole issue; it then resold it to a bank at a 5 percent discount (and thus loss); the bank then sold the issue in turn to a syndicate, with a 2 percent markup, and the syndicate then sold the issue at par to the public, taking a 3 percent commission.

283 *loan-sharking:* Parks, *George Merrick*, 317. Usually loan-sharking is the providing of loans at a usurious interest rate, but it can also be the act of providing loans in return for extraordinary and unjustifiable compensation, as was the case here.

284 *not be paid off until 1961:* Millas and Uguccioni, *Coral Gables: Miami Riviera*, 31.

284 *only 1,812 lots:* In a statement released to the press on March 13, 1926, Merrick said there were 2,500 houses built or under construction. "Tells Great Plans for Coral Gables: Southern Records Broken, Says G. E. Merrick, Owner—Sales Since Jan. $10,000,000," *New York Times*, March 13, 1926.

284 *"It grieves me":* Clifton D. Benson to George Merrick, September 15, 1935, Merrick Collection, University of Miami, quoted in Parks, *George Merrick*, 318.

285 *quit drinking:* Parks, *George Merrick*, 319.

285 *struggling to pay:* Ibid., 325.

285 *"Merrick's feet are on the ground":* Quoted in ibid., 325.

285 *he considered himself a failure:* Harner, *Florida's Promoters*, 65.

286 *The value of his estate:* Ramya Radhakrishnan, "Biography Sheds Light on Coral Gables Founder George Merrick," *Miami Hurricane*, January 28–January 31, 2016, 12.

286 *"the ladder of success":* "Tributes Expressed by Leaders," *Miami Herald*, n.d., ca. March 27, 1942, Merrick Collection, HistoryMiami Museum.

287 *"a domineering attitude":* "Mrs. Sartor Asks Divorce Decree," *Miami Daily News*, May 1, 1949, Merrick Collection, HistoryMiami Museum.

287 *She was down to $3:* Ron Laytner, "Jane Fisher: Lonely Legacy for Miami Beach's First Lady," *Miami Herald*, September 29, 1968.

287 *"I've had it all":* Redford, *Billion-Dollar Sandbar*, 286.

287 *die of a heart attack:* Jane Fisher, *Fabulous Hoosier*, 180.

22
A LEGACY OF GREED AND FOLLY

288 *"Was it thirst for power?":* Jane Fisher, *Fabulous Hoosier*, 190.

288 *"to see steam shovels throwing dirt":* Said to Irving Collins, son of John Collins, quoted in Redford, *Billion-Dollar Sandbar*, 180.

289 *securitization of subprime mortgages:* Turner, *Florida Land Boom*, 4.

289 *5.5 million people:* "Miami, Florida Population 2019, World Population Review, accessed October 5, 2018, worldpopulationreview.com/us-cities/miami.

290   *"We have a finite environment"*: Mark Riley Cardwell, "Attenborough: Poor Countries Are Just as Concerned About the Environment," *Guardian* (US edition) online, October 16, 2013, https://www.theguardian.com/environment/2013/oct/16/attenborough-poorer-countries-concerned-environment.

290   *committed environmentalists*: Others included Dr. Frank Craighead, Johnny Jones, Timothy Keyers, Dr. Gerald Parker, and Dr. Durbin Tabb.

291   *"The endless acres of saw grass"*: Douglas, *Everglades*, 349.

292   *the high drama of its ecology*: See Michael P. Branch, "Our Lady of the Glades: Marjory Stoneman Douglas and *The Everglades: River of Grass*," *Marjorie Kinnan Rawlings Journal of Florida Literature* 8 (1997): 23.

292   *"They're not saved yet"*: Quoted in Sandra Wallus Sammons, *Marjory Stoneman Douglas and the Florida Everglades*, 43.

293   *"a squat little woman"*: Betsy S. Hilbert, "Marjorie Stoneman Douglas and an Antidote to Despair," *Marjorie Kinnan Rawlings Journal of Florida Literature* 8 (1997): 52.

293   *"I'll talk about the Everglades"*: Douglas, *Voice of the River*, 230.

293   *"It was very sorrowful"*: Ibid., 238.

293   *a similar decline in bird numbers*: Lodge, *Everglades Handbook*, 307.

293   *6,250 pairs*: Ibid.

293   *The book remained unfinished*: Here is an excerpt from her Hudson biography: "It was said that he alone, among a very few first nature writers, had brought to scientists a new way of thinking about birds and to the public in general a new awareness of the value of endangered nature as the beautiful basic wealth of mankind." The typescript is in the Marjory Stoneman Douglas Collection at the University of Miami. W. H. Hudson typescript, 2.

294   *"scare the bejesus"*: Rothchild, *Up for Grabs*, 215.

294   *"she was a prophet"*: Margaria Fichter, "Pioneering Environmentalist Marjory Stoneman Douglas Dies at 108," *Miami Herald*, May 14, 1998.

294   *the Presidential Medal of Freedom*: The citation read: "Marjory Stoneman Douglas personifies passionate commitment. Her crusade to preserve and restore the Everglades has enhanced our Nation's respect for our precious environment, reminding all of us of nature's delicate balance. Grateful Americans honor the 'Grandmother of the Glades' by following her splendid example in safeguarding America's beauty and splendor for generations to come."

294   *no stove*: She cooked off a dual hot plate.

294   *author and activist*: Davis, in *Everglades Providence*, 324, describes Douglas as an ecofeminist.

295   *"outstanding habitat for greed"*: Michael Grunwald, *The Swamp: The Everglades, Florida, and the Politics of Paradise*, 394.

295   *among the supreme artistic achievements*: Tindall, "Bubble in the Sun," 111.

295 *"It has charm": Miami Herald*, November 3, 1955, quoted in Mormino, *Land of Sunshine, State of Dreams*, 41.

296 *"Deregulated capitalism":* Paul Samuelson, "Financial Crisis Work of 'Fiendish Monsters,'" *Economist's View.*

296 *"The evils of an economic depression":* Babson, *Actions and Reactions*, 374.

297 *Thirteen new counties:* The list of counties created is: Charlotte, Glades, Collier, Dixie, Gilchrist, Gulf, Hardee, Hendry, Highlands, Indian River, Marton, Sarasota, and Union.

298 *"Very simple":* Fuller, *This Was Florida's Boom*, 62.

AFTERWORD

300 *a desire for air-conditioning:* The Mizner houses can be sensitively modernized, adding central air-conditioning and new and more convenient kitchens in ways that retain the structure's architectural integrity, romantic appeal, and financial value. And today, the Mizner imprimatur on a house adds more than just cachet; it bestows on it the status of a rare commodity and thus that of a valuable investment asset, as well as a work of art. For example, Mizner's Villa Tranquilla at 640 S. Ocean Boulevard, built in 1923 for Dr. DeGrimm Renfro at a construction cost of some $65,000, sold in June 2017 for $36,150,000. This represents a back-of-the-envelope compound annual rate of investment return over the ninety-four-year period of 7 percent, which is a solid return given that the period encompassed both the Depression and the Great Recession and a handful of other stock market and real estate corrections. The Kennedy house, La Guerida, which Joe and Rose Kennedy purchased for $120,000 in 1932 and added a wing to, sold for $31 million in 2015, a 6.2 percent annual rate of return. El Solano, the John Lennon and Yoko Ono house, which Mizner built for himself at a cost of less than $50,000, sold in 2016 for $23 million, a 6.6 percent annual rate of return. Of course, these calculations overlook the costs of upkeep, the property taxes, the cost of renovations and extensions, and ignore the impact of inflation. Collado Hueco, situated on 3.3 acres along Ocean Boulevard and owned for many years by the late shopping mall developer Alfred Taubman and his wife, Judith, was listed in 2018 for $58 million. It was constructed for less than $100,000, although additions were added later. Some forty of the Mizner homes have survived.

300 *"it was too big":* Curl, introduction in Mizner, *Florida Architecture of Addison Mizner*, xxiii.

301 *She failed to sell it:* Ibid., xxii.

301 *depressed after a series of strokes:* He had his chauffeur drive him down a deserted Florida road. Then he climbed out, walked off into the shrubbery, and shot himself through the roof of his mouth with a .38 revolver.

301   *The exiled Duke and Duchess:* Amory, *Last Resorts*, 402.

301   *killed himself:* "Robert R. Young Commits Suicide," *New York Times*, January 26, 1958, 1.

302   *shy and reclusive:* Curl, introduction, in Mizner, *Florida Architecture of Addison Mizner*, xxv.

302   *"as eager and delightful as ever":* Waugh, "Miznerland" (unpublished typescript).

302   *"Sue them!":* Augustus Mayhew, "The Coconuts! Palm Beach Social History," *New York Social Diary*, May 23, 2009.

303   *"carefree, wacky Horrie":* Showalter, *Many Mizners: California Clan Extraordinary*, 62.

304   *"marvelous Miznerland":* Waugh, "Miznerland" (unpublished typescript), chap. 10, 2–6; see also Showalter, *Many Mizners: California Clan Extraordinary*, 62.

IMAGE CREDITS

Page 5

Top: University of Miami Library, Special Collections, Marjory Stoneman Douglas Papers Collection No. ASM0060 Series IV. Photographs Container Box No. 37, Folder No. 74

Middle: Photographic collection and photographer: Fishbaugh, W. A. (William A.), b. ca. 1873, State Archives of Florida, Florida Memory

Bottom: Courtesy of Tampa-Hillsborough County Public Library System

Page 6

Top: Courtesy of Tampa-Hillsborough County Public Library System

Middle: Tamiami Trail Blazers Scrapbook, Russell Kay Papers, Special and Area Studies Collections, George A. Smathers Libraries, University of Florida, Gainesville, Florida

Bottom: Matlack, Claude Carson, photographer, Circa 1920. View of Seminole Indians poling in three dugout canoes. Claude Matlack Photograph Collection. History-Miami Museum, Matlack 45–30.

Page 7

Top: Florida Photographic Collection, Florida Memory

Bottom: Courtesy of Historical Society of Palm Beach County

Page 8

Top: The Granger Collection LTD d/b/a GRANGER—Historical Picture Archive

Middle: Otto Bettman Archives courtesy of Getty Images

Bottom: Louise Cromwell by unknown photographer, ca. 1911. From the U.S. Library of Congress

Page 9

Top: Courtesy of Tampa-Hillsborough County Public Library System

Middle: Looking down a very busy East Flagler Street—Miami, Florida, 1925. Black & white photoprint, 8 x 10 in. State Archives of Florida, Florida Memory

Bottom: Romer, Gleason Waite, 1887–1971, "Overtown Dwellings," University of Miami Library, Special Collections

Page 10

Top: Miami Beach developer Carl Graham Fisher with his Packard in Elkhart, Indiana, 1915. Black & white photoprint, 8 x 10 in. State Archives of Florida, Florida Memory

Middle: Courtesy of Montauk Library

Bottom: Carl G. Fisher driving a speedboat, 1920. Black & white photograph, 8 x 10 in. State Archives of Florida, Florida Memory

Page 11

Top: Underwood Archives/UIG/Shutterstock

Middle: Matlack, Claude Carson, 1878–1944. Rosie being used as a golf tee—Miami Beach, Florida, 1927. Black & white photoprint, 8 x 10 in. State Archives of Florida, Florida Memory

Bottom: Photo by Hulton Archive courtesy of Getty Images

Page 12

Top: Gloria Swanson, James Abbe's photo, 1921

Middle: Fishbaugh, W. A. (William Arthur), 1873–1950. Construction of the Miami Biltmore Hotel—Coral Gables, Florida, 1925. Black & white photoprint, 8 x 10 in. State Archives of Florida, Florida Memory

Bottom: Photo by Transcendental Graphics courtesy of Getty Images

Page 13

Top: Courtesy of Historical Society of Palm Beach County

Bottom: Romer, G. W. (Gleason Waite), 1887–1971. Capsized "Prinz Valdemar"—Miami, Florida, 1926. Black & white photoprint, 8 x 10 in. State Archives of Florida, Florida Memory

Page 14

Top and bottom: Otto Bettman Archives courtesy of Getty Images

Page 15

Top: Photo by Edward Steichen courtesy of Getty Images

Bottom: Devastation after the hurricane at Miami Beach, 1926. Black & white photograph, 8 x 10 in. State Archives of Florida, Florida Memory

Page 16

Top: Worth Avenue shopping arcade—Palm Beach, Florida, ca 1928. Black & white photonegative, 4 x 5 in. State Archives of Florida, Florida Memory

Bottom: Kathy Willens/AP/Shutterstock

INTERIOR

Page vi

Gregg M. Turner Railroad Collection at Florida Gulf Coast University Archives, Special Collections & Digital Initiatives, "Map of the Florida East Coast Railway"

INDEX